MW01277122

Alexander Hamilton:
A Friend to America

Volume 1

Essays on Hamilton's life and times, based on
writings by Hamilton, Eliza, Washington,
Angelica, Burr, and their
contemporaries

Dianne L. Durante

NOTES

The links (underlined in the text) are available at the end of the volume and online at http://diannedurantewriter.com/ hafav1/

ABOUT THE AUTHOR

For more on the author, visit http://diannedurantewriter.com/about/ the Amazon Author Page for Dianne L. Durante, and my Patreon page at https://www.patreon.com/diannedurante.

I'm happy to hear comments, corrections, and suggestions (email above), and I'll be delirious with delight if you write a review on Amazon!

COVER IMAGE

Carl Conrads, *Alexander Hamilton,* 1880. Full-size plaster model at Museum of American Finance. Photo copyright © 2017 Dianne L. Durante. The finished granite sculpture is in Central Park, just west of the Metropolitan Museum of Art.

First published in book form via CreateSpace, December 2017.

This issue published via Ingram / LightningSource 5/19/2018.

Table of Contents

Introduction

The two volumes (728 pages) of *Alexander Hamilton: Friend to America* supplement my 92-page *Alexander Hamilton: A Brief Biography*. Here's how such a big tail came to be wagging such a small dog.

SCULPTURES

Since 2002, I've been researching and writing about outdoor sculpture in New York City. When Ron Chernow's *Alexander Hamilton* appeared in 2004, I was eager to learn why New Yorkers had erected four lifesize sculptures of Hamilton. I enjoyed Hamilton's company so much that I worked up a walking tour of the sculptures, focusing on the relationship between the important events of Hamilton's life and the ideas that drove him. For me (writer's bias!), the best way to get to know someone is to become familiar with what he wrote. On the tour, volunteers read aloud excerpts from Hamilton's writings. In 2012, I turned my tour notes into a Kindle book—*Alexander Hamilton: A Brief Biography*—and then toddled off to work on other projects.

MUSICAL

In 2015, along came *Hamilton: An American Musical*. By the time I listened to the soundtrack in January 2016 (see Chapter 1), tickets were scarce and expensive. I compensated by writing blog posts on DianneDuranteWriter.com. Once a week for sixteen months, I linked lines in the musical to writings by Hamilton and his contemporaries. Since I love visuals, I found early illustrations for the posts. I tackled the difference between art and history, and why we need both. When dealing with disputed points (e.g., Alexander's "death wish"), I talked about the process of writing history.

After I discovered the line-by-line *Hamilton* annotations on Genius.com, I began to focus less on matching lyrics to Hamilton's writings and more on stitching together an image of Hamilton's life and ideas via his own words. Because my time for research was limited, I chose not to delve into secondary sources. Instead, I read as many primary sources (original writings of Hamilton and others) as I could cram into each week.

That turned out to be quite a lot. Before I gave my talk on Hamilton in 2004, I spent hours poring over the 27-volume printed edition of

Hamilton's works. This time around, not only did I read most of Hamilton's letters and essays online—I read the letters he was replying to, and eyewitness accounts of events he participated in.

I've tried to allow Hamilton, Washington, Angelica, Eliza, Madison, and their contemporaries speak for themselves. The lengthy excerpts from their writings are the backbone of *Hamilton: A Friend to America,* and make it unique among the hundreds of published works on Hamilton. (For those unaccustomed to such long stretches of eighteenth-century prose, I've broken up the quotes by highlighting the key sections in red.)

If you're a fan of the musical, you'll recognize that the order of the early posts is based on the sequence of events used by Lin-Manuel Miranda. Aaron Burr, Hercules Mulligan, John Laurens, and the Marquis de Lafayette appear in Chapters 3-6 because they appear near the beginning of Act I. I hope you'll enjoy delving into the real lives of the characters. I'm still surprised and delighted by how much history Lin-Manuel Miranda managed to fit into *Hamilton: An American Musical*.

If you're a fan of the Founding Fathers rather than the Broadway musical, the extensive primary sources in *Alexander Hamilton: A Friend to America* will give you a new perspective on America during and just after the Revolution. To read them in chronological order, check out the cross-references in *Alexander Hamilton: A Brief Biography*.

A side note: I kept posts that were filler (such as Chapter 10) because if I deleted them, I'd have to change hundreds of cross-references—a horrifying thought. Another horrifying thought: making corrections to the blog posts (which are still online) as well as the printed version. The printed version is the up-to-date one.

HIGHLIGHTS

Some of my favorites topics:

- Alexander's "death wish": what's the evidence? (Chapters 8, 9, and 24)

- Alexander and Angelica: yes, no, maybe? (Chapters 12, 53, and 59)

- What made Hamilton's first essay (*Vindication*, 1774) so attention-grabbing? (Chapters 8 and 14)

- Duels: what were the rules? (Chapters 27 and 28)

- Hamilton's economic policies: was he a laissez- faire capitalist? A proponent of Big Government? Where did he draw the line between politics and economics? (Chapters 60, 61, and 62)
- Maria Reynolds: what the hell was he thinking? (Chapters 63A, 63B, and 63C)

PERMISSIONS

As first published, the blog posts included many lines from the musical. The producers of *Hamilton: An American Musical* denied my request to use the lyrics in the printed version. Hence I've stripped the lyrics from both books and blog posts. The few lyrics that remain fall under fair use.

WHY "A FRIEND TO AMERICA"?

Seventeen-year-old Alexander Hamilton signed his first political pamphlet, *A Full Vindication of the Measures of Congress* (see Chapters 8 and 14), as "A Friend to America." His pen name nicely sums up the range of his achievements: writing in defense of the American colonies and the new nation, acting as Washington's aide-de-camp, promoting business, supporting the Constitution, and organizing the financial system of the new government. The man wasn't perfect, but he was damn good.

REFERENCES

I hope that someone is, at this very moment, working out a way to make hyperlinks easy to translate into footnotes. Lacking that, I've left the hyperlinks underlined in the printed text and created pages on DianneDuranteWriter.com with clickable links. As a back-up, the links are also printed at the end of each volume.

ACKNOWLEDGMENTS

I've thanked a number of scholars in the text below. I'd like to also thank my husband, who was willing to discuss Hamilton and *Hamilton* for hours and hours. Thanks to my daughter, Allegra, whose Photoshop expertise made the cover much more attractive. And thanks to my sister / copy editor Jan Robinson, who caught many errors. If you find others, email me (DuranteDianne@gmail.com) and I'll fix them in a future printing.

CHAPTER 1
My World Turned Upside Down

Originally published on January 28, 2016.

How does a fifty-something opera fan fall in love with a hip-hop Broadway show?

Not easily.

The first clip I heard from *Hamilton: An American Musical* was the opening number, "<u>Alexander Hamilton</u>." It was so far out of my Mozart-Beethoven-and-Rossini-loving comfort zone that I didn't even know if "hip hop" was the right musical term for it. Strike one.

Also, Alexander Hamilton is my favorite Founding Father: an excellent writer, a (sort of) capitalist, and a New Yorker. But for the past century or so, he's been the most neglected and reviled of the Founding Fathers. A hit show in ultra-liberal New York City: how likely is it that Hamilton is going to be shown as my kind of hero? Strike two.

Fortunately, my friends refuse to let me wallow in my own ignorance. One of them saw *Hamilton* at the Public Theater and has been raving about the show ever since. He listened patiently while I explained (several times) why it was absolutely inconceivable that I would like *Hamilton*. Then he handed me the soundtrack and suggested I listen before deciding.

Well. Ahem.

I still haven't seen *Hamilton: An American Musical*. The difference is that now I really, really mind that I haven't seen it. I tear up every time I listen to "The Unimaginable." (The track is actually called "It's Quiet Uptown," but I never think of it by that name.) I jump up singing, ready to tackle the world, at "My Shot." To my amazement, although political debates generally leave me queasy, I can enjoy them if they involve the Founding Fathers, rapping.

So first of all: thanks, Lin-Manuel Miranda, for expanding my self-imposed horizons!

WAITING FOR IT

Tickets are sold out through August, and I don't have the income to patronize scalpers. I plan to cope with my impatience by writing. My niche is outdoor sculpture in New York City. There are four sculptures of Hamilton here—more than of anyone else. In researching them, I've read a fair number of Hamilton's writings. Over the next months, I'll be posting writings by Hamilton and his contemporaries that are related to the lyrics of *Hamilton: An American Musical*. For good measure, I'll toss in some illustrations of Hamilton and his times that I collected while putting together the Guides Who Know <u>Monuments of Manhattan</u> videos on two of the Hamilton sculptures in New York.

TWO WARNINGS

1. You do *not* (not, not, ***not***) (did I say, **NOT**) need historical notes such as I'm writing in order to enjoy *Hamilton: An American Musical* or its soundtrack. As legions of fans will tell you, the musical stands on its own as a work of art.
2. These comments are purely unofficial, my personal take on a work of art that I enjoy very much.

MORE

• Want to visit all four Hamilton sculptures in Manhattan? See Chapter 7.

• Find other fascinating figures represented in sculptures in Manhattan by reading <u>*Outdoor Monuments of Manhattan: A Historical Guide*</u> (or buy the book from <u>Amazon</u>). And check out the samples of <u>Monuments of Manhattan,</u> a Guides Who Know videoguide available for Android and iPhones.

"Smells like new money, dresses like fake royalty" ... This is my favorite Hamilton sculpture in NYC, for the defiant look, the posture, and the texture on the frock coat.

William Ordway Partridge, Alexander Hamilton, dedicated 1893. It's at 287 Convent Ave. at 141st St., where Hamilton's home, The Grange, used to stand. The Grange is now around the corner and down the hill, in St. Nicholas Park (414 W. 141st St.)—go visit, it'll make your toes tingle to stand where Hamilton stood. Photo copyright © 2007 Dianne L. Durante.

CHAPTER 2
The Hurricane Letter, 1772

The opening number of *Hamilton: An American Musical*, "Alexander Hamilton," has brief references to every important aspect of Hamilton's life and character: his being illegitimate and an orphan, his ambition, his constant rushing, his desire to change the world. It's brilliant. But I think it'll be more fun to discuss each of those separately, later, so here, I want to share Hamilton's "Hurricane Letter," which is almost the earliest of Hamilton's 32 volumes (!) of writings. In it, he describes the storm that blasted across St. Croix in 1772. (If you know any 15-year-olds who could write a piece like this after surviving a meteorological catastrophe, you should nudge them in the direction of a writing career.)

Published in St. Croix's *Royal Danish American Gazette*, the "Hurricane Letter" roused such enthusiasm that locals raised a fund to send young Alexander to the College of New Jersey—now Princeton University—for a proper education.

Saint Croix, September 6, 1772

Honoured Sir,

I take up my pen just to give you an imperfect account of the most dreadful hurricane that memory or any records whatever can trace, which happened here on the 31st ultimo at night.

It began about dusk, at North, and raged very violently till ten o'clock. Then ensued a sudden and unexpected interval, which lasted about an hour. Meanwhile the wind was shifting round to the South West point, from whence it returned with redoubled fury and continued so till near three o'clock in the morning. Good God! what horror and destruction—it's impossible for me to describe—or you to form any idea of it. It seemed as if a total dissolution of nature was taking place. The roaring of the sea and wind—fiery meteors flying about in the air—the prodigious glare of almost perpetual lightning—the crash of the falling houses—and the ear-piercing shrieks of the distressed, were sufficient to strike astonishment into Angels. A great part of the buildings throughout the Island are levelled to the ground—almost all the rest very much shattered—several persons killed and numbers utterly ruined—whole families running about the streets unknowing where to find a place of shelter—the sick exposed to the keenness of water and air—without a bed to lie upon—or a dry covering to their bodies—our harbour is entirely bare. In a word, misery in all its most hideous shapes spread over the whole face of the country.— A strong smell of gunpowder added somewhat to the terrors of the night; and it was observed that the rain was surprisingly salt. Indeed, the water is so brackish and full of sulphur that there is hardly any drinking it.

THE LESS FAMOUS PART OF THE LETTER

The rest of the letter is a religious diatribe that's almost worthy of Aaron Burr's grandfather, fire-and-brimstone preacher Jonathan Edwards. This part of the letter isn't referred to in *Hamilton: The Musical*, and I can understand why. If you're going to tell the story of a whole life in a couple hours, you have to be laser-sharp about picking events and words that explain why your guy did what he did. Otherwise you'll end up with a sprawling mess.

Judging from his later writings, although Hamilton did believe in God, religion didn't dominate his life. He didn't constantly seek divine guidance or explain away his faults and errors as part of a Higher Plan. He seldom went to church. So why read this part of the "Hurricane Letter"? Because it shows that even as a teenager, Hamilton was

A charming miniature. The back bears the inscription, "A. Hamilton, Drawn from life Jan. 11, 1773." This photo, taken ca. 1900-1920, is at the Library of Congress, but the location of the miniature itself is unknown. It's impossible to say whether this is actually young Alexander.

passionate and imaginative, and (in an age that lacked PowerPoint!) capable of creating extraordinarily vivid and persuasive images in the minds of his listeners.

Here's young Alexander, continuing.

My reflections and feelings on this frightful and melancholy occasion are set forth in following self-discourse.

Where now, Oh! vile worm, is all thy boasted fortitude and resolution? what is become of thy arrogance and self-sufficiency?—why dost thou tremble and stand aghast? how humble—how helpless—how contemptible you now appear. And for why? the jarring of the elements—the discord of clouds? Oh, impotent presumptuous fool! how darest thou offend that omnipotence, whose nod alone were sufficient to quell the destruction that hovers over thee, or crush thee into atoms? See thy wretched helpless state and learn to know thyself. Learn to know thy best support. Despise thyself and adore thy God. How sweet—how unutterably sweet were now the voice of an approving conscience;—then couldst thou say—hence ye idle alarms—why do I shrink? What have I to fear? A pleasing calm suspense! a short repose from calamity to end in eternal bliss?—let the earth rend, let the planets forsake their course—let the sun be extinguished, and the heavens burst asunder—yet what have I to dread? my staff can never be broken—in omnipotence I trust.

He who gave the winds to blow and the lightnings to rage—even him I have always loved and served—his precepts have I observed—his commandments have I obeyed—and his perfections have I adored.—He will snatch me from ruin—he will exalt me to the fellowship of Angels and Seraphs, and to the fulness of never ending joys.

But alas! how different, how deplorable—how gloomy the prospect—death comes rushing on in triumph veiled in a mantle of ten-fold darkness. His unrelenting scythe, pointed and ready for the stroke.—On his right hand sits destruction, hurling the winds and belching forth flames;—calamity on his left threatening famine, disease, distress of all kinds.— And Oh! thou wretch, look still a little further; see the gulf of eternal mystery open—there mayest thou shortly plunge— the just reward of thy vileness.—Alas! whither canst thou fly? where hide thyself? thou canst not call upon thy God;—

thy life has been a continual warfare with him.

Hark! ruin and confusion on every side.—Tis thy turn next: but one short moment—even now—Oh Lord help—Jesus be merciful!

Thus did I reflect, and thus at every gust of the wind did I conclude,—till it pleased the Almighty to allay it.—Nor did my emotions proceed either from the suggestion of too much natural fear, or a conscience overburdened with crimes of an uncommon cast.—I thank God this was not the case. The scenes of horror exhibited around us, naturally awakened such ideas in every thinking breast, and aggravated the deformity of every failing of our lives. It were a lamentable insensibility indeed, not to have had such feelings,—and I think inconsistent with human nature.

Our distressed helpless condition taught us humility and a contempt of ourselves.—The horrors of the night—the prospect of an immediate cruel death—or, as one may say, of being crushed by the Almighty in his anger—filled us with terror. And everything that had tended to weaken our interest with Him, upbraided us, in the strongest colours, with our baseness and folly.—That which, in a calm unruffled temper, we call a natural cause, seemed then like the correction of the Deity.—Our imagination represented him as an incensed master, executing vengeance on the crimes of his servants.—The father and benefactor were forgot, and in that view, a consciousness of our guilt filled us with despair.

But see, the Lord relents—he hears our prayers—the Lightning ceases—the winds are appeased—the warring elements are reconciled, and all things promise peace.—The darkness is dispelled—and drooping nature revives at the approaching dawn. Look back, Oh, my soul—look back and tremble.—Rejoice at thy deliverance, and humble thyself in the presence of thy deliverer.

Yet hold, Oh, vain mortal!—check thy ill-timed joy. Art thou so selfish as to exult because thy lot is happy in a season of universal woe?—Hast thou no feelings for the miseries of thy fellow-creatures, and art thou incapable of the soft pangs of sympathetic sorrow?—Look around thee and shudder at the view.—See desolation and ruin wherever thou turnest thine eye. See thy fellow-creatures pale and lifeless; their bodies mangled—their souls snatched into eternity—unexpecting—alas! perhaps unprepared!—Hark the bitter groans of distress—see sickness and infirmities exposed to the inclemencies of wind and water—see tender infancy pinched with hunger and hanging to the mother's knee for food!—see the unhappy mother's anxiety—her poverty denies relief—her breast heaves with pangs of maternal pity—her heart is bursting—the tears gush down her cheeks—Oh sights of woe! Oh distress unspeakable!—my heart bleeds—but I have no power to solace!—Oh ye, who revel in affluence, see the afflictions of humanity, and bestow your superfluity to ease them.—Say not, we have suffered also, and with-hold your compassion. What are your sufferings compared to these? Ye have still more than enough left.—Act wisely.—Succour the miserable and lay up a treasure in Heaven.

I am afraid, sir, you will think this description more the effort of imagination, than a true picture of realities. But I can affirm with the greatest truth, that there is not a single circumstance touched upon which I have not absolutely been an eye-witness to.

Our General has several very salutary and human regulations, and both in his public and private measures has shown himself the man.

MORE

• See <u>here</u> for notes on the letter's recipient and its publication.

CHAPTER 3
Aaron Burr (1756-1836)

"I WISH THERE WAS A WAR ..."

The earliest surviving letter by Hamilton is dated November 11, 1769. It was written by 12-year-old Alexander, who had lost his mother a year earlier, to his friend (half-brother?) Edward Stevens, who was a year older and was studying at King's College in New York. You can hear Alexander's ambition even then: there's a million things he hasn't done.

Dear Edward

    This just serves to acknowledge receipt of yours per Cap Lowndes which was delivered me Yesterday. The truth of Cap Lightbourn & Lowndes information is now verifyd by the Presence of your Father and Sister for whose safe arrival I Pray, and that they may convey that Satisfaction to your Soul that must naturally flow from the sight of Absent Friends in health, and shall for news this way refer you to them. As to what you say respecting your having soon the happiness of seeing us all, I wish, for an accomplishment of your hopes provided they are Concomitant with your welfare, otherwise not, tho doubt whether I shall be Present or not for to confess my weakness, Ned, my Ambition is prevalent that I contemn the grov'ling and condition of a Clerk or the like, to which my Fortune &c. condemns me and would willingly risk my life tho' not my Character to exalt my Station. Im confident, Ned that my Youth excludes me from any hopes of immediate Preferment nor do I desire it, but I mean to prepare the way for futurity. Im no Philosopher you see and may be jusly said to Build Castles in the Air. My Folly makes me ashamd and beg youll Conceal it, yet Neddy we have seen such Schemes successfull when the Projector

is Constant I shall Conclude saying I wish there was a War.
    I am   Dr Edward   Yours   Alex Hamilton
    PS   I this moment receivd yours by William Smith and
am pleasd to see you Give such Close Application to Study.
(Here)

After the "Hurricane Letter" was published three years later, in 1772,
Hamilton went to the Elizabethtown Academy (Elizabeth, N.J.), a
prep school, for intensive tutoring. The powers that be at Princeton
refused to allow him an accelerated course of study. So in late 1773,
Hamilton headed to King's College, established in 1754. It was re-
named Columbia after the American Revolution.

From lower left: King's College in 1770 (in lower Manhattan); King's
College seal; Daniel Chester French's Alma Mater at Columbia University,
with a detail of the scepter in her hand. Photos of Alma Mater
copyright © 2014 Dianne L. Durante

FICTIONAL VERSIONS OF BURR

Halfway through my fourth listen of "Aaron Burr, Sir," I remembered
that decades ago, I read Gore Vidal's Burr. On rereading it, I still
found it very entertaining, but I often felt as if I was looking at the
optical illusion on the facing page.
    For my writing on outdoor sculptures in New York City for the past
15+ years, I've read dozens of biographies, many of them quite biased.
It's part of my job as a historian to integrate what such bios say with
my other knowledge, in order to figure out where the truth lies. In
all those years of research, I've never felt my point of view flick-
er from positive to negative and back again as I did when reading

Vase and faces optical illusion. Photo: Brocken Inaglory, Wikipedia

Vidal's *Burr.* Vidal is a great story-teller; so is Lin-Manuel Miranda; and who tells your story really does matter.

THE REAL BURR

The best general source for the lives of notable Americans is the <u>American National Biography Online</u> (a subscription service). Its articles are well-written, authoritative, and perhaps best of all, they include a reading / reference list that tells where the subject's papers are (if any survive) and gives brief comments on all the major biographies.

Snippets from the ANB's entry on Burr that surprised me:
• Burr's grandfather was Jonathan Edwards, one of the most prominent practitioners of hellfire-and-brimstone preaching. In "<u>Sinners in the Hands of an Angry God</u>," 1741, Reverend Edwards told unrepentant sinners:

> That World of Misery, that Lake of burning Brimstone is extended abroad under you. There is the dreadful Pit of the glowing Flames of the Wrath of God; there is Hell's wide gaping Mouth open; and you have nothing to stand upon, not any Thing to take hold of: there is nothing between you and Hell but the Air; 'tis only the Power and meer Pleasure of God that holds you up.

• Burr's father (who died of a fever when Aaron was 2 years old) was one of the founders of the College of New Jersey and its second president, serving 1748-1757. He presided over its first commencement and over the college's move from Elizabeth to Princeton (where it eventually changed its name). Given his father's status, it's not surprising that when Aaron, Jr. entered Princeton at age 13, he was granted special privileges.

• Burr's mother died seven months after his father. The grandparents who took in the orphaned Aaron and his only sister, Sally, died soon after; the children were then raised by an uncle. Sally, who was constantly ailing even as a young woman, died in 1787 at age 33. Burr's wife Theodosia, whom he married in 1782, died in 1794 of stomach cancer. Daughter Theodosia, his only offspring to survive childhood, died at barely 30 in a shipwreck—or perhaps was murdered by pirates. Much as I love the ideas and the sense of life of the eighteenth century, I wouldn't want to live (and quickly die) then.

• In 1833, at age 77, Burr married Eliza Bowen Jumel, a widow who owned the Morris-Jumel Mansion in northern Manhattan. The Mansion is a great place to visit if you like walking in the footsteps of history: in the autumn of 1776, Washington briefly had his headquarters there. Eliza Bowen Jumel Burr filed for a divorce within a year of marriage. It was granted the day Burr died, September 14, 1836.

Hellfire-and-brimstone preacher; President of Princeton; Aaron Jr. ca. 1794 and 1802; daughter Theodosia

MORE

• The National Archives Founders Online site lets you search tens of thousands of documents by the Founding Fathers, by author, recipient, period, or keyword. What an amazing resource! By searching there, I see that Hamilton wrote to Burr on mundane legal matters in 1784-1786 and again in 1802-3. The letters they exchanged in 1804 (two from Hamilton, three from Burr) are also available.

CHAPTER 4
John Laurens (1754-1782)

John Laurens didn't live to see the end of the American Revolution. He died at age 27, killed by the British ten months after Yorktown—which was only recognized in hindsight as the final battle of the American Revolutionary War. In fact, after Cornwallis's surrender on October 19, 1781, thirty thousand British troops remained in America, occupying the key coastal cities of New York, Charleston, and Savannah. Laurens died on August 27, 1782, in a skirmish near his home town of Charleston.

Miniature of John Laurens by Charles Wilson Peale

Laurens (1754-1782) was only a few years older than Hamilton, and from August 1777 to mid-1778, both served on Washington's staff. After the Battle of Brandywine in September 1777, the Marquis de Lafayette remarked, "It was not his fault that he was not killed or wounded ... he did every thing that was necessary to procure one or t'other." (Quoted in the *American National Biography* from a letter of Laurens's father Henry, who was a South Carolina delegate to the Continental Congress.)

Had he lived, John Laurens might have been a prominent Founding Father and a powerful force in the abolitionist movement. At Valley Forge in the winter of 1777-1778, he conceived the idea of granting slaves freedom if they would volunteer to serve in the American army.

His letter below, written February 2, 1778, was part of an ongoing discussion with his father about the project. Congress authorized the formation of black regiments in March 1779, but the South Carolina legislature repeatedly rejected the idea.

Before you start reading: pay attention to the way Laurens characterizes slaves, as opposed to how he reports that those arguing against him do. In the late 18th century most Americans, and especially Southerners, were racists: they believed that blacks were born inferior. I'm a big fan of Ayn Rand, who rejected racism:"Racism claims ... that a man's convictions, values and character are determined before he is born, by physical factors beyond his control."

Laurens, on the other hand, thinks slaves deserve "the rights of humanity." He believes they have been trampled and oppressed, debased by servitude, and have in self-defense developed the habit of accepting what they were not able to change. But Laurens believes their wretched state is only the result of the way they've been treated, and that if given the choice to be free, they will take it.

By the standards of his time, then, Laurens had startlingly advanced ideas. Kudos to him for having the guts to fight for them in a time and place that was highly antagonistic. From this letter, it's clear that even his father and Commander-in-Chief George Washington weren't 100% behind him on his project.

Headquarters, 2d Feb., 1778

The more I reflect upon the difficulties and delays which are likely to attend the completing our Continental regiments, the more anxiously is my mind bent upon the scheme, which I lately communicated to you. The obstacles to the execution of it had presented themselves to me, but by no means appeared insurmountable. I was aware of having that monstrous popular prejudice, open-mouthed against me, of under taking to transform beings almost irrational, into well disciplined soldiers, of being obliged to combat the arguments, and perhaps the intrigues, of interested persons. But zeal for the public service, and an ardent desire to assert the rights of humanity, determined me to engage in this arduous business, with the sanction of your consent. My own perseverance, aided by the countenance of a few virtuous men, will, I hope, enable me to accomplish it.

You seem to think, my dear father, that men reconciled by long habit to the miseries of their condition, would prefer their ignominious bonds to the untasted sweets of liberty, especially when offer'd upon the terms which I propose.

I confess, indeed, that the minds of this unhappy species must be debased by a servitude, from which they can hope for no relief but death, and that every motive to action but fear, must be nearly extinguished in them. But do you think they are so perfectly moulded to their state as to be insensible that a better exists? Will the galling comparison between them selves and their masters leave them unenlightened in this respect? Can their self love be so totally annihilated as not frequently to induce ardent wishes for a change?

You will accuse me, perhaps, my dearest friend, of consulting my own feelings too much; but I am tempted to believe that this trampled people have so much human left in them, as to be capable of aspiring to the rights of men by noble exertions, if some friend to mankind would point the road, and give them a prospect of success. If I am mistaken in this, I would avail myself, even of their weakness, and, conquering one fear by another, produce equal good to the public. You will ask in this view, how do you consult the benefit of the slaves? I answer, that like other men, they are the creatures of habit. Their cowardly ideas will be gradually effaced, and they will be modified anew. Their being rescued from a state of perpetual humiliation, and being advanced, as it were, in the scale of being, will compensate the dangers incident to their new state.

The hope that will spring in each man's mind, respecting his own escape, will prevent his being miserable. Those who fall in battle will not lose much; those who survive will obtain their reward. Habits of subordination, patience under fatigues, sufferings and privations of every kind, are soldierly qualifications, which these men possess in an eminent degree.

Upon the whole, my dearest friend and father, I hope that my plan for serving my country and the oppressed negro race will not appear to you the chimera of a young mind, deceived by false apearance of moral beauty, but a laudable sacrifice of private interest, to justice and the public good.

You say, that my resources would be small, on account of the proportion of women and children. I do not know whether I am right, for I speak from impulse, and have not reasoned upon the matter. I say, altho my plan is at once to give freedom to the negroes, and gain soldiers to the states; in case of concurrence, I sh'd sacrifice the former interest, and therefore w'd change the women and children for able-bodied men. The more of these I could obtain, the better; but forty might be a good foundation to begin upon. [NOTE: I'm not sure what he's proposing here. DD]

It is a pity that some such plan as I propose could not be more extensively executed by public authority. A well chosen body of 5,000 black men, properly officer'd, to act as light troops, in addition to our present establishment, might give us decisive success in the next campaign.

I have long deplored the wretched state of these men, and considered in their history, the bloody wars excited in Africa, to furnish America with slaves the groans of despairing multitudes, toiling for the luxuries of merciless tyrants. [NOTE: Something's wrong with the syntax here; if I had access to the original print version, I'd check if something's missing. Or perhaps, writing in haste, Laurens simply made an error. DD]

I have had the pleasure of conversing with you, sometimes, upon the means of restoring them to their rights. When can it be better done, than when their enfranchisement may be made conducive to the public good, and be modified, as not to overpower their weak minds?

You ask, what is the general's opinion, upon this subject? He is convinced, that the numerous tribes of blacks in the southern parts of the continent, offer a resource to use that should not be neglected. With respect to my particular plan, he only objects to it, with the arguments of pity for a man who would be less rich than he might be ...." (From *The Army Correspondence of Colonel John Laurens in the Years 1777-8, with a Memoir by William Gilmore Simms*, 1867; quoted in Wm. Thomas Sherman, "...Your Dutiful Son, John Laurens")

LAURENS AND HAMILTON

This is the point where a Hamilton scholar or someone with an LGBTQ ax to grind would discuss whether Hamilton and Laurens had a homosexual relationship. I've read their surviving letters to each other, which would be the only reliable evidence. The letters don't support such a relationship. You (by which I mean, "not I") can have a long-winded debate about the expression of affection in eighteenth-century prose and whether their families destroyed any "incriminating" letters, but it won't get you any closer to the historical truth—whatever that was.

MORE

• The letter above is from a <u>selection</u> of John Laurens's letters to his father, published with a short introduction by Wm. Thomas Sherman. These letters are not available (yet?) on the <u>Founders Archive</u> site.

CHAPTER 5

Marquis de Lafayette (1757-1834)

Lord Acton wrote that Lafayette taught his compatriots the American "theory of revolution, not their theory of government—their cutting, not their sewing." Gouverneur Morris told George Washington that Lafayette "left America, you know, when his education was but half-finished. What he learnt there he knows well, but he did not learn to be a government maker." What did these two astute political observers mean?

Marquis de Lafayette as a young man. Image: Wikipedia

When he sailed to America in 1776, violating a direct order from his king, the nineteen-year-old Marquis de Lafayette (Marie Joseph Paul Yves Roch Gilbert du Montier Lafayette) was handsome, charismatic, and extraordinarily wealthy. To the wife he left behind he explained, "The happiness of America is intimately connected with the happiness of all mankind; she is destined to become the safe and venerable asylum of virtue, of honesty, of tolerance, and of peaceful liberty."

Lafayette's bravery at the Battle of Brandywine made him a favorite of Washington. In an army where men still tended to think of themselves as residents of separate states rather than of a new nation, Lafayette became one of the few figures admired from New Hampshire all the way to Georgia: "Our Marquis," they called him. Benjamin

Left: Declaration of the Rights of Man, drafted by the Marquis de Lafayette and Thomas Jefferson. Right: Lafayette giving a speech in 1790. Both images: Wikipedia

Franklin gave Lafayette credit for persuading the French king to sign a treaty of alliance with the United States. The ammunition and troops that arrived because of that treaty were a definitive factor in the American victory. When Cornwallis surrendered at Yorktown in 1781, Lafayette stood in a well-earned position at Washington's side.

Back home in France, a hero to nobles and bourgeois alike, Lafayette eagerly set out to introduce American-style liberty to his native land. In July 1789 he proposed to the National Assembly the Declaration of the Rights of Man and Citizens, co-authored with his friend Thomas Jefferson.

But when the Declaration was approved two months later, it had been substantially altered. Jefferson was strongly influenced by Locke, who emphasized individual rights. In France the favored political philosopher was Rousseau, who argued that the state is the agent of the General Will, and has the right and obligation to override individual rights if the public good demands it. (Hamilton wrote a letter to Lafayette on 10/6/1789 that begins, "I have seen with a mixture of Pleasure and apprehension the Progress of the events which have lately taken Place in your Country ..." Well worth reading, <u>here</u>.)

Without Locke's ideas as groundwork, a government on the American model was impossible. Lafayette knew how to lead an army to displace the old regime, but didn't know the principles necessary to set up a new, improved government. Hence, writing to Washington in March 1792, Lafayette admitted that the French constitution was not as good as the American one, but optimistically predicted that it would succeed nevertheless.

> Although warlike preparations are going on, it is very doubtful whether our neighbours will attempt to stifle so very catching a thing as liberty. The danger for us lies in our state of anarchy ... That liberty and equality will be preserved in France, there is no doubt; in case there were, you well know that I would not, if they fall, survive them. But you may be assured, that we shall emerge from this unpleasant situation, either by an honorable defence, or by internal improvements. . . . The success of our revolution cannot be questioned.— <u>Letter of Lafayette to George Washington,</u> 3/15/1792

Even as Lafayette wrote, events were spinning out of control. Demagogues roused the Paris mobs. Heads rolled. Extremists in the National Assembly overthrew the monarchy, imprisoned the royal family, and charged thirty-five-year-old Lafayette with treason. He fled France— only to be imprisoned as soon as he crossed the border to Belgium. Lafayette had offended his fellow revolutionaries, but he had horrified European monarchs, whose thrones were tottering in the shockwaves of France's Revolution.

Execution of Marie Antoinette, 1793.

Medal created for Lafayette's visit to the United States in 1824. Portrait of Lafayette later in life (Wikipedia)

When he finally returned to France after five years in prison, Lafayette was so weak he could barely walk. Yet he never gave up. When Jefferson offered him the governorship of the newly purchased Louisiana Territory in 1803, Lafayette sighed that he could not leave while he had "even the smallest hope" of bringing liberty to France.

In 1824, President Monroe invited Lafayette to return to the United States for the celebration of America's 50th anniversary. Lafayette visited every one of the 24 states, and was greeted enthusiastically from North Carolina to Maine and Missouri as one of the last surviving heroes of the American Revolution. He lived until 1834.

MORE

• The first time I heard of Lafayette was as the handsome and heroic leader of a band of patriots in *The Young Rebels*. Alas, the show was up against *Lassie* and *The Wonderful World of Disney;* it had only a half-season run, 1970-1971.

• More on Lafayette's imprisonment at Olmutz is here. In 1794, Angelica Schuyler Church and her husband John Barker Church paid a physician and his assistant to help Lafayette escape from Olmutz. Unfortunately, Lafayette was recaptured.

• The essay above is from *Outdoor Monuments of Manhattan: A Historical Guide*, with illustrations from the Guides Who Know Monuments of Manahttan app. Both were inspired by the *Marquis de Lafayette* in Union Square, sculpted by Bartholdi (of *Statue of Liberty* fame).

Left: Bartholdi, Marquis de Lafayette, 1873. Union Square Park.
Right: Bartholdi, Lafayette and Washington. 1890. Morningside Park.
Both photos © Dianne L. Durante 2012

• A Bartholdi sculpture of Lafayette meeting George Washington stands at Morningside Avenue and 114th Street. On this one, see the New York City Parks Dept. page here, and a Daily Beast article here.

• And for good measure: the Green in Morristown, New Jersey (near where Washington had winter headquarters 1779-80) has a sculpture of Washington, Lafayette, and, yes, Hamilton—with space for you for join their circle. Isn't it grand to know topnotch lifesize bronze sculptures are still being created? This is the work of StudioEIS.

Lafayette, Hamilton, and Washington. Morristown Green, NJ. Sculpture by StudioEIS, Brooklyn, 2007. Photos copyright © 2007 Dianne L. Durante

CHAPTER 6
Hercules Mulligan (1740-1825)

On November 25, 1783—the day the British finally evacuated New York—General George Washington rode down Broadway with New York Governor George Clinton, amid the applause of thousands. Then Washington quietly rode off to 23 Queen St. (now 218 Pearl St.) to have breakfast with a fashionable tailor named Hercules Mulligan (1740-1825). Why? During the British occupation of Manhattan, intelligence gleaned by Mulligan from loose-lipped British officers had prevented the capture of Washington at least twice. (The stories are told here and here.) To show his gratitude, Washington not only breakfasted with Mulligan: he ordered a complete civilian wardrobe from him.

Can't find any images of Washington out of uniform ca. 1783. Pity.

SOURCES ON MULLIGAN'S LIFE

From a historian's point of view, it's inconvenient when a hero lives near his friends: he never has to write to them. Sixteen-year-old Alexander Hamilton arrived in New York in 1773 carrying a letter of recommendation to Kartwright & Company in New York, one of whose principals was Hugh Mulligan. After Hamilton enrolled in King's College, he lived for some time at the home of Hugh's brother Hercules. They remained good friends. It may have been Hamilton who recruited Mulligan to spy for General Washington. But except for the Revolutionary War years and Hamilton's stint as Secretary of the Treasury, Hamilton and Mulligan lived near enough to each other for regular visits. No correspondence between them exists.

With one exception (see below), nothing written by Hercules survives. None of his contemporaries wrote anything substantive about him. Michael J. O'Brien managed to fill a 190-page biography with an elaborate array of genealogical details and historical background, but the book has a Hercules Mulligan-shaped hole where its subject should be. Aside from the spying episode, all I learned from the bio was:

1. Hercules was well known, sociable, and considered trustworthy. His name frequently occurs on legal documents (for example, as executor of a will). Even more frequently, it appears on lists of members of committees and clubs. By the 1760s, he was a member of the Sons of Liberty, and he joined many other revolutionary groups after that. (It's just as well his British military customers couldn't check out out his activities on Facebook!)

2. From 1774 to 1787, Hercules and his wife Elizabeth had three sons and five daughters. However many sets of corsets his wife wore, they don't seem to have been an impediment.

So Hercules Mulligan in *Hamilton* is the character Lin-Manuel Miranda needed him to be. I'm fine with that. Hmmm, maybe I'll write more next week on why I don't obsess over historical accuracy in works of art ... (See Chapter 43.)

MULLIGAN'S "NARRATIVE"

The only piece of writing that we have by Hercules Mulligan is a record of his memories of Alexander Hamilton that he jotted down around 1810-1815, at the request of John C. Hamilton (Alexander's fourth son), who was writing a biography of his father. This was 35 years or so after the events Mulligan was describing. Not surprisingly, he gets some dates and details wrong—for example, he says Hamilton enrolled at King's College in October 1775 rather than 1773.

The "Narrative" doesn't add much to our knowledge of Alexander Hamilton, but I enjoyed hearing Mulligan's "voice," so I'll share a couple bits of it.

Hamilton saves the president of King's College

In May 1775, when news reached New York of the Battle of Lexington and Concord, a mob set off to the home of Dr. Myles Cooper, the outspoken Loyalist who was president of King's College. Hamilton, a student at King's, was already an ardent patriot, but he was also very wary of mob action: see his letter of 11/26/1775 to John Jay. (I've kept Mulligan's charmingly erratic spelling and punctuation.)

> Dr. Cooper, President of King's Colledge, was a tory and an obnoxious man and the mob went to the Colledge with the intention of tarring & feathering him or riding him upon a rail. Mr. H got on the stoop of the President's House and harrangued them in order to give him time [to] escape out

of the back of the House which he did & went on Board a Frigate Lying in the North river.

Dr. Cooper's description of this event—in verse!—is here.

Hamilton, Mulligan, and other patriots steal cannons

In August 1775, the British warship *Asia* sailed into New York Harbor. Patriots feared the cannon on the Battery might be captured and turned on the city.

A dozen or so volunteers managed to drag some of the cannons away from the waterfront. Here's Mulligan's account—the only one I've seen of this incident.

> While in Colledge he joined a volunteer uniform company which was commanded by Capt. Fleming. It having been determined by the Committee of Safety that the Cannon which were on the Battery should be removed to a place of

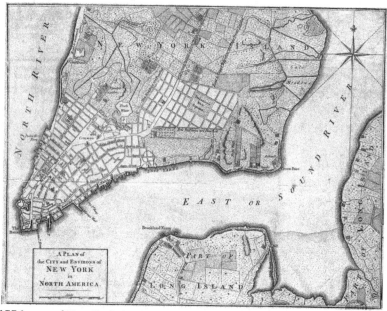

1776 map of New York. Image: Wikipedia. The Battery is toward the lower left. Broadway runs north from it; Trinity Church (an earlier version) is left of the "dway" in "The Broadway Street." The Commons (modern City Hall Park) further north on Broadway, was the site of rabble-rousing speeches. Queen St., where Hercules Mulligan had his tailor shop, runs one block in from the southeast side of the island. I love old maps!

greater safety, this Company with others were engaged in
making the removal when (28 Augt 75) the Asia fired upon
the City and I recollect well that Mr. Hamilton was there,
for I was engaged in hauling off one of the Cannons, when
Mr. H came up and gave me his musket to hold, & he took
hold of the rope. The punt of the Asia had before approached
the Battery and was fired upon and a man was killed, she
returned to the ship and the fire was then opened upon us.
Hamilton at the first firing was away with the Cannon. I left
his musket in the Battery & retreated, as he was returning
I met him and he asked for his piece. I told him where I
had left it, and he went for it, notwithstanding the firing
continued, with as much unconcern as if the vessel had not
been there.

And for those of us who gotta have visuals: here's Hercules Mulligan's signature, reproduced at the end of his "Narrative" in O'Brien's biography.

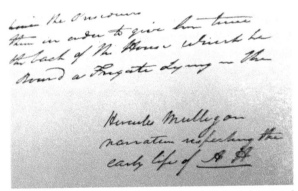

Signature of Hercules Mulligan, from O'Brien's biography.

MORE

• The excerpts from "Narrative of Hercules Mulligan of the City of New York" that I've quoted above are about a quarter of the whole narrative, which is printed in full in Nathan Schachner, "Alexander Hamilton Viewed by His Friends: The Narratives of Robert Troup and Hercules Mulligan," *The William and Mary Quarterly* IV: 2 (April 1947), pp. 203-225 (accessible via JSTOR—thanks to Professor Carrie-Ann Biondi for getting me a copy of this article!). Schachner also provides a scholarly appraisal of the value of the Mulligan and Troup narratives. For more information about the capture of the cannons on the Battery, see the Founders Online. The 1776 date it gives for the Battery cannons incident must be wrong—by late August 1776, there was far more than one British warship in New York harbor.

• Michael J. O'Brien's *Hercules Mulligan, Confidential Correspondent of General Washington* (New York, 1937) is the only biography of Mulligan. O'Brien seems to have been at least as interested in cataloging Irish contributions to the American Revolution as in writing about Hercules. The online articles about Mulligan are all derived from O'Brien's bio: see this one from Fox News, this one from The Daily Beast, and this one from a site about Irish emigrants.

• Hercules Mulligan might have advertised in the newspapers of the time, but 18th-century newspapers are still mostly on microfilm, hence not easily accessible or searchable. The *New York Journal* for 1773-1775 is an exception, but each page is saved separately, and there's no index. If you have the energy to go through it and you find a Hercules ad, let me know!

• You know you can look up all these episodes in Chernow, right? The Cooper incident is pp. 63-6 and 69 (with a wonderful excerpt from Hamilton's letter to John Jay on mobs). The cannons on the Battery episode is on p. 67.

CHAPTER 7
Hamilton-Related Places to Visit

If you need a dose of Hamilton after *Hamilton,* here's half a dozen places to visit where you can take selfies with Alexander or walk in his footsteps. But first …

BURIED IN TRINITY CHURCH

Hamilton's grave is the obvious place to visit, but if the *New York Times* article of 3/6/16 is any indication, most of you guys are missing the money shot.

When he got back to New York after the Revolutionary War, Hamilton wrote the charter of the city's (and state's) first bank: the Bank of New York, established 1784. He also served as its legal adviser.

The Bank of New York survives as part of BNY Mellon, whose headquarters is at 1 Wall Street, looming over Trinity Churchyard. So the shot you should be taking is the one on the following page.

While you're at Trinity Churchyard: also on the following page is a photo of the vault that Hercules Mulligan is buried in, with Hamilton's grave in the background. The marker is for the Whalie and Mulligan families.

THE *NEW YORK POST*

Bonus points, here and below, if you can manage to get yourself into the picture while holding a copy of the *New York Post.* Yes, Hamilton supported Jefferson over Burr in the election of 1800. But Hamilton still disagreed with Jefferson on many issues, and he established the *New York Post* in 1801 to critique the Jefferson administration.

Extra bonus points if you take the photo on a day when the *New York Post's* front page flaunts a Maria Reynolds-style scandal. It was a little more sedate when Hamilton ran it!

Above: Hamilton's grave in Trinity Churchyard and 1 Wall St.,
headquarters of BNY Mellon. Below: Vault in which Hercules Mulligan
is buried, with Hamilton's grave in the distance.
Photos copyright © 2017 Dianne L. Durante

First issue of the New York Post, 1801.

THE GRANGE

Hamilton built a home for his family in the country, a brisk hour-and-a-half commute (by horse-drawn carriage) from the downtown bustle. The two-year project was completed in 1802. The Grange has been shifted twice; it's now in a park just off St. Nicholas Avenue at 141st St. Outside the house, you're not walking in Alexander and Eliza's footsteps. Inside, depending on whether the floorboards have been replaced, you might be.

I love the style and furnishings of this house. Even if you aren't a Hamilton fan, it's a beautiful place to visit.

The Grange, from a 19th-c. illustration; and the Grange today (Photo copyright © 2011 Dianne L. Durante)

Dining room at the Grange. Photo copyright © 2014 Dianne L. Durante

HAMILTON SCULPTURES IN MANHATTAN

Manhattan has four lifesize sculptures of Hamilton—more than of any-one except Washington. Washington edges him out with five ... *if* you count the figures on the Washington Arch as two separate sculptures.

All four sculptures show Hamilton as an orator—appropri-ate since he discoursed frequently and persuasively, and published voluminously.

A handy PDF of the four Hamilton sculptures in New York is on the Forgotten Delights site. Shorter info on the sculptures (in chrono-logical order by dedication) is below.

Hamilton sculpture #1 (Central Park)

A fifteen-foot-tall marble Hamilton—in a toga!—was destroyed in the Great Fire of 1835. That makes this the earliest Hamilton sculpture still standing in New York. In 1880, it was presented to the city by Al-exander's fourth son, John Church Hamilton, who devoted decades to writing a seven-volume biography of his father. This is the only sculp-ture that refers to Hamilton's service in the Revolutionary War: on its pedestal are a sword, scabbard, and chapeau de bras (a type of mili-tary hat).

This sculpture stands in Central Park, just west of the Metropolitan Museum. For more about it, see the excerpt from my *Outdoor Mon-uments of Manhattan: A Historical Guide,* and the "More" page for the Guides Who Know Monuments of Manhattan app, which includes the guillotining of a sculptor and the *New York Times's* description of a mass transit nightmare the day this sculpture was dedicated.

Hamilton sculpture #2 (near the Grange)

Of the four Hamilton sculptures in Manhattan, this is my favorite: the liveliest and the best dressed. I wish some wealthy *Hamilton* fan would pay to have it moved around the corner and down the hill to the Grange. It looks lost in front of a garden (where the Grange used to stand) and a church. Don't miss the inscriptions on the pedestal.

The "More" page for the Guides Who Know Monuments of Man-hattan app has more info on the original location of this sculpture.

Carl Conrads, Hamilton, 1880.
Central Park.
Photos copyright © 2014
Dianne L. Durante

*William Ordway Partridge, Alexander Hamilton, 1893. At the former site of
Hamilton Grange, 287 Convent Ave. (north of 141st St.).
Photo copyright © 2004 Dianne L. Durante*

Hamilton sculpture #3 (Columbia University)

This one stands on the grounds of Columbia University, which once
upon a time was way downtown and known as King's College. Hamilton attended King's from 1774 to 1776, then headed off to war before
he received his degree.

This sculpture has been in front of Hamilton Hall since 1908. Due
west across the South Field stands *Thomas Jefferson*, by the same

Above: William Ordway Partridge, Alexander Hamilton, 1908. Columbia University. Below: Adolph A. Weinman, Alexander Hamilton, dedicated 1941. Museum of the City of New York. Photos copyright © 2014 Dianne L. Durante

sculptor, dedicated in 1914. In the dark of night the wicked words go flying.

The Jefferson sculpture is in *Outdoor Monuments of Manhattan:* see also here and here.

Hamilton Sculpture #4 (Museum of the City of New York)

This *Hamilton,* on the north end of the facade of the Museum of the City of New York (Fifth Avenue at 103rd St.), is balanced at the south end by *DeWitt Clinton.* Clinton was largely responsible for the Erie Canal, which routed the Midwest's agricultural produce through New York. Together, the two figures celebrate New York's role as the commercial capital of America.

For more on this sculpture, see ForgottenDelights.

Hamilton Sculpture #5 (Museum of American Finance)

For the Hamilton exhibition at New-York Historical Society in 2004, a pair of bronzes were commissioned: Hamilton (wearing his glasses!) facing off against Burr. This pair is now at the Museum of American Finance, which doesn't seem to have any photos on its website. Meanwhile, you can see Hamilton here; or Google "Statues Duel Hamilton Burr."

Thanks to Prof. Carrie-Ann Biondi for alerting me to this one, and Iris Bell for reminding me that a Google search turns up many more images.

HAMILTON SCULPTURES NEAR NEW YORK

Hamilton Sculpture #6 (Morristown, N.J.)

Yes, and don't be a wuss: get on a bus or train and go visit the Morristown Green. You can put your arm around this one when you're taking your selfie.

For more pics and more on this sculpture, see Chapter 5, on Lafayette.

Hamilton sculpture #7 (Paterson Great Falls)

A sculpture of Hamilton (recently refurbished) overlooks Paterson Great Falls, whose water power Hamilton and the Society of Useful Manufactures harnessed to create an industrial center in 1792.

Left: head of Hamilton, from Lafayette, Hamilton, and Washington.
Morristown Green, NJ. Sculpture by StudioEIS, Brooklyn, NY. Photo ©
2007 Dianne L. Durante Right: Franklin Simmons, Alexander Hamilton,
1905-1906. Great Falls Overlook Park, Paterson, NJ. Photo: Smithsonian
Institution via Wikimedia.

For reminding me of this sculpture and the following one, and for alerting me to the *New York Times* article that spurred me to write this post, many thanks to Rand Scholet of the Alexander Hamilton Awareness Society.

Hamilton sculpture #8 (Philadelphia)

The National Constitution Center in Philadelphia has full-size bronzes of all 42 of the delegates to the Constitutional Convention in 1787. Go have a photo op with Hamilton, Washington, Madison, and your other favorite Founding Fathers. The NCC's Wikipedia article and Wikimedia page have better photos than the NCC's site.

The NCC bronzes were created by StudioEIS, the same people who created the group of Washington, Hamilton, and Lafayette on the Morristown Green. They're famed for their meticulous historical research and execution.

Hamilton Sculpture #9 (Hamilton, Ohio)

This is the largest sculpture of Hamilton to date: 12 feet tall. Its official title is *The American Cape: Alexander Hamilton as Orator.* The sculptor, Kristen Visbal, kindly sent two images and permission to publish them; see also this page.

Above: Hamilton at National Constitution Center. Sculptures: StudioEIS, Brooklyn. Photo: Midnightdreary / Wikimedia. Below: National Constituion Center, Signers Hall—I think that's Alexander between the 2nd and 3rd doors, all by his lonesome. Philadelphia: Signers' Hall.
Photo: Ziko van Dijk / Wikipedia.

Kristen Visbal, American Cape: Hamilton as Orator, in Hamilton, OH.
Photo courtesy Kristen Visbal.

FIND A HAMILTON NEAR YOU

To see what Hamilton sculptures are near you, search the Smithsonian American Art Museum's extensive <u>Art Inventories Catalog</u>.

MORE

• I first got interested in Hamilton ca. 2002, when I began writing on outdoor sculpture in New York City, and wondered why Hamilton (whom I only knew as the face on the $10 bill) had as many sculptures as Washington. In 2004, the bicentennial of Hamilton's death, I delivered a biography in segments, as a walking tour of three Hamilton sculptures. *Alexander Hamilton: A Brief Biography* is an informal transcript of the tour. One of my favorite parts was the lengthy quotes from Hamilton, which I persuaded audience members to read. For the Kindle book, I added a timeline that sets Hamilton's life in the context of American and European history.

• Two of the Hamilton sculptures above are in my book *Outdoor Monuments of Manhattan: A Historical Guide*. The videoguide version, <u>Monuments of Manhattan</u>, is available for Android (preview <u>here</u>, purchase <u>here</u>) and iPhone (preview <u>here</u>, purchase <u>here</u>). You can also look up any of these works on the New York City Parks Department's monuments pages.

• If you want to visit all the Founding Fathers sculptures in Manhattan (plus others before 1800), a handy list is <u>here.</u>

• The Bank of New York (est. 1784) isn't the bank that Washington, Jefferson, Madison and Hamilton—and later Philip!—sing about. That one was a national bank, established in 1791. I thrashed out Hamilton's reasons for wanting a national bank for my 2004 tour, and lemme tell you, it was hard work for a humanities major. If you want the short version, see Chapter 4 of *Alexander Hamilton: A Brief Biography* (with cross-references to other chapters on the bank) and Chapter 44B.

CHAPTER 8
Hamilton's First Published Political Writing, 1774

Have you stopped to think about the way "My Shot" builds on the opening number of *Hamilton: An American Musical?* It sets Alexander Hamilton up as a hero eager to change the world, and sets up the foreboding that drives him to be non-stop. Helluva number, and one of my favorites, for reasons I'll explain in a bit.

But first, some entertaining sarcasm from Hamilton himself. Shift yourself back to the time when a clever soundbite wouldn't send you viral on the Interwebs. What gets you attention—citywide or colony-wide—is well-written, persuasive prose. If it's witty, too, even better.

A STIRRING OF REBELLION IN THE COLONIES

The *Vindication* was 17-year-old Hamilton's first lengthy political tract, running to 35 pages in print. In eighteenth-century fashion, the title also functions as the table of contents and the dust-jacket blurb: "Vindication of the Measures of Congress, from the Calumnies of their Enemies; in answer to a letter, under the signature of A.W. Farmer. Whereby his sophistry is exposed, his cavils confuted, his artifices detected, and his wit ridiculed; in a general address to the inhabitants of America, and a particular address to the farmers of the Province of New-York. Veritas magna est & praevalebit. Truth is powerful, and will prevail."

> Before I conclude this part of my address, I will answer two very singular interrogatories proposed by the Farmer, "Can we think (says he) to threaten, and bully, and frighten the supreme government of the nation into a compliance with our demands? Can we expect to force submission to our peevish and petulant humours, by exciting clamours and riots in England?" No, gentle Sir. We neither desire, nor endeavour to threaten, bully, or frighten any persons into a compliance with our demands. We have no peevish and petulant humours to be submitted to. All we aim at, is to convince your high and mighty masters, the ministry, that

we are not such asses as to let them ride us as they please. We are determined to shew them, that we know the value of freedom; nor shall their rapacity extort, that inestimable jewel from us, without a manly and virtuous struggle. But for your part, sweet Sir! tho' we cannot much applaud your wisdom, yet we are compelled to admire your valour, which leads you to hope you may be able to swear, threaten, bully and frighten all America into a compliance with your sinister designs. When properly accoutered and armed with your formidable hiccory cudgel, what may not the ministry expect from such a champion? alas! for the poor committee gentlemen, how I tremble when I reflect on the many wounds and scars they must receive from your tremendous arm! Alas! for their supporters and abettors; a very large part indeed of the continent; but what of that? they must all be soundly drubbed with that confounded hiccory cudgel; for surely you would not undertake to drub one of them, without knowing yourself able to treat all their friends and adherents in the same manner; since 'tis plain you would bring them all upon your back. (Full text is at Founders Online.)

Also from the *Vindication,* here's Hamilton's passionate appeal to his fellow New Yorkers to fight for what they value, to "take their shot"— at this point metaphorically, in the form of an embargo on goods to

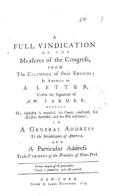

Hamilton's Vindication of the Measures of Congress, *1774, published anonymously*

Britain. He's speaking to farmers, who were worried that the export ban would destroy their livelihood.

> Is it not better, I ask, to suffer a few present inconveniencies, than to put yourselves in the way of losing every thing that is precious. Your lives, your property, your religion are all at stake. I do my duty. I warn you of your danger. If you should still be so mad, as to bring destruction upon yourselves; if you should still neglect what you owe to God and man, you cannot plead ignorance in your excuse. Your consciences will reproach you for your folly, and your children's children will curse you.
>
> You are told, the schemes of our Congress will ruin you. You are told, they have not considered your interest; but have neglected, or betrayed you. It is endeavoured to make you look upon some of the wisest and best men in the America, as rogues and rebels. What will not wicked men attempt! They will scruple nothing, that may serve their purposes. In truth, my friends, it is very unlikely any of us shall suffer much; but let the worst happen, the farmers will be better off, than other people.

Incidentally, the Congress in question is the First Continental Congress, whose "rogues and rebels" included John Adams, Samuel Adams, John Jay, Patrick Henry, and George Washington.

This chapter is already long, but do go to Founders Online and read the second paragraph—the one starting with "And first, let me ask these restless spirits, whence arises that violent antipathy they seem to entertain, not only to the natural rights of mankind; but to common sense and common modesty." I used this paragraph in my walking tour of Hamilton sculptures years back (more on that here). Read aloud and with passion, it's magnificent.

HAMILTON'S DEATH WISH?

I would like to express how profoundly dissatisfied I am that no New York library has the *Royal Danish American Gazette* from 1776, and that no institution which owns it has digitized it. I want to read in full the letter Chernow quotes (p. 72):

> It is uncertain whether it may ever be in my power to send you another line.... I am going into the army and perhaps ere long may be destined to seal with my blood the sentiments

defended by my pen. Be it so, if heaven decree it. I was born to die and my reason and conscience tell me it is impossible to die in a better or more important cause." (Cited by Chernow, p. 742, footnote 35, as "Extract of a Letter from a Gentleman in New York, dated February 18th," published 3/20/1776.)

Newton, in the recent *Alexander Hamilton: The Formative Years*, questions whether Hamilton wrote this anonymously published letter. Still, I'd like to read the whole thing.

RISE UP AND PULL DOWN

By the time the Schuyler Sisters appear (Track 5 of *Hamilton*), the Declaration of Independence has already been published. This chapter seems a good place to mention that when the Declaration was read in New York in July 1776, a mob led by the Sons of Liberty rushed from the Commons (City Hall) down to Bowling Green, where they yanked down a statue of King George III made of gilded lead. The lead was hauled off to Connecticut to be cast into bullets.

Three-quarters of a century later, the event was painted (rather … imaginatively) by Johannes Adam Simon Oertel. This article has fascinating details on the painting and the popular engraving done from it. Don't miss the list of George's surviving bits and pieces, including

Statue of George III pulled down at Bowling Green, 1776. Engraving after a painting by Johannes Adam Simon Oertel at New-York Historical Society. Photo of this engraving: Library of Congress

his horse's tail and several other chunks at the New-York Historical Society, which also has Oertel's oil and a 20th-century sketched reconstruction of what the King George sculpture actually looked like. For the modern reconstruction (3D!) see this post.

ARTISTIC INTERPRETATION / INSPIRATION

Jumping ahead more than two centuries: the *Hamilton* soundtrack's liner notes acknowledge elements of three songs in "My Shot": "Shook Ones Part 2" (lyrics here), "Going Back to Cali," and "You've Got to Be Carefully Taught."

It seems to me that most of us listen to our parents' favorite songs until we're old enough to own a music player, and that we stop listening to new music after we hit our forties—which is coincidentally when our kids start finding their own music. My parents, whose favorite singers included Frank Sinatra and Bing Crosby, thought the Beatles were long-haired hippie freaks whose music would never last. Me and rap …. Well.

With that as an introduction, perhaps you'll understand why the third song, from Rogers and Hammerstein's *South Pacific,* is the only one of those songs that I'd want to hear again. But it was fascinating to see what Miranda did with the first two – like hearing a favorite performer do a riff on a piece I didn't think I particularly liked.

MY REASONS FOR LOVING *HAMILTON: AN AMERICAN MUSICAL*

I was hooked on *Hamilton: The Musical* from the moment I heard "My Shot." It has become my go-to song when I need to gather up my nerve and commit to a choice.

Untold numbers of people have weighed in with what they love about *Hamilton: An American Musical,* but none of them have named what sent the album to the top of my own playlist when so many other candidates are jostling for the position. Since I enjoy peeling my psyche like an onion, here's what I've come up with. This is, of course, very much my own take. If you don't agree, make a snorting noise and go read someone else's blog.

1.The music is rhythmic, fast-paced, and often lyrical, which means I can hold it in my head and sing it. When music meanders so does my mind, usually in a diametrically opposed direction.

2. Lyrics. When I was 10 and there wasn't much music competing for space in my brain, a cute pop lyric with a catchy tune would stick in my mind. ("Hey, hey, we're the Monkees!" ?!?) But I grew up to be a polyglot polysyllabic philologist. I love the texture and precision of words. Common ones used in unusual ways. Uncommon ones that I seldom have the chance to use in conversation. Old-fashioned literary devices such as alliteration and assonance and consonance ("revolutionary manumission abolitionists"!). I'm amused by word play such as making "monarchy" almost rhyme with "anarchy". Combine unusual vocabulary with rhymes that come so fast they almost trip over themselves, and I'm hooked.

I can see the rap influence in the rhythm and rhymes and energy of *Hamilton*, but a great gulf separates the lyrics of "My Shot" from most hip-hop, rap, or mainstream pop lyrics.

3. Once is not enough. The words "my shot" are the start of a sequence. They're referred to in the Lee duel, at Yorktown, in Philip's duel, and in the Hamilton/Burr duel. The music reinforces the connections made by the words. The same happens with other key words and phrases, such as "satisfied," "just you wait," "rise up," and "history has its eyes on you." I love that, because it means that on the second (fourth, fifty-third) listening, I see layers of meaning that I didn't grasp at first, as the lyrics twist, intertwine, and echo.

4. The positive sense of life. I am scarily susceptible to having my mood altered by music. Put me on hold with heavy metal and I turn into one mean mother. The mood throughout *Hamilton* is upbeat. Hamilton has strong opinions on what's good and right. He uses all his considerable mental and physical energy to fight for it, and quite often, he achieves it. Such is the force of his personality that when he dies, Eliza and others remember his achievements and pick up the torch. If you think that's a minor point: imagine the difference if the curtain dropped as soon as Burr fired his shot.

Take away any one of these four elements and I'd still like the soundtrack, but I wouldn't be addicted. I still haven't seen the show live, so I can't say more than that, can I?

MORE

• For more on "sense of life," see my essay "Vitamins, Minerals, and Harry Potter" or, even better, the discussion of "sense of life" by Ayn Rand.

• The book *Hamilton: The Revolution*, by Lin-Manuel Miranda and Jeremy McCarter, will be published next month (4/12/16). It promises to trace the musical's "development from an improbable performance at the White House to its landmark opening night on Broadway six years later. In addition, Miranda has written more than 200 funny, revealing footnotes for his award-winning libretto.

CHAPTER 9

Hamilton's Death Wish, Revisited

In Chapter 8, I expressed my profound dissatisfaction at not being able to read in full a letter published in early 1776 in the *Royal Danish American Gazette,* which <u>Chernow</u> (p. 72) uses to argue that Hamilton had premonitions of death. "It is uncertain whether it may ever be in my power to send you another line…. ," says the anonymous writer. "I am going into the army and perhaps ere long may be destined to seal with my blood the sentiments defended by my pen. Be it so, if heaven decree it. I was born to die and my reason and conscience tell me it is impossible to die in a better or more important cause."

Barely a week later, I've read the letter and (because I like you!) I'm transcribing it below. Before we get to it, though, I want to talk about the source.

A NOTE ON THE ATTRIBUTION OF ANONYMOUS LETTERS

I'm not at all sure the letter in the *Royal Danish American Gazette* is by Hamilton, and I'm not at all sure Hamilton had premonitions of death or had what Chernow calls "a swooning fascination with martyrdom." <u>Chernow</u> quotes two early sources for this facet of Hamilton's character (pp. 71-72). One is a series of essays published anonymously in New York under the title "The Monitor"; the other is the *Gazette* letter.

Here's what makes my historian-hackles twitch: not all anonymous patriotic works published in New York were written by Hamilton. The colonies had many highly literate patriots, a fair number of them in New York.

The *Gazette* letter has been attributed to Hamilton partly because he was in New York in February 1776, and had ties to the West Indies. But in New York—one of the colonies' major ports—many people had ties with the West Indies, through trade and/or family relationships.

As for the Monitor essays, a comparison of sentence length and word length against all Hamilton's confirmed writings suggests that these are not his work. (See the graph in <u>Newton</u>.) I'm not particularly fond of statistical interpretations of history. I find this graph persuasive for a very personal reason: I once contracted to write a high-school textbook and was ordered to radically change my sentence structure and vocabulary. It was excruciatingly difficult.

Seven-eighths of the fun of being a historian is surveying the evidence and drawing one's own conclusions. My take is: if the Monitor essays and the *Gazette* letter aren't Hamilton's, then there's no evidence that Hamilton was driven by premonitions of death or a fascination with martyrdom. I see him as driven by his intelligence and by his desire to see the right things done the right way.

Historians often politely disagree. Rest assured that although I don't see eye to eye with him on this point, Mr. Chernow and I remain on the same terms as before I published this. To wit: he doesn't know me from Adam.

All that said, in *Hamilton: An American Musical* the repeated premonitions of death make for great theater: it's another theme running through the show. See the end of Chapter 8 on why those recurring threads make me love the musical.

THE ROYAL DANISH AMERICAN GAZETTE LETTER

And now, here's the transcription, with paragraphing and punctuation unchanged.

> Royal Danish American Gazette, March 20, 1776
> Christianstaed.
>
> Extract of a letter from a Gentleman in New York, dated February 18th.
>
> "It is not long since I paid my respects to you. Opportunities from this place are like to be so scarce for the future, that I cannot forbear embracing the present. It is uncertain whether it may ever be in my power to send you another line, not only from the forementioned cause; but from my own approaching circumstances.—I am going into the army; and perhaps, ere long, may be destined to seal with my blood, the sentiments defended by my pen—Be it so, if Heaven decree it—I was born to die; and my reason and conscience tell me it is impossible to die in a better, or more important cause. Since my last, we have met with no small loss, in the death of the immortal Montgomery, who bravely fell in an assault upon Quebec.—This man deserves as much applause as the renowned Wolff.—He encountered much greater difficulties and endured much greater fatigues, conducting an expedition under every disadvantage imaginable, in the

midst of winter in that inclement country.—His humanity, generosity, patience, fortitude and courage have never been excelled by any man—His prudence in the last instance is somewhat questionable; though much is to be said in his justification even on that score, from the necessity of his situation. By his death the expedition received a severe blow; though I trust not a fatal one. The remainder of our army still holds Carleton besieged; and large reinforcements are pouring in to them, with all possible dispatch. Before Carleton can receive any fresh forces, I flatter myself the place will be ours. Much depends upon it. General Lee is here with a body of Provincials, his design is to put this province in a state of defence against the spring, as it is expected it will be the chief seat of war. We have possessed ourselves of all the military stores in the province; a valuable acquisition; consisting chiefly of a parcel of fine cannon with their appurtenances. Gen. Clinton from Boston with a small body of forces was here lately—It is supposed he intended to have landed on Long Island, where he expected to have been joined by numbers of the inhabitants; but finding Lee had gotten the start of him, he thought it adviseable to move off to the Southward; to North Carolina, it is imagined, as the English papers announce a design of sending five regiments thither.—This city is at present evacuated by above one half of its inhabitants; under the influence of a general panic, from the appearance of Clinton and the apprehension of the men of war firing upon the city in consequence of Lee's intended fortifications—Clinton is now gone; and as to the last supposition, I believe the servants of the Ministry here are sensible of the impolicy of destroying towns as has been heretofore done—You may receive it as an infallible truth, that were this city once destroyed by them, the colonies would be lost to Britain for ever. The Ministry are driving the colonies into independence. The sound of that word was, a few months ago, as terrible as slavery to American ears; but at present the idea obtains a rapid currency. The people seem disposed to cry out for it, before their leaders will think the necessity sufficiently urgent to justify it.—Six months more, if peace be not made, will do the business; perhaps less—The cry now is, let our ports be thrown open to all nations except Great-Britain—This it is believed will be done in the spring, if an accommodation do not prevent it. You must see the immediate tendency of such a measure. Whom can Britain blame but herself?—When the colonies are irrecoverably lost, she will feel the folly of her present wicked oppression.

MORE

• Thanks to Shoshana Milgram for reminding me that scholars like to share. Thanks to Rand Scholet of the <u>Alexander Hamilton Awareness Society</u> for putting me in touch with Michael Newton, author of *<u>Alexander Hamilton: The Formative Years</u>*. Thanks most of all to Mr. Newton, who sent photos of the *Gazette* article that were taken from the display on a microfilm reader, and who pointed me to the section in his book that analyzes the Monitor essays.

• The high-school text I wrote and had to simplify is *<u>Internationalism</u>*. It was good when I handed the manuscript in; less good after the editors had a thwack at it; but even now, useful if you need to bone up quickly on U.S. foreign affairs after World War II.

• The other one eighth of the fun of being a historian is seeing how the pieces of the big picture come together. That comes after the other seven eights, but it's worth the wait. Every. Single. Time.

CHAPTER 10
Wait

Dear Alexander,

What to say? I'm having a torrid marriage with a man much, much younger than you, and our 30th anniversary is almost here. I need to take a week off to finish my gift—an anniversary book full of writing and photos and web pages swiped from the <u>Wayback Machine,</u>

This much fun is probably not legal, even in Jersey.

Can't wait to see you again, next week –

Dianne

CHAPTER 11
Thomas Paine's *Common Sense*, 1776

The pamphlet *Common Sense,* which Angelica mentions in "The Schuyler Sisters," was published anonymously in Philadelphia, on January 10, 1776. Within a few months, British expatriate Thomas Paine was known to be the author. Although others had made many of the same points (but see the note under More, below), Paine's confidence in America's potential and his plain-spoken but forceful writing made copies of *Common Sense* fly off booksellers' shelves.

Ranking books according to the percentage of people who read them, *Common Sense* remains the best-selling book in American history. In 1776, the colonies had a population of about 2.5 million. About 100,000 copies of *Common Sense* were sold within 3 months. That number soon rose to half a million. The book was frequently read aloud and shared, so its effective circulation was much wider.

Not everyone agreed with Paine (see the second John Adams excerpt below), but *Common Sense* provided a focal point for discussion. Hamilton's *Vindication of the Measures of Congress,* 1774 (see Chapter 14), discussed a wide range of topics that concerned the colonists: taxes, trade embargoes, petitions, events in Boston, the merits of the British Parliament vs. the British king. After *Common Sense* appeared, the debate shifted to one question: whether or not the colonies ought to be independent.

Common Sense has four sections:
- Of the Origin and Design of Government in general, with concise Remarks on the English Constitution
- Of Monarchy and Hereditary Succession
- Thoughts on the Present State of American Affairs
- On the Present Ability of America, with some Miscellaneous Reflections

I recently read *Common Sense,* for the first time ever as far as I can recall. (What were my American History teachers thinking?) The first and second sections were interesting as a reminder that people really did believe monarchs were anointed by God, and therefore rebellion

Left: [Thomas Paine], Common Sense. Philadelphia: R. Bell, 1776. This copy of the first edition has the title-page signature of an early owner, one W. Hamilton. (Not our guy, but pretty cool anyway.).
Right: William Sharp (1749–1824), Thomas Paine; engraving after a portrait by George Romney, 1793.

against a king was a rebellion against God. However, most of my favorite quotes are from the third and fourth sections. I'll give some of them later in the chapter. But first, a few contemporary reactions, by people who were as excited as Angelica was about reading *Common Sense.*

CHARLES LEE

On January 24, 1776, Major General Charles Lee wrote to General George Washington:

> Have You seen the pamphlet Common Sense? I never saw such a masterly irresistible performance—it will if I mistake not, in concurrence with the transcendant folly and wickedness of the Ministry give the coup de grace to G. Britain—in short I own myself convinc'd by the arguments of the necessity of seperation.

The whole letter, with Lee's charmingly erratic spelling and punctuation, is here. For Lee and the Battle of Monmouth, see Chapters 22, 23, 24, 26.)

JOHN ADAMS, FEBRUARY 1776

When *Common Sense* was published in Philadelphia in January 1776, John Adams was in the city as a Massachusetts delegate to the Continental Congress. He wrote to his beloved wife Abigail on February 18, 1776:

> I sent you from New York a Pamphlet intituled Common Sense, written in Vindication of Doctrines which there is Reason to expect that the further Encroachments of Tyranny and Depredations of Oppression, will soon make the common Faith: unless the cunning Ministry, by proposing Negociations and Terms of Reconciliation, should divert the present Current from its Channell. (More here)

GENERAL GEORGE WASHINGTON, APRIL 1776

Washington not only read *Common Sense,* but observed its profound impact on his countrymen:

> No man does, no man can, wish the restoration of peace more fervently than I do; but I hope, whenever made, it will be upon such terms, as will reflect honor upon the councils and wisdom of America. With you, I think a change in the American representation necessary. Frequent appeals to the people can be attended with no bad, but may have very salutary effects. My countrymen I know, from their form of government, and steady attachment heretofore to royalty, will come reluctantly into the idea of independence, but time and persecution bring many wonderful things to pass; and by private letters, which I have lately received from Virginia, I find "Common Sense" is working a powerful change there in the minds of many men. (Letter to Joseph Reed, April 1, 1776, from *The Writings of George Washington*

JOHN ADAMS, CA. 1801

A quarter century after *Common Sense* appeared, Adams began jotting down autobiographical notes regarding events in Philadelphia during the spring of 1776. By that time he was less enthusiastic about *Common Sense* and its author.

> I dreaded the Effect so popular a pamphlet might have, among the People, and determined to do all in my Power, to counter Act the Effect of it. My continued Occupations in Congress, allowed me no time to write any thing of any Length: but I found moments to write a small pamphlet

which Mr. Richard Henry Lee, to whom I shewed it, liked so well that he insisted on my permitting him to publish it: He accordingly got Mr. Dunlap to print it, under the Tittle of Thoughts on Government in a Letter from a Gentleman to his Friend. Common Sense was published without a Name: and I thought it best to suppress my name too: but as common Sense when it first appeared was generally by the public ascribed to me or Mr. Samuel Adams, I soon regretted that my name did not appear. ...

—Paine soon after the Appearance of my Pamphlet hurried away to my Lodgings and spent an Evening with me. His Business was to reprehend me for publishing my Pamphlet. Said he was afraid it would do hurt, and that it was repugnant to the plan he had proposed in his Common Sense. I told him it was true it was repugnant and for that reason, I had written it and consented to the publication of it: for I was as much afraid of his Work [as] he was of mine. His plan was so democratical, without any restraint or even an Attempt at any Equilibrium or Counterpoise, that it must produce confusion and every Evil Work. I told him further, that his Reasoning from the Old Testament was ridiculous, and I could hardly think him sincere. At this he laughed, and said he had taken his Ideas in that part from Milton: and then expressed a Contempt of the Old Testament and indeed of the Bible at large, which surprized me. He saw that I did not relish this, and soon check'd himself, with these Words "However I have some thoughts of publishing my Thoughts on Religion, but I believe it will be best to postpone it, to the latter part of Life." ...

The third part of Common Sense which relates wholly to the Question of Independence, was clearly written and contained a tollerable Summary of the Arguments which I had been repeating again and again in Congress for nine months. But I am bold to say there is not a Fact nor a Reason stated in it, which had not been frequently urged in Congress. The Temper and Wishes of the People, supplied every thing at that time: and the Phrases, suitable for an Emigrant from New Gate, or one who had chiefly associated with such Company, such as "The Royal Brute of England," "The Blood upon his Soul," and a few others of equal delicacy, had as much Weight with the People as his Arguments. It has been a general Opinion, that this Pamphlet was of great Importance in the Revolution. I doubted it at the time and have doubted it to this day. It probably converted some to the Doctrine of Independence, and gave others an Excuse for declaring in favour of it. (More here)

In *Patriots: The Men Who Started the American Revolution* (a very readable introduction to the Founding Fathers and the Revolution), A.J. Langguth bases much of his description of Paine in Philadelphia on Adams's notes.

MY FAVORITE QUOTES FROM COMMON SENSE
The whole text of *Common Sense* is available on Project Gutenberg.

Time vs. reason

> Perhaps the sentiments contained in the following pages, are not YET sufficiently fashionable to procure them general favour; a long habit of not thinking a thing WRONG, gives it a superficial appearance of being RIGHT, and raises at first a formidable outcry in defense of custom. But the tumult soon subsides. Time makes more converts than reason.

Sad, but true for most people.

Society vs. government

> Some writers have so confounded society with government, as to leave little or no distinction between them; whereas they are not only different, but have different origins. Society is produced by our wants, and government by our wickedness; the former promotes our happiness POSITIVELY by uniting our affections, the latter NEGATIVELY by restraining our vices. The one encourages intercourse, the other creates distinctions. The first a patron, the last a punisher.

Interesting distinction, isn't it?

"The blood of the slain, the weeping voice of nature cries, 'Tis time to part"

> Europe is too thickly planted with kingdoms to be long at peace, and whenever a war breaks out between England

and any foreign power, the trade of America goes to ruin, because of her connection with Britain. The next war may not turn out like the last, and should it not, the advocates for reconciliation now will be wishing for separation then, because, neutrality in that case, would be a safer convoy than a man of war. Every thing that is right or natural pleads for separation. The blood of the slain, the weeping voice of nature cries, 'Tis time to part. Even the distance at which the Almighty hath placed England and America, is a strong and natural proof, that the authority of the one, over the other, was never the design of Heaven.

A very persuasive argument, given events in Boston in 1775.

It is not in the power of Britain or of Europe to conquer America, if she do not conquer herself by delay and timidity.

I just can't seem to edit this next excerpt down ... And I don't really want to. It gives you a feel for the flow of Paine's argument, the emotion he packed into it, and the impact of having ideas expressed in powerful prose suitable for reading aloud.

It is the good fortune of many to live distant from the scene of sorrow; the evil is not sufficient brought to their doors to make them feel the precariousness with which all American property is possessed. But let our imaginations transport us for a few moments to Boston, that seat of wretchedness will teach us wisdom, and instruct us for ever to renounce a power in whom we can have no trust. The inhabitants of that unfortunate city, who but a few months ago were in ease and affluence, have now, no other alternative than to stay and starve, or turn out to beg. Endangered by the fire of their friends if they continue within the city, and plundered by the soldiery if they leave it. In their present condition they are prisoners without the hope of redemption, and in a general attack for their relief, they would be exposed to the fury of both armies.

Men of passive tempers look somewhat lightly over the offences of Britain, and, still hoping for the best, are apt to call out, "Come, come, we shall be friends again, for all this." But examine the passions and feelings of mankind, Bring the doctrine of reconciliation to the touchstone of nature, and then tell me, whether you can hereafter love, honour, and faithfully serve the power that hath carried fire and sword into your land? If you cannot do all these, then are you only deceiving yourselves, and by your delay bringing ruin upon posterity. Your future connection with Britain, whom you can neither love nor honour, will be forced and unnatural, and being formed only on the plan of present convenience, will in a little time fall into a relapse more wretched than the first. But if you say, you can still pass the violations over, then I ask, Hath your house been burnt? Hath your property been destroyed before your face? Are your wife and children destitute of a bed to lie on, or bread to live on? Have you lost a parent or a child by their hands, and yourself the ruined and wretched survivor? If you have not, then are you not a judge of those who have. But if you have, and still can shake hands with the murderers, then are you unworthy of the name of husband, father, friend, or lover, and whatever may be your rank or title in life, you have the heart of a coward, and the spirit of a sycophant.

This is not inflaming or exaggerating matters, but trying them by those feelings and affections which nature justifies, and without which, we should be incapable of discharging the social duties of life, or enjoying the felicities of it. I mean not to exhibit horror for the purpose of provoking revenge, but to awaken us from fatal and unmanly slumbers, that we may pursue determinately some fixed object. It is not in the power of Britain or of Europe to conquer America, if she do not conquer herself by delay and timidity. The present winter is worth an age if rightly employed, but if lost or neglected, the whole continent will partake of the misfortune; and there is no punishment which that man will not deserve, be he who, or what, or where he will, that may be the means of sacrificing a season so precious and useful.

It is repugnant to reason, to the universal order of things to all examples from former ages, to suppose, that this continent can longer remain subject to any external power. The most sanguine in Britain does not think so. The utmost stretch of human wisdom cannot, at this time, compass a plan short of separation, which can promise the continent even a year's security. Reconciliation is now a fallacious dream. Nature hath deserted the connexion, and Art cannot supply her place. For, as Milton wisely expresses, "never can true reconcilement grow where wounds of deadly hate have pierced so deep."

Every quiet method for peace hath been ineffectual. Our prayers have been rejected with disdain; and only tended to convince us, that nothing flatters vanity, or confirms obstinacy in Kings more than repeated petitioning—and nothing hath contributed more than that very measure to make the Kings of Europe absolute: Witness Denmark and Sweden. Wherefore, since nothing but blows will do, for God's sake, let us come to a final separation, and not leave the next generation to be cutting throats, under the violated unmeaning names of parent and child.

To say, they will never attempt it again is idle and visionary, we thought so at the repeal of the stamp-act, yet a year or two undeceived us; as well may we suppose that nations, which have been once defeated, will never renew the quarrel.

As to government matters, it is not in the power of Britain to do this continent justice: The business of it will soon be too weighty, and intricate, to be managed with any tolerable degree of convenience, by a power, so distant from us, and so very ignorant of us; for if they cannot conquer us, they cannot govern us. To be always running three or four thousand miles with a tale or a petition, waiting four or five months for an answer, which when obtained requires five or six more to explain it in, will in a few years be looked upon as folly and childishness—There was a time when it was proper, and there is a proper time for it to cease.

Small islands not capable of protecting themselves, are the proper objects for kingdoms to take under their care; but there is something very absurd, in supposing a continent to be perpetually governed by an island. In no instance hath nature made the satellite larger than its primary planet, and as England and America, with respect to each other, reverses the common order of nature, it is evident they belong to different systems: England to Europe, America to itself.

I am not induced by motives of pride, party, or resentment to espouse the doctrine of separation and independance; I am clearly, positively, and conscientiously persuaded that it is the true interest of this continent to be so; that every thing short of that is mere patchwork, that it can afford no lasting felicity,—that it is leaving the sword to our children, and shrinking back at a time, when, a little more, a little farther, would have rendered this continent the glory of the earth.

As Britain hath not manifested the least inclination towards a compromise, we may be assured that no terms can be obtained worthy the acceptance of the continent, or any ways equal to the expence of blood and treasure we have been already put to.

The object, contended for, ought always to bear some just proportion to the expence. The removal of North, or the whole detestable junto, is a matter unworthy the millions we have expended. A temporary stoppage of trade, was an inconvenience, which would have sufficiently ballanced the repeal of all the acts complained of, had such repeals been obtained; but if the whole continent must take up arms, if every man must be a soldier, it is scarcely worth our while to fight against a contemptible ministry only. Dearly, dearly, do we pay for the repeal of the acts, if that is all we fight for; for in a just estimation, it is as great a folly to pay a Bunker-hill price for law, as for land. As I have always considered the independancy of this continent, as an event, which sooner or later must arrive, so from the late rapid progress of the continent to maturity, the event could not be far off. Wherefore, on the breaking out of hostilities, it was not worth the while to have disputed a matter, which time would have finally redressed, unless we meant to be in earnest; otherwise, it is like wasting an estate on a suit at law, to regulate the trespasses of a tenant, whose lease is just expiring. No man was a warmer wisher for reconciliation than myself, before the fatal nineteenth of April 1775, but the moment the event of that day was made known, I rejected the hardened, sullen tempered Pharaoh of England for ever; and disdain the wretch, that with the pretended title of father of his people can unfeelingly hear of their slaughter, and composedly sleep with their blood upon his soul.

The need for a declaration of independence

And finally, here's Paine's summary. Read it, and then read the Declaration of Independence.

To Conclude, however strange it may appear to some, or however unwilling they may be to think so, matters not, but many strong and striking reasons may be given, to shew, that nothing can settle our affairs so expeditiously as an open and determined declaration for independance. Some of which are,

First.—It is the custom of nations, when any two are at war, for some other powers, not engaged in the quarrel, to step in as mediators, and bring about the preliminaries of a peace: but while America calls herself the Subject of Great-Britain, no power, however well disposed she may be, can offer her mediation. Wherefore, in our present state we may quarrel on for ever.

Secondly.—It is unreasonable to suppose, that France or Spain will give us any kind of assistance, if we mean only, to make use of that assistance for the purpose of repairing the breach, and strengthening the connection between Britain and America; because, those powers would be sufferers by the consequences.

Thirdly.—While we profess ourselves the subjects of Britain, we must, in the eye of foreign nations, be considered as rebels. The precedent is somewhat dangerous to their peace, for men to be in arms under the name of subjects; we, on the spot, can solve the paradox: but to unite resistance and subjection, requires an idea much too refined for common understanding.

Fourthly.—Were a manifesto to be published, and despatched to foreign courts, setting forth the miseries we have endured, and the peaceable methods we have ineffectually used for redress; declaring, at the same time, that not being able, any longer, to live happily or safely under the cruel disposition of the British court, we had been driven to the necessity of breaking off all connections with her; at the same time, assuring all such courts of our peaceable disposition towards them, and of our desire of entering into trade with them: Such a memorial would produce more good effects to this Continent, than if a ship were freighted with petitions to Britain.

Under our present denomination of British subjects, we can neither be received nor heard abroad: The custom of all courts is against us, and will be so, until, by an independance, we take rank with other nations.

These proceedings may at first appear strange and difficult; but, like all other steps which we have already passed over, will in a little time become familiar and agreeable; and, until an independance is declared, the Continent will feel itself like a man who continues putting off some unpleasant business from day to day, yet knows it must be done, hates to set about it, wishes it over, and is continually haunted with the thoughts of its necessity.

MORE

• As a historian, I'm always on the look-out for facts and context I've missed. It's what all good historians do: expand their knowledge and integrate it with what they already know. I realized early on in this series of blog posts that due to time constraints (the job that pays the mortgage), I wouldn't be able to read widely in secondary sources. That meant my grasp of the historical context might not always be correct. So I was thrilled when Gary Berton of the Thomas Paine National Historical Association emailed me a correction to my first paragraph in this essay:

Common Sense did not just reiterate the points made before him in stronger language. He introduced to the world what would become the foundations of democracy, which Adams and Hamilton denounced: one-person, one-vote; no rule by elites; monarchy is not only absurd but illegal; we can't base our government on tradition or religion (he denounced the concept of original sin); representative democracy; a constitution designed to protect rights; and more. These formed the basis for the age of democratic revolutions which morphed into the progressive struggles under industrial capitalism. (Quoted with Mr. Berton's permission)

• For the context of Common Sense, see Chapter 15.

• Thomas Paine used to live at what is now 309 Bleecker St.—currently the home of the Reiss store, between Grove and 7th Avenue. Read the details in the excellent blog post by Daytonian in Manhattan.

• A relief plaque with a portrait of Paine commemorates his residence at a nearby house on Grove Street: see the blog post by Forgotten New York.

CHAPTER 12
Angelica Schuyler (1756-1814)

In 1776, the "old money" families in New York—the ones that had been around in Dutch times and had continued to thrive for a century under the British—were the Van Rensselaers, the Van Cortlandts, and the Schuylers. Angelica's parentage was a trifecta: a Schuyler married to a Van Rensselaer, with Van Cortlandts for paternal grandmother and maternal step-grandmother.

PAPA SCHUYLER

Philip Schuyler (1733-1804), Angelica's father, was elected to the Second Continental Congress in 1775, and soon afterward was appointed a major-general in the Continental Army. From 1789 to 1791, he served as one of of New York's first senators. Bumped out of office by Aaron Burr, Schuyler returned to the Senate from 1797 to 1798.

MAMA SCHUYLER

Angelica's mother, Catherine Van Rensselaer Schuyler (1734-1803), bore 15 children: five daughters and three sons survived to childhood. Family tradition said that in 1777, when British troops were marching toward the family's country home in Saratoga, Mama Schuyler torched the wheat fields to deny them food. In 1852 Emanuel Gottlieb Leutze,

Mansions built by Philip Schuyler still stand in <u>Albany</u> and <u>Saratoga</u>. Both photos: Wikipedia / Matt Wade Photography

whom you jolly well ought to know for his _Washington Crossing the Delaware,_ painted Mama Schuyler as an incendiary patriot. He based her face on a <u>portrait now at the New-York Historical Society</u>. No documentation has been found to support the family tradition—but it makes for a charming picture.

Left: Emmanuel Gottlieb Leutze, Mrs. Schuyler Burning Her Wheat Fields on the Approach of the British, 1852. Photo: Los Angeles County Museum of Art. Right: Angelica's mother, Catherine Van Rensselaer Schuyler. Photo: New-York Historical Society

ANGELICA'S MARRIAGE

Angelica, the eldest Schuyler child, was born in 1756—a year or so earlier than Alexander Hamilton, if you accept 1757 as the year of his birth. By all accounts, Angelica's intelligence, beauty, wit, and charm were remarkable. But this isn't an era when being the wittiest and prettiest girl in the room would get you noticed, if the room you were in was a pauper's hovel. In fact, during the eighteenth century—before the Industrial Revolution, before the rise of capitalism and corporations, when divorce meant social disgrace – the usual way to seal a merger of fortunes was by a marriage. Angelica's parents would have expected their children to marry people they approved of, who would enhance or at least preserve the family's status and/or wealth.

Angelica circumvented that expectation by eloping in 1777 with John Barker Church (1748-1818), an Englishman who made a fortune as a supplier to the Continental and French armies. (Mama Schuyler refused to meet Angelica and John until the grandparents intervened.) Soon after the Revolutionary War ended, Church was sent as U.S. envoy to France from 1783 to 1785. Angelica and her family moved to Paris, where she became friends with Benjamin Franklin, Thomas Jefferson, and the Marquis de Lafayette. Later the

Church family relocated to London, where John was elected to Parliament. Except for a brief visit in 1789 to see Washington's inauguration as first president of the United States, Angelica's family lived in Europe until 1797.

In 1799, John Barker Church became one of twelve founding directors of the Manhattan Company. The ostensible purpose of the Company—which was the brainchild of Aaron Burr—was to bring fresh water to Manhattan. But through a loophole in the legislation, the directors intended to create a bank that would be in direct competition with the Bank of New York, which Hamilton had helped establish in 1784 (now BNY Mellon; see Chapter 7 and Chapter 44B). The water never flowed, but the bank survived and (mostly) prospered, evolving into Chase Manhattan and then J.P. Morgan Chase. Later in 1799, Church accused fellow-director Burr of taking bribes. The two dueled in Weehawken. Both emerged unscathed. The oft-repeated story that they used the same pistols as Burr and Hamilton fired five years later is apparently not true.

ANGELICA'S INTELLECT

The painting on the following page shows Angelica with her son in 1785; it was painted by John Trumbull, whom you jolly well ought to know for his *Declaration of Independence*, his *Washington Before the Battle of Trenton*, and his *Surrender of Lord Cornwallis at Yorktown* (in which Alexander Hamilton makes a profile appearance: see Chapter 37).

I love seeing Angelica in that painting ... but what sort of mind did she have? What did she think and say?

Unfortunately, few of her letters have survived. Among those I've seen, my favorite is this one, written to Eliza from London on 7/30/1794.

> I have a letter my dear Eliza from my worthy friend M. de Talleyrand who expresses to me his gratitude for an introduction to you and my Amiable, by my Amiable you know that I mean your Husband, for I love him very much and if you were as generous as the old Romans, you would lend him to me for a little while, but do not be jealous, my dear Eliza, since I am more solicitous to promote his laudable ambition, than any person in the world, and there is no summit of true glory which I do not desire he may attain; provided always that he pleases to give me a little chit-chat, and sometimes to say, I wish our dear Angelica was

here. Talleyrand and Beaumetz write in raptures to all their friends of your kindness, and Colonel Hamilton's abilities and manners, and I receive innumerable compliments on his and your account.

Ah! Bess! you were a lucky girl to get so clever and so good a companion.

Mr Jay has been perfecctly well received at Court and by the Ministers, as yet no material business is done. The people are anxious for a peace with America, and the allied armies are beat out of Flanders and on the Rhine. These circumstances may determine the Minister to be just and wise. Mr. Jay dined with Mr. Fox at our house a few days after his arrival.

Mr. Morris is building a palace, do you think Monsieur l'Enfant would send me a drawing of it? Merely from curiosity, for one wishes to see the plan of a house which it is said, will cost, when furnished 40,000 pounds Sterling. [Quoted in _An Intimate Life of Alexander Hamilton_, by Allan McLane Hamilton; it's not clear whether this is the entire letter]

This is the letter paraphrased in _Hamilton: An American Muscial_ as, "If you really loved me, you would share him." It's one of the pieces

John Trumbull, Angelica Schuyler Church, Her Son Philip, and a Servant, 1785. Private collection. Photo: Wikipedia.

of evidence most frequently cited by those who believe Angelica and
Alexander had an affair. There is no indisputable evidence of such an
affair. It's worth noting, too, that this letter wasn't written in 1780,
when Alexander and Eliza met and married, but fourteen years later.
... As a historian, I suppose I ought to present you with all the evidence and balance all the possibilities. As a woman, I simply can't
imagine Angelica—who was close friends with Eliza all her life (there
is plenty of evidence of that)—jumping into bed with Alexander, at the
risk of losing both Eliza and Alexander. Done talking about that now.
(Or not: see Chapters 53 and 59.)

Let's get back to the rest of the letter. Angelica displays an impressive knowledge of politics and culture. The "Mr. Jay" who dined
at her home was the same one who collaborated on *The Federalist
Papers* with Hamilton and Madison (Chapters 52 through 57). He was
in London negotiating what became known as "Jay's Treaty," which
settled significant disputes between the United States and Great Britain over military occupation, debts, and trade.

The Mr. Morris who was building a palace was financier Robert
Morris, who signed the Declaration of Independence and the Constitution. Morris turned down Washington's offer of the position
of secretary of the Treasury, and recommended Hamilton for it. (See
Chapter 31.) Morris's enormous mansion in Philadelphia, filling the
entire block between Walnut, Chestnut, 7th, and 8th Streets, was left
incomplete when he went bankrupt a few years later. L'Enfant, whom
Angelica mentions with casual familiarity, later designed the plan for
the city of Washington, D.C.

All this political and social savvy was displayed in a letter to her
sister—not intended for publication or meant to impress. You want to
see a mind at work, look at Angelica.

ANGELICA AND THOMAS JEFFERSON

More letters survive to Angelica than from her—and the letters
to her were written by luminaries. This one from Hamilton, dated
12/6/1787 (part of a much longer letter) has also fueled discussions about their possible affair:

> I seldom write to a lady without fancying the relation of
> lover and mistress. It has a very inspiring effect. And in
> your case the dullest materials could not help feeling that
> propensity. I have a great opinion of your discernment and

therefore I venture to rant. If you read this letter in a certain mood, you will easily divine that in which I write it.

But Thomas Jefferson seems to have been equally enamored of Angelica. After she visited him in Paris, he wrote on 2/17/1788:

> The morning you left us, all was wrong, even the sunshine was provoking, with which I never quarreled before. I took it into my head he shone only to throw light on our loss: to present a cheerfulness not at all in unison with my mind. I mounted my horse earlier than common. I took by instinct the road you had taken. … I think I have discovered a method of preventing this dejection of mind on any future parting. It is this. When you come again I will employ myself in finding or fancying that you have some faults. & I will draw a veil over all your good qualities if I can find one large enough. (More here)

The Marquis de Lafayette wrote lengthy epistles to Angelica. George Washington, too, was on quite good terms with her: see this letter of 12/4/1798. Personally, I'm inclined to make allowances for the effusive prose style of the eighteenth century, rather than assuming Angelica rolled into bed with all those fond Founding Fathers.

MORE

• This site claims that Angelica is buried in Trinity Churchyard, not far from Alexander Hamilton—but some guides at Trinity Church say not. HT to Carrie-Ann Biondi for letting me know that.

• For an example of the convoluted Van Rensselaer / Van Cortlandt / Schuyler relationships, see the provenance of this elegant 17th-century teapot, which may be the earliest surviving teapot to have been made in New York. It belonged to Angelica's mother, so let's go right ahead and imagine Angelica drinking tea poured from it.

Angelica's signature, from an 1811 letter to the Prince of Wales, at University of Virginia. See A Guide to the Papers of Angelica Schuyler Church.

• For information on Angelica's mother and father, I've treated the entries in the <u>American National Biography</u> as definitive: it's certainly more reliable than Wikipedia. On the other hand, how can the article on Hamilton not cite <u>Chernow's biography of Hamilton</u> (2004) or <u>Michael Newton's extraordinarily thorough work on his formative years</u> (2015)? The Oxford University Press (which runs ANB) needs to set a repeating <u>GQueues</u> reminder to tell its scholars to update their articles.

Teapot by Kiliaen Van Rensselaer, ca. 1690.
Photo: New-York Historical Society

• The most cohesive account of Angelica's correspondence that I've seen is <u>on this WordPress site</u>. I do wish someone would proof that page and add the missing spaces. (Cranky today, aren't we?)

• The University of Virginia recently bought from Angelica's descendants a treasure-trove of letters to her, some of which are cited above. The page for the exhibition "<u>Muse and Confidante</u>" includes links to images of many of the letters. This <u>charming fangirl blog post</u> has yet more images.

• Angelica was introduced to Jefferson by Maria Cosway, a mutual friend. I had never heard of Cosway until I saw a 2014 production by Salon-Sanctuary, "<u>More Between Heaven and Earth: Thomas Jefferson, Maria Cosway, and the Music and Philosophy of the Enlightenment</u>." It was held at the reconstructed Fraunces Tavern, and it was exceedingly enjoyable. If you're a fan of 18th-century prose style and music, get your name added to the mailing list for <u>Salon-Sanctuary</u>, in case they do a reprise, or set up a Google alert. I only heard of it because I know the <u>people who did the jaw-droppingly beautiful costumes</u>.

CHAPTER 13
New York, New York (1625-1783)

New York is the greatest city in the world: no argument from me. But greatness has to start somewhere …

Here's the Dutch settlement at the southern end of Manhattan a few years before Peter Stuyvesant was sent by the West India Company to manage New Netherland. The Dutch colony stretched from Schenectady to the southern end of Delaware, with its headquarters at New Amsterdam.

Settlement of lower Manhattan, 1642:
a later map, with the 1811 street grid superimposed.

The image below shows what seems to have been the grandest building in the city during the 17th century. According to <u>Shorto,</u> it was the City Tavern until 1653, when the town was granted a municipal government. At that point it became City Hall. (There's a joke there somewhere.) Shorto says the pavement at Pearl Street and Coenties Slip has an outline of the building, which is now on my must-stand-there list.

First City Hall. Erected 1642, taken down in 1700. From an old print in Valentine's Manual for 1852.

City Hall, ca. 1542-1700 (19th-century rendition).

In the map below, you can see the Fort Amsterdam at the south end of Manhattan, which looks impressive.

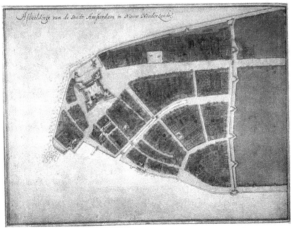

The 1660 Castello Plan of New Amsterdam.

Not so much. When four British men-of-war sailed into the harbor in 1664 to grab the island for King Charles II, Peter Stuyvesant wrote to his employers:

We have no soldiers, we have no gunpowder, we are short of food. Furthermore the citizens are completely disheartened. They cannot see that there is the slightest chance of relief in the case of a siege, and if the island falls into the hands of the invaders, they fear for the lives of themselves and their wives and their children. It is clearly apparent that this town cannot possibly hope to hold out for more than a very few days. (More here)

The letter never reached the West India Company: no Dutch ship managed to evade the British men-of-war. Here's the town just before it was surrendered to the British.

View of New Amsterdam, 1664. (Love the windmill!)

New Amsterdam became New York. Fort Amsterdam became Fort George, and the area under its battery of guns became … Well, you can guess.

On the 1729 map—when the British had been in control for six decades—the town has grown, but you're still in the country by the time you reach the pond that became the site of the notorious Five Points (Canal / Centre / Bowery / Park Row). Queen Street, where Hercules Mulligan eventually had his tailor shop (see Chapter 6), is near the river on the east side.

Below it is a view of New York a dozen years before the Revolution—1764, the year between the end of the French and Indian War

View of New York almost 60 years after the British took it over:
a 1729 map.

New York ca. 1764.

and the passage of the much-resented Quartering Act and Stamp Act. Fort George is front and center, flying an British flag of extraordinary dimensions.

THE REVOLUTION IN NEW YORK

In April 1775, Americans clashed with British troops at Lexington and Concord, in Massachusetts. Two months later, Washington was named commander-in-chief of the Continental Army and Boston was besieged. Boston's situation provoked many New Yorkers to flee their city for fear of similar reprisals. By mid-1776, when the British fleet sailed into New York Harbor, the city's population is estimated to have plummeted from about 20,000 to about 5,000.

In September—a week after the Continental Army fled and the British occupied the city—a devastating fire ripped north from the Battery. It destroyed some 500 buildings, probably a third of the city's total. As the British searched for arsonists, Nathan Hale was hauled in as a suspicious character, and hanged as a spy the following day.

The red area on the map below marks the fire damage.

Manhattan showing in red the extent of damage
from the Great Fire of 1776.

Nothing was done to repair this damage during the British occupation: soldiers have other priorities.

A sensible person would end this here ... what the hell.

Here's a selection of the few Revolutionary War-era buildings in Manhattan that are still standing, or have been more-or-less-faithfully reconstructed—working south to north.

1. Fraunces Tavern

On November 25, 1783, General George Washington rode down Broadway to reclaim the city after the British finally evacuated it. (Pics here.) Then he visited tailor and ex-spy Hercules Mulligan (Chapter 6). For the next ten days Washington resided at Fraunces Tavern, 54 Pearl St. (near Broad). He held a farewell dinner for his officers there on Decemer 4.

The Tavern was built in 1719. What stands on the site now is, according to the _AIA Guide to New York City_, "a highly conjectural construction—not a restoration—based on 'typical' buildings of 'the period,' parts of remaining walls, and a lot of guesswork" (p. 15 in the 4th ed.). Today the building contains an upscale restaurant and a gift shop.

Fraunces Tavern, from the cover of a 1920 guidebook.

2. Trinity Church (and St. Paul's Chapel)

Alexander and Eliza were members of Trinity Church, on Broadway at Wall Street, whose current home dates to 1839. Trinity was one of the hundreds of buildings lost during the Great Fire of September 1776. St. Paul's Chapel (209 Broadway, at Fulton) was just barely outside the conflagration. Its construction date of 1766 makes it the oldest church standing in Manhattan.

At the entrance to St. Paul's is a memorial to General Richard Montgomery, who died in 1775 during the American invasion of Canada. (Yes, we did.) Philip Schuyler was nominally in command of that invasion, and Aaron Burr served under Montgomery. Inside St Paul's, beneath the Great Seal of the United States, is the pew where President George Washington sat when he attended services in New York.

St Paul's Chapel: exterior, monument to Montgomery, and Washington's pew. The inscription on the base of the monument reads, "This Monument is erected by the order of CONGRESS 25th Janry. 1776 to transmit to Posterity a grateful remembrance of the patriotism conduct enterprize & perseverance of Major General RICHARD MONTGOMERY, who after a series of successes amidst the most discouraging Difficulties Fell in the attack on QUEBEC 31st Decbr. 1775, Aged 37 Years." Below it is a line in Latin stating that the plaque was designed and carved in Paris; I can't read the date in the photo I have at hand. Photos: Wikipedia

3. The Libery Pole

If you stand on the west side of City Hall and crane your eyes skyward, you'll see a flagpole that bears at its top a gilded plaque with the word "Liberty." In April 1766, when the Stamp Act was repealed, the colonists believed it was due to the efforts of King George III. Grateful New Yorkers commissioned a gilded statue of him for Bowling Green (see Chapter 8)– and a crowd of rowdy patriots stuck a pine tree on the northwestern corner of the Commons (now City Hall Park), proclaiming it a liberty pole. It bore a sign reading "George III, Pitt and Liberty." On the one-year anniversary of the repeal, British regulars hacked down the tree. The Sons of Liberty raised another the very next day, axe-proofing it with iron bands. British soldiers knocked it down. Two days later the Sons of Liberty set up a third pole, and refused to let the British soldiers patrol or drill. George III told the governor of New York to refuse to sign any legislation passed by the Assembly until New Yorkers became properly submissive again. (See Ellis, pp. 150-1.) The current pole dates to 1921.

Liberty Pole in City Hall Park.
Photos copyright © 2017 Dianne L. Durante

4. Prison Ship Martyrs' Monument

The massively destructive fire of 1776 resulted in a shortage of buildings to house citizens and troops. When American prisoners-of-war from the Battle of Long Island and the Battle of Fort Washington were brought to Manhattan, they were shoved by the hundreds into large, sturdy, but unaccommodating buildings such as sugar warehouses. A window from the Rhinelander Sugar Factory is preserved near One Police Plaza. It's Revolutionary War vintage, but the prisoners were probably kept in a warehouse owned by the Livingstons. See the <u>Daytonian in Manhattan</u> for a thorough discussion with lots of pics, and read <u>this chilling description</u> from a survivor.

Washington did not make a practice of prisoner exchanges: well-trained British soldiers returned to their units would have been sent back out to capture or kill more Americans. So the number of prisoners in New York—which was the British army's headquarters in the

Livingston Sugar House on Liberty Street, used as a prison during the Revolutionary War. Image: Wikipedia.

colonies—continually grew. Eventually many of these prisoners were shifted out of Manhattan, locked up in prison hulks in Wallabout Bay. That's on the Brooklyn shore between where the Manhattan and Williamsburg Bridges now stand.

During the course of the Revolution, some 6,800 American soldiers died in battle. It's estimated that 11,000 died as prisoners of war in New York. The <u>Prison Ship Martyrs' Monument</u> in Fort Greene is a belated tribute to them.

HMS Jersey, dismasted and rudderless, was used to house American prisoners in Wallabout Bay during the Revolutionary War.
Image: Wikipedia.

5. The Morris-Jumel Mansion

The <u>Morris-Jumel Mansion</u> (65 Jumel Terrace, near Sylvan Terrace, at about 161st St.) is Manhattan's oldest house, built in 1765. During the Battle of Harlem Heights in 1776, it was Washington's headquarters. In 1790, as president, he held a dinner there whose guests included John Adams, Thomas Jefferson, and Alexander Hamilton. Aaron Burr (Chapter 3) later married the woman who owned it.

Morris-Jumel Mansion, from a 1936 survey. Photo: Library of Congress via Wikipedia. Awesome photos of the interior <u>here</u>.

6.Reconstruction of a Hessian hut

You'd be surprised what obscure places you find when you home-school a kid in New York. So:

The Dyckman family returned to Manhattan in 1783 to find that the British had burned down their farmhouse. In 1785, they rebuilt nearby, at what's now 4881 Broadway (204th St.). Dyckman House is the oldest farmhouse standing in Manhattan; but then, there's not much competition in that category, is there? When the farmhouse was being restored in the early 20th century, excavation of the area around it turned up the foundations of 60 huts that had housed Hessian mercenaries during the Revolutionary War. One "Hessian hut" was rebuilt. See the excellent Daytonian in Manhattan post on the farmhouse and the hut.

Most American soldiers would have considered these luxury accommodations.

Hessian Hut reconstruction behind Dyckman House.
Photos copyright © 2013 Dianne L. Durante

UPWARD MOBILITY IN NEW YORK

Russell Shorto argues that New York became a place where anyone could rise above his station because of a unique combination of Dutch and English ideas. In 1653, the States General of Holland granted New Amsterdam a municipal government, in reaction to the *Remonstrance* of Adriaen van der Donck (an amazing character). Men could become citizens as "small burghers"—they could even pay the

18-stiver fee for that status in installments (forms here). As they prospered, they could rise to the status of great burgher (fee of 3 guilders), which gave them a voice in setting policy. That sort of social mobility wasn't common in Europe. Nor was the tolerance for different races and creeds that was practiced in this out-of-the-way trading post.

In 1664, the name of the town changed from New Amsterdam to New York. But the people were the same. By the Articles of Capitulation that were signed when the British took over, the traders stayed put, and their systems of government and business remained intact. If it ain't broke, don't fix it: as Shorto points out, the melting pot that was New Amsterdam was turning a nice profit, and that's why the British wanted to control it.

The English who came to New York in the 17th and early 18th centuries brought with them a firm conviction in individual rights (life, liberty, property), based largely on the writings of John Locke. Together, individual rights and social mobility made for a place where anyone could remake himself into a new and better man.

MORE

• This interview with historian David McCullough about New York during the Revolutionary War is fascinating.

• Russell Shorto's *Island at the Center of the World* did for the Dutch settlement on Manhattan almost as much as *Hamilton: An American Musical* did for Alexander Hamilton.

• My favorite survey of the history of New York up to the 1960s is Edward Robb Ellis's *The Epic of New York City*. Burrows and Wallace's *Gotham: A History of New York to 1898* has a jaw-dropping depth of research, but it's an extremely long, dense read; I prefer my history more narrative than statistical.

• The Grange wasn't built until 1802. See Chapter 7.

• If you want to visit the sculptures of all the Founding Fathers that stand in Manhattan (plus others figures who date before 1800), a handy list is here.

CHAPTER 14

Hamilton vs. Seabury, 1774-1775

By 1774, 45-year-old Reverend Samuel Seabury (1729-1796) was a veteran of verbal combat. Assigned to a church in New Jersey from 1754 to 1757, he became embroiled in the debate over whether King's College in New York (est. 1754) should be nondenominational or run by the Church of England. As an Anglican, Seabury naturally favored the Church of England. His side won.

From 1767 to 1776, as rector of St Peter's Church in Westchester, he proclaimed the dire need for an American bishop. The New York papers covered opposing sides of that debate with articles such as "The American Whig," "A Whip for the American Whig," and "A Kick for the Whipper."

As the colonists became ever more discontented with British rule, Seabury insisted that he had pledged his loyalty to the crown when he was ordained: the head of the Church of England was the king of England. (You remember the business about Henry VIII's divorce, right?) In November 1774, under the name A.W. Farmer – A Westchester Farmer—Seabury published _Free Thoughts on the Proceedings of the Continental Congress_. In it, he attacked Congress's October 1774 resolution to boycott British goods.

Of the three rebuttals to _Free Thoughts_ that quickly appeared, the only one Seabury deigned to answer was the anonymous _A Full Vindication of the Measures of the Congress, from the Calumnnies of their Enemies, in Answer to a letter, under the Signature of A.W. Farmer._ The _Vindication_ was Alexander Hamilton's first venture into the political arena. It ran to 35 pages. Seabury replied to the _Vindication,_ and Hamilton responded with _The Farmer Refuted,_ a hefty 78-page work published in February 1775.

Let's all make a loud, screechy noise and rewind ourselves to 1774. Hamilton isn't famous and revered: he's a not-quite-18-year-old college student. Here's the question to answer, without the benefit of hindsight: what is it about Hamilton's _Vindication_ that makes such an impact on his fellow colonists? In particular, whom do Seabury and Hamilton address, and what sort of arguments do they use?

SAMUEL SEABURY

Seabury's opening volley is that the colonies are a scene of "confusion and discord," and that the Continental Congress has "ignorantly misunderstood, carelessly neglected, or basely betrayed the interests of all the Colonies." His structure is a discussion of the likely short-term and long-term effects of the Congress's non-importation, non-exportation, and non-consumption agreements.

Sometimes Seabury is very specific: for example, in his projections of what will happen to sales of flax-seed, grain and sheep once the boycott is in force. Sometimes he paints a broader picture: Our feeble efforts won't harm Great Britain, who commands the seas and will find other trading partners. The prices of staples here in New York will rise if fewer staples are imported. The debts of us farmers will rise when we're unable to export our goods.

Seabury is not above trying to get what he wants by crying shame — in fact, it's his first major argument. Do we really want to assert ourselves in a way that will harm people in Britain and its other colonies?

> The manufacturers of Great-Britain, the inhabitants of Ireland, and of the West-Indies, have done us no injury. They have been no ways instrumental in bringing our distresses upon us. Shall we then revenge ourselves upon them? Shall we endeavour to starve them into a compliance with our humours? Shall we, without any provocation, tempt or force them into riots and insurrections, which must be attended with the ruin of many—probably with the death of some of them? Shall we attempt to unsettle the whole British

Rev. Samuel Seabury, and his Free Thoughts, 1774. The line above the year of printing says, "Hear me, for I WILL speak!"

Government–to throw all into confusion, because our self-will is not complied with? Because the ill-projected, ill-conducted, abominable scheme of some of the colonists, to form a republican government independent of Great-Britain, cannot otherwise succeed?–Good God! can we look forward to the ruin, destruction, and desolation of the whole British Empire, without one relenting thought? Can we contemplate it with pleasure; and promote it with all our might and vigour, and at the same time call ourselves his Majesty's most dutiful and loyal subjects? Whatever the Gentlemen of the Congress may think of the matter, the spirit that dictated such a measure, was not the spirit of humanity.

Another Seabury favorite is scare tactics:

We have no trade but under the protection of Great-Britain. We can trade nowhere but where she pleases. We have no influence abroad, no ambassadors, no consuls, no fleet to protect our ships in passing the seas, nor our merchants and people in foreign countries. Should our mad schemes take place, our sailors, ship-carpenters, carmen, sail-makers, riggers, miners, smelters, forge-men, and workers in bar-iron, &c. would be immediately out of employ; and we should have twenty mobs and riots in our own country, before one would happen in Britain or Ireland. Want of food will make these people mad, and they will come in troops upon our farms, and take that by force which they have not money to purchase. And who could blame them? Justice, indeed, might hang them; but the sympathetic eye would drop the tear of humanity on their grave.

Seabury closes with a plea for his fellow farmers to petition their (British-approved) general assemblies:

Let me intreat you, my Friends, to have nothing to do with these men, or with any of the same stamp. Peace and quietness suit you best. Confusion, and Discord, and Violence, and War, are sure destruction to the farmer. Without peace he cannot till his lands; unless protected by the laws, he cannot carry his produce to market. Peace indeed is departed from us for the present, and the protection of the laws has ceased. But I trust in God, there is yet one method left, which, by prudent management, will free us from all our difficulties; restore peace again to our dwellings, and give us the

firm security of the laws for our protection. Renounce all
dependence on Congresses, and Committees. They have
neglected, or betrayed your interests. Turn then your eyes
to your constitutional representatives. They are the true, and
legal, and have been hitherto, the faithful defenders of your
rights, and liberties; and you have no reason to think but that
they will ever be so. ...

Whatever you may be taught by designing men to think of
the government at home [i.e., the British Parliament], they,
I am certain, would embrace us with the arms of friendship;
they would press us to their bosoms, to their hearts, would
we give them a fair opportunity. This opportunity our
Assembly alone can give them. And this opportunity, I trust,
they will give them, unless we prevent all possibility of
accommodation, by our own perverseness, and ill conduct.
And then, God only knows where our distresses may
terminate.

November 16, 1774—A.W. Farmer

Seabury's pamphlet is sharply focused on the proposed boycott of British goods. He addresses himself specifically to farmers (as producers,
debtors, and country folk), pitting them against businessmen (as mid-
dlemen, creditors, and City slickers). He closes with the dire warning
of evils to come.

He is, in fact, both decisive and divisive.

ALEXANDER HAMILTON

Seventeen-year-old Hamilton opens his response to *Free
Thoughts* with with feigned incredulity:

It was hardly to be expected that any man could be so
presumptuous, as openly to controvert the equity, wisdom,
and authority of the measures, adopted by the congress
... But lest they should have a tendency to mislead, and
prejudice the minds of a few; it cannot be deemed altogether
useless to bestow some notice upon them.

Having hooked those of his readers who were already inclined to be
rebellious, he moves the discussion from specific acts of the Continental Congress to a broad philosophical abstraction: the nature of man

and man's rights. This is my favorite paragraph in the *Vindication*, and since I didn't quote it in Chapter 8, I'll do it here:

> And first, let me ask these restless spirits, whence arises that violent antipathy they seem to entertain, not only to the natural rights of mankind; but to common sense and common modesty. That they are enemies to the natural rights of mankind is manifest, because they wish to see one part of their species enslaved by another. That they have an invincible aversion to common sense is apparent in many respects: They endeavour to persuade us, that the absolute sovereignty of parliament does not imply our absolute slavery; that it is a Christian duty to submit to be plundered of all we have, merely because some of our fellow-subjects are wicked enough to require it of us, that slavery, so far from being a great evil, is a great blessing; and even, that our contest with Britain is founded entirely upon the petty duty of 3 pence per pound on East India tea; whereas the whole world knows, it is built upon this interesting question, whether the inhabitants of Great-Britain have a right to dispose of the lives and properties of the inhabitants of America, or not?

Then Hamilton proceeds to define his terms ("The only distinction between freedom and slavery consists in this …"), state his principle ("That Americans are intitled to freedom, is incontestible upon every

Vindication of the Measures of Congress, 1774.

rational principle"), and address what he sees as the major disagree-
ment with Great Britain ("What then is the subject of our controversy
with the mother country?"). He runs through the history of the dis-
agreement ("In the infancy of the present dispute ..."), and presently makes one of his strongest points in favor of non-importation and
non-exportation:

> There is no law, either of nature, or of the civil society in
> which we live, that obliges us to purchase, and make use
> of the products and manufactures of a different land, or
> people. It is indeed a dictate of humanity to contribute to
> the support and happiness of our fellow creatures and more
> especially those who are allied to us by the ties of blood,
> interest, and mutual protection; but humanity does not
> require us to sacrifice our own security and welfare to the
> convenience, or advantage of others. Self preservation is the
> first principle of our nature. When our lives and properties
> are at stake, it would be foolish and unnatural to refrain from
> such measures as might preserve them, because they would
> be detrimental to others.

Hamilton discusses the principles that make for good policy ("To render it agreeable to good policy, three things are requisite ...") and the
results of becoming enslaved to Britain ("Should Americans submit to
become the vassals of their fellow-subjects in Great Britain ..."). In
my Library of America edition of Hamilton's works, this first part of
the *Vindication* occupies pp. 10-30: the first two-thirds of the essay.

Only after he's established the terms of the debate does Hamilton
address Seabury's specific (very, very specific) points, on pp. 30-41.
He wraps up his comments on Seabury's *Free Thoughts* with:

> I say, it is enough to make a man mad, to hear such ridiculous
> quibbles offered instead of sound argument; but so it is, the
> piece I am writing against contains nothing else. When a
> man grows warm, he has a confounded itch for swearing.
> I have been going, above twenty times, to rap out an oath,
> by him that made me, but I have checked myself, with this
> reflection, that it is rather unmannerly, to treat him that
> made us with so much freedom. Thus have I examined and
> confuted, all the cavils and objections, of any consequence,
> stated by this Farmer. I have only passed over such things,
> as are of little weight, the fallacy of which will easily appear.

Hamilton, like Seabury, opens his pamphlet with "Friends and Countrymen." But he signs it with "A Friend to America," rather than "A W[estchester] Farmer." He's aiming at a much wider audience than Seabury did: not a specific profession, location, or social or economic status, but all the colonists.

And that, my dears, is how to blow us all away. Set a hook. Define your terms. State your principles. Show how they apply to the current situation. Wrap it up on a positive note. This is surely the reason Hamilton's *Vindication* launched him into the top rank of the writers of the Revolution and early Republic: the pamphlet makes a logical, reasoned argument on broad principles, and can be read as an independent work even by those who have arrived late to the debate.

Damn. Now that I've read the *Vindication,* I'm going to be angry, nauseous, or both every time I listen to a speech by our current crop of presidential candidates.

MORE

• Seabury was kidnapped by Isaac Sears in November 1775, on the same expedition in which Sears and his men destroyed the printing office of James Rivington, who published both *Free Thoughts* and *A Vindication.* (The Sears expedition spurred Hamilton to write to John Jay what became one of his more famous letters, discussing the passions of mobs. It's good reading for an election year.) In 1776 Seabury fled to Long Island, staying behind enemy lines until the end of the war.

• Speaking of things that come back to bite you on the ass: In 1783, Seabury was elected first bishop of Connecticut. Church of England bishops in London refused to consecrate him because as a citizen of the new United States, he could not swear an oath of loyalty to King George III. After a few months, Seabury rode off to Scotland, where he was consecrated by a group of dissident Anglican bishops whose predecessors had refused to swear loyalty to William and Mary a century earlier. Their successors had been refusing loyalty oaths to British monarchs ever since, and were happy to consecrate Seabury. For more on Seabury, see the American National Biography (by subscription) and this article.

• Thomas Paine's *Common Sense* came out in January 1776, a year after the Seabury-Hamilton exchange, and changed the terms of debate by focusing on the question: Should these colonies be independent? (See Chapter 11.)

CHAPTER 15

A Revue of Royal & Revolutionary Rhetoric,
1756-1776

In Several Violent Acts and Interludes,
with Important and incendiary dialogue in (of course) red.

Setting: A world before the Industrial Revolution and capitalism, with countries ruled by kings and assorted other tyrants. To become prosperous, they do not compete with each other to lure inventors who create railroads, assembly-line automobiles, or iPhones—they grab what they can get from each other, in a zero-sum wealth game.

PRELUDE

• 1756-1763: Seven Years' War, known in the United States as the French and Indian War. Letter from Robert Dinwiddie, Governor of Virginia, to the commandant of the French Forces on the Ohio, October 31, 1753:

> The Lands upon the River Ohio, in the Western Part of the Colony of Virginia, are so notoriously known to be the Property of the Crown of Great-Britain; that it is a Matter of equal Concern and Surprize to me, to hear that a Body of French Forces are erecting Fortresses, and making Settlements upon that River, within his Majesty's Dominions. The many and repeated Complaints I have received in these Acts of Hostility, lay me under the Necessity of sending, in the Name of the King my Master, the Bearer hereof, George Washington, Esq; one of the Adjutants General of the Forces of this Dominion, to complain to you of the Encroachments thus made ... (from Journal of George Washington, 1753)

To give a sense of the scale of this conflict: at a single engagement, the Battle of Kunersdorf in 1759, some 50,000 Prussians met 65,000

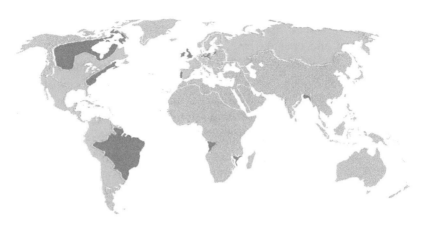

Major combatants in the Seven Years' War, 1756-1763. Blue: Great Britain, Prussia, and Portugal, and their colonies. Green: France, Spain, Austria, Russia, Sweden, and their colonies. Map: Wikipedia

Russians and Austrians on the field. At least 13,000 soldiers died in that *one* battle. Even the royals who were on the winning side in the Seven Years' War incurred massive debts as they sent soldiers hither and yon, and quartered, fed, and armed them.

ACT I: BRITISH TAXATION, 1765-1770

• 1765, March 22: Stamp Act. "An act for granting and applying certain stamp duties, and other duties, in the British colonies and plantations in America, towards further defraying the expences of defending, protecting, and securing the same."

• 1766, March 18: Stamp Act repealed *and* Declaratory Act passed.

> Whereas several of the houses of representatives in His Majesty's colonies and plantations in America have of late, against law, claimed to themselves, or to the general assemblies of the same, the sole and exclusive right of imposing duties and taxes upon His Majesty's subjects in the said colonies and plantations … [T]he said colonies and plantations in America have been, are, and of right ought to be, subordinate unto, and dependent upon the imperial crown and Parliament of Great Britain; … [who] had, hath, and of right ought to have, full power and authority to make laws and statutes of sufficient force and validity to bind

the colonies and people of America, subjects of the crown of Great Britain, in all cases whatsoever. And be it further declared and enacted by the authority aforesaid, That all resolutions, votes, orders, and proceedings, in any of the said colonies or plantations, whereby the power and authority of the Parliament of Great Britain to make laws and statutes as aforesaid is denied, or drawn into question, are, and are hereby declared to be, utterly null and void to all intents and purposes whatsoever.

• 1767, November 20: <u>Townshend Acts</u> levy taxes on paper, paint, lead, glass, and tea.

Whereas it is expedient that a revenue should be raised in your Majesty's dominions in America, for making a more certain and adequate provision for defraying the charge of the administration of justice, and the support of civil government, in such provinces where it shall be found necessary; and towards further defraying the expenses of defending, protecting, and securing, the said dominions..."

• 1770, March 5: Boston Massacre. Residents attack British soldiers sent to enforce the Townshend Acts. <u>Captain Preston,</u> the British officer in charge, reported:

On this a general attack was made on the men by a great number of heavy clubs and snowballs being thrown at them, by which all our lives were in imminent danger, some persons at the same time from behind calling out, damn your bloods—why don't you fire. Instantly three or four of the soldiers fired, one after another, and directly after three more in the same confusion and hurry. The mob then ran away, except three unhappy men who instantly expired."

From an <u>anonymous report printed in Boston</u>:
THE   HORRID   MASSACRE   IN   BOSTON, PERPETRATED IN THE EVENING OF THE FIFTH DAY OF MARCH, 1770, BY SOLDIERS OF THE TWENTY-NINTH REGIMENT WHICH WITH THE FOURTEENTH REGIMENT WERE THEN QUARTERED THERE; WITH SOME OBSERVATIONS ON THE STATE OF THINGS PRIOR TO THAT CATASTROPHE. ... Captain Preston is said to have ordered them to fire, and to have repeated that order. One gun was fired first; then others in succession

HAMILTON: A FRIEND TO AMERICA, VOL. 1

and with deliberation, till ten or a dozen guns were fired; or till that number of discharges were made from the guns that were fired. By which means eleven persons were killed and wounded, as above represented."

• 1770, April 2: repeal of Townshend Acts, except for the tax on tea.

ACT II: THE TEA ACT AND THE BOSTON TEA PARTY, 1773-1774

• 1773, May 10: Parliament passes the Tea Act, an attempt to help the struggling British East India Company to keep its head above water ... oops.

• 1773, December 2: the Sons of Liberty in Boston publish a notice:

> Friends! Brethren! Countrymen! THAT worst of plagues, the detested T E A shipped for this port by the East India Company, is now arrived in this Harbor: the hour of destruction or manly opposition to the machinations of tyranny stares you in the face. Every friend to his country, to himself and posterity, is now called upon to meet at Faneuil Hall at nine o'clock THIS DAY (at which time the bells will ring) to make a united and successful resistance to this last, worst and most destructive measure of administration.

• 1773, December 16: Boston Tea Party. More on the circumstances surrounding it here – including a poem in urging everyone stop drinking drink tea. In his diary the following day, John Adams wrote:

> This is the most magnificent Movement of all. There is a Dignity, a Majesty, a Sublimity, in this last Effort of the Patriots, that I greatly admire.

• 1774, March 25: Parliament shuts down the port of Boston. Benjamin Franklin, writing anonymously in a London paper, said:

> Now, my Lord, if the Port of Boston is to remain shut till the People in that Province acknowledge the Right of Parliament to impose any Taxes or Duties whatever, except for the Regulation of Commerce, it must remain shut till the very Name of a British Parliament if forgotten among them. You may shut up their Ports, one by one, as the Minister has lately threatened. You may reduce their Cities to Ashes, but the Flame of Liberty in North America shall not be extinguished. Cruelty and Oppression and Revenge shall

only serve as Oil to increase the Fire. A great Country of hardy Peasants is not to be subdued. In the Grave which we dig for the Inhabitants of Boston, Confidence and Friendship shall expire, Commerce and Peace shall rest together. (More here)

• 1774, September—October: first Continental Congress, meeting in Philadelphia, states the rights of the colonists and resolves to boycott British goods.

> That the inhabitants of the English colonies in North-America, by the immutable laws of nature, the principles of the English constitution, and the several charters or compacts, have the following RIGHTS:
> *Resolved*, N.C.D. 1. That they are entitled to life, liberty and property: and they have never ceded to any foreign power whatever, a right to dispose of either without their consent.
> *Resolved*, N.C.D. 2. That our ancestors, who first settled these colonies, were at the time of their emigration from the mother country, entitled to all the rights, liberties, and immunities of free and natural-born subjects, within the realm of England.

ACT III: OPENING SALVOS, 1774-1775

• 1774, November: Seabury's *Free Thoughts on the Proceedings of the Continental Congress* ("Congress has "ignorantly misunderstood, carelessly neglected, or basely betrayed the interests of all the Colonies") provokes Hamilton's *Full Vindication of the Measures of the Congress* in December ("And first, let me ask these restless spirits, whence arises that violent antipathy they seem to entertain, not only to the natural rights of mankind; but to common sense and common modesty?") [on both these, see Chapter 14], and then Hamilton's *The Farmer Refuted* (February 1775):

> The origin of all civil government, justly established, must be a voluntary compact, between the rulers and the ruled; and must be liable to such limitations, as are necessary for the security of the absolute rights of the latter; for what original title can any man or set of men have, to govern others, except their own consent?

• 1775, April 19: Battle of Lexington and Concord. First open armed conflict between colonists and British soldiers: approximately 49 Americans and 73 British were killed.

• 1775, June 17: <u>Congress</u> to George Washington:

> We, reposing special trust and confidence in your patriotism, valor, conduct, and fidelity, do, by these presents, constitute and appoint you to be General and Commander in chief, of the army of the United Colonies, and of all the forces now raised, or to be raised, by them, and of all others who shall voluntarily offer their service, and join the said Army for the Defence of American liberty, and for repelling every hostile invasion thereof: And you are hereby vested with full power and authority to act as you shall think for the good and welfare of the service." [Washington's reply is <u>here</u>]

ACT IV: ATTEMPTS AT RECONCILIATION, 1775

• 1775, July 8: Congress sent King George III the "<u>Olive Branch Petition,</u>" drafted by Thomas Jefferson, toned down by John Dickinson ("Mr. Jefferson, Mr. Lee, Mr. Hopkins, Dr. Franklin, why have you joined this... incendiary little man, this BOSTON radical? This demagogue, this *madman?*"—sorry, <u>different musical</u>). The Olive Branch Petition begins:

> We, your Majesty's faithful subjects … acknowledge Great Britain as "a power the most extraordinary the world had ever known." We are truly shocked that after all we contributed to the late [Seven Years'] war, Parliament is attacking us. We blame "the delusive pretences, fruitless terrors, and unavailing severities" of your ministers, "those artful and cruel enemies who abuse your royal confidence and authority, for the purpose of effecting our destruction." We would like harmony restored so we can be happy British subjects for generations to come.

• 1775, August 23: George III, having refused to look at the Olive Branch Petition, responds to the hostilities at Lexington and Concord with the <u>Proclamation of Rebellion</u>. Some in the colonies have proceeded to "open and avowed rebellion," encouraged by "counsels and comfort of divers wicked and desperate persons." We decree that civil and military officials in the colonies are to suppress the rebellion and bring the traitors to justice. "Our obedient and loyal subjects" are to

102

DURANTE

inform on any who "shall be found carrying on correspondence with, or in any manner or degree aiding or abetting the persons now in open arms and rebellion against our Government."

• 1775, October 27: The <u>King elaborates on the Proclamation of Rebellion</u> in a speech to Parliament.

Those who have long too successfully laboured to inflame my people in America by gross misrepresentations, and to infuse into their minds a system of opinions, repugnant to the true constitution of the colonies, and to their subordinate relation to Great-Britain, now openly avow their revolt, hostility and rebellion. They have raised troops, and are collecting a naval force; they have seized the public revenue, and assumed to themselves legislative, executive and judicial powers, which they already exercise in the most arbitrary manner, over the persons and property of their fellow-subjects: And altho' many of these unhappy people may still retain their loyalty, and may be too wise not to see the fatal consequence of this usurpation, and wish to resist it, yet the torrent of violence has been strong enough to compel their acquiescence, till a sufficient force shall appear to support them. The authors

King George III's speech to Parliament, October 27, 1775

and promoters of this desperate conspiracy have, in the conduct of it, derived great advantage from the difference of our intentions and theirs. They meant only to amuse by vague expressions of attachment to the Parent State, and the strongest protestations of loyalty to me, whilst they were preparing for a general revolt. ... [To be a subject of Great Britain is to be] the freest member of any civil society in the known world. ... When the unhappy and deluded multitude, against whom this force will be directed, shall become sensible of their error, I shall be ready to receive the misled with tenderness and mercy!

• 1775, December 6: the Constitutional Congress responds to the king's August 23 Proclamation of Rebellion.

We, the Delegates of the thirteen United Colonies in North America [look, a move toward a collective name for what had been 13 separate colonies!] ... What allegiance is it that we forget? Allegiance to Parliament? We never owed—we never owned it. Allegiance to our King? Our words have ever avowed it,—our conduct has ever been consistent with it. ... By the British Constitution, our best inheritance, rights, as well as duties descend upon us: We cannot violate the latter by defending the former. [Damn fine rhetorical flourish!] ... We view [the King] as the Constitution represents him. That tells us he can do no wrong. ... We will not, on our part, lose the distinction between the King and his Ministers. ...[Congress and the people of these United Colonies regret to see] Britons fight against Britons, and the descendants of Britons.

ACT V: INDEPENDENCE, 1776

• 1776, January 10: Publication of Thomas Paine's *Common Sense*. Paine soon added an appendix:

Since the publication of the first edition of this pamphlet, or rather, on the same day on which it came out, the King's Speech [of October 27, 1775] made its appearance in this city. Had the spirit of prophecy directed the birth of this production, it could not have brought it forth, at a more seasonable juncture, or a more necessary time. The bloody mindedness of the one, shew the necessity of pursuing the doctrine of the other. Men read by way of revenge. And the Speech, instead of terrifying, prepared a way for the manly principles of Independance."

More on *Common Sense* in Chapter 11. The full text of Paine's pamphlet is here.

• 1776, July 4: Congress adopts the Declaration of Independence, drafted by the Committee of Five: Thomas Jefferson, John Adams, Benjamin Franklin, Robert R. Livingston, and Roger Sherman.

In CONGRESS, July 4, 1776. The unanimous Declaration

Earliest known draft of the Declaration of Independence, June 1776, in Jefferson's handwriting with suggestions / corrections by the Committee of Five. Photo: Library of Congress via Wikipedia

of the thirteen United States of America, When in the Course of human events, it becomes necessary for one people to dissolve the political bands which have connected them with another, and to assume among the powers of the earth, the separate and equal station to which the Laws of Nature and of Nature's God entitle them, a decent respect to the opinions of mankind requires that they should declare the causes which impel them to the separation.

We hold these truths to be self-evident, that all men are created equal, that they are endowed by their Creator with certain unalienable Rights, that among these are Life, Liberty and the pursuit of Happiness.

That to secure these rights, Governments are instituted among Men, deriving their just powers from the consent of the governed, That whenever any Form of Government becomes destructive of these ends, it is the Right of the People to alter or to abolish it, and to institute new Government, laying its foundation on such principles and organizing its powers in such form, as to them shall seem most likely to effect their Safety and Happiness. Prudence, indeed, will dictate that Governments long established should not be changed for light and transient causes; and accordingly all experience hath shewn, that mankind are more disposed to suffer, while evils are sufferable, than to right themselves by abolishing the forms to which they are accustomed. But when a long train of abuses and usurpations, pursuing invariably the same Object evinces a design to reduce them under absolute Despotism, it is their right, it is their duty, to throw off such Government, and to provide new Guards for their future security.

Such has been the patient sufferance of these Colonies; and such is now the necessity which constrains them to alter their former Systems of Government. The history of the present King of Great Britain is a history of repeated injuries and usurpations, all having in direct object the establishment of an absolute Tyranny over these States. To prove this, let Facts be submitted to a candid world.

He has refused his Assent to Laws, the most wholesome and necessary for the public good. ... (full text here)

Declaration of Independence, drafted in May-June 1776, adopted by Congress July 4, 1776

EPILOGUE: KING GEORGE III

• After the surrender of Lord Cornwallis at Yorktown in 1781, King George drafted a <u>letter of abdication</u>. He never submitted it ... but he never burned it and stomped on the ashes, either.

> His Majesty with much sorrow finds he can be of no further utility to his native country, which drives him to the painful step of quitting it forever. In consequence, His Majesty resigns the Crown of Great Britain to his son and lawful successor George, Prince of Wales, whose endeavours for the prosperity of the British Empire, he hopes will prove more successful.

• King George III had bouts of mental instability in 1783, 1788, and 1804.

• In 1811 George III lapsed into mental instability and didn't recover. A regent was assigned to rule Great Britain, and George spent the last decade of his life (he died in 1820) in the care of the mad-doctors.

King George III in 1762, by Ramsay; and in 1817. Images: Wikipedia

MORE

• The *Boston Tea Party Opera*?!? Yes! Check it out <u>here</u>.

• The portable desk on which Jefferson drafted the Declaration of Independence: doesn't it make your fingers tingle?

Jefferson's portable writing desk, on which he drafted the Declaration of Independence, 1776. Smithsonian Institution. Photo: Wikipedia

CHAPTER 16
Hamilton Joins Washington's Staff, 1777

GENERAL WASHINGTON ASKS CONGRESS FOR HELP

Commander-in-Chief <u>George Washington to John Hancock</u>, President of the Continental Congress:

New York July the 11th 1776

As I am truly sensible the time of Congress is much taken up with a variety of Important matters, It is with unwillingness and pain I ever repeat a request after having once made It, or take the liberty of Enforcing any opinion of mine after It is once given, but as the establishing of some Office for auditing accounts is a matter of exceeding importance to the public Interest I would beg leave once more to call the attention of Congress to an appointment competent to the purposes. Two motives induce me to urge the matter, first a conviction of the utility of the measure—Secondly that I may stand exculpated, If hereafter It should appear that money has been improperly expended and necessaries for the army obtained upon unreasonable Terms. For me whose time is employed from the hour of my rising, till I retire to bed again, to go into an examination of the amounts of such an Army as this, with any degree of precision and exactness, without neglecting other matters of equal importance is utterly impracticable ...

A prisoner belonging to the 10th Regimt taken yesterday, Informs that they hourly expect Admiral Howe and his Fleet, he adds that a Vessell has arrived from them, and the prevailing Opinion is that an Attack will be made immediately on their arrival.

By a Letter from Genl Ward I am Informed, that the small pox has broke out at Boston and Infected some of the Troops. I have wrote him to place the Invalids under an Officer to remain till they are well, and to use every possible precaution to prevent the Troops coming from thence bringing the Infection. The distresses and calamities we have already suffered by this disorder in one part of our Army, I hope will excite his utmost care that they may not be Increased. I have the honor to be with sentiments of the greatest esteem Sir Yr Most Obed. Servt.

Two weeks later, <u>Washington wrote to Congress</u> that he needed to increase the number of men on his staff.

New York July 25th 1776
    Disagreeable as it is to me, and unpleasing as it may be to Congress to multiply Officers, I find myself under the unavoidable necessity of asking an Increase of my Aid de Camps—The augmentation of my Command—the Increase of my Correspondance—the Orders to give—the Instructions to draw, cut out more business than I am able to execute in time, with propriety. The business of so many different departments centering with me, & by me to be handed on to Congress for their information, added to the Intercourse I am obliged to keep up with the adjacent States and incidental occurrences, all of which requiring confidential (& not hack) writers to execute, renders it impossible in the present state of things for my family to discharge the several duties expected of me with that precission and dispatch that I could wish—what will it be then when we come into a more active Scene, and I am called upon from twenty different places perhaps at the same Instant?

Charles Wilson Peale, George Washington as Commander-in-Chief, 1776. Peale's diary notes that he was working on this portrait when Congress passed the Declaration of Independence. Brooklyn Museum of Art. Photo:Wikipedia

Congress will do me the justice to believe, I hope, that it is not my Inclination or wish to run the Continent to any unnecessary expence. and those who better know me, will not suspect that shew, and parade can have any Influence on my Mind in this Instance. A Conviction of the necessity of it, for the regular discharge of the trust reposed in me is the Governing motive for the application, and as such is Submitted to Congress by, Sir Yr Most Obedt & Most Hble Servt

Go: Washington

Washington had <u>33 aides-de-camp</u> over the course of the Revolutionary War. Alexander Hamilton joined their number early in 1777, nine months after Washington wrote the letter above.

Head-Quarters, Morristown [New Jersey] March 1, 1777.

Alexander Hamilton Esquire is appointed Aide-De-Camp to the Commander in Chief; and is to be respected and obeyed as such.

Extract of General Orders

Alexd Scammell   Adjt. Genl.

JOHNSON ON WASHINGTON'S STAFF

Have I mentioned how much I adore <u>Paul Johnson's brief biography of Washington</u>? More than most historians I've read, Johnson (a Brit)

Washington's study at the <u>Ford Mansion</u> in Morristown, NJ, his headquarters from December 1779 to June 1780. Photo: Wikipedia

puts Washington and the American Revolution into a worldwide context. Here are Johnson's comments on Washington's staff.

> In Alexander Hamilton, a lawyer from the West Indies and a fierce and brilliant field commander, Washington discovered a superb chief of staff from 1777 to 1781 (his nominal position was secretary), who presided over a score of aides-de-camp, half of them Virginians. These young men, each ranked a colonel, he called his military family, the martial equivalent to his personal family at Mount Vernon. He treated them with love and tenderness, and they worshipped him and (with one or two exceptions) served him with fanatical loyalty. Thus Washington, entirely as a result of his personal qualities—not too much to say his charisma—possessed, for the first time in history, a first-class general staff, who understood his mind and methods and could carry out his intentions religiously. This was something none of the British commanders had; indeed, it was denied to the two outstanding generals of the next generation, Napoleon and Wellington. But, in strict military terms, it was all Washington had. In all other respects he was outnumbered, outgunned, and outfinanced.

MORE

• There's a charming illustration of how crucial protocol can be in Washington's letter of July 14, 1776, in which he reports that he has refused to accept a letter from newly arrived General Howe because it was addressed to "George Washington Esqr."

• Washington knew the value of art for reminding people of their values. He ordered that his favorite play, Addison's *Cato,* be performed for the troops at Valley Forge in April and May 1778. *Cato* is credited with inspiring famous lines by Patrick Henry, Nathan Hale, and Washington. (Quotes from it at the end of this post on the Pergamon exhibition at the Metropolitan Museum.) Congress, disapproving of such "frivolities," in October 1778 passed a resolution: "Whereas frequenting play houses and theatrical entertainments has a fatal tendency to divert the minds of the people from a due attention to the means necessary for the defence of their country, and the preservation of their liberties: Resolved, That any person holding an office under the United States, who shall act, promote, encourage or attend such plays, shall be deemed unworthy to hold such office, and shall be accordingly dismissed." Fascinatingly detailed article on Congress's opposition to the theater here.

• Mount Vernon commissioned reconstructions of Washington at ages 19, 45, and 57. Here they are lined up at StudioEIS, where they were created. For more on these reconstructions, see the *New York Times* article from 2006, "Coming Soon to Mount Vernon, 3 Georges" and Jeffrey Schwartz's excellent article "Putting a Face on the First President," in *Scientific American,* February 2006 (available by subscription).

Forensic reconstructions of George Washington at ages 57, 19, and 45, by StudioEIS for Mount Vernon. Photo: StudioEIS

• In *Hamilton,* Washington refers to himself as "the very model of a modern major general," a reference to the famous patter song from Gilbert and Sullivan's 1879 operetta *Pirates of Penzance.* This video shows the lyrics (you'll need them the first 5 times or so) and has the traditional ending, where the singer sees how fast he can do the song before his tongue falls out. Rap isn't new in that respect. The 1983 movie features Kevin Kline as the Pirate King (signing up right now, I am), Angela Lansbury, Linda Ronstadt, and Rex Smith. My particular favorite among the patter songs is from Ruddigore (here with Vincent Price!). But I digress. Basingstoke.

CHAPTER 17

The Battle of Long Island
and the American Retreat, 1776

"View of the Narrows between Long Island & Staten Island with Our
Fleet at Anchor & Lord Howe Coming In", July 12, 1776, by Lieutenant
Archibald Robertson (1745-1813) of the Royal Engineers. Lord Howe's
HMS Eagle is top right. More here

THE BRITISH FLEET ARRIVES

General George Washington to John Hancock, President of the Continental Congress:

> New York July the 3d 1776
>> Sir
>> Since I had the honor of addressing you and on the same day, several Ships more arrived within the Hook, making the number that came in then a hundred & Ten, and there remains no doubt of the whole of the Fleet from Hallifax being now here. Yesterday evening fifty of them came up the Bay, and Anchored on the Staten Island side. ...
>> Our reinforcement of Militia is but yet small. I cannot ascertain the amount not having got a return. However I trust if the Enemy make an Attack they will meet with a repulse,

as I have the pleasure to inform you, that an agreable spirit and willingness for Action seem to animate and pervade the whole of our Troops. ...

I must entreat your attention to an Application I made some time ago for Flints, we are extremely deficient in this necessary Article, and shall be greatly distressed if we cannot obtain a Supply. Of Lead we have a sufficient quantity for the whole Campaign taken off the Houses here.

Esteeming It of Infinite advantage to prevent the Enemy from getting fresh provisions and Horses for their Waggons, Artillery &c. I gave orders to a party of our men on Staten Island since writing Genl Herd to drive the Stock off, without waiting for the assistance or direction of the Committees there, lest their slow mode of transacting business might produce too much delay ...

I have the Honor to be with Sentiments of the greatest Esteem Sir Your Most Obedt Servt

Go: Washington (full text here)

Did you notice that the commander-in-chief is personally writing to Congress begging for flints for firearms? No wonder he asked for a larger staff (more right-hand men) a few weeks later (Chapter 16).

Washington literally didn't know the half of what he was facing: more than 300 ships transporting 32,000 men. When the

General William Howe, ca. 1777. Image: Wikipedia

British disembarked on Staten Island, it was the largest amphibious attack of the eighteenth century, unsurpassed until the Normandy Invasion in 1944. (NOTE: I'm taking the ship and troop numbers from Chernow's *Hamilton,* p. 76, but I wish I had a good contemporary source on them! Yo, anybody?)

Depending on the wind, the British could have either landed in Brooklyn and marched through it toward New York, or sailed north to land directly in Manhattan. (For maps of the city at that time, see Chapter 13.) Washington split his force of 20,000 so he could defend both possible landing points.

ANOTHER NOTE: I'm going to use modern street and neighborhood names below, because I like picturing the Revolutionary War military actions overlaid on today's grid. So ...

THE BRITISH INVADE BROOKLYN

A bit earlier than 1776—something like 18,000 years ago – the Wisconsin Ice Sheet retreated, leaving a glacial moraine in Brooklyn. At its western end, the moraine includes a ridge that runs from the area around the Green-Wood Cemetery northeast through Jamaica. The ridge is that brownish area on the map below.

Unless you're the noble Duke of York, you don't march your men to the top of the hill and march them down again. (Mom joke. That

Battle of Long Island, August 27, 1776. Image: Wikipedia

song, animated <u>here</u>, is even older than "The World Turned Upside Down": see Chapter 38.) If you're moving thousands of men, you look for passes through the hills.

General Howe ordered his troops ferried across to Brooklyn at about the point where the Verrazzano Narrows Bridge now stands. Then he split them, sending some northeast roughly along the path of the Brooklyn Queens Expressway, where they ran into the American defenses at a pass just north of the Green-Wood Cemetery. Another British contingent headed northeast through what's now Bensonhurst and Borough Park. That contingent split, with one part attacking American defenses at a pass in Prospect Park.

The final contingent—the largest, with some 10,000 men – was the one that caused the Americans to lose the Battle of Brooklyn. It marched down Flatbush and then northeast up Flatlands. Way out there where Jamaica, East New York, and Bushwick Avenues meet (think LIRR Jamaica Station), the British troops marched through Jamaica Pass. The Americans had not defended that one: it lay five miles away, and the Americans were already spread thin. These British troops swung around to approach the American forces from the east while Howe's other contingents continued their attack from the south. At 8 a.m., two cannons boomed, indicating that the last contingent was in place. The trap snapped shut. By noon, the Americans were on the run.

Lord Stirling attacks the British during the Battle of Long Island, August 27, 1776; the building is known today as the Old Stone House. Painting by Alonso Chappel, 1858. Image: Wikipedia

Below is the account of Michael Graham, an 18-year-old American militia volunteer who fought at the Battle of Long Island. It's long and not particularly well written, but read it anyway: as an expression of the desperation and despair felt by the American troops surrounded by British regulars, it's difficult to top. Graham is describing the fighting between Lord Stirling's American troops and the British near the Old Stone House, just west of Prospect Park. The swamp he mentions is the area around the Gowanus Canal.

On the next morning, the battle commenced about the break of day or perhaps a little before. At the Narrows, where Lord Stirling commanded, there was a pretty heavy cannonading kept up and occasionally the firing of small arms, and from the sound appeared to be moving slowly towards Brooklyn. This continued for hours. At length the firing commenced above us and kept spreading until it became general almost in every direction. We continued at our post until I think about twelve o'clock, when an officer came and told us to make our escape, for we were surrounded. We immediately retreated towards our camp. We had went but a small distance before we saw the enemy paraded in the road before us. We turned to the left and posted ourselves behind a stone fence; from the movements of the enemy, we had soon to move from this position. Here we got parted, and I neither saw officers or men belonging to our party (with the exception of one man) during the balance of that day. I had went but a small distance before I came to a party of our men making a bold stand. I stopped and took one fire at the enemy, but they came on with such rapidity that I retreated back in the woods. Here I met Colonel Miles, a regular officer from Pennsylvania, and Lieutenant Sloan, a full cousin of my own. As soon as I had loaded my gun, I left them (Colonel Miles was taken prisoner and Lieutenant Sloan killed), as the firing had ceased where I had retreated from. I returned to near the same place. I had not been at this place I think more than one minute before the British came in a different direction from where they were when I retreated, firing platoons as they marched. I turned and took one fire at them and then made my escape as fast as I could. By this time our troops were routed in every direction. It is impossible for me to describe the confusion and horror of the scene that ensued:

the artillery flying with the chains over the horses' backs, our men running in almost every direction, and run which way they would, they were almost sure to meet the British or Hessians. And the enemy huzzahing when they took prisoners made it truly a day of distress to the Americans. I escaped by getting behind the British that had been engaged with Lord Stirling and entered a swamp or marsh through which a great many of our men were retreating. Some of them were mired and crying to their fellows for God's sake to help them out; but every man was intent on his own safety and no assistance was rendered. At the side of the marsh there was a pond which I took to be a millpond. Numbers, as they came to this pond, jumped in, and some were drowned. Soon after I entered the marsh, a cannonading commenced from our batteries on the British, and they retreated, and I got safely into camp. Out of the eight men that were taken from the company to which I belonged the day before the battle on guard, I only escaped. The others were either killed or taken prisoners. At the time, I could not account for how it was that our troops were so completely surrounded but have since understood there was another road across the ridge several miles above Flatbush that was left unoccupied by our troops. Here the British passed and got betwixt them and Brooklyn unobserved. This accounts for the disaster of that day. (Online here.)

THE MARYLAND 400

With the British attacking from several sides, Lord Stirling chose the best-trained and best-equipped unit in the American army to remain with him, covering the retreat of the rest of his troops from the Stone House across the Gowanus swamp to Brooklyn Heights to meet Washington and his troops. For hours, Sitrling and a few hundred members of the Maryland Regiment fought an holding action against 2,000 British troops. Two hundred fifty-six of them died. Only a dozen survived. Washington, taking a last look at the battle from the heights, is said to have lamented, "Good God, what brave fellows I must this day lose."

History is a series of what-if moments ... but some are more decisive than others. If the British had kept marching and trapped the Americans against the river in Brooklyn Heights, the British would have killed or captured the American army's commander-in-chief and most of his troops. The American Revolution would have gone down in history as an unsuccessful rebellion, rather than as the War of Independence. So if you visit the <u>monument to the Maryland 400</u> in the southern end of Prospect Park, take off your hat, salute, or bow your head: do whatever it is you do to show profound respect.

RETREAT TO MANHATTAN

On the night of August 29-30, 1776, the American troops were ferried from Brooklyn to Manhattan. Washington wrote to John Hancock, President of the Continental Congress.

> New York Augt 31st 1776
>   Sir
>   Inclination as well as duty would have Induced me to give Congress the earliest Information of my removal and that of the Troops from Long Island & Its dependencies to this City the night before last, But the extreme fatigue which myself and Family have undergone as much from the Weather since the Engagement on the 27th rendered me & them entirely unfit to take pen in hand—Since Monday scarce any of us have been out of the Lines till our passage across the East River was effected Yesterday morning & for Forty Eight Hours preceding that I had hardly been of[f] my Horse and never closed my Eyes so that I was quite unfit to write or dictate till this Morning.
>   Our Retreat was made without any Loss of Men or Ammunition and in better order than I expected from Troops in the situation ours were—We brought off all our Cannon & Stores, except a few heavy peices, which in the condition the earth was by a long continued rain, we found upon Trial impracticable—The Wheels of the Carriages sinking up to the Hobs, rendered it impossible for our whole force to drag them—We left but little provisions on the Island except some Cattle which had been driven within our Lines and which after many attempts to force across the Water we found Impossible to effect, circumstanced as we were …
>   In the Engagement on the 27th Generals Sullivan & Stirling were made prisoners … Nor have I been yet able to obtain an exact account of Our Loss, we suppose It from

700 to a Thousand, killed & taken—Genl Sullivan says Lord Howe is extremely desirous of seeing some of the Members of Congress for which purpose he was allowed to come out & to communicate to them what was passed between him & his Lordship—I have consented to his going to Philadelphia, as I do not mean or conceive It right to withold or prevent him from giving such information as he possesses in this Instance. ...

I am with my best regards to Congress Their & Your Most Obedt He Servt

Go: Washington (More here)

Hostilities paused for ten days while Howe went to New Jersey to speak to delegates from Congress. On September 11, 1776, Edward Rutledge reported the results to Washington:

I must beg Leave to inform you that our Conferrence with Lord Howe has been attended with no immediate Advantages—He declared that he had no Powers to consider us as Independt States, and we easily discover'd that were we still Dependt we would have nothing to expect from those with which he is vested—He talk'd altogether in generals, that he came out here to consult, advise, & confer with Gentlemen of the greatest Influence in the Colonies about their Complaints, that the King would revise the Acts of Parliament & royal Instructions upon such Reports as should be made and appear'd to fix our Redress upon his Majesty's good Will & Pleasure—This kind of Conversation lasted for several Hours & as I have already said without any Effect—Our Reliance continues therefore to be (under God) on your Wisdom & Fortitude & that of your Forces—That you may be as succesful as I know you are worthy is my most sincere wish ... (More here)

KIPS BAY

On September 15, British troops landed in Manhattan and fought the Americans at Kips Bay. This map drawn by the British after they occupied Manhattan happens to be the earliest accurate topographical map of the island. Kips Bay is below the "N" in "North River," if you can read that tiny print. Or look for the first large cove as you work your way up the east side of the island.

British Headquarters Map. North is to the right. Photo: <u>Welikia</u>

General Washington to John Hancock, September 16, 1776, from Col. Roger Morris's House [i.e., the <u>Morris-Jumel Mansion</u>]:

About Eleven OClock those in the East River began a most severe and Heavy Cannonade to scour the Grounds and cover the landing of their Troops between Turtle-Bay and the City, where Breast Works had been thrown up to oppose them. As soon as I heard the Firing, I road with all possible dispatch towards the place of landing when to my great surprize and Mortification I found the Troops that had been posted in the Lines retreating with the utmost precipitation and those ordered to support them, parson's & Fellows's Brigades, flying in every direction and in the greatest confusion, notwithstanding the exertions of their Generals to form them. I used every means in my power to rally and get them into some order but my attempts were fruitless and ineffectual, and on the appearance of a small party of the Enemy, not more than Sixty or Seventy, their disorder increased and they ran away in the greatest confusion without firing a Single Shot—Finding that no confidence was to be placed in these Brigades and apprehending that another part of the Enemy might pass over to Harlem plains and cut off the retreat to this place, I sent orders to secure the Heights in the best manner with the Troops that were stationed on and near them, which being done, the retreat was effected with but little or no loss of Men, tho of a considerable part of our Baggage occasioned by this disgracefull and dastardly conduct—Most of our Heavy Cannon and a part of our Stores and provisions which we were about removing was unavoidably left in the City, tho every means after It had been determined in Council to evacuate the post, had been used to prevent It. We are now encamped with the Main body of the Army on the Heights of Harlem where I should hope the Enemy would meet with a defeat in case of an Attack, If the Generality of our Troops would behave with tolerable bravery, but experience to my extreme affliction has convinced me that this is rather to be wished for than expected; However I trust, that there are many who will act like men, and shew themselves worthy of the blessings of Freedom. I have sent out some reconoitring parties to gain Intelligence If possible of the disposition of the Enemy and shall inform Congress of every material event by the earliest Opportunity. I have the Honor to be with the highest respect Sir Your Most Obedt Sert. (More here)

It was at the Battle of Kips Bay that Washington, losing his temper, is reported to have said, "Are these the men with which I am to defend America?" The line is quoted in Flexner's biography of Washington and McCullough's 1776. I'd love to have the reference to the original source—anyone own either?

RETREAT TO HARLEM

General Orders from General Washington for September 17, 1776, at Headquarters, Harlem Heights:

Parole: Leitch. Countersign: Virginia.
    The General most heartily thanks the troops commanded Yesterday, by Major Leitch, who first advanced upon the enemy, and the others who so resolutely supported them— The Behaviour of Yesterday was such a Contrast, to that of some Troops the day before, as must shew what may be done, where Officers & soldiers will exert themselves—Once more therefore, the General calls upon officers, and men, to act up to the noble cause in which they are engaged, and to support the Honor and Liberties of their Country. ... (More here)

AMERICANS SEEK FRENCH AID

A week after the orders above, on September 30, 1776, Congress dispatched Benjamin Franklin and Charles Lee as American commissioners to France. Along with Silas Deane (who was already in Paris), they were tasked with negotiating a treaty to get French aid against France's old foe, Great Britain. The treaty was signed on February 6, 1778, delivered to Congress on May 2, 1778, and ratified by

John Trumbull, portrait of Benjamin Franklin as ambassador to France,
wearing his oh-so-American fur hat and plain Quaker clothing. Yale
University Art Gallery.

Congress two days later. But that was long in the future in the autumn
of 1776.

RETREAT TO WESTCHESTER

On October 20, 1776, General Washington wrote to Robert R. Livingston from a farmhouse in Westchester County. Livingston was one of
the Committee of Five who drafted the Declaration of Independence.

> Dear Sir,
>
> I wish I had leizure to write you fully on the subject of yr
> last Letter—the moving state of the Army, and the extreame
> hurry in which I have been Involved for these Eight days,
> will only allow me time to acknowledge the receipt of yr
> favour, and to thank you (as I shall always do) for Any hints
> you may please to communicate, as I have great reliance
> upon your judgment; & knowledge of the Country, (which I
> wish to God I was as much master of) ...
>
> Let me Intreat you my Dear Sir, to use your Influence
> to send, without delay, Provisions for this Army, towards
> the White Plains—upon a strict scrutiny, I find an alarming
> deficiency herein, occasioned by the Commissary's placing
> too much confidence in his Water Carriage, and the Stock
> he had laid in at the Saw pits &ca (which but too probably
> may be cut of from us, althô upon the first knowledge I had

of Its being there, I ordered it to be remov'd)—We want both Flour, & Beef; & I entreat your exertions to forward them. I must also entreat you to send us a Number of Teams the more the better to aid in removing the Army as occasion requires. We are amazingly distress'd on Acct of the want of them—We can move nothing for want of them—In short Sir, our Situation is really distressing. I have orderd Lord Sterling with upwards of 2000 Men to the White Plains to prevent the Enemys taking possession of it, & for security of Our Stores there; but the Troops were obliged to March without their Tents, or Baggage. In exceeding great haste, & much sincerety I am Dr Sir Yr Most Obedt and obligd Sert

   Go: Washington   (More <u>here</u>)

MORE

• Re Battering down the Battery: I haven't seen references to fighting there between the British and Americans summer and autumn of 1776. Hercules Mulligan's account of his time with Alexander Hamilton describes them stealing cannon from the Battery in 1775, though. (See Chapter 6.)

CHAPTER 18

Hamilton as a Bachelor
and Meeting Elizabeth Schuyler, 1777-1780

A NOTE ON LONG-DISTANCE RELATIONSHIPS IN THE 18TH CENTURY

In the 1770s, there is no Snapchat or Twitter, no email or phone. If you can't talk to someone face to face, you have to send a letter. And if there's a war going on, it's not easy to figure out how to deliver a letter. So you're likely to write longer letters, not lots of short ones.

I could cut the letters below substantially, but then you'd have my interpretation of what's important about Hamilton's attitude toward the ladies, and I'd rather let you make your own judgment—although I will tell you occasionally what I think the main points are. Pour a cup of coffee, pull up a chair, and read on.

KITTY LIVINGSTON

When Hamilton came to Elizabethtown, New Jersey to study in 1772, he met William Livingston and his family, including daughter Catharine ("Kitty"). By 1777, Livingston had served on the Continental Congress and was governor of New Jersey. When Hamilton wrote the following letter to Kitty in early April 1777, he had been on General Washington's staff for just over a month. The army was still in winter quarters at Morristown, N.J.

Alexander had been asked to write to Kitty and discuss politics with her. I suspect that one of the reasons he was so reliably popular with women is that he was happy to treat women as equals in discussions of politics and the military. By contrast, Thomas Jefferson, who later corresponded with Angelica, told her: "You will preserve, from temper and inclination, the happy privilege of the ladies to leave to the rougher sex and to the newspapers their party squabbles and reproaches." (May 24, 1797; quoted here)—essentially, "Don't worry your pretty head about politics."

Here's what Alexander wrote to Kitty Livingston. Main points: I'm happy to discuss politics with you, but I want to keep my options open for discussing other matters, including romance; there is not much

Catharine (Kitty) Livingston (1751-1813). Image: <u>Find-a-Grave</u>

news to report on the military front, but we'd all like to win, because among other benefits it will allow people to think about things such as matrimony.

Morris Town [New Jersey] April 11th. 1777
    I take pleasure in transmitting you a letter, committed to my care, by your Sister Miss Suky, and in executing a promise, I gave her, of making an advance towards a correspondence with you. She says you discover, in all your letters to her, a relish for politics, which she thinks my situation qualifies me better for gratifying, than would be in her power; and from a desire to accommodate you in this particular, as well as to get rid of what she calls a difficult task to herself, and to give me an opportunity of enjoying the felicity which must naturally attend it, she wishes me to engage on the footing of a political correspondent.
    Though I am perfectly willing to harmonize with your inclination, in this respect, without making the cynical inquiry, whether it proceed from sympathy in the concerns of the public, or merely from female curiosity, yet I will not consent to be limited to any particular subject. I challenge you to meet me in whatever path you dare; and if you have no objection, for variety and amusement, we will even sometimes make excursions in the flowery walks, and roseate bowers of Cupid. You know, I am renowned for gallantry, and shall always be able to entertain you with a choice collection of the prettiest things imaginable. I fancy my knowlege of

you affords me a tolerably just idea of your taste, but lest I should be mistaken I shall take it kind, if you will give me such intimations of it, as will remove all doubt, and save me the trouble of finding it out with certainty myself. This will be the more obliging, as, without it, I should have a most arduous task on my hands, at least, if connoisseurs in the sex say true, according to whose representations, contrary to the vulgar opinion, woman is not a simple, but a most complex, intricate and enigmatical being.

After knowing exactly your taste, and whether you are of a romantic, or discreet temper, as to love affairs, I will endeavour to regulate myself by it. If you would choose to be a goddess, and to be worshipped as such, I will torture my imagination for the best arguments, the nature of the case will admit, to prove you so. You shall be one of the graces, or Diana, or Venus, or something surpassing them all. And after your deification, I will cull out of every poet of my acquaintance, the choicest delicacies, they possess, as offerings at your Goddesships' shrine. But if, conformable to your usual discernment, you are content with being a mere mortal, and require no other incense, than is justly due to you, I will talk to you like one [in] his sober senses; and, though it may be straining the point a little, I will even stipulate to pay you all the rational tribute properly applicable to a fine girl.

But amidst my amorous transports, let me not forget, that I am also to perform the part of a politician and intelligencer. This however will not take up much time, as the present situation of things gives birth to very little worth notice, though it seems pregnant with something of importance. The enemy, from some late movements, appear to be brooding mischief, which must soon break out, but I hope it will turn to their own ruin. To speak plainly, there is reason to believe, they are upon the point of attempting some important entreprize. Philadelphia in the opinion of most people, is their object. I hope they may be disappointed.

Of this, I am pretty confident, that the ensuing campaign will effectually put to death all their hopes; and establish the success of our cause beyond a doubt. You and I, as well as our neighbours, are deeply interested to pray for victory, and its necessary attendant peace; as, among other good effects, they would remove those obstacles, which now lie in the way

of that most delectable thing, called matrimony;—a state, which, with a kind of magnetic force, attracts every breast to it, in which sensibility has a place, in spite of the resistance it encounters in the dull admonitions of prudence, which is so prudish and perverse a dame, as to be at perpetual variance with it. With my best respects to Mr. & Mrs. Jay, I beg you will believe me to be,   Your assured friend & servant
    Alexr. Hamilton (More here)

THE IDEAL WIFE

In April 1779, from Middlebrook, New Jersey, Hamilton wrote to his friend John Laurens (see Chapter 4), who had been dispatched to South Carolina in hopes he would be allowed to raise a battalion of black soldiers. At the beginning of the letter, Hamilton talks about how much their friendship means to him:

> Cold in my professions, warm in my friendships, I wish, my Dear Laurens, it might be in my power, by action rather than words, to convince you that I love you. I shall only tell you that 'till you bade us Adieu, I hardly knew the value you had taught my heart to set upon you. Indeed, my friend, it was not well done. You know the opinion I entertain of mankind, and how much it is my desire to preserve myself free from particular attachments, and to keep my happiness independent on the caprice of others. You should not have taken advantage of my sensibility to steal into my affections without my consent. But as you have done it and as we are generally indulgent to those we love, I shall not scruple to pardon the fraud you have committed, on condition that for my sake, if not for your own, you will always continue to merit the partiality, which you have so artfully instilled into me.

After a paragraph on Laurens's promotion and another on news of Laurens's wife, who was in England, Hamilton continues:

> And Now my Dear as we are upon the subject of wife, I empower and command you to get me one in Carolina. Such a wife as I want will, I know, be difficult to be found, but if you succeed, it will be the stronger proof of your zeal and dexterity. Take her description—She must be young, handsome (I lay most stress upon a good

Miniature of John Laurens by Charles Wilson Peale

shape) sensible (a little learning will do), well bred (but she must have an aversion to the word ton) chaste and tender (I am an enthusiast in my notions of fidelity and fondness) of some good nature, a great deal of generosity (she must neither love money nor scolding, for I dislike equally a termagent and an œconomist). In politics, I am indifferent what side she may be of; I think I have arguments that will easily convert her to mine. As to religion a moderate stock will satisfy me. She must believe in god and hate a saint. But as to fortune, the larger stock of that the better. You know my temper and circumstances and will therefore pay special attention to this article in the treaty. Though I run no risk of going to Purgatory for my avarice; yet as money is an essential ingredient to happiness in this world—as I have not much of my own and as I am very little calculated to get more either by my address or industry; it must needs be, that my wife, if I get one, bring at least a sufficiency to administer to her own extravagancies. NB You will be pleased to recollect in your negotiations that I have no invincible antipathy to the maidenly beauties & that I am willing to take the trouble of them upon myself.

If you should not readily meet with a lady that you think answers my description you can only advertise in the public papers and doub[t]less you will hear of many competitors for most of the qualifications required, who will be glad to become candidates for such a prize as I am. To excite their emulation, it will be necessary for you to give an account of the lover—his size, make, quality of mind and body, achievements, expectations, fortune, &c. In drawing my picture, you will no doubt be civil to your friend; mind you do justice to the length of my nose and don't forget, that I———— –. [NOTE: The Founders Archive notes, "At some points in this letter H's words have been crossed out so that it is impossible to decipher them; and at the top of the first page, a penciled note, which was presumably written by J. C. Hamilton, reads: "I must not publish the whole of this."]

After reviewing what I have written, I am ready to ask myself what could have put it into my head to hazard this Jeu de follie. Do I want a wife? No—I have plagues enough without desiring to add to the number that greatest of all; and if I were silly enough to do it, I should take care how I employ a proxy. Did I mean to show my wit? If I did, I am sure I have missed my aim. Did I only intend to frisk? In this I have succeeded, but I have done more. I have gratified my feelings, by lengthening out the only kind of intercourse now in my power with my friend. Adieu

Yours.

A Hamilton (More here)

ELIZABETH SCHUYLER

Elizabeth Schuyler (1757-1854), the second daughter of Philip Schuyler and Catherine Van Rensselaer Schuyler, was raised in the family of a politician, patriot, and soldier. She may have met Alexander Hamilton at the Schuyler mansion in Albany in 1777. In early February 1780, 22-year-old Eliza arrived at Morristown, New Jersey, where Washington, his staff, and the American army were in winter quarters. She stayed with her uncle, Washington's personal physician, just down the road from headquarters.

Eliza's older sister Angelica (see Chapter 12) was described by James McHenry in 1782 (in a letter to Hamilton) as "a fine woman. She charms in all companies. No one has seen her, of either sex, who has not been pleased with her and she pleased everyone, chiefly, by means of those qualities which made you the husband of her sister." But by February 1780, Angelica had eloped with John Barker Church: she didn't come to Morristown.

Eliza seems to have made quite an impression on Washington's staff, especially Hamilton, who fell hard and fast. He wrote the letter below to the Schuylers' third daughter, Margarita ("and Peggy!"), in February 1780, when he had known Eliza barely a month.

[Morristown, New Jersey, February, 1780]

In obedience to Miss Schuylers commands I do myself the pleasure to inclose you a letter, which she has been so obliging as to commit to my care, and I beg your permission to assure you that many motives conspire to render this commission peculiarly agreeable. Besides the general one of being in the service of the ladies which alone would be sufficient, even to a man of less zeal than myself, I have others of a more particular nature. I venture to tell you in confidence, that by some odd contrivance or other, your sister has found out the secret of interesting me in every thing that concerns her; and though I have not the happiness of a personal acquaintance with you, I have had the good fortune to see several very pretty pictures of your person and mind which have inspired me with a more than common partiality for both. Among others your sister carries a beautiful copy constantly about her elegantly drawn by herself, of which she has two or three times favoured me with a sight. You

Elizabeth Schuyler Hamilton, 1787. <u>Museum of the City of New York</u>.
Image: Wikipedia

will no doubt admit it as a full proof of my frankness and good opinion of you, that I with so little ceremony introduce myself to your acquaintance and at the first step make you my confident. But I hope I run no risk of its being thought an impeachment of my discretion. Phlegmatists may say I take too great a license at first setting out, and witlings may sneer and wonder how a man the least acquainted with the world should show so great facility in his confidences—to a lady. But the idea I have formed of your character places it in my estimation above the insipid maxims of the former or the ill-natured jibes of the latter.

I have already confessed the influence your sister has gained over me; yet notwithstanding this, I have some things of a very serious and heinous nature to lay to her charge. She is most unmercifully handsome and so perverse that she has none of those pretty affectations which are the prerogatives of beauty. Her good sense is destitute of that happy mixture of vanity and ostentation which would make it conspicuous to the whole tribe of fools and foplings as well as to men of understanding so that as the matter now stands it is very little known beyond the circle of these. She has good nature affability and vivacity unembellished with that charming frivolousiness which is justly deemed one of the principal accomplishments of a belle. In short she is so strange a creature that she possesses all the beauties virtues and graces of her sex without any of those amiable defects, which from their general prevalence are esteemed by connoisseurs necessary shades in the character of a fine woman. The most determined adversaries of Hymen [i.e., marriage] can find in her no pretext for their hostility, and there are several of my friends, philosophers who railed at love as a weakness, men of the world who laughed at it as a phantasie, whom she has presumptuously and daringly compelled to acknowlege its power and surrender at discretion. I can the better assert the truth of this, as I am myself of the number. She has had the address to overset all the wise resolutions I had been framing for more than four years past, and from a rational sort of being and a professed contemner of Cupid has in a trice metamorphosed me into the veriest inamorato you perhaps ever saw.

These are a few specimens of the mischiefs, and enormities she has committed the little time she has made her appearance among us. I should never have done, were I to attempt to give you a catalogue of the whole, of all the hearts she has vanquished, of all the heads she has turned, of all the philosophers she has unmade, or of all the inconstants she has fixed to the great prejudice of the general service of the female world. It is essential to the safety of the state and to the tranquillity of the army that one of two things take place; either that she be immediately removed from our neighbourhood, or that some other nymph qualified to maintain an equal sway come into it. By dividing her empire it will be weakened and she will be much less dangerous when she has a rival equal in charms to dispute the prize with her. I solicit your aid to (Letter ends abruptly; what survives is <u>here</u>)

ASKING FOR PERMISSION TO MARRY

Alexander and Eliza asked Eliza's parents for permission to wed sometime in February or March, a month or so after they met at Morristown. Here's the opening paragraph of the letter with Papa Schuyler's reply. The rest of the letter discusses political and military matters.

Philadelphia April 8th 1780
    Dear Sir
    Yesterday I had the pleasure to receive a line from Mrs Schuyler in answer to mine on the subject of the one you delivered me at Morris town; she consents to Comply with your and her daughters wishes. You will see the Impropriety of taking the dernier pas where you are. Mrs. Schuyler did not see her Eldest daughter married. That also gave me pain, and we wish not to Experience It a Second time. I shall probably be at Camp In a few days, when we will adjust all matters. ...
    Adieu my Love to Betsy, make the same to Mrs. Cochran, my best wishes to all at head Quarters,
    I am Dr Sir sincerely Yours   &c &c
    Ph. Schuyler (More <u>here</u>)

Philip Schuyler. Mirror-image copy of a portrait of Philip Schuyler. Painted by Jacob H. Lazarus (1822-91) from a miniature painted by John Trumbull. Image: Wikipedia

HAMILTON ANNOUNCES HIS ENGAGEMENT

Sometime between April 1779 and June 1780, John Laurens was captured by the British. When Alexander wrote the letter below, Laurens had been released on parole, on the condition that he remain in Pennsylvania. The first paragraph of the letter (which I've cut below) deals with a possible exchange of prisoners; the second and third with recent military actions. After that, Alexander expresses discouragement with his fellow Americans, and then—almost in passing—tells of his engagement.

[Ramapo, New Jersey, June 30, 1780]
You have heard how the enemy made an incursion into the Jerseys and made an excursion out of it, how the Continental troops and Militia behaved with singular spirit, how the enemys Vessels have been dancing up and down the North [i.e., Hudson] River, and how they have at length thought proper to sit down quietly in New York. You have also heard how we have made a very good show with very little substance. My Dear Laurens, our countrymen have all the folly of the ass and all the passiveness of the sheep in their compositions. They are determined not to be free and they can neither be frightened, discouraged nor persuaded to change their resolution. If we are saved France and Spain must save us. I have the most pigmy-feelings at the idea, and I almost wish to hide my disgrace in universal ruin. Don't think I rave; for the conduct of the states is enough most pitiful that can be imagined. ...
We have now before us a golden opportunity: we have applied to the states for means completely within their power;

we have done everything that could operate on their fears and on their hopes. They have complied by halves, and if we attempt any thing, we must do it on the principle of despair; when we had it in our power to do it with a moral certainty of success, if we had properly exerted our resources. We are however still trying to rouse them, and it is still possible we may have a glorious campaign. I wish as far as you think yourself at liberty you would give me a confidential view of the progress of your affairs Southward.

Have you not heard that I am on the point of becoming a benedict? I confess my sins. I am guilty. Next fall completes my doom. I give up my liberty to Miss Schuyler. She is a good hearted girl who I am sure will never play the termagant; though not a genius she has good sense enough to be agreeable, and though not a beauty, she has fine black eyes—is rather handsome and has every other requisite of the exterior to make a lover happy. And believe me, I am lover in earnest, though I do not speak of the perfections of my Mistress in the enthusiasm of Chivalry.

Is it true that you are confined to Pensylvania? Cannot you pay us a visit? If you can, hasten to give us a pleasure which we shall relish with the sensibility of the sincerest friendship.

Adieu God bless you.

A Hamilton

The lads all sympathize with you and send you the assurances of their love. (More here)

"Becoming a Benedict" probably refers to *Much Ado about Nothing,* whose Benedick swears he'll never marry. (Act One; search "bachelor")

This sounds lukewarm, but remember this is a time when it's not considered acceptable to got into details about one's deepest emotions. Alexander's son John C. Hamilton heavily censored many of his father's letters before publishing them, and even scribbled out passages on the original letters to make them illegible—and that was 50 years or so later.

MORE

• Want to see some writing in Alexander's hand? See this site.

CHAPTER 19

Alexander and Eliza's
Engagement and Wedding, 1780

"EMPLOY ALL YOUR LEISURE IN READING"

By early July 1780, Alexander and Eliza had been engaged for several months. For Alexander's list of requirements for a wife, his letter to sister Peggy about Eliza, and Papa Schuyler's permission to marry, see Chapter 18. Since February, Eliza had been staying in Morristown with Dr. Cochran, George Washington's personal physician. When the army left winter quarters, she set out for her parents' home in Albany— and then we have letters from Alexander to her.

In the letter below, Alexander reminds Eliza of her promise to read widely so that they can have long talks about important subjects. It's exactly the same attitude he showed to Kitty Livingston back in 1777, when he was a carefree bachelor: he's willing, even eager, to talk with women as equals, on politics and other matters. (See Chapter 18.)

> [Preakness, New Jersey, July 2–4, 1780]
>
> I have been wishing my love for an opportunity of writing to you, but none has offered. The inclosed [see below] was sent to you at Morris Town, but missed you; as it contains ideas that often occur to me, I send it now. Last evening Doctor Cochran delivered me the dear lines you wrote me from Nicholson's. I shall impatiently long to hear of your arrival at Albany and the state of your health. I am perfectly well, proof against any thing that can assail mine. We have no change in our affairs since you left us. I should regret the time already lost in inactivity if it did not bring us nearer to that sweet reunion for which we so ardently wish. I never look forward to that period without sensations I cannot describe.
>
> I love you more and more every hour. The sweet softness and delicacy of your mind and manners, the elevation of your sentiments, the real goodness of your heart, its tenderness to

me, the beauties of your face and person, your unpretending good sense and that innocent simplicity and frankness which pervade your actions; all these appear to me with increasing amiableness and place you in my estimation above all the rest of your sex.

I entreat you my Charmer, not to neglect the charges I gave you particularly that of taking care of your self, and that of employing all your leisure in reading. Nature has been very kind to you; do not neglect to cultivate her gifts and to enable yourself to make the distinguished figure in all respects to which you are intitled to aspire. You excel most of your sex in all the amiable qualities; endeavour to excel them equally in the splendid ones. You can do it if you please and I shall take pride in it. It will be a fund too, to diversify our enjoyments and amusements and fill all our moments to advantage.

I have received a letter from my Laurens [who had been captured by the British and was released on parole in Pennsylvania] solicitg an interview on the Pensylvania Boundary. The General has half consented to its taking place. I hope to be permitted to meet him; if so, I will go to Philadelphia and then you may depend, I shall not forget the picture you requested.

Yrs. my Angel with inviolable   Affection

Alex Hamilton

July 2d. 80

It is now the fourth and no opportunity has offered. I open my letter just to tell you your Papa has been unwell with a touch of the Quinsey; but is now almost perfectly recovered. He hoped to be at Hd. Qrs. to day. He is eight miles off. I saw him last evening and heard from him this morning. I mention this lest you should hear of his indisposition through an exaggerated channel and be unnecessarily alarmed. Affectionately present me to yr Mama.

Adieu my love (More here)

The "inclosed" that Alexander refers to above may be the poem that Allan McLane Hamilton reported was written on a slip of paper that Eliza treasured.

But few letters remain which enable us to mark the advance of Hamilton's wooing, but a little verse is in my possession which was found in a tiny bag hanging from his wife's
neck after her death, and which she had evidently always
worn, and it was quite probably given to her when they were
together this winter.[1] What is apparently a sonnet was
written upon a piece of torn and yellow paper, fragments of
which had been sewn together with ordinary thread.

ANSWER TO THE INQUIRY WHY I SIGHED

Before no mortal ever knew
A love like mine so tender—true—
Completely wretched—you away—
And but half blessed e'en while you stay.

If present love [illegible] face
Deny you to my fond embrace
No joy unmixed my bosom warms
But when my angel's in my arms."

[1] 1779–80.

From *Intimate Life of Alexander Hamilton,* 1910, p. 126.

"DO YOU SOBERLY RELISH THE PLEASURE OF BEING A POOR MAN'S WIFE?"

A month after the letter above, Alexander wrote to Eliza again. Main points: 1) Please write me! And let's number our letters so we know if we miss any. 2) I'll quit the army if you ask me to, but please don't. 3) Here's the state of the war. 4) I don't have a fortune: can you handle that?

[Teaneck, New Jersey, August, 1780]

Impatiently My Dearest have I been expecting the return of your father to bring me a letter from my charmer with the answers you have been good enough to promise me to the little questions asked in mine by him. I long to see the workings of my Betseys heart, and I promise my self I shall have ample gratification to my fondness in the sweet familiarity of her pen. She will there I hope paint me her feelings without reserve—even in those tender moments of pillowed retirement, when her soul abstracted from every other object, delivers itself up to Love and to me—yet with all that delicacy which suits the purity of her mind and which is so conspicuous in whatever she does.

It is now a week my Betsey since I have heard from you. In that time I have written you twice. I think it will be adviseable in future to number our letters, for I have reason to suspect they do not all meet with fair play. This is number one.

[Richard Kidder] Meade just comes in and interrupts me by sending his love to you. He tells you he has written a long letter to his widow asking her opinion of the propriety of quitting the service; and that if she does not disapprove it, he will certainly take his final leave after the campaign. You see what a fine opportunity she has to be enrolled in the catalogue of heroines, and I dare say she will set you an example of fortitude and patriotism. I know too you have so much of the Portia in you, that you will not be out done in this line by any of your sex, and that if you saw me inclined to quit the service of your country, you would dissuade me from it. I have promised you, you recollect, to conform to your wishes, and I persist in this intention. It remains with you to show whether you are a Roman or an American wife. [NOTE: He's probably referring to Portia, the steadfast wife of Brutus, who is described in Plutarch's *Life of Brutus*—rather than Portia in the Merchant of Venice.]

Though I am not sanguine in expecting it, I am not without hopes this Winter will produce a peace and then you must submit to the mortification of enjoying more domestic happiness and less fame. This I know you will not like, but we cannot always have things as we wish.

The affairs of England are in so bad a plight that if no fortunate events attend her this campaign, it would seem impossible for her to proceed in the war. But she is an obstinate old dame, and seems determined to ruin her whole family, rather than to let Miss America go on flirting it with her new lovers, with whom, as giddy young girls often do, she eloped in contempt of her mothers authority. I know you will be ready to justify her conduct and to tell me the ill treatment she received was enough to make any girl of spirit act in the same manner. But I will one day cure you of these refractory notions about the right of resistance, (of which I foresee you will be apt to make a very dangerous application), and teach you the great advantage and absolute necessity of implicit obedience.

But now we are talking of times to come, tell me my pretty damsel have you made up your mind upon the subject of housekeeping? Do you soberly relish the pleasure of being a poor mans wife? Have you learned to think a home spun preferable to a brocade and the rumbling of a waggon wheel to the musical rattling of a coach and six? Will you be able to see with perfect composure your old acquaintances flaunting it in gay life, tripping it along in elegance and splendor, while you hold an humble station and have no other enjoyments than the sober comforts of a good wife? Can you in short be an Aquileia and chearfully plant turnips with me, if fortune should so order it? If you cannot my Dear we are playing a comedy of all in the wrong, and you should correct the mistake before we begin to act the tragedy of the unhappy couple. [NOTE: I can't sort out who Aquileia is, but among the Romans, turnips were the cheapest and most rustic food known.]

I propose you a set of new questions my lovely girl; but though they are asked with an air of levity, they merit a very serious consideration, for on their being resolved in the affirmative stripped of all the colorings of a fond imagination our happiness may absolutely depend. I have not concealed my circumstances from my Betsey; they are far from splendid; they may possibly even be worse than I expect, for every day brings me fresh proof of the knavery of those to whom my little affairs are entrusted. They have already filed down what was in their hands more than one half, and I am told they go on diminishing it, 'till I fear they will reduce it below my former fears. [NOTE: He's talking about the subscription set up for him by the citizens of St. Croix, after the "hurricane letter"; see Chapter 2.] An indifference to property enters into my character too much, and what affects me now as my Betsey is concerned in it, I should have laughed at or not thought of at all a year ago. But I have thoroughly examined my own heart. Beloved by you, I can be happy in any situation, and can struggle with every embarrassment of fortune with patience and firmness. I cannot however forbear entreating you to realize our union on the dark side and satisfy, without deceiving yourself, how far your affection for me can make you happy in a privation of those elegancies to which you have been accustomed. If fortune should smile upon us, it will do us no harm to have been prepared for adversity; if she frowns upon us, by being prepared, we shall encounter it without the chagrin of disappointment. Your future rank in life is a perfect lottery; you may move in an exalted you may move in a very humble sphere; the last is most probable; examine well your heart. And in doing it, dont figure to yourself a cottage in romance, with the spontaneous bounties of nature courting you to enjoyment. Dont imagine yourself a shepherdess, your hair embroidered with flowers a crook in your hand tending your flock under a shady tree, by the side of a cool fountain, your faithful shepherd sitting near and entertaining you with gentle tales of love. These are pretty dreams and very apt to enter into the heads of lovers when they think of a connection without the advantages of fortune. But they must not be indulged. You must apply your situation to real life, and think how you should feel in scenes of which you may find examples every day. So far My Dear Betsey as the tenderest affection can compensate for other inconveniences in making your estimate, you cannot give too large a credit for this article. My heart overflows with every thing for you, that admiration, esteem and love can inspire. I would this moment give the world to be near you only to kiss your sweet hand. Believe what I say to be truth and imagine what are my feelings when I say it. Let it awake your sympathy and let our hearts melt in a prayer to be soon united, never more to be separated.

Adieu loveliest of your sex

AH

Instead of inclosing your letter to your father I inclose his to you because I do not know whether he may not be on his way here. If he is at home he will tell you the military news. If he has set out for camp, you may open and read my letters to him. The one from Mr. Mathews [delegate to Congress from South Carolina] you will return by the first opportunity. (More here; also Library of America, pp. 66-9)

"ALL THE PROOFS I HAVE OF YOUR TENDERNESS AND READINESS TO SHARE EVERY KIND OF FORTUNE"

The main points: 1) I'm very sorry if I insulted you by asking whether you could bear to live in poverty: it's because I don't have a high opinion of most men and women. 2) Everyone at camp has fallen in love with the same cute girl, but she has no soul, so she doesn't tempt me.

[Liberty Pole, New Jersey, September 3, 1780]

I wrote you last night the inclosed hasty note in expectation that your papa would take his leave of us this morning early; a violent storm in which our house is tumbling about our ears prevents him. He and Meade are propping the house (I mean the Marquis), and I sit down to indulge the pleasure I always feel in writing to you.

The little song you sent me I have read over and over. It is very pretty and contains precisely those sentiments I would wish my betsey to feel, and she tells me it is an exact copy of her heart. [NOTE: That letter apparently doesn't survive.] You seem by sympathy to have anticipated the inquiries I made in one of mine lately, and to have answered them all by this little song; a pretty method indeed when I am asking a set of sober questions, of the greatest importance, to answer me with a song. I confess however that they scarcely deserved a better and that if you should in reality refer me to your song, I shall be very well served. For after all the proofs I have of your tenderness and readiness to share every kind of fortune with me it is a presumptuous diffidence of your heart to propose the examination I did. But be assured My angel it is not a diffidence of my betsey's heart, but of a female heart, that dictated the questions. I am ready to believe everything in favour of yours; but am restrained by the experience I have had of human nature, and of the softer part of it. Some of your sex possess every requisite to please delight, and inspire esteem friendship and affection; but there are too few of this description. We are full of vices. They are full of weaknesses; though I will not agree with the poet that they are, "Matter too soft, a lasting mark to bear. And best distinguished by black brown or fair." Nor will I join in the exclamation of Adam against the Creators having formed woman, "a fair defect of nature." Yet I have reason to think that these portraits are applicable to too many of the sex; and though I am satisfied, whenever I trust my senses and my judgment that you are one of the exceptions, I cannot forbear having moments when I feel a disposition to make a more perfect discovery of your temper, and character. In one of those moments I wrote the letter in question.

Do not however I entreat you suppose that I entertain an ill opinion of all your sex. I have a much worse of my own. I have seen more of yours that merited esteem and love, but the truth is, My Dear girl, there are very few of either that are not very worthless. You know my sentiments on this head. I think I have found a precious jewel. I pray you do not think your sex injured and undertake to be their champion; for it will be taking an unfair advantage of your influence over me.

We have been fortunate of late in Quarters. I gave you a description of a fair one in those we had at Tappan. We have found another here; a pretty little dutch girl of fifteen. Every body makes love to her, and she receives every body kindly. She grants every thing that is asked and has too much simplicity to refuse any thing; but she has so much innocence to shield her, that the most determined rake would not dare to take advantage of her simplicity. This you will say is a very favourable character; but I have summed up all her excellencies—beauty, innocence, youth, simplicity. If all her sex were like her, I would become a disciple of Mahomet. I am persuaded she has no soul; and as I am squeamish enough to require a soul in a woman, I run no great risk of becoming one of her captives.

You see I give you an account of all the pretty females I meet with; you tell me nothing of the pretty fellows you see. I suppose you will pretend there is none of them engages the least of your attention, but you know I have been told you were something of a coquette, and I shall take care what degree of credit, I give to this pretence. When your sister returns home, I shall try to get her in my interest and make her tell me of all your flirtations. Have you heard any thing more of what I hinted to you about [François Louis Teisseydre, Marquis de] Fleury? When she returns, give my love to her and tell her, I expected, she would have outstripped you in the Hymenial line.

Adieu My love

A Hamilton (More <u>here</u>)

"WHAT HAVE WE TO DO WITH ANYTHING BUT LOVE?"

Main points: 1) Why don't you write me? 2) Here's the military news. 3) We need a new form of government. 4) I've given up the idea of suicide if we lose this war, but how would you feel about moving to Switzerland?

[Bergen County, New Jersey, September 6, 1780]

I wrote you My Dear Betsey a long letter or rather two long letters by your father. I have not since received any of yours. I hope I shall not be much longer without thus

enjoying this only privilege of our separation. [The Founders
Archive notes: "The remainder of this paragraph, consisting
of fourteen lines, has been crossed out in such a way that
it is impossible to decipher the writing. These lines were
presumably crossed out by J. C. Hamilton."]

Most people here are groaning under a very disagreeable
piece of intelligence just come from the Southward; that
Gates has had a total defeat near Cambden in South Carolina.
Cornwallis and he met in the night of the 15th. by accident
marching to the same point. The advanced guards skirmished
and the two armies halted and formed 'till morning. In the
morning a battle ensued, in which the Militia and Gates
with them immediately run away and left the Continental
troops to contend with the enemy's whole force. They did
it obstinately, and probably are most of them cut off. Gates
however who writes to Congress seems to know very little
what has become of his army. He showed that age and the
long labors and fatigues of a military life had not in the least
impaired his activity; for in three days and a half, he reached
Hills borough, one hundred and eighty miles from the scene
of action, leaving all his troops to take care of themselves,
and get out of the scrape as well as they could. He has
confirmed in this instance the opinion I always had of him.

This event will have very serious consequences to the
Southward. Peoples imaginations have already given up
North Carolina and Virginia; but I do not believe either of
them will fall. I am certain Virginia cannot. This misfortune
affects me less than others, because it is not in my temper to
repine at evils that are past, but to endeavour to draw good
out of them, and because I think our safety depends on a
total change of system, and this change of system will only
be produced by misfortune.

Pardon me my love for talking politics to you. What have
we to do with any thing but love? Go the world as it will,
in each others arms we cannot but be happy. If America
were lost we should be happy in some other clime more
favourable to human rights. What think you of Geneva as
a retreat? 'Tis a charming place; where nature and society
are in their greatest perfection. I was once determined to let
my existence and American liberty end together. My Betsey
has given me a motive to outlive my pride, I had almost said

my honor; but America must not be witness to my disgrace. As it is always well to be prepared for the worst, I talk to you in this strain; not that I think it probable we shall fail in the contest; for notwithstanding all our perplexities, I think the chances are without comparison in our favour; and that my Aquileia and I will plant our turnips in her native land. [NOTE: Again with the cheap veggies!]
    Adieu my lovely girl
    A Hamilton (More <u>here</u>)

"I SHALL NEVER MAKE YOU BLUSH"

In a letter of 9/25/1780, after telling Eliza of Benedict Arnold's treachery and Arnold's wife's distraught behavior, Alexander writes:

Could I forgive Arnold for sacrificing his honor reputation and duty I could not forgive him for acting a part that must have forfieted the esteem of so fine a woman. At present she almost forgets his crime in his misfortune, and her horror at the guilt of the traitor is lost in her love of the man. But a virtuous mind cannot long esteem a base one, and time will make her despise, if it cannot make her hate.

Indeed my angelic Betsey, I would not for the world do any thing that would hazard your esteem. 'Tis to me a jewel of inestimable price & I think you may rely I shall never make you blush.

Thank you for all the goodness of which your letters are expressive, and I entreat you my lovely girl to believe that my tenderness for you every day increases and that no time or circumstances can abate it. I quarrel wit the hours that they do not fly more rapidly and give us to each other. (More <u>here</u>)

"I HAVE TALENTS AND A GOOD HEART, BUT WHY AM I NOT HANDSOME?"

Main points: 1) Here's the story on Major Andre and the traitor Benedict Arnold. 2) I want to be a better man for your sake.

[Tappan, New York, October 2, 1780]
    Since my last to you, I have received your letters No. 3 & 4; the others are yet on the way. Though it is too late to have the advantage of novelty, to comply with my promise, I send

you my account of Arnold's affair; and to justify myself to your sentiments, I must inform you that I urged a compliance with Andre's request to be shot and I do not think it would have had an ill effect; but some people are only sensible to motives of policy, and sometimes from a narrow disposition mistake it. ...

I fear you will admire the picture so much as to forget the painter. I wished myself possessed of André's accomplishments for your sake; for I would wish to charm you in every sense. You cannot conceive my avidity for every thing that would endear me more to you. I shall never be satisfied with giving you pleasure, and I am mortified that I do not unite in myself every valuable and agreeable qualification. I do not my love affect modesty. I am conscious of the advantages I possess. I know I have talents and a good heart; but why am I not handsome? Why have I not every acquirement that can embellish human nature? Why have I not fortune, that I might hereafter have more leisure than I shall have to cultivate those improvements for which I am not entirely unfit?

Tis not the vanity of excelling others, but the desire of pleasing my Betsey that dictates these wishes. In her eyes I should wish to be the first the most amiable the most accomplished of my sex; but I will make up all I want in love.

Two days since, the bundle directed to your papa was delivered to me. I beg you to present my affectionate compliments with it to your mama.

I am in very good health and shall be in very good spirits when I meet my Betsey.

Adieu

A Hamilton ... (More here)

THE WEDDING

Alexander and Eliza were married on December 14, 1780, at Albany. The miniature on the next page, by Charles Wilson Peale, was perhaps commissioned by Eliza. She probably embroidered the mat, which is rather lovely.

On December 19, 1780, Hamilton wrote to General Washington:

Ivory miniature of Alexander Hamilton by Charles Wilson Peale, possibly painted in 1780 on the occasion of Hamilton's marriage. The embroidered mat has been attributed to Eliza. Image: <u>Columbia University</u>.

Mrs. Hamilton presents her respectful compliments to Mrs. Washington and yourself. After the holidays we shall be at Head Quarters.

I believe I imparted to you General Schuylers wish that you could make it convenient to pay a visit with Mrs. Washington this winter. He and Mrs. Schuyler have several times repeated their inquiries and wishes. I have told them I was afraid your business would not permit you. If it should, I shall be happy you will enable me to let them know about what period will suit; when the slaying [ahem, Alexander: SLEIGHING] arrives, it will be an affair of two days up and two days down.

With the most respectful attachment I have the honor to be   Yr. Excellys. Obed ser

A Hamilton (More <u>here</u>)

Washington replied on December 27, 1780:

Mrs. Washington most cordially joins me, in compliments of congratulations to Mrs. Hamilton & yourself, on the late happy event of your marriage & in wishes to see you both at head Quarters. We beg of you to present our respectful

compliments to Generl. Schuyler, his Lady & Family &
offer them strong assurances of the pleasure we should feel,
at seeing them at New Windsor.

   With much truth and great personal regard   I am Dr
Hamilton   Yr affecte. frd & Servt
   Go: Washington (More <u>here</u>)

MORE

• Last week I finished *Hamilton: The Revolution,* by Lin-Manuel Miranda and Jeremy McCarter. Having worked for a dealer in old and
rare books for several decades, I love the fact that the printed version
is done in eighteenth-century style: large quarto format, raised bands,
spine labels, deckle edges. After seeing the fabulous photos, I almost
feel like I've seen the show ... Mmmm, no, not really. Still trying the
lottery. But the book does include excellent photos. Aside from the
lyrics with notes by Miranda, it also has a series of enlightening essays
on the conception and production of the show. Highly recommended.

CHAPTER 20
Hamilton Asks for a Military Command, 1780

Alexander and Eliza were married in December, 1780 (see Chapter 19). A month earlier, with the prospect of a wife and family to support, Hamilton wrote to George Washington to remind him that he urgently wanted a military command. Hamilton suggested which regiments the men could be drawn from without offending his fellow officers, and laid out an objective for the newly created force, plus an alternative.

Ironically (with 20/20 hindsight, much of history is ironic), the knowledge, clarity, and breadth of vision that made Hamilton able to sketch out this plan also made him far too valuable for Washington to send out into the field.

November 22. 1780
Dear Sir,
    Sometime last fall when I spoke to your Excellency about going to the Southward, I explained to you candidly my feelings with respect to military reputation, and how much it was my object to act a conspicuous part in some enterprise that might perhaps raise my character as a soldier above mediocrity. You were so good as to say you would be glad to furnish me with an occasion. When the expedition to Staten Island was on foot a favourable one seemed to offer. There was a batalion without a field officer, the command of which I thought, as it was accidental, might be given to me without an inconvenience. I made an application for it through the Marquis, who informe me of your refusal on two principles—one that giving me a whole batalion might be a subject of dissatisfaction, the other that if an accident should happen to me in the present state of your family, you would be embarrassed for the necessary assistance.
    The project you now have in contemplation affords another opportunity. I have a variety of reasons that press me to desire ardently to have it in my power to improve it. I take the liberty to observe that the command may now be proportioned to my rank, and that the second objection ceases

to operate, as during the period of establishing our winter quarters there will be a suspension of material business; besides which, my peculiar situation will, in any case call me away from the army in a few days and Mr Harrison may be expected back early next month. [NOTE: Hamilton was taking leave to travel to Albany, to marry Eliza.]

My command may consist of an hundred and fifty or two hundred men composed of fifty men of Major Gibbs's corps, fifty from Col Meig's regiment, and fifty or an hundred more from the light infantry: Major Gibbs to be my Major. The hundred men from here may move on friday morning towards [blank space in manuscript], which will strengthen the appearances for Staten Island to form a junction on the other side of the Passaick.

I suggest this mode to avoid the complaints that might arise from composing my party wholly of the light infantry, which might give umbrage to the officers of that corps, who, on this plan, can have no just subject for it.

The primary idea may be, if circumstances permit to attempt with my detachment Bayard's Hill. Should we arrive early enough to undertake it, I should prefer it to any thing else, both for the brilliancy of the attempt in itself and the decisive consequences of which its success would be productive. If we arrive too late to make this eligible (as there is reason to apprehend) my corps may form the van of one of the other attacks; and Bayards Hill will be a pretext for my being employed in the affair, on a supposition of my knowing the ground, which is partly true.

I flatter myself also that my military character stands so well in the army as to reconcile the officers in general to the measure. All circumstances considered, I venture to say any exception which might be taken would be unreasonable.

I take this method of making the request to avoid the embarrassment of a personal explanation. I shall only add that however much I have the matter at heart, I wish your Excellency intirely to consult your own inclination; and not from a disposition to oblige me, to do any thing that may be disagreeable to you. It will, nevertheless, make me peculiarly happy if your wishes correspond with mine. I have the honor to be very sincerely and respectfully Yr Excellencys Most Obed. servant

A. Hamilton (More here)

LAFAYETTE RECOMMENDS HAMILTON FOR A PROMOTION

Hamilton and Lafayette became close friends while working at Washington's headquarters. When Alexander Scammell resigned as adjutant general, Lafayette wrote to Washington recommending Hamilton for the position.

11/28/1780

As you have been pleased to consult me on the choice of an adjutant-general, I will repeat here, my dear general, that though I have a claim upon General [Edward] Hand, in every other point of view, his zeal, obedience, and love of discipline, have given me a very good opinion of him.

Colonel [William Stephens] Smith has been by me wholly employed in that line, and I can assure you that he will perfectly answer your purpose.

Unless, however, you were to cast your eye on a man who, I think, would suit better than any other in the world. Hamilton is, I confess, the officer whom I should like to see in that station. With equal advantages, his services deserve from you the preference to any other. His knowledge of your opinions and intentions on military arrangements, his love of discipline, the superiority he would have over all the others, principally when both armies shall operate together, and his uncommon abilities, are calculated to render him perfectly agreeable to you. His utility would be increased by this preferment; and on other points he could render important services. An adjutant-general ought always to be with the commander-in-chief. Hamilton should, therefore, remain in your family, and his great industry in business would render him perfectly serviceable in all circumstances. On every public or private account, my dear general, I would advise you to take him. (Quoted here)

Just before Hamilton set off for Albany, Lafayette relayed his recommendation to Hamilton.

Paramus [New Jersey] Novr. 28. 1780

Dear Hamilton,

Here I arrived last night and am going to set out for Philadelphia. Gouvion goes strait to New Windsor and by him I write to the General, I speak of Hand & Smith whom I recommend [for the adjutant general position] and add—

"If however you was to cast your-eye on a Man who I think would suit better than any other in the World Hamilton is, I confess the officer whom I would like best to see in my _____ [blank in manuscript] ." Then I go on with the idea that at equal advantages you deserve from him the preference, that your advantages are the greatest, I speak of a cooperation, of your being in the family, & conclude that on every public & private account I advise him to take you.

I know the general's friendship and gratitude for you, My Dear Hamilton, both are greater than you perhaps imagine. I am sure he needs only to be told that something will suit you and when he thinks he can do it he certainly will. Before this campaign I was your friend and very intimate friend, agreable to the ideas of the World. Since my second voyage, my sentiment has increased to such a point, the world knows nothing about. To shew both from want and from scorn of expressions I shall only tell you. Adieu   Yrs

La Fayette (More <u>here</u>)

Brigadier General Edward Hand was chosen for the position of adjutant general.

WORDING

I tend to look for primary sources—a historian's turn of mind. I realized this past week that I haven't been commenting on the lyrics to the musical, because I'm not sure I can do it without lapsing into bone-dry academic prose. I've been working not to sound academic for ... Hmphf. Nearly as long as Lin-Manuel Miranda has been alive.

But I do like a challenge, and one of the reasons I'm addicted to the musical is the way Miranda weaves words together: so let's see if I can share my delight without suffering an academic relapse.

"Give me a command": in the musical, Hamilton's passionate desire to lead men in the field is the reason he leaves Washington's staff. Washington's a very sympathetic character and features prominently in both acts, so the motive for Hamilton's break with him has to be established early and made completely believable. And here it is in "Helpless," high on the list of material advantages that Hamilton doesn't have:

Eliza, I don't have a dollar to my name

An acre of land, a troop to command, a dollop of fame ...

At the wedding feast, Hamilton greets Burr with, "I wish I had your command instead of manning George's journal." In "Stay Alive," Hamilton asks Washington to let him lead men in the field: "Entrust me with a command."

Given this set-up, when we get to "Meet Me Inside," it's not a surprise that Washington's refusal to give Hamilton a field command is the reason Hamilton leaves Washington's staff.

We have letters from Hamilton explaining why he left Washington's staff (Chapter 30); he doesn't cite the lack of command as the reason. But *Hamilton: An American Musical* is a drama, not a history book. For it to work on stage, the characters' actions have to be justified to the point of seeming inevitable. If you think that repetition of "command" is accidental, then you'll never write a musical that's nominated for sixteen Tonys.

MORE

• Amazon popped up a recommendation for Nathaniel Philbrick's *Valiant Ambition.* I'm enjoying it very much—like the Vidal book on Aaron Burr (see Chapter 3), it makes me shift perspective and get a better understanding of the whole. I've always focused on Washington's actions during the Revolutionary War. Philbrick (who writes very well) is filling in my knowledge of topics such as the Battle of Saratoga and the Conway Cabal. If you finish it before I do, don't tell me the ending. Seriously! Facts are facts, and history is history, but where a historian or biographer ends his story makes an enormous difference. (I already said that, when explaining why the finale of *Hamilton* affects my attitude to the whole musical: here, in the "My Heart Went 'Boom'" section.)

• A recent article in the *Wall Street Journal* attempted to show how similar the *Hamilton* lyrics are to rap. If you read the words rather than listen to the rhythm and stare cross-eyed at the multicolor graphics, all the article "proves" is that the *Hamilton* lyrics are miles above rap's usual level. (HT Iris Bell for the article.)

*The United States of America laid down from the best authorities,
agreeable to the Peace of 1783. Image: Library of Congress*

CHAPTER 21
Young Philip, 1782

I'd meant to write on the Battle of Monmouth this week, but I'm skipping ahead a bit, to the song after "Yorktown," because it's a perfect Father's Day song. Not bad for mothers, either. Have a listen.

Dead people don't have charisma, but in the following letter, you can get a sense of Alexander's charm and humor in the paragraph that begins, "You reproach me with not having said enough ..." He's writing to Richard Kidder Meade, who had served with him on Washington's staff until 1780.

> Albany Augt 27th. 1782
>
> I thank you my dear Meade for your letter of the first of this month which you will perceive has travelled much faster than has been usual with our letters. Our correspondence hitherto has been unfortunate, nor in fact can either of us compliment himself on his punctuality but you were right in concluding that however indolence or accident may interrupt our intercourse, nothing will interrupt our friendship. Mine for you is built on the solid basis of a full conviction that you deserve it and that it is reciprocal and it is the more firmly fixed because you have few competitors. Experience is a continued comment on the worthlessness of the human race and the few exceptions we find have the greater right to be valued in proportion as they are rare. I know few men estimable, fewer amiable & when I meet with one of the last description it is not in my power to withhold my affection.
>
> You reproach me with not having said enough about our little stranger. When I wrote last I was not sufficiently acquainted with him to give you his character. ... He is truly a very fine young gentleman, the most agreable in his conversation and manners of any I ever knew—nor less remarkable for his intelligence and sweetness of temper. You are not to imagine by my beginning with his mental qualifications that he is defective in personal. It is agreed on all hands, that he is handsome, his features are good, his eye is not only sprightly and expressive but it is full of benignity.

His attitude in sitting is by connoisseurs esteemed graceful and he has a method of waving his hand that announces the future orator. He stands however rather awkwardly and his legs have not all the delicate slimness of his fathers. It is feared He may never excel as much in dancing which is probably the only accomplishment in which he will not be a model. If he has any fault in manners, he laughs too much. He has now passed his Seventh Month. [NOTE: Philip was born January 22, 1782.]

I am glad to find your prospect of being settled approaches. I am sure you will realize all the happiness you promise yourself with your amiable partner. I wish Fortune had not cast our lots at such a distance, Mrs. Meade you, Betsy & myself would make a most affectionate & most happy partie quarré.

As to myself I shall sit down in New York when it opens & the period we are told approaches. [NOTE: The British did not evacuate New York until November 1783.] No man looks forward to a Peace with more pleasure than I do, though no man would sacrifice less to it than myself, If I were not convinced the people sigh for peace. I have been studying the Law for some months and have lately been licenced as an attorney. I wish to prepare myself by October for Examination as a Counsellor but some public avocations may possibly prevent me.

I had almost forgotten to tell you, that I have been pretty unanimously elected by the legislature of this state, a member of Congress to begin to serve in November. I do not hope to reform the State although I shall endeavour to do all the good I can.

Suffer Betsey & me to present our love to Mrs. Meade; she has a sisterly affection for you. ...

God Bless you

A Hamilton (More <u>here</u>)

The man was non-stop.

Philip Schuyler Hamilton, 1782-1801

CHAPTER 22
General Charles Lee, 1773-1777,
and Valley Forge, 1777-1778

Until I read Philbrick's *Valiant Ambition,* I hadn't realized how much dissent there was among American generals during the Revolutionary War. The fact that they managed to cooperate long enough to defeat the British is astonishing. But in an odd way, their disagreements give me hope (as do the rifts between the Founding Fathers). All is not lost today, if these far-from-perfect men could accomplish so much.

And on the subject of far-from-perfect men: let's talk about Charles Lee (1731-1782). When the Revolutionary War broke out, Lee had much more military experience than George Washington. Born in Chester, England, to a British officer, Lee joined the army at age 14. He served in the French and Indian Wars, then in Portugal. While Great Britain was at peace (it did happen, once in a while), Lee hired himself out to the king of Poland, where he rose to the rank of major general; at home, he never rose higher than lieutenant colonel.

Lee vociferously opposed King George III's treatment of the colonies. In 1773 he moved to America and bought property in Virginia (now West Virginia). He also traveled throughout the colonies, meeting George Washington, Patrick Henry, and John Adams, among others.

Despite Lee's military experience, in 1775 it was George Washington whom the Continental Congress named commander-in-chief. But

General Charles Lee, from a contemporary engraving

Washington was only in charge of part of the army. General Lee was sent to command the southern army, in South Carolina. His success in defending Fort Moultrie (near Charleston) on June 18, 1776, made him a hero—particularly after Washington's disastrous defeat at the Battle of Long Island in August 1776. Soon Lee, Horatio Gates, and other American generals were jockeying to replace Washington as commander-in-chief.

And then there came the fall of Fort Washington, the last patriot stronghold in Manhattan. Against General Washington's better judgment, he allowed General Greene to persuade him to try to hold it. The British captured it in a matter of hours on November 16, 1776, along with more than 2,800 American soldiers and provisions that the Continental Army desperately needed. Across the Hudson, Fort Lee (named for none other than Charles Lee) was abandoned four days later.

1901 Relief commemorating the Battle of Fort Washington, Washington Heights. Image: Pilettes / Wikipedia. The inscription is transcribed here.

LEE ON WASHINGTON

Soon after the loss of Forts Washington and Lee, Washington opened a letter to his trusted aide Joseph Reed. He assumed it was official business. Instead, he found a letter from Charles Lee, dated November 30, 1776, replying to a letter by Reed:

> I receiv'd your most obliging flattering letter—lament with you that fatal indecision of mind which in war is a much greater disqualification than stupidity or even want of personal courage—accident may put a decisive Blunderer in the right—but eternal defeat and miscarriage must attend the man of the best parts if curs'd with indecision. The General recommends in so pressing a manner as almost to amount to an order to bring over the Continental Troops under my command—which recommendation or order throws me into the greatest dilemma from sev'ral considerations ... I only wait myself for this busyness I mention of Rogers & Co being over—shall then fly to you—for to confess a truth I really think our Chief will do better with me than without me. ... (More here, note 1)

It's a telling indication of the chain of command in the American army that General Washington can only *recommend* that Lee join him!

Two weeks later, Lee was still meandering his way to meet Washington. On December 13, 1776, he spent the night three miles from Washington's encampment, at a comfortable inn at Basking Ridge. From there he wrote to his friend General Horatio Gates:

> The ingenious manoeuvre of Fort Washington has completely unhinged the goodly fabrick we had been building. There never was so damned a stroke; entre nous, a certain great man is most damnably deficient. He has thrown me into a situation where I have my choice of difficulties. If I stay in this Province, I risk myself and Army; and if I do not stay, the Province is lost forever. I have neither guards, cavalry, medicines, money, shoes, or stockings. I must act with the greatest circumspection. Tories are in my front, rear, and on my flanks. The mass of the people is strangely contaminated. In short, unless something which I do not expect turns up, we are lost. Our counsels have been weak to the last degree. As to what relates to yourself, if you think you can be in time to aid the General, I would have you, by

all means, go. You will, at least, save your Army. It is said
that the Whigs are determined to set fire to Philadelphia. If
they strike this decisive stroke, the day will be our own; but
unless it is done, all chance of liberty, in any part of the
globe, is forever vanished. (More here)

What do you suppose would have happened to the morale of
Lee's troops if their commander spoke like this in front of them?
There's a difference between acknowledging a difficult situation and
predicting immediate and eternal catastrophe if the current effort fails.

Washington wrote to Lee the following day (12/14/1776):

I last night received your Letter of the 11th Instt by Major
Dehart. I am much surprized that you should be in any doubt
respecting the Route you should take after the information
you have had upon that Head as well by Letter as from Majr
Hoops who was dispatched for the purpose. ... I have so
frequently mentioned our situation, and the necessity of
your aid, that it is painfull to me to add a word upon the
Subject. Let me once more request and entreat you to march
immediately for Pitts Town ...

The Congress have adjourned from Philadelphia, to meet
at Baltimore on the 20th Inst. & sensible of the importance
of the former have directed it to be defended to the utmost
extremity to prevent the Enemy from possessing it. the
fatal consequences that must attend it's loss are but too
obvious to every one. Your arrival may be the means of
saving it, Nothing but a respectable force, I am certain from
melancholy experience can induce the Militia to come in
and give their Aid. (More here)

Washington, too, knows that to lose Philadelphia would be a devastating blow to the United States, and he's practically begging Lee to
bring his troops to help defend it.

LEE'S CAPTIVITY

But Lee could not help defend Philadelphia, because a British patrol
captured him at the tavern in Basking Ridge, as he was writing letters in his nightgown. He spent the next 16 months imprisoned in
New York.

Three months into his captivity, Major General Charles Lee wrote
out for General William Howe a plan for how the British could win
the war. It begins:

Capture of Major General Charles Lee by the British, from a monument to Lord Harcourt in St. George's Chapel, Windsor, England. Image here.

As on the one hand it appears to me that by the continuance of the War America has no chance of obtaining the ends She proposes to herself; that altho by struggling She may put the Mother Country to very serious expence both in blood and Money, yet She must in the end, after great desolation havock and slaughter be reduc'd to submit to terms much harder than might probably be granted at present—and as on the other hand Great Britain tho' ultimately victorious, must suffer very heavily even in the process of her victories, every life lost and every guinea spent being in fact worse than thrown away … and as I am not only perswaded from the high opinion I have of the humanity and good sense of Lord and General Howe that the terms of accommodation will be as moderate as their powers will admit …

He goes on to list specific places the British should attack in order to defeat the rebellious colonists.

To bring matters to a conclusion, it is necessary to unhinge or dissolve, if I may so express myself, the whole system or machine of resistance, or in other terms, Congress Government—this system or machine, as affairs now stand, depends entirely on the circumstances and disposition of the People of Maryland Virginia and Pensylvania – if the Province of Maryland or the greater part of it is reduc'd or submits and the People of Virginia are prevented or intimidated from marching aid to the Pensylvania Army the whole machine is dissolv'd and a period put to the War, to accomplish which, is, the object of the scheme which I now take the liberty of offering to the consideration of his Lordship and the General, and if it is adopted in full I am so

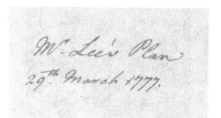

Cover title for the plan General Lee wrote for General Howe, March 29, 1777. See George H. Moore's 1860 publication.

confident of the success that I wou'd stake my life on the issue …

I would propose that four thousand men [British soldiers] be immediately embark'd in transports, one half of which shou'd proceed up the Patomac and take post at Alexandria, the other half up Chesepeak Bay and possess themselves of Annapolis. They will most probably meet with no opposition in taking possession of these Posts, and when possess'd they are so very strong by nature that a few hours work and some trifling artillery will secure them against the attacks of a much greater force than can possibly be brought down against them …

This breathtakingly treasonous document, written throughout in Lee's own hand, was only discovered and published in 1860 (whole document and background here; quotes are from pp. 84-88).

PAINE'S "AMERICAN CRISIS"

On December 23, 1776, in the aftermath of the Battle of Long Island and the loss of Forts Washington and Lee, Thomas Paine (now a volunteer in the Continental Army) published the first essay in his series "The American Crisis."

These are the times that try men's souls. The summer soldier and the sunshine patriot will, in this crisis, shrink from the service of their country; but he that stands it now, deserves the love and thanks of man and woman. Tyranny, like hell, is not easily conquered; yet we have this consolation with us, that the harder the conflict, the more glorious the triumph. What we obtain too cheap, we esteem too lightly: it is dearness only that gives every thing its value. … (Yes, you should read the rest: here.)

Emanuel Leutze, Washington Crossing the Delaware, 1851. Image: MetMuseum.org. It's 21 feet wide, so yes, you should go see it. And maybe I should do a tour soon of American art ... Shall I?

Washington had the opening of this essay read to his troops three days later, on December 26, 1776, as they prepared to cross the Delaware to attack the Hessian soldiers at Trenton.

WASHINGTON AT VALLEY FORGE

While General Lee was languishing in New York from mid-December 1776 through early 1778, Washington and his army fought at Trenton, Princeton, Brandywine, and Germantown, lost Philadelphia to the British in September 1777, and settled down to wait out the winter 20 miles from Philadelphia, at a place called Valley Forge. From there, on December 23, 1777, Washington wrote to Henry Laurens, president of the Continental Congress:

> Sir: Full as I was in my representation of matters in the Commys. departmt. yesterday, fresh, and more powerful reasons oblige me to add, that I am now convinced, beyond a doubt that unless some great and capital change suddenly takes place in that line, this Army must inevitably be reduced to one or other of these three things. Starve, dissolve, or disperse, in order to obtain subsistence in the best manner they can; rest assured Sir this is not an exaggerated picture, but that I have abundant reason to support what I say.
>
> Yesterday afternoon receiving information that the Enemy, in force, had left the City, and were advancing towards Derby with apparent design to forage, and draw

Subsistance from that part of the Country, I order'd the Troops to be in readiness, that I might give every opposition in my power; when, behold! to my great mortification, I was not only informed, but convinced, that the Men were unable to stir on Acct. of Provision, and that a dangerous Mutiny begun the Night before, and [which] with difficulty was suppressed by the spirited exertion's of some officers was still much to be apprehended on acct. of their want of this Article. ...

I can assure those Gentlemen that it is a much easier and less distressing thing to draw remonstrances in a comfortable room by a good fire side than to occupy a cold bleak hill and sleep under frost and Snow without Cloaths or Blankets; however, although they seem to have little feeling for the naked, and distressed Soldier, I feel superabundantly for them, and from my Soul pity those miseries, wch. it is neither in my power to relieve or prevent. (More here)

The Continental Congress, which had decamped to Lancaster and then York, Pennsylvania, had its own challenges. Henry Laurens wrote to his son John (one of Washington's aides, and a good friend of Alexander Hamilton; see Chapter 4) in January 1778: "Our whole frame is shattered. We are tottering and without the immediate exertions of wisdom and fortitude we must fall flat down." (More here, pp. 267-9)

LEE RETURNS TO THE AMERICAN ARMY

After Charles Lee was released on a prisoner exchange in the spring of 1778, he was reinstated as second-ranking general in the Continental Army. (Of course, no one on the American side knew of that treasonous document written for General Howe.) In June, as the British prepared to evacuate Philadelphia, Lee was one of the senior advisers in the council of war that Washington held to discuss whether the American army should attack the British as they marched overland to New York.

Drumroll.

Next up: the Battle of Monmouth.

MORE

• During the French and Indian War, Lee married the daughter of a Seneca chief. Among the Senecas, his name was Ounewaterika, "Boiling Water."

• More on Thomas Paine in Chapters 11 (on *Common Sense*) and 15 (on the lead-up to the Revolution).

• Highly recommended: Nathaniel Philbrick, *Valiant Ambition: George Washington, Benedict Arnold, and the Fate of the American Revolution,* which tells the Revolutionary War from a very different perspective. It's not the first book you should read on the subject, but it's a great spur to integration if you've read about many of the featured players.

Major General Charles Lee, in an early engraving.

CHAPTER 23
The Battle of Monmouth, June 1778

When Lee was released in early 1778, he resumed his position as second-ranking general in the Continental Army. (On Lee's military career and capture by the British, see Chapter 22.) In late June, as the British prepared to evacuate Philadelphia, Washington and his commanders discussed whether to attack them as they marched the hundred miles to New York. The council of war, wrote Hamilton some days later, "would have done honor to the most honourable society of midwives, and to them only" (see below).

LAFAYETTE TAKES THE LEAD

Lee and some others opposed an attack. But on June 26, Washington decided to send out a small force (4,000 men) to harass the rearguard of the 12-mile-long British column, giving the rest of the Continental Army time to reach the British forces. Major General Lafayette was given command of this advance force.

Side note: I had never thought about communication during battles in this era. Most of the army was on foot, and with tens of thousands of men in the field, that meant they were spread out over a considerable distance. No satellite phones, cell phones, radios, telegraph lines. Washington dictated messages to his staff (his aides-de-camp: Hamilton, Laurens, and others) and sent one of them off on horseback to carry the message to the officer in charge in a certain area. The commanders were expected to keep Washington informed of major changes in the situation—verbally via a staff member, if they were in the heat of battle. As a historian I'm happy that many such orders survive; but I can't help being amazed that battles were fought and won under those conditions.

So: Lafayette was given command of the advance force. Then General Lee changed his mind, apparently for social rather than military reasons (6/25/1778):

> Dr General
>   When I first assented to the Marquis of Fayette's taking the command of the present detachment, I confess I viewd

it in a very different light than I do at present I considerd it as a more proper busyness of a Young Volunteering General than of the Second in command in the Army—but I find that it is considerd in a different manner; They say that a Corps consisting of six thoushand Men, the greater part chosen, is undoubtedly the most honourable command next to the Commander in Chief, that my ceding it woud of course have an odd appearance I must intreat therefore, (after making a thoushand apologies for the trouble my rash assent has occasion'd to you) that if this detachment does march that I may have the command of it—so far personally, but to speak as an Officer—I do not think that this detachment ought to march at all, untill at least the head of the Enemy's right column has pass'd Cranbury—then if it is necessary to march the whole Army, I cannot see any impropriety in the Marquis's commanding this detachment or a greater as advance Guard of the Army—but if this detachment with Maxwells Corps Scotts, Morgans and Jacksons are to be considerd as a seperate chosen active Corps and put under the Marquis's Command until the Enemy leave the Jerseys—both Myself and Lord Steuben will be disgrac'd. I am, Dr General Yours (More here)

Washington replied (6/26/1778), "Your uneasiness, on account of the command of yesterday's detachment, fills me with concern, as it is not in my power, fully, to remove it without wounding the feelings of the Marquiss de la Fayette—I have thought of an expedient, which though not quite equal to either of your views, may in some measure answer both ..." Lee was given command of the entire advance force, with Lafayette serving under him. (More here.)

Lafayette, in the field and eager to go, wrote to Washington later in the day. His spelling is, as always, charmingly erratic.

I would be very happy if we could attak them before they halt for I have no notion of taking one other moment but this off the march—if I Can not overtake them we could lay at some distance and attak to morrow Morning provided they do'nt escape in the night which I much fear as our intelligences are not the best ones; I have sent Some partys out and I will get some more light by them.

I fancy your excellency will move down with the army, and if we are at a Convenient distance from you I have nothing to fear in striking a blow if opportunity is offered,

I believe that in our present strength provided they do'nt escape we may do Some thing. ...

Sir, I want to repeat you in writing what I have told to you, which is that if you believe it, or if it is believed necessary or useful to the good of the Service and the honor of General lee to Send him down with a couple of thousand men or any force more, I will chearfully obey and Serve him not only out of duty but out of what I owe to that gentleman's character ... (More here)

The next day, June 27, 1778, Lee reported to Washington that he had taken up position near Englishtown (letter here).

GRUNT'S-EYE VIEW OF THE BATTLE OF MONMOUTH

Joseph Plumb Martin, a private in the Continental Army, had a remarkable knack of being present at crucial battles in the Revolutionary War. On June 28, 1778, he was with the army as it approached the British rearguard. Here's the battle from a grunt's-eye view:

It was ten or eleven o'clock before we got through ... and came into the open fields. The first cleared land we came to was an Indian cornfield, surrounded on the east, west and north sides by thick tall trees. The sun shining full upon the field, the soil of which was sandy, the mouth of a heated oven seemed to me to be but a trifle hotter than this ploughed field; it was almost impossible to breathe. We had to fall back again as soon as we could, into the woods. By the time we had got under the shade of the trees and had taken breath, of which we had been almost deprived, we received orders to retreat, as all the left wing of the army, that part being under the command of General Lee, were retreating. Grating as this order was to our feelings, we were obliged to comply.

We had not retreated far before we came to a defile, a muddy, sloughy brook. While the artillery were passing this place, we sat down by the roadside. In a few minutes the Commander in Chief and suite crossed the road just where we were sitting. I heard him ask our officers "by whose order the troops were retreating," and being answered, "by General Lee's," he said something, but as he was moving forward all the time this was passing, he was too far off for me to hear it distinctly. Those that were nearer to him said that his words were "d——n him." Whether he did thus express himself

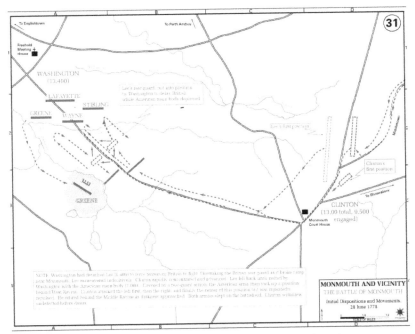

Battle of Monmouth, June 28, 1778. Map: Wikipedia

or not I do not know. It was certainly very unlike him, but he seemed at the instant to be in a great passion; his looks if not his words seemed to indicate as much. After passing us, he rode on to the plain field and took an observation of the advancing enemy. He remained there some time upon his old English charger, while the shot from the British artillery were rending up the earth all around him. After he had taken a view of the enemy, he returned and ordered the two Connecticut brigades to make a stand at a fence, in order to keep the enemy in check while the artillery and other troops crossed the before-mentioned defile. … (More here)

BATTLING GENERALS

Lee responded to Washington's exasperated comments on the battle-field in a letter of June 30, 1778, that drips with sarcasm:

Sir

From the knowledge I have of your Excys character—I must conclude that nothing but the misinformation of some very stupid, or misrepresentation of some very wicked person coud have occasioned your making use of so very singular expressions as you did on my coming up to the ground where you had taken post—They implyd that I was guilty either of disobedience of orders, of want of conduct, or want of courage. Your Excellency will therefore infinitely oblige me by letting me know on which of these three articles you ground your charge—that I may prepare for my justification which I have the happiness to be confident I can do to the army, to the Congress, to America, and to the world in general. Your excellency must give me leave to observe that neither yourself nor those about your person, could from your situation be in the least judges of the merits or demerits of our measures—And to speak with a becoming pride, I can assert that to these manouvers the success of the day was entirely owing—I can boldly say, that had we remained on the first ground, or had we advanced, or had the retreat been conducted in a manner different from what it was, this whole army and the interests of America would have risked being sacrificed. I ever had (and hope ever shall have the greatest respect and veneration for General Washington) I think him endowed with many great and good qualities, but in this instance I must pronounce that he has been guilty of an act of cruel injustice towards a man who certainly has some pretensions to the regard of every servant of this country—And I think Sir, I have a right to demand

Emmanuel Leutze, The Battle of Monmouth, ante 1853. Original is at University of California at Berkeley. Image: Wikipedia.

some reparation for the injury committed—and unless I can obtain it, I must in justice to myself, when this campaign is closed, (which I believe will close the war) retire from a service at the head of which is placed a man capable of offering such injuries. But at the same time in justice to you I must repeat that I from my soul believe, that it was not a motion of your own breast, but instigaged by some of those dirty earwigs who will for ever insinuate themselves near persons in high office—for I really am convinced that when General Washington acts from himself no man in his army will have reason to complain of injustice or indecorum. I am, Sir, and hope I ever shall have reason to continue your most sincerely devoted humble servt

Charles Lee (More here)

Washington sent a succinct reply the same day (6/30/1778):

I received your letter (dated thro' mistake the 1st of July) expressed as I conceive, in terms highly improper. I am not conscious of having made use of any very singular expressions at the time of my meeting you, as you intimate. What I recollect to have said, was dictated by duty and warranted by the occasion. As soon as circumstances will permit, you shall have an opportunity, either of justifying yourself to the army, to Congress, to America, and to the world in General; or of convincing them that you were guilty of a breach of orders and of misbehaviour before the enemy on the 28th Inst. in not attacking them as you had been directed and in making an unnecessary, disorderly, and shameful retreat. I am Sir your most obt servt

Go: Washington (More here)

Lee replied later in the day (6/30/1778) more briefly, and with even more polite venom:

[Y]ou cannot afford me greater pleasure than in giving me the opportunity of shewing to America the sufficiency of her respective servants—I trust that temporary power of office and the tinsel dignity attending it will not be able by all the mists they can raise to affuscate the bright rays of truth, in the mean time your Excellency can have no objection to my retiring from the army—I am Sir your most obt hble servt

Charles Lee (More here)

Washington replied even more briefly, later the same day (6/30/1778):

> Sir
>
> Your letter by Colo. Fitzgerald and also one of this date have been duly received. I have sent Colo. Scammel, the Adjutant General to put you in arrest, who will deliver you a copy of the charges on which you will be tryed. I am Sir Yr most obt servt
>
> Go: Washington (More here)

General Lee's court-martial ran from July 4 to August 12, 1778; we have a transcript, which is as close as you and I will ever get to hearing Hamilton, Laurens, and Lee talk. (Excerpts in Chapter 24.)

LAURENS: "A RAPIDITY AND INDECISION CALCULATED TO RUIN US"

Soon after the Battle of Monmouth, John Laurens and Alexander Hamilton wrote accounts of it. Laurens wrote (6/30/1778) to his father Henry, president of the Continental Congress, probably in the expectation that the letter's contents would be shared with the Congress. Read the description very carefully until your eyes glaze over with the sheer confusion of it, and then you'll have some sense of what it must have been like on the battlefield that scorching June day. Then you can skim the rest of the battlefield details and just focus on the interaction between Laurens and Lee.

> I was exceedingly chagrined that public business prevented my writing to you from the Field of battle, when the General sent his dispatches to Congress—the delay however will be attended with this advantage that I shall be better able to give you an account of the enemys loss—tho I must even now content myself with a very succinct relation of this affair—the situation of the two Armies on Sunday was as follows—Genl Washington with the main body of our army was at 4 miles distance from Englishtown—Genl Lee with a chosen advanced Corps was at that Town—the Enemy were retreating down the Road which leads to Middle Town ...
>
> I was with a small party of horse reconnoitring the enemy in an open space before Monmouth when I perceived two parties of the enemy advancing by files in the woods on our right and left, with a View as I imagined of enveloping our small party, or preparing the way for a skirmish of their horse—I immediately wrote an account of what I had seen

to the General—and expressed my anxiety on account of
the languid appearance of the continental troops under Gen
Lee—some person in the mean time reported to Genl Lee that
the Enemy were advancing upon us in two Columns—and I
was informed that he had in consequence ordered Varnums
brigade which was in front to repass a bridge which it had
passed—I went myself & assured him of the real state of
the case—his reply to me was, that his accounts had been
so contradictory, that he was utterly at a loss what part to
take—I repeated my account to him in positive distinct
terms and returned to make farther discoveries—I found that
the two parties had been withdrawn from the woods and that
the enemy were preparing to leave Monmouth—I wrote a
second time to Genl Washington—Genl Lee at length gave
orders to advance—the Enemy were forming themselves
on the Middletown Road, with their light infantry in front,
and Cavalry on the left flank—while a scattering distant fire
was commenced between our flanking parties and theirs—I
was impatient, and uneasy at seeing that no disposition was
made, and endeavored to find out Genl Lee to inform him of
what was doing, and know what was his disposition—he told
me that he was going to order some troops to march below
the Enemy and cut off their retreat—two Pieces of Artillery
were posted on our right without a single foot soldier to
support them—our men were formed piecemeal in front of
the Enemy—and there appeared to be no general plan or
disposition—calculated on that of the Enemy, the nature of
the ground, or any of the other principles which generally
govern in these cases—the Enemy began a cannonade from
two parts of their line—their whole body of horse made
a furious charge upon a small party of our Cavalry and
dissipated them, and drove them till the appearance of our
infantry and a judicious discharge or two of Artillery made
them retire precipitately—three Regiments of ours that had
advanced in a plain open country towards the enemys left
flank, were ordered by Gen Lee to retire and occupy the
village of Monmouth they were no sooner formed there, than
they were ordered to quit that post and gain the woods—
one order succeeded another, with a rapidity and indecision
calculated to ruin us—the enemy had changed their front
and were advancing in full march toward us—our men were
fatigued, with the excessive heat—the artillery horses were

not in condition to make a brisk retreat—a new position
was ordered—but not generally communicated—for part of
the Troops were forming on the right of the ground, while
others were marching away, and all the Artillery driving
off—the enemy after a short halt resumed their pursuit—no
Cannon was left to check their progress—a Regiment was
ordered to form behind a fence and as speedily commanded
to retire—all this disgraceful retreating—passed without the
firing of a Musket—over ground which might have been
disputed Inch by Inch—we passed a defile—and arrived at
an eminence beyond which was defended on one hand by
an impracticable fen—on the other by thick woods where
our men must have fought to advantage—here fortunately
for the honor of the Army, and the welfare of America—
Genl. Washington met the troops retreating—in disorder,
and without any plan to make an opposition—he ordered
some pieces of Artillery to be brought up to defend the
pass—and some troops to form and protect the pieces—the
Artillery was too distant to be brought up readily so that
there was but little opposition given here—a few shot though
and a little skirmishing in the wood checked the Enemys
career—The Genl expressed his astonishment at this
unaccountable Retreat, Mr Lee indecently replied that the
attack was contrary to his advice and opinion in council—
we were obliged to retire to a position which though hastily
reconnoitred, proved an excellent one—two Regiments were
formed behind a fence in front of the position—the enemys
horse advanced in full charge with admirable bravery—to
the distance of forty paces—when a general discharge from
these two Regiments—did great execution among them,
and made them fly with the greatest precipitation—the
Grenadiers succeeded to the attack—in this spot the action
was hottest, and there was considerable Slaughter of British
Grenadiers—The General ordered Woodfords brigade with
some Artillery to take possession of an eminence on the
enemys left and cannonade from thence—this produced an
excellent effect—the enemy were prevented from advancing
on us—and confined themselves to cannonade with a shew
of turning our left flank—our artillery answered theirs—
with the greatest vigour—the general seeing that our left
flank was secure—as the ground was open and commanded

by it—so that the enemy could not attempt to turn us without exposing their own flank to a heavy fire from our artillery, and causing to pass in review before us, the force employed for turning us—in the mean time Genl Lee continued retreating—Baron Steuben was order'd to form the broken troops in the rear—The Cannonade was incessant, and the General ordered parties to advance from time to time, and engage the British Grenadiers—and Guards—the horse shewed themselves no more—the Grenadiers shewed their backs and retreated every where with precipitation— they returned however again to the charge and were again repulsed—they finally retreated and got over the strong pass where as I mentioned before Genl Washington first rallied the troops—we advanced in force and continued Masters of the ground—the Standards of Liberty were planted in Triumph on the field of battle—we remained looking at each other with the defile between us till dark—& they stole off in silence at midnight— (More here)

HAMILTON: "SUCCESS SO FAR INFERIOR TO WHAT WE IN ALL PROBABILITY SHOULD HAVE HAD"

Alexander Hamilton, who was also carrying messages to and from Washington, described the battle to Elias Boudinot a week later (7/5/1778). Boudinot (1740-1821) was a friend from Hamilton's days in Elizabethtown, and at this time a delegate from New Jersey to the Continental Congress.

My dear Sir,
   You will by this time imagine that I have forgotten my promise of writing to you, as I have been so long silent on an occasion, which most people will be fond of celebrating to their friends. The truth is, I have no passion for scribbling [REALLY, Alex?!] and I know you will be at no loss for the fullest information. But that you may not have a right to accuse me of negligence, I will impose upon myself the drugery of saying something about the transactions of the 28th, in which the American arms gained very signal advantages; and might have gained much more signal ones.
   Indeed, I can hardly persuade myself to be in good humour with success so far inferior to what we, in all probability should have had, had not the finest opportunity America

ever possessed been fooled away by a man, in whom she has placed a large share of the most ill judged confidence. You will have heard enough to know, that I mean General Lee. This man is either a driveler in the business of soldiership or something much worse. To let you fully into the silly and pitiful game he has been playing, I will take the tale up from the beginning; expecting you will consider what I say, as in the most perfect confidence.

When we came to Hopewell Township, The General unluckily called a council of war, the result of which would have done honor to the most honorab[le] society of midwives, and to them only. The purport was, that we should keep at a comfortable distance from the enemy, and keep up a vain parade of annoying them by detachment. In persuance of this idea, a detachment of 1500 men was sent off under General Scot to join the other troops near the enemy's lines. General Lee was primum mobile of this sage plan; and was even opposed to sending so considerable a force. The General, on mature reconsideration of what had been resolved on, determined to persue a different line of conduct at all hazards. With this view; he marched the army the next morning towards Kingston and there made another detachment of 1000 men under General Wayne; and formed all the detached troops into an advanced corps under the command of the Marquis De la fayette. The project was, that this advanced corps should take the first opportunity to attack the enemy's rear on the march, to be supported or covered as circumstances should require by the whole army.

General Lee's conduct with respect to the command of this corps was truly childish. According to the incorrect notions of our army his seniority would have intitled him to the command of the advanced corps; but he in the first instance declined it, in favour of the Marquis. Some of his friends having blamed him for doing it, and Lord Stirling having shown a disposition to interpose his claim, General Lee very inconsistently reasserted his pretensions. The matter was a second time accommodated; General Lee and Lord Stirling agreed to let the Marquis command. General Lee a little time after, recanted again and became very importunate. The General, who had all along observed the greatest candor in the matter, grew tired of such fickle behaviour and ordered the Marquis to proceed.

The enemy in marching from Allen Town had changed their disposition and thrown all their best troops in the rear; this made it necessary, to strike a stroke with propriety, to reinforce the advanced corps. Two brigades were detached for this purpose, and the General, willing to accommodate General Lee, sent him with them to take the command of the whole advanced corps, which rendezvoused the forenoon of the 27th at English Town, consisting of at least 5000 rank & file, most of them select troops. General Lee's orders were, the moment he received intelligence of the enemy's march to persue them & to attack their rear.

This intelligence was received about five oClock the morning of the 28th. and General Lee put his troops in motion accordingly. The main body did the same. The advanced corps came up with the enemys rear a mile or two beyond the court House; I saw the enemy drawn up, and am persuaded there were not a thousand men; their front from different accounts was then ten miles off. However favourable this situation may seem for an attack it was not made; but after changing their position two or three times by retrograde movements our advanced corps got into a general confused retreat and even route would hardly be too strong an expression. Not a word of all this was officially communicated to the General; as we approached the supposed place of action we heard some flying rumours of what had happened in consequence of which the General rode forward and found the troops retiring in the greatest disorder and the enemy pressing upon their rear. I never saw the general to so much advantage. His coolness and firmness were admirable. He instantly took measures for checking the enemy's advance, and giving time for the army, which was very near, to form and make a proper disposition. He then rode back and had the troops formed on a very advantageous piece of ground; in which and in other transactions of the day General Greene & Lord Stirling rendered very essential service, and did themselves great honor. The sequel is, we beat the enemy and killed and wounded at least a thousand of their best troops. America owes a great deal to General Washington for this day's work; a general route dismay and disgrace would have attended the whole army in any other hands but his. By his own good sense and fortitude he turned the fate of the day. Other officers have great merit in performing their parts well; but he directed the whole with the skill of a Master workman. He did not hug himself at a distance and leave an Arnold to win laurels for him [NOTE: a reference to Benedict Arnold's valor at Saratoga, when fighting under General Horatio Gates]; but by his own presence, he brought order out of confusion, animated his troops and led them to success.

A great number of our officers distinguished themselves this day. ... In short one can hardly name particulars without doing injustice to the rest. The behaviour of the officers and men in general was such as could not easily be surpassed. Our troops, after the first impulse from mismanagement, behaved with more spirit & moved with greater order than the British troops. You know my way of thinking about our army, and that I am not apt to flatter it. I assure you I never was pleased with them before this day.

What part our family acted let others say. I hope you will not suspec[t] me of vanity when I tell you that one of them Fitsgerald, had a slight contusion with a Musket ball, another, Laurens, had a slight contusion also—and his horse killed—a third, Hamilton, had his horse wounded in the first part of the action with a musket ball. If the rest escaped, it is only to be ascribed to better fortune, not more prudence in keeping out of the way. ...

What think you now of General Lee? You will be ready to join me in condemning him: And yet, I fear a Court Martial will not do it. A certain preconceived and preposterous opinion of his being a very great man will operate much in his favour. Some people are very industrious in making interest for him. Whatever a court Martial may decide, I shall continue to believe and say—his conduct was monstrous and unpardonable. ... (More here)

MORE

• The Battle of Monmouth gave rise to the story of Molly Pitcher, whom most of us know only as the name of a rest stop on the New Jersey Turnpike.

• Joseph Plumb Martin's account of the Revolutionary War is here.

CHAPTER 24

Charles Lee on Trial, July-August 1778

In which we see Alexander Hamilton in a frenzy of valor,
and Dianne indulging in a historiographical rant.

Most prominent American leaders during the Revolutionary War period wrote well, often brilliantly—but the transcript of the testimony
at General Charles Lee's court-martial is as close as we'll ever get
to hearing some of them *speak*. Although Lee's court-martial doesn't
figure in *Hamilton: An American Musical,* it shows a facet of Hamilton that made me rethink my comments in Chapters 8 adn 9. Excerpts
from the testimony are below; the full transcript is <u>here</u>.

Lee's court-martial stretched from July 4 to August 9, 1778, shifting along with the army from New Brunswick to Morgantown to Paramus, Peeksill, and North Castle. Presiding was Major-General Lord
Stirling, whom we last met leading the Maryland 400 at the Battle of
Brooklyn (Chapter 17). Nearly 40 witnesses were called, including
members of Washington's staff (Alexander Hamilton, John Laurens,
and others), members of Lee's staff, and officers who had commanded various parts of the battlefield.

A question for military historians: was it normal to have eight generals or brigadier-generals at the same battle, in an army of 11,000?
And those were only the ones called to testify at Lee's trial. There may
have been more.

THE BATTLE OF MONMOUTH: OVERVIEW

Here's the CliffsNotes version of the Battle of Monmouth. (Eyewitness accounts of bits and pieces of it are in Chapter 23.) In June
1778, 11,000 or so British soldiers plus hundreds of Tories and a 12-
mile baggage train set out overland from Philadelphia to New York. At
Washington's council of war, Lee (who was second-ranking general
in the army) and others argued against a direct attack on the British.
After much debate, Major General Lafayette was sent ahead with a
force of 4,000 to delay the British by harassing their rearguard. Lee
then decided that honor required he hold command of that advance
guard. He was sent forward with another thousand men and given

command of the whole advance guard. When they met the British on June 28, Lee's men retreated in some disorder. Washington, arriving with the main body of the Continental Army, saw the retreating soldiers and, meeting Lee, demanded to know why he was falling back. Lee claimed that his intelligence about the enemy's strength was mistaken and that his subordinates had disobeyed orders; he also pointed out that he had advised against an attack. Washington rallied the troops and gave Lee command of a much smaller force.

The Americans fought the British to a stalemate. Overnight, the British slipped away. In British military history, the Battle of Monmouth was a mere skirmish. For the Americans, who had been drilled by Baron von Steuben all winter at Valley Forge, it was one of the earliest proofs that they could successfully confront the mighty British army. John Laurens wrote to his father that "the Standards of Liberty were planted in Triumph on the field of battle" (Chapter 23).

Meanwhile, in the aftermath of the battle, Lee sent a series of venomous letters to Washington (also Chapter 23). On June 30, Lee was arrested. He was charged with disobeying orders in not attacking the enemy; allowing his troops to retreat in an unnecessary and sometimes disorderly manner; and being disrespectful to the commander-in-chief.

HAMILTON'S TESTIMONY AT LEE'S COURT-MARTIAL

Hamilton's testimony appears in the printed transcript of the Lee court-martial on pp. 11-12, 13-14, and 66-72. It's long and interesting, but understanding most of it would require more than the CliffsNotes version of the battle; so I'm only going to give you the bits that Lee responds to later.

Q. Did you fall in with General Lee's troops afterwards? [i.e., after Lee met Washington]

A. I came up with them in their retreat a little time before the stand was made, by which the enemy received their first check. I heard General Washington say to General Lee, that it would be necessary for him (General Washington) to leave the ground and form the main body of the army, while I understood he recommended to General Lee to remain there, and take measures for checking the advance of the enemy; General Lee replied, he should obey his orders, and would not be the first man to leave the field. I was some little time after this, near General Lee, during which, however, I heard no measures directed, nor saw any taken by him to answer the purpose before-mentioned. (p. 68)

Pages 69-70:

Q, Were the troops, when you fell in with them the second time, retreating in order or disorder, and in what particular manner?

A. The corps that I saw were in themselves in tolerable good order, but seemed to be marching without system or design, as chance should direct; in short, I saw nothing like a general plan or combined disposition for a retreat; in this, however, the hurry of the occasion made it very difficult to have a distinct conception.

Q.: Was there any body drawn up in their rear to cover their retreat that you saw?

A. I saw no such thing.

Q. Were the orders that you heard General Lee give that day, given distinct and clear?

A. I recollect to have heard General Lee give two orders; at both times he seemed to be under a hurry of mind.

Q. Did General Lee, to your knowledge, advise General Washington of his retreat?

A. He did not, to my knowledge.

Pages 71-72

General Lee's question.—Did you not express in the field an idea diametrically reverse of my state of mind, from what you have before mentioned in your testimony?

A. I did not. I said something to you in the field expressive of an opinion, that there appeared in you no want of that degree of self-possession, which proceeds from a want of personal intrepidity. I had no idea in my present evidence of insinuating the most distant charge of this nature, but only to designate that there appeared a certain hurry of spirits, which may proceed from a temper not so calm and steady as is necessary to support a man in such critical circumstances.

OTHER TESTIMONY AT LEE'S COURT-MARTIAL

Lt. Colonel Tilghman, a member of Washington's staff, also testified about Washington's meeting with Lee in the field (pp. 91-3):

> General Washington desired Colonel Shreve to march his men over the morass, halt them on the hill, and refresh them. Major Howell was in the rear of the regiment; he expressed himself with great warmth at the troops coming off, and said he had never seen the like. At the head of the next column General Lee was himself, when General Washington rode up to him, with some degree of astonishment, and asked him what was the meaning of this? General Lee answered, as Dr. M'Henry has mentioned, Sir, sir. I took it that General Lee did not hear the question distinctly. Upon General Washington's repeating the question, General Lee answered, that from a variety of contradictory intelligence, and that from his orders not being obeyed, matters were thrown into confusion, and that he did not choose to beard the British army with troops in such a situation. He said that besides, the thing was against his own opinion. General Washington answered, whatever his opinion might have been, he expected his orders would have been obeyed, and then rode on towards the rear of the retreating troops.

Dr. Griffiths testified that on the battlefield, Lee was telling all and sundry that there was no need to fight, given that the French alliance would win the war (pp. 94-95):

> I recollect perfectly well overtaking General Lee the 28th of June, about one hour and a half after the action commenced, about half way between the Meeting-house and English-Town, as near as I can recollect, as he was retiring at the head of his column. I asked the General, when I first overtook him, what appearance or what face things wore? his answer was, as I expected. I heard the General repeat the same to a number of persons at English-Town, who had asked him the same question, in almost the same words. From what followed in conversation, I thought his expectation was, that the day would be disgraceful to the American arms ; and as sure as we did attack, we would be beat, and he went on to assign reasons for it; the superiority of the enemy in point of discipline, that they outflanked us in cavalry, and

that they outmanoeuvered us, were urged by General Lee. General Lee asserted that his advice had ever been contrary to a general action, for the reasons I have already mentioned, and that it was impolitic or imprudent to risk anything, when we were sure of succeeding in the main point; that the connection with France would secure our independency, and the American arms wanted no addition to their reputation.

LEE'S CLOSING SPEECH AT HIS COURT-MARTIAL

Lee began his closing speech by arguing that he was exercising his discretionary powers (pp. 199-200):

> Before I enter into a narration of what was performed or was not performed on the 28th of June, by the body of troops under my command, it is necessary to make as clear as possible to the Court, the nature and spirit of the orders I received from his Excellency, at least to explain my idea of them; for it must appear, from the evidence of the different commentators on these orders, that they were by no means precise and positive, but in a great measure discretionary, at least I conceived them as such, and am inclined to think that the Court will consider them in the same light. The several councils of war, held both in Pennsylvania and on this side of the Delaware, on the subject of the operations to be pursued in the Jerseys, reprobated the idea of risking a general engagement, as a measure highly absurd in the present, or rather then, circumstances of America …
>
> But, whatever may have been the good sense of these Councils, I shall readily allow that they ought to have little or no weight with an officer, if subsequent orders from the Commander-in-Chief, or even a hint communicated, had been of such a nature, as to give reason to think that the idea had been discarded, and that the General had adopted a plan repugnant to these Councils; but I had not the least reason to think that he had discarded this idea. No letter I received, no conversation I ever held with him, indicated an intention or wish to court a general engagement; if he had, I protest solemnly, that, whatever I might have thought of the wisdom of the plan, I should have turned my thoughts solely to the execution.

Lee had his feelings hurt by the way Washington accosted him on the field (p. 219-20):

> When I arrived first in his [Washington's] presence, conscious of having done nothing that could draw on the least censure, but rather flattering myself with his congratulation and applause, I confess I was disconcerted, astonished and confounded by the words and manner in which his Excellency accosted me; it was so novel and unexpected from a man, whose discretion, humanity and decorum I had from the first of our acquaintance stood in admiration of, that I was for some time incapable of making any coherent answer to questions so abrupt and in a great measure to me unintelligible. The terms, I think, were these— "I desire to know, sir, what is the reason—whence arises this disorder and confusion ?" The manner in which he expressed them was much stronger and more severe than the expressions themselves. When I recovered myself sufficiently, I answered, that I saw or knew of no confusion but what naturally arose from disobedience of orders, contradictory intelligence, and the impertinence and presumption of individuals, who were vested with no authority, intruding themselves in matters above them and out of their sphere. That the retreat, in the first instance, was contrary to my intentions, contrary to my orders, and contrary to my wishes. I even particularized ...

HAMILTON'S DEATH WISH, REVISITED (YET AGAIN)

I find it fascinating that the only witness whose testimony Lee attempted to disparage in his concluding remarks was Alexander Hamilton. Hamilton's comment about Lee being in a "hurry of mind" seems to have struck a nerve: if you read the transcript, you'll notice Lee asks witness after witness to testify that he was calm, cool, and collected. He seems, in fact, more concerned with how he appeared than with how he was doing.

Lee gives quite a lengthy description of his interaction with Hamilton on the battlefield, apparently aiming to make Hamilton look foolhardy and himself braver, by comparison. You may have to read the lines 4-5 twice (I did) before you realize what an exceptionally nasty backhanded compliment it is.

There is one part of Colonel Hamilton's evidence I cannot help animadverting upon; it has hurt me because it is even an impeachment of my qualifications as an officer, and it has hurt me the more, as it comes from a man of esteemed sense, and whose valor I myself was a witness of, although it is not that sort of valor, unless by practice and philosophy he can correct, will ever be of any great use to the community. The Colonel is pleased to allow me personal intrepidity, but that there appeared in me that hurry of spirits which may proceed from a temper not so calm and steady as is necessary to support a man in such critical circumstances. Now, in answer to all this fine language, I shall only repeat, as nearly as possible, the conversation that passed between us. When General Washington asked me whether I would remain in front and retain the command, or he should take it, and I had answered that I undoubtedly would, and that he should see that I myself should be one of the last to leave the field, Colonel Hamilton flourishing his sword, immediately exclaimed : That's right, my dear General, and I will stay, and we will all die here on this spot. I must observe, that this hill was by no means a position to risk anything further than the troops then halted on it, with which I intended to cover my corps in their passage over the bridge, and give the enemy a check, to gain time for General Washington to make a disposition of the army. As this was the principle on which the hill was defended, I could but be surprised at his expression, but observing him much flustered and in a sort of frenzy of valor, I calmly requested him to observe me well and to tell me if I did not appear tranquil and master of my faculties; his answer was, that he must own that I was entirely possessed of myself; well, then (said I), you must allow me to be a proper judge of what I ought to do. Sir (I added) if you will take pains to examine that hill in our front, you will perceive that it so eminently commands this we are on, that it would be unpardonable to risk anything more on it than what necessity will oblige us; as to myself, I am as ready to die as what you possibly can be, but I am responsible for something more than my own person, I am responsible to the General and to the continent for the troops I have been entrusted with. When I have taken proper measures to get the main body of them in a good position, I will die with you on this spot, if you please. If Colonel Hamilton's sentiments were really opposite to what his precise words were, I cannot help thinking it somewhat extraordinary that he and Colonel Laurens should have seen with so very different optics from those of every other gentleman who had an opportunity of observing me that day. (pp. 229-31)

Here comes the rant. (Some of you are only here for the rant, right?)

What happened at the Battle of Monmouth is as real and definite as what happened to me yesterday on the subway. However, not every aspect of what happened at Monmouth on June 28, 1778 was recorded and preserved. As any policeman will tell you, the accounts of excited eyewitnesses can vary widely.

If enough evidence is found, we can discover the historical truth. But for me, the historical truth is almost a side issue: the point is the journey to it. Seeking out information and deciding what's reliable. Integrating new information: does it agree with or contradict what I already know? If it contradicts, how do I resolve that? This is a skill that's as valuable when I'm listening to a politician talk today as when I'm studying 18th-century battles. And then, once I've discovered the facts, there's the question of how they should be judged in their own context, and in my time: a whole 'nother matter, plunging into thickets of thorny ethical questions.

The point is: Real historians don't spend their time memorizing dates and statistics. They seek out information, integrate, and keep seeking and integrating for, like, ever. If you're not willing to do that, or if it makes you nervous that history isn't rote memorization, then leave your historian's hat on the desk and close the door quietly behind you.

All right, now that it's just us: in Chapter 9, I said that I didn't see compelling evidence that Hamilton longed for martyrdom. Lee's description of him on the battlefield makes me willing to allow that Hamilton wouldn't have objected to "dying on the battlefield in glory." It makes sense, in fact, since Hamilton's closest friends were military men, for whom courage in the face of death is a requirement, and glorious death in battle is, if not a goal, at least an honorable end.

Hamilton didn't fall in love with Eliza and become part of the Schuyler family for another 18 months—February, 1780. In fact, in one of the letters he wrote to her (September 6, 1780), he said that "I was once determined to let my existence and American liberty end together. My Betsey has given me a motive to outlive my pride, I had almost said my honor...." (See Chapter 19.)

Whether thoughts of martyrdom and death are threads that run through the rest of his life—that I can't decide until I've seen more supporting evidence from his later writings. And I'm good with that, because I enjoy the journey to the truth.

THE VERDICT OF LEE'S COURT-MARTIAL

On August 9, 1778, the court returned its verdict:

> The Court having considered the first charge against Major-General Lee, the evidence and his defence, are of opinion, that he is guilty of disobedience of orders, in not attacking the enemy on the 28th of June, agreeable to repeated instructions; being a breach of the latter part of article 5th, section 2d of the Articles of War.
>
> The Court having considered the second charge against Major-General Lee, the evidence and his defence, are of opinion, he is guilty of misbehavior before the enemy on the 28th of June, by making unnecessary, and in some few instances, a disorderly retreat; being a breach of the 13th article of the 13th section of the Articles of War.
>
> The Court having considered the third charge against Major-General Lee, are of opinion, that he is guilty of disrespect to the Commander-in-Chief in two letters dated the 1st of July and the 28th of June; being a breach of the 2d article, section 2d of the Articles of War.
>
> The Court do sentence Major-General Lee to be suspended from any command in the armies of the United States of North America, for the term of twelve months. (pp. 238-9)

MORE

• Lee's court martial (full text as PDF)

CHAPTER 25
A Modern Hamilton Portrait

On Wednesday July 20, 2016, a bronze bust of Alexander Hamilton by Zenos Frudakis (a noted American sculptor) came up at <u>auction in Philadelphia, at Freeman's</u>. I asked Zenos's wife Rosalie, a long-time member of the ForgottenDelights / DianneDuranteWriter mailing list, if she could send me extra pics—the one I saw on the auction house's website had some glare. This one's much better.

See it on Zenos's website <u>here</u>. A video, so you can get the full 3-D effect, is <u>here</u>.

Alexander Hamilton, by Zenos Frudakis. Photo: Zenos Frudakis

FREEDOM

While you're on Zenos's site, have a look at his *Freedom,* which
I ***adore***, and which is all by itself a reason to visit Philadelphia (16th
and Vine, 20 feet long by 8 feet high). Details here.

*Zenos Frudakis, Freedom. 16th & Vine Sts., Philadelphia.
Photo: Zenos Frudakis.*

CHAPTER 26
Meanwhile: Aaron Burr, 1778-1783

Forty-seven-year-old General Charles Lee, who had been a career military man since age 14, was bitterly angry when a court martial after the Battle of Monmouth found him guilty of disobeying orders, allowing a disorderly retreat, and disrespecting Commander-in-Chief Washington. (See Chapter 24.) Lieutenant Colonel Aaron Burr, who fought at Monmouth (June 28, 1778; Chapter 23), was not called as a witness during the court martial. He did write a letter in support of Lee. We don't have Burr's letter, but we have Lee's thanking him:

October 1778

Dear Sir,

As you are so kind as to interest yourself so warmly in my favour, I cannot resist the temptation of writing you a few lines. Till these two days, I was convinced the Congress would unanimously have rescinded the absurd, shameful sentence of the court-martial; but, within these two days, I am taught to think that equity is to be put out of the question, and the decision of the affair to be put entirely on the strength of party; and, for my own part, I do not see how it is possible, if the least decency or regard for national dignity has place, that it can be called a party business.

I wish I could send you the trial [transcript], and will the moment I can obtain one. I think myself, and I dare say you will think on the perusal, that the affair redounds more to my honour, and the disgrace of my persecutors, than, in the warmth of indignation, either I or my aid-de-camps have represented it. As I have no idea that a proper reparation will be made to my injured reputation, it is my intent, whether the sentence is reversed or not reversed, to resign my commission, retire to Virginia, and learn to hoe tobacco, which I find is the best school to form a consummate general. This is a discovery I have lately made. Adieu. Dear sir, believe me to be your most

Sincerely obliged servant,

C. Lee (Matthew L. Davis, *Memoirs of Aaron Burr*, I, pp. 94-5)

For more on Lee's career before the Battle of Monmouth, see Chapter 22.

BURR GOES ON LEAVE

At about this time, Aaron Burr wrote to General Washington reporting that his health was so poor that he needed to retire temporarily from active service.

Elizabethtown, N.J., 24th Oct. 1778

Sir:

The excessive heat and occasional fatigues of the preceding campaign, have so impaired my health and constitution as to render me incapable of immediate service. I have, for three months past, taken every advisable step for my recovery, but have the mortification to find, upon my return to duty, a return of sickness, and that every relapse is more dangerous than the former. I have consulted several physicians; they all assure me that a few months retirement and attention to my health are the only probable means to restore it. A conviction of this truth, and of my present inability to discharge the duties of my office, induce me to beg your Excellency's permission to retire from pay and duty till my health will permit, and the nature of service shall more particularly require my attention, provided such permission can be given without subjecting me to any disadvantage in point of my present rank and command, or any I might acquire during the interval of my absence.

I shall still feel and hold myself liable to [be] called into service at your Excellency's pleasure, precisely as if in full pay, and barely on furlough; reserving to myself only the privilege of judging of the sufficiency of my health during the present appearance of inactivity. My anxiety to be out of pay arises in no measure from intention or wish to avoid any requisite service. But too great a regard to malicious surmises, and a delicacy perhaps censurable, might otherwise hurry me unnecessarily into service, to the prejudice of my health, and without any advantage to the public, as I have had the misfortune already to experience. ...

I am, with respect, Your humble servant,

A. Burr (More here)

Washington replied on October 26:

You, in my opinion, carry your Ideas of delicacy too far when you propose to drop your pay while the recovery of your Health necessarily requires your absence from the Service. It is not customary and it would be unjust. You therefore have leave to retire untill your health is so far re-established as to enable you to do your duty. (More here, n.1)

Burr retained his commission as lieutenant colonel until February 1779, when he wrote to Washington, "The Reasons I did myself the Honour to mention to your Excellency ... still exist and determine me to resign my Rank and Command in the Army." He didn't reappear in Hamilton's life until after the war, back in New York.

BURR AND THEODOSIA

Burr had met Theodosia Bartow Prevost in August 1778 (soon after the Battle of Monmouth) and spent more time with her after he had resigned his commission. She wrote to him in May 1781:

Our being the subject of much inquiry, conjecture, and calumny, is no more than we ought to expect. My attention to you was ever pointed enough to attract the observation of those who visited the house. Your esteem more than compensated for the worst they could say. When I am sensible I can make you and myself happy, I will readily join you to suppress their malice. But, till I am confident of this, I cannot think of our union. Till then I shall take shelter under the roof of my dear mother, where, by joining stock, we shall have sufficient to stem the torrent of adversity. (More here)

Theodosia had married Swiss-born British army officer Jacques Prevost in 1763, and bore him five children. She remained at her family home (the Hermitage, in Ho-Ho-Kus, N.J.) when Prevost was sent south as British governor of Georgia in 1778, and then on to Jamaica. There he was seriously wounded in 1780, and died in October 1781. Burr and Theodosia were married on July 2, 1782. (Information on Burr's courtship is here.) Their daughter Theodosia (later Theodosia Burr Alston) was born June 21, 1783.

I wanted to include a portrait of Theodosia Bartow Prevost Burr, but there seems to be none, at least not online. The genealogy site WikiTree shows a painting that also appears on the site of the Hermitage, Theodosia's home. But on that site, the painting is not captioned, and the file name that appears when I hit "save image" is "Ann Stillwell" (i.e., Theodosia's mother).

MORE

• Theodosia's home is a museum: the Hermitage in Ho-Ho-Kus, N.J.

CHAPTER 27

Dueling Codes, Part 1

This chapter, I thought blithely, will be fast and easy. Wouldn't every gentleman carry a pocket-sized copy of the Code Duello for reference in affairs of honor? I'll find a printed dueling code and show some screenshots of an edition Alexander Hamilton might have seen, and that'll be it for "The Ten Duel Commandments."

In my folder of notes for upcoming posts, I found a print-out from a PBS page on the "Code Duello." It says this code was

> drawn up and settled at Clonmel Summer Assizes, 1777, by gentlemen-delegates of Tipperary, Galway, Sligo, Mayo and Roscommon, and prescribed for general adoption throughout Ireland. The Code was generally also followed in England and on the Continent with some slight variations. In America, the principal rules were followed, although occasionally there were some glaring deviations.

Woohoo, 1777! That's early enough (barely) that it could have been used not only by Burr and Hamilton in 1804, but conceivably by Charles Lee and John Laurens in their 1778 duel.

But I'm a cautious, scholarly type. I prefer to go back to the original printed version to see the context and to make sure nothing has been cut.

The short version: I can't find *any* dueling codes printed in the 18th century. The earliest ones date to the 1820s. Furthermore, several of the "Ten Duel Commandments" aren't in any of the four dueling codes that I have found. Which leads me to the question that's been obsessing me for two weeks: where did the "Ten Duel Commandments" come from, and what's their purpose in *Hamilton: An American Musical?*

Hush, Lin-Manuel, I know you know the answer. And yes, I'll be mentioning Joanne Freeman's *Affairs of Honor* presently.

The rest of you: part of the reason I spend time looking at primary sources is so that I can spend more time thinking about the musical, i.e., about art, which is one of my very favorite things to do. If the dueling codes don't interest you, skip to the end of Chapter 28 for thoughts on the role of the commandments in the musical.

THE DUEL COMMANDMENTS IN THE HAMILTON MUSICAL

Here are the "Ten Duel Commandments," paraphrased so I don't get into trouble for quoting a whole song. The cast recording with lyrics is here.

1. Demand satisfaction; if the offender apologizes, the matter ends. Otherwise …
2. Find a second to act on your behalf.
3. Have the seconds meet to negotiate a peace, or to set a time and place for the duel.
4. If the seconds don't reach an agreement, get a set of dueling pistols and pay a physician to come to the dueling ground. Have him turn around so he can deny seeing anything illegal.
5. Duel early in the day, and at a place that's high and dry.
6. Leave a note for your next of kin. Say your prayers.
7. Confess your sins and get ready to fight.
8. Have your seconds try one last time to negotiate a peace.
9. Look your opponent in the eye, take aim, gather your courage.
10. Count ten paces, fire!

I've found four dueling codes: Royal, Irish, French, American. I'll give you the context for each, and we'll see which of the Ten Duel Commandments appear in which codes.

THE ROYAL CODE, BY JOSEPH HAMILTON

NOTE: Alexander Hamilton's family was from Scotland. Joseph Hamilton lived at Annadale Cottage, near Dublin, Ireland. When Joseph Hamilton describes the Hamilton-Burr duel (which he does in several places, in two different works), he mentions no family connection. That strongly suggests there was none.

The Royal Code first appears in Joseph Hamilton's 1829 work, *The Only Approved Guide through All the Stages of a Quarrel: Containing the Royal Code of Honor; Reflections upon Duelling; and the Outline of a Court for the Adjustment of Disputes; With Anecdotes, Documents and Cases, Interesting to Christian Moralists Who Decline the Combat; to Experienced Duellists, and to Benevolent Legislators. The Only Approved Guide* is currently available from Dover under the title *The Duelling Code.*

Joseph Hamilton, Some Short and Useful Reflections upon Duelling, 1823: frontispiece and title page. In case you miss the reason the father is lying dead on the sofa, a huge painting of duelists hangs on the wall above him.

The backstory is crucial for understanding the Royal Code. Joseph (calling him "Hamilton" is just too confusing) was vehemently opposed to dueling. Back in 1823, he published <u>*Some Short and Useful Reflections upon Duelling*</u>. His attitude is obvious from the frontispiece (above).

In <u>*The Only Approved Guide through All Stages of a Quarrel*</u>, published in 1829—six years after *Some Short and Useful Reflections* – Joseph also makes his position quite clear:

> Before we composed our short reflections upon duelling, with a view to the total abolition of the practice, we carefully perused almost every publication which had appeared upon the subject [i.e., against duelling], and endeavoured to condense into the smallest possible compass, all the arguments which had been urged by the Christian, the moralist, and the man of common sense. We sent copies of that work to several courts in Christendom, and were unsuccessful in our effort to induce a simultaneous movement on the subject. … [Many told him], "It is impossible to eradicate this most pernicious custom." (p. 16)

What to do when men refuse to give up such a barbarous custom?

> Having failed in our endeavours to promote the abolition of the practice, we were next induced to try if we could lessen its attendant evils. We found, in several thousand anecdotes and cases, which we had collected during thirty years, a

mass of evidence that the grossest atrocities and errors were committed hourly on the subject. We conceived that such atrocities and errors might possibly in future be prevented, by the extensive circulation of a well-digested code of laws, in which the highest tone of chivalry and honour might be intimately associated with justice, humanity, and common sense; and we were encouraged by several experienced friends, as well as by Plato's strong assurance, that it is truly honourable to contrive how the worst things can be turned into better.

After carefully perusing our collection of remarkable quarrels ... we sketched out a code, consisting of twenty articles, which we submitted to experienced friends in Ireland. We next forwarded manuscript copies to the first political, military, and literary characters of the age, and received the most complimentary assurances of approbation. In May, 1824, we forwarded printed copies for the several courts of Europe and America, as well as to the conductors of the public press, for the purpose of inducing the transmission of such corrections and additions as might, if possible, render it deserving of universal acceptation; and we have now the satisfaction of presenting to the world a collection of highly-applauded rules, for the government of principals and seconds, in our ROYAL CODE OF HONOUR. (pp. 17-18)

I eagerly read the sixty items in Joseph's Royal Code to see if any of the rules coincided with the Ten Duel Commandments. Hmmm, not so much. Joseph frequently mentions seconds, but no rule explicitly states that you should seek one. In Rule 24, he notes that the duel should be held where there's easy access to a surgeon, but he doesn't say that one should be present at the duel (Commandment 4). He states in Rule 32 that a duel shouldn't be scheduled until each participant has had the chance to "make a proper disposition of his property and trusts, for the advantage of his family, constituents, clients, wards, or creditors." That's not the same as "Leave a note for your next of kin" (Commandment 6). (Incidentally, Rule 43 prohibits those who don't normally wear spectacles from wearing them at a duel.)

So: does the Royal Code have the equivalent of any of the Ten Duel Commandments? Yup. Wanna guess which? Numbers 3 and 8, both of which deal with negotiating peace. For example:

Rule XXIV. When bosom friends, fathers of large, or unprovided families, or very inexperienced youths are about to fight, the Seconds must be doubly justified in their solicitude for reconciliation.

By my count, **twenty-four (out of sixty)** of Joseph's rules mention reparation, reconciliation, and/or valid reasons for refusing to duel. Not surprising, given that Joseph was so opposed to dueling.

We can judge the popularity of Joseph Hamilton's Royal Code by the fact that the 1829 first edition of *The Only Approved Guide through All the Stages of a Quarrel* remained the sole edition until Dover began publishing <u>reprints</u> in 2007.

THE IRISH CODE

Next up: the Code Duello on that <u>PBS page</u> that I mentioned at the beginning of this chapter. PBS cites as its source *American Duels and Hostile Encounters,* Chilton Books, 1963. Tut, tut, PBS: is that the best you can do for a scholarly citation? Never mind: I can probably track down an early edition just by Googling the opening words or a distinctive phrase.

Hmph, not so easy. The first reference I find is a reprint of the 1777 code in John Lyde Wilson's <u>*The Code of Honor, or, Rules for the Government of Principals and Seconds in Duelling,*</u> 1838. Wilson, a Southerner, made up his own set of rules (the "American Code": see below). He notes at the end of his book, "Since the above Code was in press, a friend has favored me with the Irish Code of Honor, which I had never seen" – so he printed those rules as an appendix to his own. Wilson says he saw the Irish code in the <u>*American Quarterly Review,*</u> "in a notice about Sir Jonah Barrington's history of his own times" (p. 35). This turns out to be Barrington's <u>*Personal Sketches of His Own Times,*</u> in two volumes, London, 1827.

All right, where did Barrington find the Irish Code?

Sir Jonah Barrington, from a 19th-c. edition of his Recollections

Sir Jonah Barrington (1756/7-1834) was a member of the Irish bar and the Irish House of Commons. In his 50s, he moved to England and then France, where he made his living as a writer. According to the authoritative *Oxford Dictionary of National Biography*, he was known for his panache and humor. Sir J (do you mind if I call you "Sir J"?) devotes a whole chapter, "The Fire-eaters" (pp. 286-318), to describing Irishmen's love of guns and fighting. Two examples:

> One of the most humane men existing, an intimate friend of mine, and at present a prominent public character, but who (as the expression then was) had frequently played both "hilt to hilt," and "muzzle to muzzle," [i.e., was a frequent duellist] was heard endeavoring to keep a little son of his quiet, who was crying for something: "Come now, do be a good boy! Come, now," said my friend, "don't cry, and I'll give you a case of nice little pistols to-morrow. Come, now, don't cry, and we'll shoot them all in the morning."—"Yes! yes! we'll shoot them all in the morning!" responded the child, drying his little eyes, and delighted at the notion." (p. 289)

And:

> He was considered in the main a peacemaker, for he did not like to see anybody fight but himself; and it was universally admitted that he never killed any man who did not well deserve it. (p. 291)

It's in this chapter on "fire-eaters" that Sir J introduces the rules of dueling. He has just explained that a society called the Knights of Tara, which existed to practice fencing as an art, had faded out of existence:

> I can not tell why it broke up: I rather think, however, the original fire-eaters thought it frivolous, or did not like their own ascendency to be rivalled. ... Soon after, a comprehensive code of the laws and points of honor was issued by the southern fire-eaters, with directions that it should be strictly observed by gentlemen throughout the kingdom, and kept in their pistol-cases, that ignorance might never be pleaded. This code was not circulated in print, but very numerous written copies were sent to the different county clubs, &c.

My father got one for his sons; and I transcribed most
(I believe not all) of it into some blank leaves. These rules
brought the whole business of duelling into a focus, and
have been much acted upon down to the present day. They
called them in Galway "the thirty-six commandments."

As far as my copy went, they appear to have run as
follows: –

The practice of duelling and points of honor settled at
Clonmell summer assizes, 1777, by the gentlemen-delegates
of Tipperary, Galway, Mayo, Sligo, and Roscommon, and
prescribed for general adoption throughout Ireland.

Rule 1.—The first offence requires the first apology ...
(pp. 293-297, reprinted on the <u>PBS page on the Code Duello</u>]

Immediately after listing these rules, Sir J relates the story of his first
duel, which occurred purely by accident: the challenger had sent his
second to the wrong man. Citing Rule 7, Sir J's second insisted that
the men were obliged to fight, since they had come to the dueling
ground. When, after having duly fired at the challenger, the curious Sir
J asked the cause of the quarrel, the challenger replied that according
to Rule 8, if an explanation was not requested *before* a shot was fired,
it could not be requested afterward.

Here's why we're spending so much time with Sir J: I think the
man has his tongue so far in his cheek that it's a wonder he can pronounce dental consonants. Sir J's *Personal Sketches* (including the
Irish Code) appeared in 1827. That's between 1824, when fellow
Irishman Joseph Hamilton circulated his draft of the Royal Code, and
1829, when Joseph Hamilton published the sixty-item Royal Code.

I think Sir J read the early draft of the Royal Code and thought,
"What namby-pamby stuff! Real Irishmen like to fight too much for
all that negotiation. Let me tell you how they actually behave." Here,
for example, is Rule 9:

All imputations of cheating at play, races, &c., to be
considered equivalent to a blow; but may be reconciled after
one shot, on admitting their falsehood, and begging pardon
publicly.

With one exception, in the Irish Code as Sir J prints it, **every single
rule that talks about shooting requires that at least one shot be
fired.** None of that sissy reconciliation and reparation business. The exception is Rule 5, which concedes that there is no need for shots *if* the
offender hands a cane to the injured party for use on the offender's
own back.

The bloodthirstiness of the Irish Code was obvious even to American Code author John Lyde Wilson, who noted, "One thing must be apparent to every reader, viz., the marked amelioration of the rules that govern in duelling at the present time."

Sir J has neatly covered his tracks by saying the rules were passed around only in manuscript copies—so you needn't bother trying to find a printed edition. And he's dated the rules fifty years back, long enough to make it difficult for his contemporaries to track down a record and contest Sir J's account.

In his 1829 *The Only Approved Guide through All the Stages of a Quarrel,* Joseph Hamilton quotes the whole of Sir J's rules (which had appeared in print a mere two years earlier) in a section entitled "Obsolete Regulations." Then he briefly states,

> Perhaps we should apologise for copying so many pages from Sir Jonah Barrington, who is generally considered an apocryphal authority (p. 168)

As I said, I think the Irish Code of 1777 is a tongue-in-cheek creation by Sir J in 1827. However, I've been known to misinterpret British humor as well as British accents, so I hauled out two substantial fencing and dueling bibliographies. (My day job is with a dealer in old and rare books: this is the kind thing I'm very experienced at.) Thimm's *Complete Bibliography of Fencing & Duelling as Practised by All European Nations from the Middle Ages to the Present Day,* 1896, has no entries for the Irish code of dueling—I've searched under every title and subject I could think of.

Levi and Gelli's *Bibliografia del Duello, con numerose note sulla questione del Duello,* 1903, mentions on pp. xxii-xxiii the recent adoption of a uniform dueling code, which makes a bad practice somewhat better. (Their exact workds: "A noi sembra evidente come evidente è la convenienza, anzi la necessità, dell'adozione di un unico razionale Codice Cavalleresco [see note 44], il quale, finchè dura il male, valga circonscriverlo ...."). Levi and Gelli's note 44 cites no printed code earlier than the 1820s. They, too, refer to Sir J as the earliest and only source for the Irish code.

I have spent only two weeks seeking evidence of early dueling codes, but Thimm, Levi, and Gelli spent years and years searching out every available work on fencing and dueling. If they didn't find earlier evidence for the Irish code, then it's a safe bet there isn't any.

But for good measure, I logged into OCLC, the best online catalogue of holdings of libraries worldwide. (WorldCat is the layman's equivalent.) I did various tricky searches for an Irish dueling code printed before Sir J's time. Again nothing.

For extra good measure—because not all books are in institutions, and because I'm indefatigable when I get the bibliographic bit between my teeth—I searched ViaLibri, my favorite aggregator site for online booksellers. Yet again, nothing.

No matter where I look, the Irish code doesn't appear until the first volume of Sir J's *Personal Sketches,* 1827.

Sir J, you witty liar, I'm done with you.

Oh, wait, I almost forgot the point of this exercise. The only rule in the Irish Code that corresponds to any of the Ten Duel Commandments is number 21. It mentions that seconds are to seek a reconciliation either before the principals meet (Commandment 3) ... or (those bloodthirsty Irish!) *"after* sufficient firing or hits, as specified."

MORE

• The credits to the *Hamilton* soundtrack and the Hamiltome list, as a source for the "Ten Duel Commandments," Biggie Smalls' "Ten Crack Commandments" (listen here, read lyrics here). If you still don't know the difference between rap and *Hamilton: An American Musical,* here's your chance to find out.

CHAPTER 28
Dueling Codes, Part 2

In Chapter 27, I looked at the Royal Code and (disdainfully, because I think it was made up as joke) at the Irish Code. This week, we move on to two other dueling codes, the French and the American, and then ask, at last: what has all this got to do with "The Ten Duel Commandments"?

THE FRENCH CODE

The French Code was published by Comte Louis Alfred Le Blanc de Chateauvillard (or Chatauvillard) in his *Essai sur le duel,* Paris 1836 (pp. 8-85 of nearly 500 pages). Chateauvillard (1800-1869), a wealthy and accomplished man, moved in the highest levels of society. He believed that even though dueling was illegal, there were rules that should be followed in affairs of honor. Those who did not abide by such rules were assassins, and should be punished as such.

Chateauvillard's code has dozens of rules, neatly divided into chapters on the challenge, seconds, types of pistol and saber duels, etc. His code was sanctioned by more than eighty peers and prominent military men and by the French minister of War—a reminder that through the 19th century, dueling was common among members of the military as well as among aristocrats like Chateauvillard. (Hamilton, a former military man who had risen to the upper class, had a double whammy when it came to duels.)

Compared to Sir Jonah Barrington's Irish code (see Chapter 27), the French code is less bloodthirsty (apologies are allowed) and more ritualized (what happens if a group offends a group?). The French rules have the feel of a stately, deadly minuet—for example, in the elaborate procedures for various types of pistol duels.

> Rule 66. On the word "March," the combatants may advance in a zigzag step, not exceeding two paces. They may take aim without firing, and, while advancing, stop when they choose, and advance again; but once having fired, both parties must halt on the spot.

Rule 67. The combatant who has not fired may now fire, but without advancing, and the party who has fired must firmly stand the fire of his antagonist, who for that purpose is allowed half a minute; if he allows a longer time to elapse, he must be disarmed by the seconds. (From the translation of the French Code in _Down the River, or Practical Lessons in the Code Duello, by an Amateur,_ 1874, p. 259)

A few rules in the French code overlap with the Ten Duel Commandments. Chateauvillard requires that one choose a second to negotiate and allows the seconds to attempt a reconciliation at the dueling ground, before shots are fired. In the translation of the French code published in _Down the River, or Practical Lessons in the Code Duello,_ those are rules 13, 14, and 18 (see Commandments 2, 3, and 8).

THE AMERICAN CODE

John Lyde Wilson published _The Code of Honor, or, Rules for the Government of Principals and Seconds in Duelling_ in 1838, barely a decade after serving as governor of South Carolina (1822-1824). Kudos to Wilson for great organization: his rules move in eight chapters from how the gentleman should behave at the moment he's insulted, on to the choice of a second, then the duties of the man challenged, the duties of principals and seconds once they arrive at the dueling ground, and how seconds should load and present weapons to the principals. The final chapter discusses degrees of insult. For example:

1. The prevailing rule is that words used in retort, although more violent and disrespectful than those first used, will not satisfy, words being no satisfaction for words.
2. When words are used, and a blow given in return, the insult is avenged, and if redress is sought, it must be from the person receiving the blow.

Several of Wilson's rules coincide with the Ten Duel Commandments. One rule gives advice on choosing a second (Chapter I, first part, #3; see Commandment 2). The seconds are advised to meet and negotiate, and if that fails, to set a time and place (Chapter II, second part; see Commandment 3). Each principal should have a surgeon and an assistant surgeon, although "the assistant surgeon may be dispensed with" (Chapter VI, #1; Commandment 4).

WHY ARE THERE NO EARLY PRINTED DUELING CODES?

There's no question that duels were common from the Renaissance on among aristocrats and military men, although for much of that time they were illegal, even if tolerated. You might assume that's why dueling handbooks are so rare. I don't think that explains it. Almost from the time Gutenberg invented the printing press, authors published works with false names and fake imprints. A book that would annoy the Grand Inquisitor of Spain might be printed anonymously in Barcelona, with a title page stating that it was printed in Amsterdam. That sort of misdirection was no more difficult than creating a fake Facebook profile. If a book was on a topic that was in demand, someone found a way to publish and distribute it.

I think dueling codes were not printed until the 1820s precisely because until the early 19th century, dueling was still widespread. For centuries, you learned the rules of dueling at your father's knee, or from aristocratic friends or military colleagues. Any man who cared enough about his honor to fight for it knew the proper way to conduct a duel.

By the 1820s, however, dueling was on the wane. Joseph Hamilton was a member of a crescendoing chorus of opposition. Courts were more consistently judging the survivor of a fatal duel to be a murderer. As dueling became less common, fewer men knew the proper procedures. I think that's when a small market for printed books on dueling developed. Those books (the American, French, and Royal

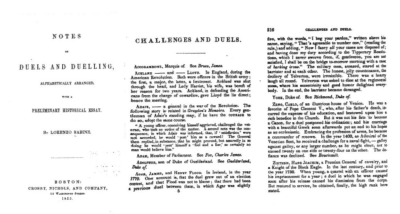

Duels from A to Zed: in Lorenzo Sabine's Notes on Duelling, *1855.*
The alphabetical list of known duels runs to
more than 300 pages (pp. 5-316).

codes) made an attempt to present a duel not as two men shooting at each other, but as a ritual with a proper procedure—justifiable if done according to the rules.

This explanation popped into my head as I read a short story that Google tossed up while I was searching for Chateauvillard's dueling code. In Guy de Maupassant's "The Coward," written in 1888, the hero is the Viscount Signoles, a handsome, stylish, graceful, and clever orphan. He practices fencing and shooting as he would any fashionable activity. "If I ever fight a duel," he thinks complacently, "I shall choose the pistol. With that weapon I am sure of killing my man." When Signoles issues a challenge—to a stranger in a cafe who had the temerity to stare at one of the Viscount's companions—Signoles is satisfied that he has fulfilled a social requirement. "He had done what he should have done; he had shown himself to be what he ought to be. His conduct would be discussed and approved; people would congratulate him." He tells his seconds that he insists on a "very serious" duel, "shots to be exchanged until some one is badly wounded." But when he's alone, he loses his nerve, obsessing about the possibility of being killed.

> From time to time, his teeth chattered with a little dry noise. He tried to read, and took up Chateauvillard's duelling-code. Then he asked himself:
> "Has my opponent frequented the shooting-galleries? Is he well-known? What's his class? How can I find out?"
> He remembered Baron de Vaux's book on pistol-shooters, and he looked it through from end to end. [His opponent] Georges Lamil's name was not mentioned. But if the fellow were not a good shot, he would not have assented so readily to that dangerous weapon and those fatal conditions! ...

For all his outward show of being a duelist, Signoles has clearly never thought about the reality of it. It's all theoretical: book learning. (I won't tell you the outcome of Maupassant's story. Go read it.)

WHY *THESE* TEN DUEL COMMANDMENTS?

I've been fascinated for a long time with what artists—sculptors, painters, composers—decide to include in their works. A work of art is created from scratch, and every detail is there by choice. In a good work of art, every detail adds something to the effect, to the message. So what I've been mulling over for the past two weeks is this: It's clear that the Ten Duel Commandments are not merely a restatement of a standard list of dueling rules. Why these ten, then, and what's their point within the musical?

Twofold, I think.

The Ten Duel Commandments are set out for the Lee-Laurens duel in Act I, but in the musical, neither Lee nor Laurens writes a letter to a loved one (Commandment 6) or looks over his life and admits errors (Commandment 7). In the Philip-Eacker duel in Act II, only Commandment 2 ("Did your friends attempt to negotiate a peace?") and Commandments 9 and 10 are mentioned (look 'em in the eye, summon your courage, count to ten).

But the commandments that are ignored in the early duels are an essential part of the set-up for the Hamilton-Burr duel. For the musical's plot, it would be lame not to have Alexander bid goodbye to Eliza—even if she doesn't know that he thinks it may be his final farewell (Commandment 6). It would be equally lame not to allow Alexander one last speech (Commandment 7)—words have always been his tools and his weapons. The set of lines beginning "I imagine death so much it feels more like a memory" are the last words he utters in the show. They sum up what he's been striving for all his life, what he has valued most, whom he has loved most. (Bloody brilliant, they are.) Commandments 6 and 7 in the musical are essential to make Alexander's last live appearance a satisfying one.

The commandments as a group have an even more important function, as a pacing technique. With the Lee-Laurens and Philip-Eacker duels, we were shown that fighting face to face with a murderous weapon was an accepted, even required way at that time to handle insults to one's honor. By saying there are ten rules and then listing them, the Ten Duel Commandments make us feel a relentless speed and inevitability. Once you start the process, its momentum carries you forward, with a force that doesn't give you much time to question whether the action is appropriate and just. At the end, when Burr fires and Hamilton falls, we don't say, "What an idiot he was to fight," but "What a tragedy that he died." That's what we need to feel, in order to regard Hamilton as a hero while the finale is sung, and after we leave the theater.

MORE

• One of the details of Hamilton's life that most moderns just can't grasp is why he would fight a duel. He had a thriving career, a wife, seven living children, and a lovely house that was just barely finished and hadn't been paid off. Why did he risk his life in a duel? In the _Hamiltome_ (p. 99, n. 1), Lin-Manuel writes, "This song owes a huge debt to _Affairs of Honor, the_ book on duelling by Joanne Freeman." I've read Freeman; she's very persuasive about the role of duels in the early American republic. She discusses the rules for duels at locations 2010-2166 or so in my Kindle version.

• A couple histories of dueling: Milligen's _History of Duelling,_ 1841. Steinmetz, _The Romance of Duelling in All Times and Countries_, 1868. _Down the River, or Practical Lessons in the Code Duello, by an Amateur,_ 1874. Early in my research for the Ten Duel Commandments chapters, I skimmed Barbara Howard, _Gentlemen's Blood: A Thousand Years of Sword and Pistol,_ 2003. It's relentlessly flippant, snide, collectivist (women are smart, men are slaves to testosterone), and has no footnotes whatsoever. Don't bother.

CHAPTER 29
The Lee-Laurens Duel, 1778-1779

Months ago, I found John Laurens's letter to Hamilton about General Charles Lee's "infamous publication," and Hamilton's account of the Lee-Laurens duel. But it took me weeks to find the "strong words from Lee" that provoked the duel. When I did find it, the insult was so subtle that I missed it on first reading.

GENERAL LEE'S STATUS

Let's rewind a bit. From the beginning of the Revolutionary War, Charles Lee was disgruntled: he felt his years of military experience made him a much more suitable commander-in-chief than George Washington. He was particularly free in commenting on Washington (Chapters 22 and 23). Court-martialed in July and August 1778 for his actions at the Battle of Monmouth (Chapter 24), Lee was found guilty of disobeying orders, allowing a disorderly retreat, and disrespecting his commander-in-chief. He was suspended from duty for twelve months.

Lee complained of his treatment to Aaron Burr in October 1778 (see Chapter 26). By that time, Lee was in Philadelphia, petitioning the Continental Congress to review his case. Here's an excerpt from a draft of one of his letters to Congress, dated 10/30/1778. (This and

General Charles Lee, from a contemporary engraving

most of the documents cited below were printed in 1873 in _Collections of the New-York Historical Society for the Year 1873_, Publication Fund Series vol. 6, 1874—cited below as "NYHS Publication Fund Series 6.")

> When it is consider'd I hold a high rank in the service of one of the most respectable Princes of Europe; that I have been honour'd with the trust of the second command in your Army; that I have hitherto serv'd with some reputation as a soldier—that I now stand charg'd, and have actually been try'd for some of the most heinous military crimes; and to the astonishment not only of myself, but I can venture to say of every man in the Army who was present at this Court, and of every Man out of the Army who has read the proceedings, found guilty of these crimes – when at the same time I am myself inflexibly perswaded that I am not only guiltless, but that the Success of the 28th of June ought principally in justice to be ascrib'd to me ... (NYHS Publication Fund Series 6, p. 244)

LEE VS. STEUBEN

Having just finished Joanne Freeman's _Affairs of Honor_, I read Lee's correspondence with an eye to the sort of comments that might provoke a challenge. Baron Steuben, like Charles Lee, was a career military man with extensive experience in European wars before he joined the Continental Army. In the early months of 1778, he was in charge of drilling Washington's troops at Valley Forge—an important step in transforming a rag-tag volunteer army into a professional army capable of fighting well-trained British soldiers. One awestruck American said Steuben looked like "the ancient fabled God of War ... The trappings of his horse, the enormous holsters of his pistols, his large size, and his strikingly martial aspect, all seemed to favor the idea." (Quoted in Chernow's _Washington: A Life_)

Baron Steuben learned that Lee had disparaged his testimony at the court martial:

> [He] has certainly shown a very laudable zeal for bringing a criminal officer to condign punishment; but the next time he takes the field of prosecution in the case of an injured community, I hope his prudence will dictate to him the necessity of being furnished with a better apparatus. (Lee Court Martial, p. 232)

Ralph Earl, Baron Friedrich Wilhelm August Heinrich Ferdinand Steuben, ca. 1786. Image: Wikipedia

You and I might have to read this twice to understand that Lee is making a criticism—never mind voicing an insult so severe that the man in question would want to meet Lee and shoot at him. Steuben found Lee's comment grossly insulting, and in a letter of 12/2/1778 called Lee out:

> Sir! It has come to my attention that at your court martial, you allowed yourself some indiscreet comments about me .... You have offended me—I demand an explanation. You will choose the place, time, and weapons, but since I do not like to draw these things out, I demand to see you as soon and as nearby as possible. (More in <u>NYHS Publication Fund Series 6,</u> pp. 253-4; my translation)

Alexander Hamilton wrote soon afterwards to Baron Steuben:

> I have read your letter to Lee, with pleasure—it was conceived in terms, which the offence merited, and if he had had any feeling must have been felt by him. Considering the pointedness and severity of your expressions, his answer [NOTE: Lee's reply doesn't seem to have survived] was certainly a very modest one and proved that he had not a violent appetite, for so close a tete a tete as you seemed disposed to insist upon. His evasions, if known to the world,

would do him very little honor. (Letter of 12/19/1778, <u>NYHS Publication Fund Series 6,</u> p. 254)

LEE'S "VINDICATION"

Meanwhile, on 12/3/1778, the day after Baron Steuben wrote his letter to Lee, Lee's "Vindication to the Public" was published in *The Pennsylvania Packet or The General Advertiser.* Here are the most offensive passages. Don't blink.

> There is but one supposition, and indeed only one (and that, for the General's honour, is too monstrous to be admitted), that would render me criminal; it is, that he had positively commanded me, that after the attack commenced, whatever were my circumstances or whatever were my numbers, from thence I should not, from any consideration, recede an inch. Now, if such I had conceived to have been his intention, so great is my opinion of the valour, zeal, and obedience of the troops, and so well I think I know myself, that I do really believe we should all have perished on the first spot ; but I never had, (it was almost impossible that I should have) an idea that such was his plan; and it is evident that it was not; consequently, in seeking a better position in our rear, I could be guilty of no disobedience. ...
>
> [W]ere the transactions of that day to pass over again, there is no one step I took which I would not again take. There is no one thing I did which does not demonstrate that I conducted myself as an obedient, prudent, and, let me add, spirited officer; and I do from my soul sincerely wish, that a court of inquiry, composed of the ablest soldiers in the world, were to sit in judgment, and enjoined to canvass with the utmost rigor every circumstance of my conduct on this day, and on their decision my reputation or infamy to be for ever established. There is, however, I confess, the strongest reason to believe (but for this omission I am no Ways responsible) that, had a proper knowledge of the theatre of action been obtained, as it might, and ought to have been, its nature and different situations, with their references studied, and, in consequence, a general plan of action wisely concerted and digested, a most important, perhaps a decisive blow might have been struck, but not by adopting any one measure that any one of my censurers has been fortunate enough to think of. ...

Lee summarizes the heroic behavior of American soldiers ever since Bunker Hill—when they were *not* under the command of Washington. Then he continues:

> With respect to the transactions on Long and York Islands, I must be silent, as I am ignorant of them; but, from some observations after I joined the army, I have reason to think the fault could not have been in the men, or in the common bulk of officers. Even the unhappy business of Fort Washington, which was attended with such abominable consequences, and which brought the affairs of America to the brink of ruin, (when the circumstances are well considered) did honour to the officers and men, devoted to the defence of this worthless and ridiculous favourite. (NYHS Publication Fund Series 6, p. 262-3)

And summing up:

> Upon the whole, I am warranted to say, what I always thought, that no disgrace or calamity has fallen on the arms of America through the whole course of the war, but what must be attributed to some other cause than to the want of valour, of disposition to obedience, or to any other military defect in the men, or the general mass of their officers in their different ranks; and I solemnly declare, that was it at my choice to select from all the nations of the earth to form an excellent and perfect army, I would, without hesitation, give the preference to the Americans. By publishing this opinion, I cannot incur the suspicion of paying my court to their vanity, as it is notoriously the language I have ever held. ... (NYHS Publication Fund Series 6, pp. 263-4)

If you read the whole the "Vindication," you'll find not a single direct, quotable attack on Washington. Perhaps you've been lucky enough not to meet a person who deals in this sort of oblique insult swaddled in compliments. Lee's contemporaries had no doubt about what he meant.

LAURENS AND HAMILTON ON LEE

Two days after Lee's "Vindication" appeared (on 12/5/1778), John Laurens wrote to Hamilton, appealing to him as a writer rather than a fellow soldier:

Miniature of John Laurens by Charles Wilson Peale

My Dear Hamilton:

You have seen, and by this time considered, General Lee's infamous publication. I have collected some hints for an answer; but I do not think, either that I can rely upon my own knowledge of facts and style to answer him fully, or that it would be prudent to undertake it without counsel. An affair of this kind ought to be passed over in total silence, or answered in a masterly manner. ... The pen of Junius is in your hand; and I think you will, without difficulty, expose, in his defence, letters, and last production, such a tissue of falsehood and inconsistency, as will satisfy the world, and put him for ever to silence. ... (More here)

Laurens, Hamilton, and other members of Washington's staff weren't the only ones disgusted by Lee's comments. General John Cadwalader wrote to General Nathanael Greene from Philadelphia on the same date, 12/5/1778:

Gen. Lee's tryal has been the subject of Conversation in all Companies for some time—Congress, I am told, have confirmed the sentence—three to one— I do not suppose he will ever serve again in our Army—I think it would have [been] better if he never had ... (NYHS Publication Fund Series 6, p. 270)

WASHINGTON ON LEE

On 12/12/1778, General Washington wrote to Joseph Reed, the newly elected president of the Supreme Executive Council of Pennsylvania (*i.e.,* governor). It's a fascinating letter because 1) Washington doesn't often put into writing his complaints about what others say of him and 2) Joseph Reed had once been Washington's trusted aide and adjutant general. In November 1776 Washington broke with Reed after accidentally opening a letter addressed to Reed from Charles Lee ("I ... lament with you that fatal indecision of mind ...": see Chapter 22.) The part of Washington's 12/12/1778 letter related to Lee is this:

> General Lee's publication in Dunlap's Gazette of the 3d inst., (and I have seen no other,) puts me in a disagreeable situation. I have neither leisure nor inclination to enter the lists with him in a news paper: and so far as his production points to personality, I can and do from my inmost soul despise it but when he has most barefacedly misrepresented facts in some places, and thrown out insinuations in others that have not the smallest foundation in truth, not to attempt a refutation is a tacit acknowledgment of the justice of his assertions; for though there are thousands who know how unsupported his piece is, there are yet tens of thousands that know nothing of the matter, and will be led naturally to conclude that bold and confident assertions, uncontradicted, must be founded in truth.
>
> It became a part of General Lee's plan, from the moment of his arrest, (though it was an event solicited by himself,) to have the world believe that he was a persecuted man, and that party was at the bottom of it. But however convenient for his purpose to establish this doctrine, I defy him or his most zealous partisans to adduce a simple instance in proof of it, unless bringing him to trial at his own request is considered in this light. I can do more; I will defy any man out of my own family [i.e., on my staff] to say that I have ever mentioned his name after his trial commenced, if it was to be avoided: and, when it was not, if I have not studiously declined expressing any sentiment of him or his behaviour. How far this conduct accords with his, let his own breast decide. If he conceives that I was opposed to him because he found himself disposed to enter into a

party against me—if he thought I stood in his road to preferment, and therefore that it was convenient to lessen me in the esteem of my countrymen, in order to pave the way for his own advancement—I have only to observe, that as I never entertained any jealousy of. or apprehension from him, so neither did I do more, than common civility and a proper respect to his rank required, to conciliate his good opinion. His temper and plans were too versatile and violent to attract my admiration: and that I have escaped the venom of his tongue and pen so long, is more to be wondered at than applauded; as it is a favour, that no officer under whose immediate commands he ever served has the happiness, (if happiness can be thus denominated) of boasting. (More in *Life and Correspondence of Joseph Reed* II, 41-43)

Well said, George; and Joe, I hope you feel very uncomfortable about your former dealings with Chuck. (I'm feeling severely uncharitable toward Joseph Reed because of what I read of his doings in Philbrick's *Valiant Ambition,* Chapters 3 and 9.)

LEE VS. LAURENS

John Laurens issued a challenge to Lee (we don't have it), to which Lee responded on 12/22/1778:

I am extremely sorry that the nature of my busyness should have laid an embargo on me so long—but as I now begin to apprehend from the delay of Congress that the ultimate determinations of my transactions with that Body will not require less than a month which is too tedious to think of I will do myself the Honour of meeting you attended by a Friend with a brace of pistols to-morrow [at] past 3. p. m. I would willingly bring a small sword at the same time, but from the effects of my fall and the quantity of Physick I have taken to baffle a fit of the Gout which I apprehended I do not think myself sufficiently strong on my legs — there is on the point and no point road, to the left hand a little on the Philad. side of the four mile stone a very convenient piece of wood, where unless it should rain I will do myself the honour of meeting you. In the meantime I am Sir, Your most Obedt. Servt. C. L. (NYHS Publication Fund Series 6, p. 283)

So essentially, Lee says: I will of course meet you to defend my honor, but if you beat me it's because I was already in such poor health that I could barely stand.

Laurens and Lee dueled the day after Lee sent that letter, on 12/23/1778. The seconds—Alexander Hamilton and Major Evan Edwards—wrote up an account that I find more chilling than anything in Freeman's *Affairs of Honor* or all those books I read for the Ten Duel Commandments posts (Chapters 27 and 28). Because their attitude seems so utterly foreign, and because that attitude is so important in Act II of the Hamilton musical, I'm including the whole letter. As always, you can skip to the red highlights if you're in a rush.

Narrative of an Affair of Honor between General Lee and Col Laurens

General Lee attended by Major Edwards and Col Laurens attended by Col Hamilton met agreeable to appointment on Wednesday afternoon half past three in a wood situate near the four mile stone on the Point no point road. Pistols having been the weapons previously fixed upon, and the combatants being provided with a brace each, it was asked in what manner they were to proceed. General Lee proposed, to advance upon one another and each fire at what time and distance he thought proper. Col Laurens expressed his preference of this mode, and agreed to the proposal accordingly.

They approached each other within about five or six paces and exchanged a shot almost at the same moment. As Col Laurens was preparing for a second discharge, General Lee declared himself wounded. Col Laurens, as if apprehending the wound to be more serious than it proved advanced towards the general to offer his support. The same was done by Col Hamilton and Major Edwards under a similar apprehension. General Lee then said the wound was inconsiderable, less than he had imagined at the first stroke of the Ball, and proposed to fire a second time. This was warmly opposed both by Col Hamilton and Major Edwards, who declared it to be their opinion, that the affair should terminate as it then stood. But General Lee repeated his desire, that there should be a second discharge and Col Laurens agreed to the proposal. Col Hamilton observed, that unless the General was influenced by motives of personal enmity, he did not think the affair ought to be persued any further; but as General Lee seemed to persist in desiring it, he was too tender of his friend's honor to persist in opposing it. The combat was then going to be renewed; but Major Edwards again declaring his opinion, that the affair ought to end where it was, General Lee then expressed his confidence in the honor of the Gentlemen concerned as seconds, and said he should be willing to comply with whatever they should cooly and deliberately determine. Col. Laurens consented to the same.

Col Hamilton and Major Edwards withdrew and conversing awhile on the subject, still concurred fully in opinion that for the most cogent reasons, the affair should terminate as it was then circumstanced. This decision was communicated to the parties and agreed to by them, upon which they immediately returned to Town; General Lee slightly wounded in the right side.

During the interview a conversation to the following purport past between General Lee and Col Laurens—On Col Hamilton's intimating the idea of personal enmity, as beforementioned, General Lee declared he had none, and had only met Col. Laurens to defend his own honor—that Mr. Laurens best knew whether there was any on his part. Col Laurens replied, that General Lee was acquainted with the motives, that had brought him there, which were that he had been informed from what he thought good authority, that General Lee had spoken of General Washington in the grossest and most opprobrious terms of personal abuse, which He Col Laurens thought himself bound to resent, as well on account of the relation he bore to General Washington as from motives of personal friendship, and respect for his character. General Lee acknowleged that he had given his opinion against General Washingtons military character to his particular friends and might perhaps do it again. He said every man had a right to give his sentiments freely of military characters, and that he did not think himself personally accountable to Col Laurens for what he had done in that respect. But said he never had spoken of General Washington in the terms mentioned, which he could not have done; as well because he had always esteemed General Washington as a man, as because such abuse would be incompatible with the character, he would ever wish to sustain as a Gentleman.

Upon the whole we think it a piece of justice to the two Gentlemen to declare, that after they met their conduct was strongly marked with all the politeness generosity coolness and firmness, that ought to characterise a transaction of this nature. (Letter here)

Colonel Robert Troup, who was aide-de-camp to Major General Horatio Gates before being named Congress's secretary of the Board of War, wrote to Gates on 1/3/1779:

Congress have confirmed the sentence of the Court Martial against General Lee, & he is suspended for a Twelvemonth. He has lately published a Piece in the Philadelphia paper which Col. Malcom had read, & pronounces extremely severe. His satyr [i.e., satire] is pointed particularly at General Washington & Family. I suppose this Piece occasioned the Duel which was fought the other Day by Gen1. Lee & Col. Laurens, the A D Camp, in Philadelphia. My Albany acquaintance says General Lee was slightly wounded in the Body, and intends to have another Pop ["another pop"?!?!] as soon as he recovers. (NYHS Publication Fund Series 6, pp. 289-90)

LEE VS. SCOURGE

The repercussions of Lee's "Vindication" continued to rumble on for some time. On 12/31/1778, *The New Jersey Gazette* published a letter from a Virginian who signed himself "Scourge," which attacked Lee: "This man is by profession what is called a Mercenary soldier, that is, a man who is altogether void of principle, who never consults conscience, but is ever guided by interest in his pursuits, and changes sides for one more farthing more added to his pay. It is difficult to ascribe any other motive of conduct to our hero than avarice." [NOTE: Lee had worked for hire for the sovereigns of Portugal and Poland, as well as Britain, before he joined the Continental Army.] In the *New Jersey Gazette,* the cover letter to the Scourge's piece ran:

The attempt of a certain General Officer lately condemned by a Court Martial for his malconduct, to raise a party in his favor, by calling in question the abilities not only of our illustrious Commander in chief, but that of all our General

William Livingston, first governor of New Jersey (1776-1790).
Image: Wikipedia

Officers—has justly raised the indignation of every honest
man — His publications are an insult to America. It is a
degree of vanity without a parallel, even to hope to raise
himself into importance, by affecting to be a competitor for
popularity with that great and good man. There is no more
similarity between their characters than there is between
virtue and vice—good and evil—And he may assure himself
that before he can raise a party in America in his favor, he
must first deprive the people of their senses, and teach them
that light and darkness are synonymous terms. ... (NYHS
Publication Fund Series 6, p. 297)

General Lee demanded that Governor William Livingston take action against the *Gazette* for publishing that letter. (We met Livingston
some months back as father of Kitty, one of the women Hamilton flirt-
ed with in 1777; see Chapter 18.) Livingston sent a tactful but repres-
sive reply to Lee (1/16/1779):

I am honoured with your favour of the 13th and can assure
you that of the merit or demerit of your conduct in the affair
of Monmouth on the 28th of June, I have not to this day
framed my opinion. I have so little leisure to attend to the
military operations of America, and am so incompetent
a judge of the qualifications necessary to constitute the
character of a General that I make no judgment at all. But
without admitting or denying that "you have made greater
sacrifices in the cause of American freedom than any officer
of our whole army without a single exception, & that it is
not less certain that you have saved our whole army more
than once from destruction" (the proofs of which are not in
my possession [ZING!!!]) I can assure you that I heartily
disapprove of all publications containing personal reflections

on the character of any Gentleman, & especially on those of your rank in the American Army. ...

I should be extremely unhappy in having reason to believe, what is frequently & perhaps injuriously reported of you, that you endeavoured to lessen the estimation in which General Washington is held by the most virtuous Citizens of America; and which estimation, not Sir, from a blind attachment to men of high rank, nor from any self interested motive whatsoever, but from a full conviction of his great personal merit & public importance, I deem it my duty to my country, to use my utmost influence to support. I am With all due respect, Sir Your most humble Servt Wil : Livingston. (NYHS Publication Fund Series 6, pp. 294-7)

At his court martial in August 1778, Charles Lee had been suspended from duty for 12 months. In January 1780 he was released from duty (i.e., fired from the army) and retired to his estate in the Shenandoah Valley, now West Virginia. On a visit to Philadelphia in late 1782, he caught a fever and died.

I think we can be done with Charles Lee now.

CADWALADER VS. CONWAY

In late 1777 and early 1778, Thomas Conway was one of the leaders in the attempt to remove Washington as commander-in-chief (the "Conway Cabal"). In summer 1778, General John Cadwalader called Conway a coward for his behavior at the Battle of Germantown in October 1777. The two dueled near Philadelphia on 7/4/1778. Cadwalader's shot smashed Conway's cheek: a severe but not fatal wound. Cadwalader is reported to have said, "I've stopped the damned rascal's tongue anyhow." (Quoted in Thomas Fleming, *Washington's Secret War*)

CHAPTER 30
Hamilton Resigns from Washington's Staff, 1781

In mid-February 1781, after four years as Washington's aide-de-camp, Hamilton resigned. The reasons behind this as well as the relationship between Washington and Hamilton are the subject of nearly as much speculation among Hamilton scholars as are Hamilton's birth date and the reason for his duel with Burr.

HAMILTON EXPLAINS HIS RESIGNATION TO A FRIEND

Hamilton gave the reason for the break in a letter to his friend James McHenry, who had once been one of Washington's aides and was now on the staff of the Marquis de Lafayette.

> [New Windsor, New York, February 18, 1781]
> I have, Dear Mac, several of your letters. I shall soon have time enough to write my friends as often as they please.
> The Great man and I have come to an open rupture. Proposals of accomodation have been made on his part but rejected. I pledge my honor to you that he will find me inflexible. He shall for once at least repent his ill-humour. Without a shadow of reason and on the slightest ground, he charged me in the most affrontive manner with treating him with disrespect. I answered very decisively—"Sir I am not conscious of it but since you have thought it necessary to tell me so, we part." I wait till more help arrives. At present there is besides myself only Tilghman, who is just recovering from a fit of illness the consequence of too close application to business.
> We have often spoken freely our sentiments to each other. Except to a very few friends our difference will be a secret; therefore be silent. I shall continue to support a popularity that has been essential, is still useful.
> Adieu my friend. May the time come when characters may be known in their true light.
> AH

Madame [i.e., Eliza] sends her friendship to you.
(Annotated letter here)

HAMILTON EXPLAINS HIS RESIGNATION TO HIS FATHER-IN-LAW

For his father-in-law, General Philip Schuyler, a more detailed explanation was in order. Alexander had married Eliza on December 14, 1780. Part of the reason this orphan immigrant was so readily accepted into the prominent and wealthy Schuyler family was surely Alexander's position since March 1, 1777 as one of the commander-in-chief's aides-de-camp (see Chapter 16). Now, two months after the wedding, Alexander has to tell General Schuyler that he's resigned from Washington's staff.

Head Quarters New Windsor [New York] Feby 18, 81
    My Dear Sir.
    Since I had the pleasure of writing you last, an unexpected change has taken place in my situation. I am no longer a member of the General's family. This information will surprise you, and the manner of the change will surprise you more. Two days ago, the General and I passed each other on the stairs; —he told me he wanted to speak to me, —I answered that I would wait upon him immediately. I went below, and delivered Mr. Tilghman a letter to be sent to the commissary, containing an order of a pressing and interesting nature. Returning to the General, I was stopped on the way by the Marquis de La Fayette, and we conversed together about a minute on a matter of business. He can testify how impatient I was to get back, and that I left him in a manner which; but for our intimacy, would have been more than abrupt. Instead of finding the General, as is usual, in his room, I met him at the head of the stairs, where accosting me in an angry tone, "Colonel Hamilton, (said he,) you have kept me waiting at the head of the stairs these ten minutes ;—I must tell you, sir, you treat me with disrespect." I replied, without petulancy, but with decision, "I am not conscious of it, sir, but since you have thought it necessary to tell me so, we part." "Very well, sir, (said he,) if it be your choice," or something to this effect, and we separated.
    I sincerely believe my absence, which gave so, much umbrage, did not last two minutes. In less than an hour after,

Tilghman came to me in the General's name, assuring me of his great confidence in my abilities, integrity, usefulness, &c, and of his desire, in a candid conversation, to heal a difference which could not have happened but in a moment of passion. I requested Mr. Tilghman to tell him,—1st. That I had taken my resolution in a manner not to be revoked. 2d. That as a conversation could serve no other purpose than to produce explanations, mutually disagreeable, though I certainly would not refuse an interview, if he desired it, yet I would be happy, if he would permit me to decline it. 3d. That though determined to leave the family, the same principles which had kept me so long in it, would continue to direct my conduct towards him when out of it. 4th. That, however, I did not wish to distress him, or the public business, by quitting him before he could derive other assistance by the return of some of the gentlemen who were absent. 5th. And that in the mean time, it depended on him, to let our behaviour to each other be the same as if nothing had happened.

He consented to decline the conversation, and thanked me for my offer of continuing my aid in the manner I had mentioned.

I have given you so particular a detail of our difference, from the desire I have to justify myself in your opinion.

Perhaps you may think I was precipitate in rejecting the overture made by the General to an accommodation. I assure you, my dear sir, it was not the effect of resentment ; it was the deliberate result of maxims I had long formed for the government of my own conduct.

I always disliked the office of an aid-de-camp, as having in it a kind of personal dependence. I refused to serve in this capacity with two Major Generals, at an early period of the war. Infected, however, with the enthusiasm of the times, an idea of the General's character overcame my scruples, and induced me to accept his invitation to enter into his family. It has been often with great difficulty that I have prevailed upon myself not to renounce it ; but while, from motives of public utility, I was doing violence to my feelings, I was always determined, if there should ever happen a breach between us, never to consent to an accommodation. I was persuaded, that when once that nice barrier, which marked the boundaries of what we owed to each other, should be thrown down, it might be propped again, but could never be restored.

The General is a very honest man ;—his competitors have slender abilities, and less integrity. His popularity has often been essential to the safety of America, and is still of great importance to it. These considerations have influenced my past conduct respecting him, and will influence my future ; —I think it is necessary he should be supported.

His estimation in your mind, whatever maybe its amount, I am persuaded has been formed on principles, which a circumstance like this cannot materially affect ; but if I thought it could diminish your friendship for him, I should almost forego the motives that urge me to justify myself to you. I wish what I have said to make no other impression, than to satisfy you I have not been in the wrong. It is also said in confidence, as a public knowledge of the breach would, in many ways, have an ill effect. It will, probably, be the policy of both sides to conceal it, and cover the separation with some plausible pretext. I am importuned by such of my friends as are privy to the affair, to listen to a reconciliation; but my resolution is unalterable.

As I cannot think of quitting the army during the war, I have a project of re-entering into the artillery, by taking Lieutenant Colonel Forrest's place, who is desirous of re tiring on half-pay. I have not, however, made up my mind upon this head, as I should be obliged to come in the youngest lieutenant colonel instead of the eldest, which I ought to have been by natural succession, had I remained in the corps; and, at the same time, to resume studies relative to the profession, which to avoid inferiority, must be laborious. If a handsome command in the campaign in the light infantry should offer itself, I shall balance between this and the artillery. My situation in the latter would be more solid and permanent; but as I hope the war will not last long enough to make it progressive, this consideration has the less force. A command for the campaign, would leave me the winter to prosecute studies relative to my future career in life.

I have written to you on this subject with all the freedom and confidence to which you have a right, and with an assurance of the interest you take in all that concerns me.

Very sincerely and affectionately, I am, dear sir,

Your most obedient servant,

A. Hamilton. [NOTE: This is the corrected version as published in John C. Hamilton's *Life of Alexander Hamilton* I, 333-336. If you like seeing how Alexander thinks, see the <u>Founders Archive version</u> of the letter, which includes corrections from the autograph draft signed at Morristown National Historical Park.]

PAPA SCHUYLER REPLIES

General Schuyler responded a week later (2/25/1781).

My Dear Sir

Last night your favor of the 18 Inst: was delivered me. I confess that the contents surprized and afflicted me, not that I discover any impropriety in your conduct in the affair in question, for of that I persuade myself you are incapable, but as it may be attended with consequences prejudical to my country which I love, which I affectionately love, and as no event tending to its detriment can be beheld by me with indifference, I should esteem myself culpable were I silent on the occasion, and must therefore intreat your attention; a candid and favorable construction I ask not, for that I am certain I shall have. Long before I had the least Intimation that you intended that connection with my family, which is so very pleasing to me, and which affords me such entire satisfaction I had studied Your Character, and that of the other Gentlemen who composed the Genrals family. I thought I discovered in all an attention to the duties of their station, in some a considerable degree of ability, but, (without a compliment for I trust there is no necessity of that between us,) in you only I found those qualifications so essentially necessary to the man who is to aid and council a commanding General, environed with difficulties of every kind, and these perhaps more, and of greater magnitude, than any other ever has had to encounter, whose correspondance must of necessity be extensive always interesting, and frequently so delicate as to require much Judgment and adress to be properly managed. The public voice has confirmed the Idea I had formed of You, but what is more consoling to me and more honorable to you, men of genius Observation and Judgement think as I do on the occasion. Your quitting your station must therefore be productive of very material

Injuries to the public, and this consideration, exclusive of others, impells me to wish that the unhappy breach should be closed, and a mutual Confidence restored. You may both of you Imagine when you seperate, that the cause will remain a secret, but I will venture to speak decidely, and say It is impossible, and I fear the Effect, especially with the French Officers, with the french Minister, and even with the french Court; these already Observe so many divisions between us; they know and acknowledge your Abilities and how necessary you are to the General. Indeed how will the loss be replaced? He will if you leave him, have not one Gentleman left sufficiently versed in the french to convey his Ideas. And if he obtains one, it is more than probable that he will be a meer interpreter, without being able to afford his General an Idea, and Incapable of conducting business with any competent degree of adress propriety or delicacy.

It is evident my Dear Sir that the General conceived himself the Agressor, and that he quickly repented of the Insult; "he wished to heal a difference which could not have happened but in a moment of passion." It falls to the lott of few men to pass thro life without one of those unguar[d]ed moments which wound the feelings of a friend; let us then impute them to the fraility of human nature, and with Sternes recording angel, drop a tear, and blot It out of the page of life. I do not mean to reprehend the maxims you have formed for your conduct; they are laudable, and tho generally approved, yet times and circumstances sometimes render a deviation necessary and Justifiable. This necessity now exists in the distresses of Your country. Make the sacrifice, the greater it is, the more glorious to you, your services are wanted, they are wanted in that particular station which You have already filled so beneficially to the public, and with such extensive reputation. I am as incapable of wishing as you are of doing, any thing injurious to those principles of honor, which If I may use the expression, are the test of virtue; my wishes, which are very earnest for a reconciliation I am convinced you will impute to their true motives, public good and the best affections of the human heart. I have a letter from the General of the 20th Instant he mentions not a syllable of this unhappy difference. ... (Rest of letter here)

WASHINGTON AND HAMILTON'S RELATIONSHIP

I always start my research with primary sources. When I move on to secondary sources, it's with the constant question: does this scholar make sense of all the primary sources? Do his explanations make the pieces whir and click and fall into place, with no leftover facts languishing off to the side?

After reading Hamilton's letters about his resignation from Washington's staff, I wanted to know who else wrote about this argument at the time. Naturally I went to Michael Newton's *Alexander Hamilton: The Formative Years.* Newton is a font of quotes from primary sources (Hamilton, his contemporaries, early biographers) and Hamilton scholars.

After reading Chapters 35-37 of Newton, I'm persuaded that the relationship between Washington and Hamilton was a business-like one rather than a father-son one, and that the break between them was not a bitter and long-enduring one. It was a matter of Hamilton having outgrown his position as an aide, exactly as he explained to Philip Schuyler.

Two of the most persuasive points in favor of this are that in letters to a few of his aides (mostly men he had known before the Revolutionary War), Washington expressed affection in a way he never did to Hamilton. Also, Hamilton remained at headquarters, continuing his duties as Washington's aide, from mid-February until April 9, 1781: hardly a situation that would have been tolerable if there had been an irreconcilable break between them.

"UNHAPPILY FOR PUBLIC AFFAIRS, THERE SEEMS TO BE LITTLE PROSPECTD OF ACTIVITY"

Hamilton didn't resign from the army, only from Washington's staff. In July 1781, five months after his break with Washington, Hamilton wrote Eliza from a camp near Dobbs Ferry. Main points: 1) I was so angry not to be given a command that I resigned my commission; 2) in Washington's name, an aide persuaded me not to resign, and promised a command as soon as feasible, and I agreed to stay; 3) I love you, and I'm in touch with your father and Angelica's husband.

> [Camp near Dobbs Ferry, New York, July 10, 1781]
> The day before yesterday, my angel, I arrived here, but for the want of an opportunity could not write you sooner. Indeed, I know of none now, but shall send this to the Quarter Master General to be forwarded by the first conveyance to

the care of Col. Hughes. Finding when I came here that nothing was said on the subject of a command, I wrote the General a letter [NOTE: it's never been found] and enclosed him my commission. This morning Tilghman came to me in his name, pressed me to retain my commission, with an assurance that he would endeavor by all means to give me a command nearly such as I could have desired in the present circumstances of the army. Though I know my Betsy would be happy to hear I had rejected this proposal, it is a pleasure my reputation would not permit me to afford her. I consented to retain my commission and accept my command.

I hope my beloved Betsy will dismiss all apprehensions for my safety; unhappily for public affairs, there seems to be little prospect of activity, and if there should be Heaven will certainly be propitious to any attachment so tender, so genuine as ours. Heaven will restore me to the bosom of my love and permit me to enjoy with new relish the delights which are centred there. It costs me a great deal to be absent from them, but the privation is certainly only temporary. I impatiently long to hear from you the state of your mind since our painful separation. Be as happy as you can, I entreat you, my amiable, my beloved wife. But let not absence deprive me of the least particle of your affection. Always remember those tender proofs I have so frequently given you of mine and preserve for me unabated the only blessing which can make life of any value to me.

I write your father all the military news. I have barely seen Mr. Carter [i.e., John Barker Church, Angelica's husband] and delivered him the letters which your amiable father committed to my care. You are of a charming family my Betsy. I shall not easily forget the marks of parting regret which appeared in both your sisters. Assure them of everything my heart is capable of feeling for the lovely sisters of a lovely wife. ...

My good, my tender, my fond, my excellent Betsy, Adieu. You know not how much it must ever cost me to pronounce this word. God bless and preserve you.

A. Hamilton (More here)

We're coming up on Yorktown (October 1781), but I want to poke around a bit in Alexander's letters from April to October 1781. Can't wait to see what turns up!

CHAPTER 31
Hamilton Tackles Economics, Summer 1781

On February 16, 1781, after a confrontation with Washington on the stairs at army headquarters, Hamilton resigned from the commander-in-chief's staff. He refused both Washington's apology and his father-in-law's plea to reconcile. (See Chapter 30.) But because Washington's staff was very much reduced—only Hamilton and Tench Tilghman were at headquarters—Hamilton remained at New Windsor until early April, writing his last letter as Washington's aide-de-camp on April 9.

What was Alexander doing between April 9 and July 31, 1781, when he was finally given a field command? Canoodling with Eliza? Taking a break upstate?

Hah.

Hamilton and Eliza had been together at the army's 1780-1781 winter quarters in New Windsor (just south of the I-84 / Newburgh–Beacon Bridge over the Hudson River). After Hamilton left Washington's staff, they moved to De Peyster's Point, just across the river. In mid-May, Alexander took Eliza to the Schuyler home in Albany—probably because the summer campaign was due to start, and Eliza was pregnant. So OK, there was some canoodling. (Philip was born January 22, 1782.)

WHAT PROVOKED HAMILTON'S RESIGNATION?

After I researched Chapter 30, it seemed plausible that Hamilton resigned as aide-de-camp because he had "outgrown" the position—rather than because he and Washington had a massive, irreconcilable argument. This week, while searching for something completely different, I found three solid reasons that Hamilton might have felt he'd outgrown his staff position.

Background: having no regular source of revenue, the Continental Congress had been issuing paper currency to pay its expenses since 1776. Lots and lots of paper currency. By May 1781, "continentals" were virtually worthless. The United States was/were (collectively and singularly) in dire financial straits. To handle the financial situation,

A sample of Continental currency, 1776. "Mind your business" is such a lovely motto for currency!

Congress finally decided to put finances in the hands of a single man, rather than a committee.

Major General John Sullivan, a delegate to Congress, wrote to Washington asking about Hamilton's qualifications as finance minister. On February 4, 1781—ten days before the rupture between Washington and Hamilton—Washington replied.

> The measure adopted by Congress of appointing a Minister of War—Finance—& for Foreign Affairs I think a very wise one. To give efficacy to it, proper characters will, no doubt, be chosen to conduct the business of these departments. How far Colo. Hamilton—of whom you ask my opinion as a financier—has turned his thoughts to that particular study I am unable to ansr because I never entered upon a discussion of this post with him—but this I can venture to advance from a thorough knowledge of him, that there are few men to be found, of his age, who has a more general knowledge than he possesses—and none whose Soul is more firmly engaged in the cause—or who exceeds him in probity & Sterling virtue. ...
>
> It is a provident foresight—a proper arrangement of business—system & order in the execution that is to be productive of that œconomy which is to defeat the efforts & hopes of Great Britain—And I am happy—thrice happy on private as well as public acct, to find that these are in train; for it will ease my Shoulders of as immense burthen

which the deranged & perplexed Situation of our Affairs
and the distresses of every department of the Army which
concentred in the Comdr in chief had placed upon them. ...
(More here)

I would dearly love to know whose handwriting that letter from Washington to Sullivan is in. (According to the Founders Archives, the letter is at Library of Congress, so it's probably digitized by now; but I couldn't find it.) Did Hamilton see Sullivan's letter and/or Washington's reply? It seems likely, since Washington's staff at the time consisted only of Hamilton and Tilghman. Tilghman had been so sick that he wrote no letters for Washington between January 12 and February 9. (See Newton, *Hamilton,* Ch. 35.)

If Hamilton saw Sullivan's letter or Washington's, then he knew he was being mentioned for one of the most prominent roles in the U.S. government.

And it wasn't the first time. In November 1780, the Marquis de Lafayette had recommended Hamilton for the newly vacant position of adjutant-general for the army. Washington passed him over.

In December 1780, Hamilton was nominated by Sullivan, and strongly seconded by Lafayette, to be sent as envoy to France. Negotiating a loan from France was a crucial task, given the financial mess the U.S. was in. Hamilton was passed over in favor of his friend John Laurens. He told Laurens he didn't mind in a letter of 2/4/1781 – coincidentally, the same day Washington replied to Sullivan's query about Hamilton's qualifications for the superintendent of finances position.

So: by mid-February 1781, 24-year-old Alexander Hamilton, an orphan immigrant from the Caribbean with two years of college and four years of experience in military administration, had been mentioned three times in three months for crucial roles of nationwide scope. Even though he didn't get the adjutant-general, envoy, or financial superintendent position, I can see that he might have felt he'd outgrown his position as Washington's subordinate. If you'd been in the running for a CEO position (never mind three), would you want to go back to being an executive secretary?

"EXTREMELY SORRY TO HAVE EMBARRASSED YOU BY MY LATE APPLICATION"

And now, back to the weeks following April 9, 1781, when Hamilton wrote his last letter for Washington.

On April 19, Hamilton wrote to General Nathanael Greene (whom he had met in 1775) asking for a field command.

[Washington's aide Robert Hanson] Harrison has left the General to be a Chief Justice of Maryland. I am about leaving him to be any thing that fortune may cast up. I mean in the military line. This, my dear General, is not an affair of calculation but of feeling. You may divine the rest, and I am sure you will keep your divinations to yourself. (More here).

Greene's reply doesn't survive.

A week later, on April 27th, Hamilton wrote to Washington pointing out that Congress had recently resolved that those who served as aides-de-camp would have the same seniority in the army as if they had served in the field. He again asked Washington for a command.

It is become necessary to me to apply to your Excellency to know in what manner you foresee you will be able to employ me in the ensuing campaign. I am ready to enter into activity whenever you think proper, though I am not anxious to do it 'till the army takes the field, as before that period I perceive no object. ...

Your Excellency knows I have been in actual service since the beginning of 76. I began in the line and had I continued there, I ought in justice to have been more advanced in rank than I now am. I believe my conduct in the different capacities in which I have acted has appeared to the officers of the army in general such as to merit their confidence and esteem; and I cannot suppose them to be so ungenerous as not to see me with pleasure put into a situation still to exercise the disposition I have always had of being useful to the United States. I mention these things only to show that I do not apprehend, the same difficulties can exist in my case (which is peculiar) that have opposed the appointment to commands of some other officers not belonging to what is called the line. ... (More here)

Washington replied from across the Hudson on the same day, April 27, citing the unrest caused recently when officers had been appointed from outside military units, rather than promoted from within.

Your letter of this date has not a little embarrassed me. You must remember the ferment in the Pensylvania line the last Campaign occasioned by the appointment of Major McPhearson; and you know the uneasiness which at this moment exists among the Eastern Officers on Acct. of the commands conferred upon Colo. Gemat and Major Galvan although it was the result of absolute necessity.

Should circumstances admit of the formation of another advanced Corps ... it can be but small and must be composed almost entirely of Eastern Troops, and to add to the discontents of the Officers of those lines by the further appointment of an Officer of your Rank to the command of it, or in it, would, I am certain, involve me in a difficulty of a very disagreeable & delicate nature; and might perhaps lead to consequences more serious than it is easy to imagine. ... I am convinced that no officer can with justice dispute your merit and abilities. ... (More here)

Hamilton's reply has a bitter tone (5/2/1781):

I am extremely sorry to have embarrassed you by my late application, and that you should think there are insuperable obstacles to a compliance with it. Having renounced my expectations, I have no other inducement for troubling Your Excellency with a second letter, than to obviate the appearance of having desired a thing inconsistent with the good of the service, while I was acquainted with the circumstances that made it so. (More here)

But getting a command matters to Hamilton. He's not about to let this go. He analyzes the cases that Washington cited and again argues that they are different from his own:

I cannot forbear repeating, that my case is peculiar and dissimilar to all the former; it is distinguished by the circumstances I have before intimated—my early entrance into the service; my having made the campaign of 76, the most disagreeable of the war at the head of a company of artillery, and having been intitled in that corps to a rank, equal in degree, more ancient in date than I now possess; my having made all the subsequent campaigns in the family of the Commander in Chief, in a constant course of important and laborious service; these are my pretensions, at this advanced period of the war, to being employed in the only way, which my situation admits ... I am incapable of wishing to obtain any object by importunity. (More here)

Two months later, on July 10, Alexander wrote to Eliza from Dobbs Ferry, reporting that he had resigned his commission because

Washington had still not given him a field command. And then, he's sorry to admit, he allowed himself to be persuaded to withdraw his resignation. (See Chapter 30. ... If I'd known where this week's post was going, I would have waited to include that letter. But I never know where I'm going, until I've dug into primary sources and found a question that whets my curiosity.)

Meanwhile ...

HAMILTON TURNS TO ECONOMICS

On April 20, eleven days after he wrote his last letter for Washington, Hamilton asked Timothy Pickering (then the army's adjutant general) to lend him several books on economics, including Hume's *Political Discourses*, Wyndham Beawes's *Lex Mercatoria Rediviva: or the Merchant's Directory,* and Malachy Postlethwayt's *The Universal Dictionary of Trade and Commerce* (letter here).

Ten days later, on April 30, 1781, Hamilton dropped into the mailbag a 12,000-word letter on finances. That's about 30 pages in print. It's the first detailed, lengthy work that Hamilton wrote on this subject. (His 1780 letter to James Duane is more on politics, although finance figures into it.) Hamilton's choice of recipient for this treatise—Robert Morris—was spot on.

Morris, a 47-year-old British-born financier, signed the Declaration of Independence and the Articles of Confederation (and later, the

Portrait of Robert Morris by Robert Edge Pine, ca. 1785

Constitution). Beginning in May 1781, he was America's superintendent of Finance—the position General Sullivan had thought Hamilton
might be suited for. Next to Washington, Robert Morris was probably the most important man in the United States. Eight years later, in
1789, it was Morris whom Washington first invited to be secretary of
the Treasury. Morris refused, and suggested Alexander Hamilton. This
letter is the beginning of the Morris-Hamilton relationship.

The outlines of Hamilton's ideas on government and government
finances were set early in his life, so let's look at some of the important
points in his 4/30/1781 letter to Morris.

At the beginning of the letter, Hamilton argues that we need a different form of government from the ever-squabbling Congressional
committees—i.e., government by men experienced in their particular
fields, such as Morris.

> I was among the first who were convinced, that an
> administration by single men was essential to the proper
> management of the affairs of this country. I am persuaded
> now it is the only resource we have to extricate ourselves
> from the distresses, which threaten the subversion of our
> cause. It is palpable that the people have lost all confidence
> in our public councils, and it is a fact of which I dare say you
> are as well apprised as my self, that our friends in Europe
> are in the same disposition. I have been in a situation that
> has enabled me to obtain a better idea of this than most
> others; and I venture to assert, that the Court of France will
> never give half the succours to this Country while Congress
> holds the reins of administration in their own hands, which
> they would grant, if these were intrusted to individuals of
> established reputation and conspicuous for probity, abilities
> and fortune.

Next point: We will win the war via finances, not battles. Notice how
very similar Hamilton's attitude is to Washington's, as expressed in
Washington's 2/4/1781 letter to General Sullivan (above). It's no
wonder President Washington and Secretary of the Treasury Hamilton
later worked together so well.

> Tis by introducing order into our finances—by restoreing
> public credit—not by gaining battles, that we are finally to
> gain our object. Tis by putting ourselves in a condition to
> continue the war not by temporary, violent and unnatural
> efforts to bring it to a decisive issue, that we shall in reality

bring it to a speedy and successful one. In the frankness of truth I believe, Sir, you are the Man best capable of performing this great work. ...

I take the liberty to submit to you some ideas, relative to the object of your department. I pretend not to be an able financier; it is a part of administration, which has been least in my way and of course has least occupied my inquires and reflections. Neither have I had leisure or materials to make accurate calculations. I have been obliged to depend on memory for important facts for want of the authorities from which they are drawn. With all these disadvantages, my plan must necessarely be crude and defective; but if it may be a basis for something more perfect, or if it contains any hints that may be of use to you, the trouble I have taken myself, or may give you, will not be misapplied. ...

Next point: Based on the money in circulation and the tax revenues of France, Great Britain, and the Netherlands, we can guess how much taxes could be collected in the United States: about a quarter of the cash in circulation. However, although America is still very productive (despite the war), little cash is in circulation.

Hamilton calculates the probable expenses of the American civil and military establishments and asks: where will we get the money?

Not from foreign loans or wealthy individuals; the American government isn't regarded as reliable enough to repay its debts. So here's what we need. This is the keystone of Hamilton's proposal, and he waxes rhetorical.

To surmount these obstacles and give individuals ability and inclination to lend, in any proportion to the wants of government, a plan must be devised, which by incorporating their means together and uniting them with those of the public, will on the foundation of that incorporation and Union, erect a mass of credit that will supply the defect of monied capitals and answer all the purposes of cash, a plan which will offer adventurers immediate advantages analagous to those they receive by employing their money in trade, and eventually greater advantages, a plan which will give them the greatest security the nature of the case will admit for what they lend, and which will not only advance their own interest and secure the independence of their country, but in its progress have the most beneficial influence upon its future commerce and be a source of national strength and wealth.

> I mean the institution of a National Bank. This I regard, in some shape or other as an expedient essential to our safety and success ... There is no other that can give to government that extensive and systematic credit, which the defect of our revenues makes indispensably necessary to its operations. The longer it is delayed, the more difficult it becomes; our affairs grow every day more relaxed and more involved; public credit hastens to a more irretrievable catastrophe; the means for executing the plan are exhausted in partial and temporary efforts.

Now, if you think the proper functions of government are limited to police, military, and the courts (I do), and if you think the government should keep its grubby tentacles out of the markets and other financial matters (I do), then you're going to be upset at the idea of a national bank. (I am.)

But here's the thing. *There are no banks in the United States in 1781.* None. Zero. Zilch. Hence when Hamilton lists the government's options for getting a loan for running expenses, he mentions foreign governments or private individuals. What he wants is an institution where money can be safely deposited, and loaned out at interest, to the government or to private individuals.

> The tendency of a national bank is to increase public and private credit. The former gives power to the state for the protection of its rights and interests, and the latter facilitates and extends the operations of commerce among individuals. Industry is increased, commodities are multiplied, agriculture and manufactures flourish, and herein consist the true wealth and prosperity of a state.

It's fascinating—and not surprising given his commercial activities as a youth—that even as early as 1781, Hamilton thinks American prosperity will depend not only on agriculture, but on manufacturing and trade. He and Jefferson would already have disagreed on this ("We plant seeds in the South") long before they came to verbal fisticuffs in Washington's cabinet.

In his 1781 letter to Morris, Hamilton goes on to describe the structure of such a bank, in 20 annotated sections. Near the end of the letter is its most famous paragraph:

> A national debt if it is not excessive will be to us a national blessing; it will be powerfull cement of our union. It will

also create a necessity for keeping up taxation to a degree which without being oppressive, will be a spur to industry; remote as we are from Europe and shall be from danger, it were otherwise to be feard our popular maxims would incline us to too great parsimony and indulgence. We labour less now than any civilized nation of Europe, and a habit of labour in the people is as essential to the health and vigor of their minds and bodies as it is conducive to the welfare of the State. We ought not to Suffer our self-love to deceive us in a comparrison, upon these points. (More here.)

Robert Morris responded from Philadelphia about a month later, on May 26, 1781:

I have read it with that attention which it justly deserves and finding many points of it to Coincide with my own Opinions on the Subject, it naturally Strengthened that Confidence which every man ought to possess to a certain degree in his own judgement. You will very Soon See the Plan of a Bank published and Subscriptions opened for its establishment …

I esteem myself much your Debtor for this piece not merely on account of the personal Respect you have been pleased to express but also on account your good Intentions and for these and the pains you have taken I not only think, but on all proper Occasions Shall Say, the Publick are also Indebted to you.

My office is new and I am Young in the execution of it. Communications from Men of Genius & abilities will always be acceptable and yours will ever Command the attention of,   Sir   Your obed hble Servt.
Robt. Morris (More here)

Morris proposed a national bank on 5/17/1781; it was chartered on 5/26, and opened its doors in Philadelphia as the Bank of North America on 1/7/1782.

WORKING WITH ELIZA

The version of Hamilton's letter to Robert Morris that the Library of Congress owns is in three different hands. The first part is in Eliza's handwriting. The middle is by an unknown hand and Hamilton. The end in Eliza's hand again. (Wish I could find an image of this manuscript. No luck so far on the Library of Congress site.)

The Founders Online page on the letter notes that the sections written by Eliza have "many spelling errors, and … such errors appear in all her other writing." Never mind: Eliza had qualities that went beyond secretarial. I do love to think of her having the chance to work with Alexander on one of his non-stop projects!

But American finances weren't the only problem that Alexander Hamilton was writing about in the summer of 1781.

THE CONTINENTALIST ESSAYS

In July 1781, Hamilton published his first political pamphlets since *A Full Vindication of the Measures of the Congress,* 1774, and *The Farmer Refuted,* 1775. (See Chapter 14 for what made Hamilton's early essays so remarkable.)

The title of Hamilton's new series – *The Continentalist* – is significant. It shows he's already pushing for a unified country rather than a loose federation of states. The Articles of Confederation had only been ratified in early 1781, but they had been the operating rule for the government since 1776. Their deficiencies were already glaringly obvious to Hamilton.

Continentalist no. 1 sets out the dangers of a weak central government.

> It would be the extreme of vanity in us not to be sensible, that we began this revolution with very vague and confined notions of the practical business of government. To the greater part of us it was a novelty ... [T]here is hardly at this time a man of information in America, who will not acknowledge, as a general proposition, that in its present form, it is unequal, either to a vigorous prosecution of the war, or to the preservation of the union in peace. ...
>
> In a government framed for durable liberty, not less regard must be paid to giving the magistrate a proper degree of authority, to make and execute the laws with rigour, than to guarding against encroachments upon the rights of the community. As too much power leads to despotism, too little leads to anarchy, and both eventually to the ruin of the people. ... (Whole issue here)

The second issue of the *Continentalist* deals with the objection that a strong central government may turn to tyranny.

> In a single state, where the sovereign power is exercised by delegation, whether it be a limitted monarchy or a republic,

the danger most commonly is, that the sovereign will become too powerful for his constituents; in fœderal governments, where different states are represented in a general council, the danger is on the other side—that the members will be an overmatch for the common head, or in other words, that it will not have sufficient influence and authority to secure the obedience of the several parts of the confederacy. (Whole issue here)

The Founders Archives has links to the rest of the *Continentalist* issues. I'll resist summarizing and commenting, because this chapter is already quite long, isn't it?

"NATURE HAS GIVEN YOU A RIGHT TO BE ESTEEMED, TO BE CHERISHED, TO BE BELOVED"

On July 13, 1781—the day after the first issue of *The Continentalist* appeared—Alexander writes to Eliza, complaining that he's bored!

I have received my angel two letters from you since my arrival in Camp with a packet of papers, and I have written to you twice since I saw you. ...

With no object of sufficient importance to occupy my attention here I am left to feel all the weight of our separation. I pass a great part of my time in company but my dissipations are a very imperfect suspension of my uneasiness. I was cherishing the melancholy pleasure of thinking of the sweets I had left behind and was so long to be deprived of, when a servant from Head Quarters presented me with your letters. I feasted for some time on the sweet effusions of tenderness they contained, and my heart returned every sensation of yours. Alas my Betsey you have divested it of every other pretender and placed your image there as the sole proprietor. I struggle with an excess which I cannot but deem a weakness and endeavour to bring myself back to reason and duty. I remonstrate with my heart on the impropriety of suffering itself to be engrossed by an individual of the human race when so many millions ought to participate in its affections and in its cares. But it constantly presents you under such amiable forms as seem too well to justify its meditated desertion of the cause of country humanity, and of glory I would say, if there were not something in the sound insipid and ridiculous when compared with the sacrifices by which it is to be attained.

Indeed Betsey, I am intirely changed—changed for the worse I confess—lost to all the public and splendid passions and absorbed in you. Amiable woman! nature has given you a right to be esteemed to be cherished, to be beloved; but she has given you no right to monopolize a man, whom, to you I may say, she has endowed with qualities to be extensively useful to society. Yes my Betsey, I will encourage my reason to dispute your empire and restrain it within proper bounds, to restore me to myself and to the community. Assist me in this; reproach me for an unmanly surrender of that to love and teach me that your esteem will be the price of my acting well my part as a member of society. ...

I write your father all the news we have. Give my love to your mother sisters and brothers. Love me and let your happiness always consist in loving

Yr. A Hamilton (More here)

On July 31, 1781, Hamilton was finally given a troop to command. By August 7, 1781, he was complaining to Timothy Pickering, the army's quartermaster, that the supplies he had required for his men had not yet arrived.

MORE

• Hamilton wrote to Laurens on 2/4/1781, congratulating him on being chosen as envoy to France. When he wrote this letter, he had been a soldier for five years, and had never been a politician. "⟨I have⟩ implicit confidence in your talent⟨s and⟩ integrity; but in the frankness of fri⟨endship⟩ allow me to suggest to you one apprehension. It is of the honest warmth of your ⟨temper.⟩ A politician My Dear friend must be at all times supple—he must often dissemble." How very ... Burrish! (See Chapter 12.)

• Robert Morris has been on our radar before, when Angelica asked Eliza (7/30/1794) to send a sketch of the grand new Morris mansion in Philadelphia (see Chapter 12). The "old" Morris mansion was used as the executive mansion by Washington and Adams from 1790-1800.

CHAPTER 32
French Aid, 1775-1781

Back in high school, I was taught that America's alliance with France was crucial for winning the Revolutionary War. Today's question: just what did the French contribute?

King Louis XVI didn't love the Americans nearly as much as he hated the British, who a decade earlier had walloped the French in the Seven Years' War (1756-1763). When the Revolutionary War broke out in 1775, the French began sending supplies (mostly gunpowder) and allowing high-ranking military men to go "on leave" to advise the Americans.

WHAT FRENCH AID COST THE FRENCH KING

Over the course of the Revolutionary War, from 1775 to 1783, the French spent 1.3 billion francs aiding the Americans. (So says Schiff, *A Great Improvisation,* p. 5.) This was twice the normal annual income of the French government. Rather than figuring out what this would be in today's currency, let's just imagine how much deep financial trouble you or I would be in if we suddenly spent twice our annual income, and still had to cover all normal living expenses.

Coping with this debt is often cited as one of the reasons for the political and economic instability in France just before the French Revolution (1789). You could say King Louis lost his head over the debt.

And by the way, here's his head. French gold coin of 1778, from King Louis XVI's reign.

THE FRANCO-AMERICAN ALLIANCE

On February 6, 1778, France and America signed the Treaty of Alliance, which had been negotiated by Benjamin Franklin, Silas Deane, and Arthur Lee. France and the United States were now officially military allies against Great Britain. Neither was to make a separate peace with the British, and American independence was to be a condition of any peace agreement. Since France was one of the leading nations in Europe at this time, in terms of wealth and population, this alliance was a major coup for the Americans.

France and the United States became commercial allies, too. By the Treaty of Amity and Commerce (also 2/6/1778), the two countries agreed to a number of mutual protections regarding commerce: most-favored-nation status, protection of cargoes in each others' territories, right to due process if contraband was seized, restoration of property stolen by pirates, and so on.

The sculpture at the Morristown Green, NJ, represents the moment when Lafayette returns to Washington with the news that France will send money and troops. Hamilton is at the center. Sculpture by StudioEIS. Photo copyright © 2017 Dianne L. Durante.

Manuscript copy of the Franco-American Alliance,
signed February 6, 1778. Image: Wikipedia

French fleet under d'Estaing approaching Newport, Rhode Island, 1778

A FRENCH FLEET ARRIVES

In August 1778—six months after the Treaty of Alliance was signed—a
French fleet under Admiral d'Estaing was sent to help the Americans.
As it approached the British-held harbor at Newport, Rhode Island,
the weather turned foul. The fleet hustled back out to sea. The Amer-
icans under General John Sullivan narrowly escaped capture by the
British. Not an auspicious start for the partnership.

In September and October 1779, Admiral d'Estaing commanded
a Franco-American force attacking Savannah, Georgia. He failed to
capture it from the British, and was recalled to France. Not an auspicious second attempt by the partnership.

LAFAYETTE AS MEDIATOR

The nineteen-year-old Marquis de Lafayette arrived in America in June 1777 and fought beside Washington until late 1778. Then he sailed back to France to help persuade King Louis XVI to send troops and money. He returned to America in April 1780, just in time to serve as Washington's liaison with Jean-Baptiste Donatien de Vimeur, Comte de Rochambeau.

Rochambeau arrived at Newport with 5,500 men and instructions from Louis XVI to put his force at Washington's disposal. He also brought hard currency to pay for all the French army's needs—a boon, given the state of American currency. (See Chapter 31.) Washington, delighted to hear of the French fleet's arrival, wrote to Rochambeau on July 16, 1780:

> Sir,
>
> I hasten to impart to you the happiness I feel at the welcome news of your arrival; and as well in the name of the American Army as in my own name to present you with an assurance, of our warmest sentiments for Allies, who have generously come to our Aid.
>
> As a citizen of the United States and as a Soldier in the cause of liberty, I thankfully acknowledge this new mark of friendship from his Most Christian Majesty—and I feel a most grateful sensibility for the flattering confidence he has been pleased to honor me with on this occasion. ...

Rochambeau (at right) reviewing troops, in a British cartoon of 1780

The Marquis De La Fayette has been by me desired from time to time to communicate such intelligence and make such prepositions as circumstances dictated. I think it so important immediately to fix our plan of operations and with as much secrecy as possible, that I have requested him to go himself to New London, where he will probably meet you. As a Genl Officer I have the greatest confidence in him—as a friend he is perfectly acquainted with my sentiments & opinions—He knows all the circumstances of our Army & the Country at large; All the information he gives and all the propositions he makes, I entreat you will consider as coming from me. I request you will settle all arrangements whatsoever with him .... (More here)

Despite their mutual regard, Washington and Rochambeau's relationship had its glitches. In September 1780, Washington felt he had to comment on the shocking treason of General Benedict Arnold, who had planned to hand the fortifications at West Point—along with Commander-in-Chief Washington and General Lafayette—over to the British.

Sir
On my arrival here a very disagreeable scene unfolded itself. By a lucky accident a conspiracy of the most dangerous kind the object of which was to sacrifice this post. has been detected. General Arnold, who has sullied his former glory by the blackest treason, has escaped to the enemy. This is an event that occasions me equal regret and mortification; but traitors are the growth of every country and in a revolution of the present nature it is more to be wondered at, that the catalogue is so small than that there have been found a few. (9/26/1780; more here)

In March 1781, Arnold—now a brigadier-general in the British army—was rampaging through Virginia. Lafayette was sent with several thousand American soldiers to harass him. The Chevalier Destouches, in Rhode Island, dispatched a few ships from the French fleet to Virginia. They were too few to trap Arnold. Crippled by gout (serves him right!), Arnold returned to New York, the British headquarters in America.

In a personal letter to his estate manager, Lund Washington, George Washington complained that those French ships had been far too few

Benedict Arnold effigy at Philadelphia, September 1780.

and far too late. The letter was waylaid by the British and published in the *New-York Gazette*.

I haven't been able to find the *Gazette's* version … but I suspect it sounded something like these comments by Washington to John Laurens (4/9/1781), who was still serving as American envoy in Paris.

> [T]he Chevr Destouches had sent a Ship of the line and two or three frigates to Chesapeak bay which not only retarded the plan I had proposd (by awaiting their return) but, ultimately, defeated the project, as the enemy in the meantime remasted the Bedford with those taken out of the Culloden & following the French fleet, arrived off the Capes of Virginia before it—where a Naval combat glorious for the French (who were inferior in Ships and Guns) but unprofitable for us who were disappointed of our object was the issue.
>
> The failure of this Expedition, (which was most flattering in the commencement of it) is much to be regretted; because a successful blow in that quarter, would, in all probability, have given a decisive turn to our Affairs in all the Southern States—Because it has been attended with considerable expence on our part, & much inconvenience to the State of Virginia, by assembling its Militia—And because the World are disappointed at not seeing Arnold in Gibbets. above all, because we stood in need of something to keep us a float, till the result of your mission is known for be assured my dear Laurens, that day does not follow night more certainly than it brings with it some additional proof of the impracticality

of carrying on the War without the aids you were directed to sollicit. (More here)

Washington's intercepted letter, as printed in the *Gazette,* was brought to Rochambeau's attention. Rochambeau repeated the part he found most disturbing, but kept his temper admirably:

> Newport, April 26th, 1781
>> Sir,
>> The New-york Gazette has published a Supposed intercepted Letter wrote, as it says by your Excellency to Mr Land Washington, and in which is this Paragraph. "It is very unlikely [NOTE: for "unfortunate"?], I say it to you in confidence that the French fleet and detachment did not undertake this present expedition at the time I proposed it. The destruction of Arnold's corps would have been unavoidable, and over before the British squadron could have put to sea: Instead of this, they have sent the small squadron that took the Romulus and some other vessels, But as I had foreseen it, it could do nothing at Portsmouth, without the help of some Land Troops."
>
> If really this Letter has been wrote by Your Excellency, I shall beg Leave to observe, that the result of this reflexion should seem to be, that We have had here the choice of two expeditions proposed, and that We have preferred the Least to a more considerable undertaking which your Excellency desired. ... I hope that your Excellency is fully persuaded that the King having put me under your orders, I shall always follow them with as much exactness as any General Officer of your Excellency's army, being bound to do so as much by my inclination as my duty. ... (More here)

To Lafayette, his most trusted liaison with the French, Washington wrote on 4/22/1781:

> I am very sorry that any letter of mine should be the subject of public discussion, or give the smallest uneasiness to any person living—The letter, to which I presume you allude, was a confidential one from me to Mr Lund Washington (with whom I have lived in perfect intimacy for near 20 Years)—I can neither avow the letter as it is published by Mr Rivington, nor declare that it is spurious, because my letter to this Gentn was wrote in great haste, and no copy of it was

taken—all I remember of the matter is, that at the time of writing it, I was a good deal chagreened to find by your letter of the 15th of March (from York Town in Virginia) that the French fleet had not, at that time, appeared within the Capes of Chesapeak; and meant (in strict confidence) to express my apprehensions and concern for the delay; but as we know that the alteration of a single word does often times, pervert the Sense, or give force to expression unintended by the letter writer, I should not be surprized at Mr Rivingtons or the Inspector of his Gazette having taken this liberty with the letter in question; especially as he, or they have, I am told, lately published a letter from me to Govr Hancock and his answer, which never had an existance but in the Gazette. That the enemy fabricated a number of Letters for me formerly, is a fact well known—that they are not less capable of doing it now few will deny. as to his asserting, that this is a genuine copy of the original—he well knows that their friends do not want to convict him of a falsehood and that ours have not the oppertunity of doing it, though both sides are knowing to his talents for lying.

In the next paragraph is one of Washington's few references to Alexander Hamilton's resignation from his staff.

The event, which you seem to speak of with regret, my friendship for you would most assuredly have induced me to impart to you in the moment it happened had it not been for the request of H—— who desired that no mention might be made of it: Why this injunction on me, while he was communicating it himself, is a little extraordinary! but I complied, & religiously fulfilled it. With every sentiment of Affecte regard I am Yrs
    Go: Washington (More here)

RENDEZVOUS WITH ROCHAMBEAU

By May 1781, the options for a joint Franco-American attack had been reduced to New York or Virginia, where Lafayette (with some 4,500 men) was harassing Lord Cornwallis. Cornwallis, who answered only to Sir Henry Clinton at British headquarters in New York, was in command of some 8,000 troops.

In August, when word arrived that a French fleet under Admiral De Grasse would be available for joint operations in the southern states from September until mid-October, the decision was made. Virginia would be the target.

The French troops marched south from Newport, meeting Washington's army in August at Philipsburg, New York. From there, they continued south in separate columns spread out over a considerable distance, to make gathering provisions on the march easier—and to confuse the British about the army's size and destination. In Maryland, many of the troops embarked on transports to carry them to the Virginia Peninsula, where Cornwallis had hunkered down at Yorktown.

Of this 500-mile odyssey, one German serving under the French wrote home:

> I hope that you have received my last letter that I had the honor to write to you while passing through Philadelphia. Since then we have traveled through a lot of country with the American army and been subjected to a lot of fatigues …
>
> The campaign has been pretty hard on us, but in return I had the satisfaction of seeing a large part of the country. Here are the names of the provinces I marched through between 2 June and September 29. We stopped at Philippsburg for 15 days, which is in the province of New York, to rest up; Rhod Island, Connecticut, Jork Statt, Jersey, Pinsilvani, Mariland, Virgini. Judge for yourself, my very dear uncle, that we were exhausted and desirous to go into winter quarters. (Wilhelm Graf von Schwerin; quoted here)

Winter quarters? Not quite yet.

Admiral De Grasse

HAMILTON GETS A COMMAND

Alexander Hamilton finally received his longed-for field command on July 31, 1781. At that point, the objective of the Franco-American army had not yet been decided, but within a month he knew where he was headed.

> Haverstraw [New York] Aug 22d. 81
>
> In my last letter My Dearest Angel I informed you that there was a greater prospect of activity now than there had been heretofore. I did this to prepare your mind for an event which I am sure will give you pain. I begged your father at the same time to intimate to you by degrees the probability of its taking place. I used this method to prevent a surprise which might be too severe to you. A part of the army My Dear girl is going to Virginia, and I must of necessity be separated at a much greater distance from my beloved wife. I cannot announce the fatal necessity without feeling every thing that a fond husband can feel. I am unhappy my Betsey. I am unhappy beyond expression, I am unhappy because I am to be so remote from you, because I am to hear from you less frequently than I have been accustomed to do. I am miserable because I know my Betsey will be so. I am wretched at the idea of flying so far from you without a single hour's interview to tell you all my pains and all my love. But I cannot ask permission to visit you. It might be thought improper to leave my corps at such a time and upon such an occasion. I cannot persuade myself to ask a favour at Head Quarters. I must go without seeing you. I must go without embracing you. Alas I must go.
>
> But let no idea other than of the distance we shall be asunder disquiet you. Though I said the prospects of activity will be greater, I said it to give your expectation a different turn and prepare you for something disagreeable. It is ten to one that our views will be disappointed by Cornwallis retiring to South Carolina by land. At all events our operations must be over by the latter end of October and I will fly to the arms of my Betsey.
>
> Let me implore you my Dear My amiable wife, let not the length of absence or the distance of situation steal from me one particle of your tenderness. It is the only treasure I possess in this world. I shall loath existence if it should be

lost or even impaired. A miser is greedy of his gold, but the comparison would be cold and poor to say I am more greedy of your love. It is the food of my hopes, the object of my wishes, the only enjoyment of my life. Neither time distance nor any other circumstance can abate that pure that holy that ardent flame which burns in my bosom for the best and sweetest of her sex. Oh heaven shield and support her. Bring us speedily together again & let us never more be separated

Adieu Adieu My Betsey

A Hamilton

I have had too little time to write this. I will write you again at large this day. Dont mention I am going to Virginia (More here)

Next week: what's the big deal about Redoubt 10? And why did they take the bullets out of their guns?

MORE

• Read more about Rochambeau and Washington on the sites of the National Park Service, the Museum of the American Revolution, and Xenophon Group. Most of the numbers and dates above are from one or the other of those articles.

CHAPTER 33
Alexander and Eliza's Rings, Handkerchiefs, and Wedding Cake

Today, September 2, 2016, is the last day of the Hamilton memorabilia exhibition at the Rare Book and Manuscripts Library in the Butler Library, Columbia University. It includes Alexander and Eliza's wedding bands.

Elizabeth and Alexander Hamilton's wedding bands (the names are engraved on them). Columbia University, Butler Library. Photo copyright © 2016 Dianne L. Durante

If you don't get chills looking at these, you're dead to me.

The exhibition also has their amazing hand-worked wedding handkerchiefs.

Since we're on the subject of weddings: the recipe for Alexander and Eliza's wedding cake (maybe?!?) has surfaced. See the article here. If you make it, let me know how it tastes. Twelve pounds of flour, 12 pounds of sugar, 4 quarts of booze: you'd better plan to have quite a large party.

MORE

• To reach the rare book room at Butler Library, you'll have to present an ID and get a day pass. No big deal. If it's past September 2, 2016, when you read this, phone the <u>Rare Book and Manuscripts Library</u> at (212) 854-5590 and ask if the exhibition run past its official closing date. Apparently that sometimes happens.

• Thanks to Judith Weiss for alerting me to the wedding-cake recipe, and to Rand Scholet of the <u>Alexander Hamilton Awareness Society</u> for alerting me to the Columbia exhibition.

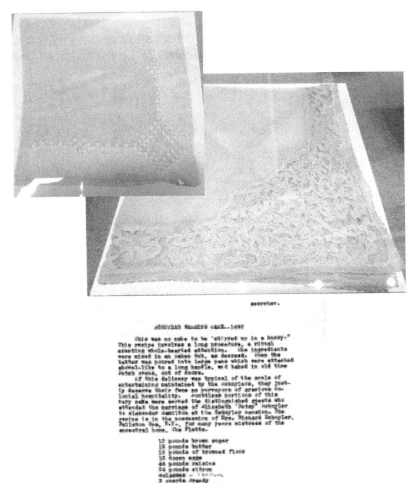

Top and center: the Hamiltons' wedding handkerchiefs. Columbia University, Butler Library. Photos copyright © 2016 Dianne L. Durante. Below: Recipe for Alexander and Eliza's wedding cake?!?

CHAPTER 34

Yorktown: August to Early October 1781

Here are the main characters on the American Revolutionary scene, in September and October 1781—skewed, of course, to those who appear in *Hamilton: An American Musical.*

THE AMERICANS

- George Washington: commander-in-chief of the Continental Army since June 1775. He has not fought the British on the battlefield since the Battle of Monmouth in June 1778 (Chapter 23). In terms of number of soldiers, finances, and supplies, his army is in bad shape, as he has repeatedly told members of Congress. (See Chapter 22.)

- John Laurens: formerly on Washington's staff, where he and Hamilton became friends. A few months ago, he returned from a mission to France, where he helped persuade Louis XVI to send more money, ammunition, and arms to the Americans. (See Chapter 31.)

- Alexander Hamilton: on 7/31/1781, he was finally given a battalion to command in the field. As of late August, he is on the move with the Continental Army and its French allies from New York to Virginia. (See the end of Chapter 32.)

Washington, Laurens, Hamilton

Lafayette, Rochambeau, De Grasse

THE FRENCH

- Marquis de Lafayette, "America's favorite fighting Frenchman": one of the few figures in the Revolution who has nationwide rather than local appeal. He has been fighting beside the Americans since 1777, when he was 19 years old. In
1779-1780, he returned to France to persuade King Louis XVI
to send soldiers, supplies, and money to the Americans. (See
Chapters 5 and 32.)

- Comte de Rochambeau: in charge of a French fleet based at
Newport, Rhode Island, since early 1780. (Again, see Chapter
32.)

- Admiral De Grasse: in charge of the 1781 West Indies fleet,
which sailed to the Caribbean to fight the British, and to collect money from the French colonies. De Grasse's fleet has
been given orders to coordinate operations with the Franco-American forces … but only until mid-October. Then the
fleet must sail back to France before winter sets in.

THE BRITISH

- Sir Henry Clinton: commander-in-chief of the British forces
in America, a ditherer who does his best not to take any action on his own responsibility. His headquarters are New York
City, which has been in British hands since August 1776. (See
Chapter 17.)

- Lord Charles Cornwallis: a brilliant soldier, chafing as second-in-command of the British forces under Clinton.

Clinton and Cornwallis

THE BRITISH RAMPAGE THROUGH THE SOUTH

In the northern United States, the British made no significant gains against Washington after 1776. In 1778, they decided to shift the theater of war to the southern states, where there were fewer people—and a greater percentage of the population was loyalist. First up: Savannah, Georgia, which Clinton and Cornwallis captured in December 1778. (Jacques Prevost was named governor of Georgia, leaving Aaron Burr free to dally with wife Theodosia: see Chapter 26.)

In May 1780, Clinton and Cornwallis captured Charleston, South Carolina. Then Clinton returned to New York, and Cornwallis battled his way northward through the Carolinas. By early 1781, he had reached Virginia. There he took command of additional troops (some of which had been serving under the traitor Benedict Arnold), bringing his force up to some 7,000 men. (See Chapter 32.)

The Marquis de Lafayette, with a force too small to meet the British on the field, desperately attempted to prevent the British from having it all their own way as they ravaged the populous and wealthy state of Virginia. "When he changes his position," explained Lafayette, "I try to give to his movements the appearance of defeat" (quoted here). Lafayette's aide, James McHenry, wrote on 7/11/1781: "Legerdemain is a very necessary science for an American general at this moment."

In early summer 1781, Clinton, fearing an attack on New York, ordered Cornwallis to send several thousand of his men to New York. Then he declared instead that Cornwallis should settle down for the winter somewhere on the Chesapeake Bay, and fortify a deep-water base for future British naval operations. Maintaining control of the Bay would give the British easy access to hundreds of square miles of vulnerable American territory.

Obeying orders and suppressing his trained military instincts, Cornwallis chose as his base Yorktown, a once thriving tobacco-shipping port on the York River that served as the harbor for Williamsburg, the capital of Virginia. (See the blue "x" on the map below.) Its 300 houses had been largely deserted since the inhabitants fled inland to escape British raids.

Uh-oh. In late August, soon after Cornwallis settled in at Yorktown, Admiral De Grasse's fleet of 29 ships arrived from the West Indies and blockaded the entrance to the York River.

When the British fleet under Admiral Graves arrived from New York, the French fleet prevented them from reaching Cornwallis at Yorktown. Not only that: at the Battle of Chesapeake (9/5/1781), the French inflicted so much damage that the British fleet limped back to New York for repairs and reinforcements.

Cornwallis and his soldiers were left with only a few ships—too few to transport them out of Yorktown. But in a letter Cornwallis received on September 29, Clinton promised to send a fleet to his rescue within a few days.

YORKTOWN'S SITUATION

Yorktown had been built as a port and a commercial center. It sat on swamp land near a harbor, and lacked any military advantages such as

Chesapeake Bay, cropped from a 1776 map of Virginia. Image courtesy David Rumsey Map Collection. Yorktown is at the blue X.

a high elevation. Cornwallis, blockaded, ordered the construction of earthwork fortifications around the town, and another line further out. Then he resigned himself to waiting for rescue. On September 16, he wrote to Clinton:

> If I had no hopes of relief I would rather risk an action than defend my half finished works but as you say Digby is hourly expected and promise every exertion to assist me I do not think myself justified in putting the fate of the war on so desperate an attempt. By examining the transports with care and turning out useless mouths my provisions will last at least six weeks from this day if we can preserve them from accidents. This place is in no state of defence. If you cannot relieve me very soon you must be prepared to hear the worst … (Quoted here)

For an escape hatch, Cornwallis fortified and posted troops at Gloucester Point, less than a mile away on the north side of the York River. (See map on facing page.) If the British fleet didn't arrive to save him, he could ferry his troops across and march north from Gloucester.

On October 2, Cornwallis received another letter from Clinton: the fleet would not be setting out until October 5 at the earliest. It would take at least a week after that to arrive.

THE AMERICANS AND FRENCH BESIEGE YORKTOWN

Meanwhile, the 15,000 or so Franco-American forces, who had been on the move since mid-August, were struggling with dire shortage of transport and food. But on September 28, 1781, they finally settled down about a mile outside Yorktown and began softening up the British with an artillery bombardment. Cornwallis, realizing that his outer defenses were too weak to withstand such bombardment for long, soon pulled nearly all his men and artillery back to the innermost defenses: the earthenworks just outside Yorktown.

On October 6, the allies began digging a trench (a.k.a. "parallel") 2,000 yards long, and 600 yards away from the British defenses. The trench was so deep that the allied troops could move through it with little danger of being hit by British fire. The dirt from the trench was used to build a parapet facing the enemy, on which artillery could be positioned. (For an eyewitness account, see *The Journal of Colonel Daniel Trabue*, pp. 111-2). By October 9th, the first trench was complete, and the new series of batteries and redoubts was bombarding the British position even more fiercely.

On October 11, the allies began construction of a second trench, this one only 300 yards from the British earthenworks.

Alexander wrote to Eliza (about 6 months pregnant) on October 12, 1781:

> Thank heaven, our affairs seem to be approaching fast to a happy period. Last night our second parallel commenced. Five days more the enemy must capitulate or abandon their present position; if they do the latter it will detain us ten days longer; and then I fly to you. Prepare to receive me in your bosom. Prepare to receive me decked in all your beauty, fondness and goodness. With reluctance I bid you adieu. Adieu My darling Wife My beloved Angel Adieu A Hamilton (More here)

The second trench ran directly toward two redoubts that the British were still manning in what had been their outermost lines. Redoubt 10 was on the banks of the York River. Redoubt 9 was about

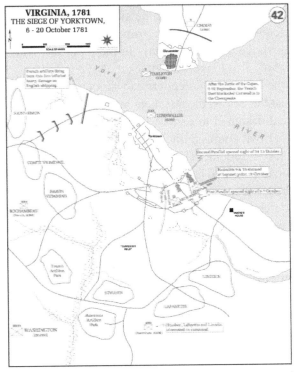

Siege of Yorktown, 1781. Image: U.S. Military Academy via Wikipedia.

a quarter mile to the west. The second trench could not be completed as long as the enemy held these two redoubts, whose position allowed them to unleash a barrage of fire at the men digging the trench. Both redoubts had to be neutralized at once, since either redoubt could fire mercilessly on the other.

So: The next step was to capture those redoubts. The order went out that the redoubts would be stormed on October 14, soon after sundown. The French were to attack Redoubt 9. The Americans, with Alexander Hamilton leading, were to attack Redoubt 10.

THE BRITISH REDOUBTS AT YORKTOWN

Let's pause here, waiting for the signal to storm the redoubts, and ask: what is it Hamilton and the other attackers are facing?

First of all: the redoubt. A redoubt is an arrangement of dirt, trees, and whatever other large obstacles the defenders can contrive that will make an approach to their position more difficult for the attackers. (The U.S. Army Heritage site has a great pic of a reconstructed redoubt at Yorktown.)

At Yorktown, Redoubt 10's outermost defense is a 15-foot-high dirt wall protected with abatis (same singular or plural). To make abatis, the defenders cut down trees, trim their branches at nastily sharp angles, then shove the trunks firmly in the outer dirt wall, spiky bits facing outward. The longer the attackers have to struggle to get past the abatis, the longer the defenders can shoot at them.

Once past the abatis, the attackers must cross the glacis, an area of rising ground designed to expose them to yet more fire from the defenders. After that comes a ditch: sharpened logs in the middle make crossing it more difficult. The side of the ditch closest to the redoubt is a steep slope (a scarp) topped with rows of sharpened logs pointing outward (the fraises). Beyond the scarp and fraises is the parapet, from which the defenders are shooting at the attackers. Redoubts 9 and 10 had a total of 65 pieces of artillery.

Once at the parapet, the attackers are in hand-to-hand combat with the defenders. At Redoubts 9 and 10, there were some 180 well-trained, battle-hardened British soldiers.

And what's coming at the attackers while they push their way through these obstacles? Considerably more than the business end of a bayonet.

REVOLUTIONARY WAR WEAPONRY

The largest cannons at Yorktown shot 18- and 24-pound balls. (Nice pic of Revolutionary War cannon at Yorktown here.) You do not want to get in the way of a cannon ball. A German soldier in service of the French reported:

> Another fatality. While working on a fortification during this siege, Soldier [Mathias] Eisenbarth from Saar Wellingen was cut in half right down the middle by an enemy cannon ball. (More here)

The good news is that at Redoubt 10, the attackers probably won't have British cannons shooting at them. Cannons send their projectiles in a long, low arc—great for long-range devastation, but not useful at close quarters.

What the attackers face instead, as they close in, are mortars and howitzers. These look like short-barreled cannon. (Nice pic of Revolutionary War howitzer at Yorktown here, mortar here.) Mortars and howitzers shoot their projectiles more steeply upwards than cannons. The projectiles fall – at murderous speed—quite nearby.

Aside from a standard cannonball, a mortar or howitzer could be loaded with an explosive shell: a 3-inch thick hollow ball packed with explosive that trailed a fuse. Shells were unpredictable in the 18th century: they might explode in the air, on impact, or soon after hitting the ground. (I'm pretty sure this 1814 image of the attack that inspired the "Star-Spangled Banner" shows such explosive shells—"the bombs bursting in air.") Daniel Trabue described them:

> The shells were made of pot metal like a jug 1-2 inch thick, without a handle, & with a big mouth. They were filled with powder, and other combustibles in such a manner that the blaze came out of the mouth, and keeps on burning until it gets to the body where the powder is, then it bursts and the pieces fly every way, and wound & kill whoever it hits. (More here, p. 112)

James Thacher, an American surgeon, described the shells on the evening of the October 15, 1781:

> The bomb-shells from the besiegers and the besieged are incessantly crossing each others' path in the air. They are clearly visible in the form of a black ball in the day, but in the night, they appear like a fiery meteor with a blazing

Alexander Hamilton in a battery at Yorktown. Painting by Alonzo Chappel (1828-1887).

tail, most beautifully brilliant, ascending majestically from the mortar to a certain altitude, and gradually descending to the spot where they are destined to execute their work of destruction. It is astonishing with what accuracy an experienced gunner will make his calculations, that a shell shall fall within a few feet of a given point, and burst at the precise time, though at a great distance. When a shell falls, it whirls round, burrows, and excavates the earth to a considerable extent, and bursting, makes dreadful havoc around. I have more than once witnessed fragments of the mangled bodies and limbs of the British soldiers thrown into the air by the bursting of our shells … (More here)

Explosive shells were enormously destructive. Joseph Plumb Martin, describing the attack on Redoubt 10, wrote:

We were now at a place where many of our large shells had burst the ground, making holes sufficient to bury an ox in. The men, having their eyes fixed upon what was transacting before them, were every now and then falling into these holes. I thought the British were killing us off at a great rate. At length, one of the holes happening to pick me up, I found out the mystery of the huge slaughter. (More here)

A mortar or howitzer could also be loaded with grapeshot: a couple dozen musket balls in a canvas bag. After firing, the bag exploded and the shot scattered, like a modern shotgun blast. (Picture here.)

By mid-October, the French and Americans had about a hundred pieces of artillery (including cannons, mortars, howitzers) firing on the British at Yorktown. As long as the ammo held out, the British were firing at least that many pieces back at the allies. A German soldier fighting for the British described the scene at Yorktown on October 11, three days before the storming of Redoubts 9 and 10:

> During these 24 hours, 3,600 shot were counted from the enemy, which they fired at the town, our line and at the ships in the harbour. These ships were miserably ruined and shot to pieces. Also the bombs and cannon balls hit many inhabitants and Negroes of the city, and marines, soldiers, and sailors. One saw men lying nearly everywhere who were mortally wounded and whose heads, arms and legs had been shot off. (Quoted here)

Artillery is relatively long-distance weaponry. If the attackers get closer, the defenders can throw hand grenades. Like explosive shells, they're unpredictable, but if that hand-sized bomb goes off at the right moment, it can take down a couple attackers.

A musket is more reliable for close-up defense, but a musket only holds one bullet, and takes about 20 seconds to reload—by which point the enemy might be on top of you. If he is, there's the business end of your bayonet, a 17-inch piece of triple-edged steel attached to the end of your 5-foot-long musket. (Triple-edged because a triangular wound is more difficult to stitch together.)

Add to all these devastating weapons the fact that medicine at this time is primitive. There's no knowledge of germs, asepsis, antibiotics. A severe wound to the head or torso usually resulted in death. A severe wound to a limb was treated with amputation and cauterization, so an infection wouldn't kill the victim.

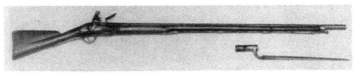

Brown Bess musket and bayonet, 18th century. Image: Wikipedia

You might argue that all these weapons were typical of 18th-century warfare, and that the soldiers at Yorktown were accustomed to such hazards. I don't think one gets accustomed to facing horrendous death just because it's common.

Are you ready to storm Redoubt 10 yet?

Raise a glass to freedom, and to all the soldiers who have, are, and will fight for it.

And now, it's 7:30 p.m. on the night of October 14, 1781, and the signal has just gone up to storm Redoubts 9 and 10.

THE ATTACK ON REDOUBT 9

Four hundred French soldiers were assigned to capture Redoubt 9. They lost the element of surprise when a German sentry heard them approaching, but waited for their pioneers to clear away the abatis before rushing forward. Within half an hour the French had captured the redoubt and taken 120 British and Hessians prisoner. Numbers of French casualties vary in the primary sources, but the total wounded and killed seems to have been just over a hundred.

Guillaume, vicomte de Deux-Ponts, who led the French, noted in his journal:

> Before starting, I had ordered that no one should fire before reaching the crest of the parapet of the redoubt; and when established upon the parapet, that no one should jump into the works before receiving the orders to do so. ...
>
> Our fire was increasing, and making terrible havoc among the enemy, who had placed themselves behind a kind of intrenchment of barrels, where they were well massed, and where all our shots told. We succeeded at the moment when I wished to give the order to leap into the redoubt and charge upon the enemy with the bayonet; then they laid down their arms, and we leaped in with more tranquillity and less risk. I shouted immediately the cry of Vive le Roi, which was repeated by all the grenadiers and chasseurs who were in good condition, by all the troops in the trenches, and to which the enemy replied by a general discharge of artillery and musketry. I never saw a sight more beautiful or more majestic. I did not stop to look at it; I had to give attention to the wounded, and directions to be observed towards the prisoners. (More here)

THE ATTACK ON REDOUBT 10

On the American side, the Marquis de Lafayette was in overall command, and he had put the 400 troops attacking Redoubt 10 under the
command of Alexander Hamilton. Hamilton assigned Lt.-Colonel
John Laurens to hustle around to the other side of the redoubt and
prevent the British from escaping in that direction.

In *Memoirs, Correspondence and Manuscripts of General Lafayette,* compiled by Lafayette much later in his life and published after
his death, he makes the following brief comment on the taking of
Redoubt 10. (As often at this period, it's written in third person.)

> It became necessary to attack two redoubts. One of these
> attacks was confided to the Baron de Viomenil, the other to
> General Lafayette. The former had expressed, in a somewhat
> boasting manner, the idea he had of the superiority of the
> French in an attack of that kind; Lafayette, a little offended,
> answered, "We are but young soldiers, and we have but one
> sort of tactic on such occasions, which is, to discharge our
> muskets, and push on straight with our bayonets." He led
> on the American troops, of whom he gave the command to
> Colonel Hamilton, with the Colonels Laurens and Gimat
> under him. The American troops took the redoubt with the
> bayonet. As the firing was still continued on the French side,
> Lafayette sent an aide-de-camp to the Baron de Viomenil,
> to ask whether he did not require some succour from the
> Americans; but the French were not long in taking possession
> also of the other redoubt … (More here)

Why did the Americans plan a bayonet charge? None of the primary
sources written by officers explain: probably too obvious to them. It
may have been done to keep an accidental discharge from warning
the British. Or perhaps it made for a faster charge—keep the soldiers
running forward, rather than having them take time to aim and reload.
According to Fleming, the British took pride in winning battles using
bayonets; so perhaps the Americans did as well.

Captain James Duncan kept a journal of events at Yorktown that
includes the storming of Redoubt 10.

> Oct 15: I have just said we were ordered yesterday to the
> trenches. The French grenadiers were ordered out the same
> time and all for the purpose of storming two redoubts on

the enemy's left. Our division arrived at the deposite of the [NOTE: manuscript is defective here] a little before dark where every man was ordered to disencumber himself of his pack. The evening was pretty dark and favored the attack. The column advanced, Col. Guinot's [i.e., Gimat's] regiment in front and ours in the rear. We had not got far before we were discovered, and now the enemy opened a fire of cannon, grape shot, shell, and musketry upon us but all to no effect. The column moved on undisturbed and took the redoubt by the bayonet without firing a single gun. The enemy made an obstinate defense but what cannot brave men do when determined. We had 7 men killed and 30 wounded. Among the latter were Col Guinot [i.e., Gimat], Maj. Barber, and Capt Olney. Fifteen men of the enemy were killed and wounded in the work; 20 were taken prisoners besides Maj. Campbell who commanded, a captain, and one ensign. The chief of the garrison made their escape during the storm by a covered way. (More here; I've added a lot of punctuation)

Captain Stephen Olney's account includes such details as how he made his way through the abatis:

The column marched in silence, with guns unloaded, and in good order. ... When we came near the front of the abatis the

Storming of Redoubt 10: you're looking at a fraise and a parapet. Later rendition via the U.S. Army Chief of Military Historians Office / Wikipedia

enemy fired a full body of musketry. At this our men broke silence and huzzaed and as the order for silence seemed broken by every one, I huzzaed with all my power saying "see how frightened they are they fire right into the air." The pioneers began to cut off the abatis which were the trunks of trees with the trunk part fixed in the ground the limbs made sharp and pointed towards us. This seemed tedious work in the dark within three rods [NOTE: about 15 yards] of the enemy and I ran to the right to look a place to crawl through, but returned in a hurry without success fearing the men would get through first; as it happened I made out to get through about the first and entered the ditch and when I found my men to the number of ten or twelve had arrived, I stepped through between two palisades, one having been shot off to make room on to the parapet, and called out in a tone as if there was no danger, "Captain Olney's company form here."

On this I had not less than six or eight bayonets pushed at me. I parried as well as I could with my espontoon [NOTE: a pike with pointy bits at the end], but they broke off the blade part and their bayonets slid along the handle of my espontoon and scaled my fingers, one bayonet pierced my thigh, another stabbed me in the abdomen just above the hip bone. One fellow fired at me and I thought the ball took effect in my arm; by the light of his gun I made a thrust with the remains of my espontoon in order to injure the sight of his eyes but as it happened I only made a hard stroke in his forehead. At this instant two of my men, John Strange and Benjamin Bennett, who had loaded their guns while they were in the ditch, came up and fired upon the enemy, who part ran away and some surrendered so that we entered the redoubt without further opposition. (More here; I've added a lot of punctuation)

Joseph Plumb Martin, whom we met as a grunt at the Battle of Monmouth (Chapter 23), was present at the storming of Redoubt 10 as a sapper. His job was to go in ahead of the troops and clear away the obstructions. Martin's account (published in 1830) includes such charming details as the fact that the watchword, "Rochambeau," if pronounced quickly sounded like "Rush-an-boys." You really should read it: here.

AFTERMATH OF THE ATTACK ON REDOUBTS 9 AND 10

Hamilton's troops suffered fewer than 50 killed and wounded. He reported to Lafayette the next day:

> The killed and wounded of the enemy did not exceed eight. Incapable of imitating examples of barbarity, and forgetting recent provocations, the soldiery spared every man, who ceased to resist. (More here)

The barbarity Hamilton refers to was a recent raid of New London, Connecticut, led by Benedict Arnold. The British brutally slaughtered 85 Americans who surrendered there. Sixty more were wounded, many mortally.

Despite the fact that we have Hamilton's own after-action report, uncertainties abound regarding Hamilton's doings before and during the storming of Redoubt 10, including whether he was originally given the command and what he did while leading the attack. If this interests you, you can't possibly do better than reading Chapters 39 and 40 in Michael Newton's *Alexander Hamilton: The Formative Years.* (No, I can't summarize, she said snappishly, casting a bleary eye at her 10-page blog post).

By the next morning (October 15), Redoubts 9 and 10 had been incorporated into the second line of trenches, and the British in Yorktown were being ceaselessly bombarded from a few hundred yards away.

Cornwallis wrote to Clinton that day:

> Sir Last evening the enemy carried my two advanced redoubts on the left by storm, and during the night have included them in their second parallel which they are at present busy in perfecting. My situation now becomes very critical; we dare not shew a gun to their old batteries and I expect that their new ones will open to morrow morning; experience has shewn that our fresh earthen works do not resist their powerful artillery, so that we shall soon be exposed to an assault, in ruined works, in a bad position and with weakened numbers. The safety of the place is therefore so precarious that I cannot recommend that the fleet and army should run great risque in endeavouring to save us. I have the honour to be & c CORNWALLIS (More here; some punctuation added)

On October 17, Saint George Tucker noted in his journal:

> An officer's Baggage by some means or other fell into our hands by the running on shore of a Boat destin'd for N. York. A Journal of the Siege to yesterday was found—In it this remarkable Conclusion—Our provisions are now nearly exhausted & our Ammunition totally. (More here)

MORE

• The 235th anniversary of the Siege of Yorktown is coming up in mid-October, with appropriate celebrations. After reading this post, how can you (and I!) not want to "learn the steps leading up to the firing of an artillery piece, followed by its firing"? Somebody better post videos!

• The numbers of troops and artillery pieces, the distances between trenches, and many other details above are taken from primary sources, which tend not to agree. For the latest scholarly thoughts on the details, read one of the many recent books on the Siege of Yorktown, such as Thomas Fleming's *Beat the Last Drum: The Siege of Yorktown*. (A well-told story, but dude, where are the footnotes and bibliography?!?!?!?)

• Captain Stephen Olney's account mentions men being chosen for "the forlorn hope." Turns out that's a military term for a small group of soldiers who take the lead in an attack, right behind the sappers, hence are more likely to suffer casualties.

• Redoubt 10 at modern Yorktown is a reconstruction. Most of the original redoubt toppled over the bluff and into the river.

CHAPTER 35
Alexander and Eliza's Wedding Cake, Revisited

In Chapter 33, which included pics of Alexander and Eliza's wedding bands and wedding kerchiefs, I gave a link to a recipe for a cake that was identified as their wedding cake. The author of the article expressed some doubt about the authenticity.

It occurred to me that I know someone who runs a website that collects manuscripts of early American recipes. I passed the Schuyler recipe along to her, asking whether it looked like an authentic 18th-century recipe, and how many people it would serve.

Within 24 hours, I had exactly the sort of answer I'd been hoping for from Steven Schmidt, principal researcher and writer for The Manuscript Cookbooks Survey (and a co-creator of the site), who has been studying historical Anglo-American cooking for over twenty-five years and has published, spoken, and consulted extensively on the subject. With his permission, I'm posting his comments.

> I am skeptical that this cake is of the 18th century—or of any time. I think the recipe is a hoax, perhaps dating from around the time of the Centennial, when lots of supposedly colonial recipes were manufactured—as also occurred in 1976.

The ingredients in the recipe are:
   12 pounds brown sugar
   12 pounds butter
   12 pounds of browned flour
   12 dozen eggs
   46 pounds raisins
   24 pounds citron
   Molasses [handwritten]—1 gallon
   3 quarts Brandy
   1 quart Jamaica Rum
   12 ounces each of cloves, allspice, cinnamon, and nutmeg, pounded fine in a mortar.
   10 teaspoons salt
   12 teaspoons pearl ash

Steve wrote:

> Molasses was not used in wedding fruitcakes until after 1820, browned flour and brown sugar debuted in fruitcakes around 1860, and I have never seen a wedding cake recipe calling for rum until nearly 1900. Also, the pearl ash is wrong. The alkali may have been on the scene as a leavening by 1780 (though there is no written record to prove its use before 1796), but chemical leavening was not countenanced in fine cakes like wedding cakes until after the Civil War. Also, 18th century wedding cakes always had currants and lots of mace (and typically rose water too), all of which are oddly absent here—and 18th century cake recipes absolutely never call for salt.

The cooking instructions in the recipe are: "Mix in large oaken tub, and bake 16 hours." Steve said:

> Finally, the business about the large oaken tub and the 16-hour baking sounds to me like someone's fantasy of "ye olden colonial baking." Even if this 125-pound cake was baked as a single loaf—and I am extremely skeptical that it was (or could be)—you can't bake any cake for 16 hours. The outside will char.
>
> Today, most people would consider a 3-ounce serving of fruitcake more than ample, which would mean this cake would serve close to 400 people. But somewhat more cake per wedding guest seems to have been allowed in early America, as 50-pound wedding cakes are fairly common in middle-class cookbooks, and I doubt that middle-class weddings typically had 150 guests.
>
> By the way, the cookbook recipes make clear that these large cakes are to be baked in multiple pans, sometimes as small as 1 quart.

I also asked Steven what a real 18th-century wedding cake recipe looked like. He replied:

> Eliza Leslie, the most popular and influential American cookbook author of the second quarter of the 19th century, outlines a recipe for "Black Cake, or Plum Cake" that can be considered a basic template for wedding cake as typically made in this country from circa 1760 to 1860.

BLACK CAKE, OR PLUM CAKE.

One pound of flour sifted.
One pound of fresh butter.
One pound of powdered white sugar.
Twelve eggs.
Two pounds of the best raisins.
Two pounds of currants.
Two table-spoonfuls of mixed spice, mace and cinnamon.
Two nutmegs powdered.
A large glass of wine ⎫
A large glass of brandy ⎬ mixed together.
Half a glass of rose-water ⎭
A pound of citron.

Mrs. Leslie's wedding cake recipe

In the 1832 edition of Leslie's cookbook, the recipe is on p. 50. The list of ingredients is followed by a full page of instructions.

(Fascinating article on Mrs. Leslie is here.) Elizabeth Fries Ellet, in *The Practical Housekeeper* (1857 ed., p. 475), paraphrases Leslie's recipe as "Plum [Cake] New England Wedding."

MORE

• The Manuscripts Cookbook Survey is a fascinating site. Hey, for our next Hamilton-themed party, why don't we whip up some authentic 18th-century recipes?

• Thanks to Szilvia Szmuk-Tanenbaum, director of the Manuscript Cookbooks Survey and a co-creator of the site, who put me in touch with Steve Schmidt.

CHAPTER 36
Yorktown: October 16-18, 1781

Like 9/11, the British surrender at Yorktown was recognized as a world-changing event at the very moment it happened. Everyone remembered where they were and what they saw and did. We have eyewitness accounts from Americans and French, British and Germans, officers and enlisted men, even one woman who followed her husband to war.

In this chapter, I'll give you a couple notes on what happened each day, and then let the eyewitnesses tell the story. (If you don't know how the players got to this point, see Chapter 34, on the earlier part of the Siege of Yorktown.)

OCTOBER 16, 1781: THE BRITISH ATTEMPT TO ESCAPE FAILS

Events of the day

• Commander-in-Chief Henry Clinton had promised General Charles Cornwallis (in a letter Cornwallis received on October 2) that the British fleet would depart from New York by October 5. On October 16 it had not yet left New York Harbor. None of the combatants at Yorktown knew that: the British fleet might sail into view at Chesapeake Bay in two days or two weeks. Hence the American and French allies were in a hurry, and the British wanted to stall.

• From their newly completed second parallel (incorporating Redoubts 9 and 10, captured by the French and Americans on the night of October 14-15: see Chapter 34), the Franco-American allies bombarded the earthworks around Yorktown from 300 yards away.

• After dark, Cornwallis began to ferry his troops across the York River to Gloucester, hoping that from there he could march overland to New York. A sudden storm forced him to cancel the plan and return to Yorktown the part of his troops that had already crossed.

Johann Doehla (German in service of the British):

> This afternoon the enemy cannonaded terribly. .... Everybody
> easily saw that we could not hold out much longer in this
> place if we did not get help soon. ("The Doehla Journal,"
> translated by Robert J. Tilden, William and Mary Quarterly
> 2nd series, 22:3 [July 1942], p. 254)

General Charles Cornwallis to Commander-in-Chief Henry Clinton
(from a letter written 10/20/1781):

> [Once the second parallel was complete,] we knew that there
> was no part of the whole front attacked on which we could
> show a single gun, and our shells were nearly expended; I
> therefore had only to chuse between preparing to surrender
> next day, or endeavouring to get off with the greatest part of
> the troops; and I determined to attempt the latter, reflecting,
> that though it should prove unsuccessful in its immediate
> object, it might, at least, delay the enemy in the prosecution
> of farther enterprizes. Sixteen large boats were prepared,
> and upon other pretexts were ordered to be in readiness to
> receive troops precisely at ten o'clock: With these I hoped to
> pass the infantry during the night; abandoning our baggage,

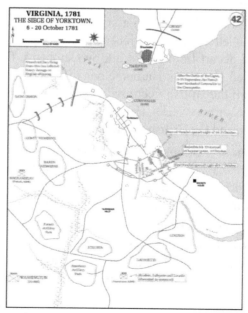

Siege of Yorktown, 1781; Gloucester is to the northeast.
Image: U.S. Military Academy via Wikipedia.

and leaving a detachment to capitulate for the town's people, and the sick and wounded; on which subject a letter was ready to be delivered to General Washington.

After making my arrangements with the utmost secrecy, the light infantry, greatest part of the guards, and part of the 23d regiment, landed at Gloucester; but at this critical moment, the weather, from being moderate and calm, changed to a violent storm of wind and rain, and drove all the boats, some of which had troops on board, down the river. It was soon evident, that the intended passage was impracticable ; and the absence of the boats rendered it equally impossible to bring back the troops that had passed, which I had ordered about two in the morning. In this situation, with my little force divided, the enemy's batteries opened at day break: The passage between this place and Gloucester was much exposed, but the boats having now returned, they were ordered to bring back the troops that had passed during the night, and they joined in the forenoon without much loss.

Our works in the meantime were going to ruin; and not having been able to strengthen them by abbatis, nor in any other manner than by a slight fraizing [see Chapter 34], which the enemy's artillery were demolishing wherever they fired, my opinion entirely coincided with that of the engineer and principal officers of the army, that they were in many places assailable in the forenoon, and that by the continuance of the same fire for a few hours longer, they would be in such a state as to render it desperate, with our numbers, to attempt to maintain them.

We at that time could not fire a single gun; only one eight-inch and little more than a hundred cohorn shells remained; a diversion by the French ships of war that lay at the mouth of York river was to be expected. Our numbers had been diminished by the enemy's fire, but particularly by sickness [malaria and smallpox]; and the strength and spirits of those in the works were much exhausted by the fatigue of constant watching and unremitting duty. Under all these circumstances, I thought it would have been wanton and inhuman to the last degree to sacrifice the lives of this small body of gallant soldiers, who had ever behaved with so much fidelity and courage, by exposing them to an assault, which, from the numbers and precaution of the enemy, could not fail to succeed. I therefore proposed to capitulate … (Quoted in Banastre Tarleton's *A History of the Campaigns of 1780 and 1781, in the Southern Provinces of North America)*

Corporal Stephan Popp (German in British service):

> We had no rest or sleep, for the enemy kept up heavy firing and pushed their lines forward within a stone's throw, with a battery of 14 guns and approaches and trenches so well made that it was only a matter of a few days before we would be completely surrounded and hemmed in under their concentrated fire. (*Popp's Journal, 1777-1783*)

OCTOBER 17: "AN OFFICER HOLDING UP A WHITE HANDKERCHIEF"

Events of the day

• Admiral Graves and the British fleet in New York City continued preparations to sail. And still, none of the combatants at Yorktown knew where this fleet was.

• Admiral De Grasse and the French fleet were still at hand, two days past the date on which their king had ordered them to set sail so that they would be home before the winter set in. The British did not seem to know that De Grasse had orders to leave in mid-October.

• Cornwallis sent a request to Washington that they discuss terms of surrender. Washington gave Cornwallis two hours to send an outline of his proposed terms. Cornwallis sent them in late afternoon.

• Fourth anniversary of the surrender of 5,800 British troops under General Burgoyne at Saratoga, New York (10/17/1777). It was one of the few American triumphs on the battlefield during the Revolutionary War, and a factor in persuading King Louis XVI to lend assistance to the United States.

Admiral Graves (British), in New York:

> The excessive want of stores and provisions and the immense repairs wanted for a crazy and shattr'd Squadron, with many cross accidents which have interven'd, has thrown back the equipment of the Squadron to a great distance. They are not quite ready – They are now very short of bread, and all the ovens will not keep up the daily consumption. Several Ships have parted their cables, others broke their anchors, and

three been on shore ... I see no end to disappointments ... (quoted in Fleming, *Beat the Last Drum*)

James Thacher (American, surgeon in the Massachusetts 16th Regiment):

> The whole of our works are now mounted with cannon and mortars; not less than one hundred pieces of heavy ordnance have been in continual operation during the last twenty-four hours. The whole peninsula trembles under the incessant thunderings of our infernal machines; we have leveled some of their works in ruins, and silenced their guns; they have almost ceased firing. We are so near as to have a distinct view of the dreadful havoc and destruction of their works, and even see the men in their lines tore to pieces by the bursting of our shells. But the scene is drawing to a close. ... (More here)

Corporal Stephan Popp (German in British service):

> The enemy opened a heavier fire than at any time and from all sides at once. The Light Infantry returned from Gloucester, reporting that it was impossible to escape in that direction ... Lord Cornwallis himself visited the works and saw how near the enemy had come. He returned to his headquarters and at once sent the first flag of truce, which was very civilly treated. The English troops at once began to destroy their tents, ruin their arms, and prepare for surrender. At 12 o'clock another flag of truce was sent,— firing ceased,—there were messages going through the lines, and we were all heartily glad the fighting was over. (*Popp's Journal, 1777-1783*)

General Cornwallis to General Washington:

> Sir: I propose a cessation of hostilities for twenty-four hours, and that two officers may be appointed by each side, to meet at Mr. Moore's house, to settle terms for the surrender of the posts of York and Gloucester. I have the honor to be, &c. (From the appendix to *Tarleton's History*)

Lt. Ebenezer Denny (American):

> In the morning, before relief came, had the pleasure of seeing a drummer mount the enemy's parapet, and beat a parley, and immediately an officer, holding up a white

handkerchief, made his appearance outside their works; the
drummer accompanied him, beating. Our batteries ceased.
An officer from our lines ran and met the other, and tied
the handkerchief over his eyes. The drummer sent back,
and the British officer conducted to a house in rear of our
lines. Firing ceased totally.

Had we not seen the drummer in his red coat when he
first mounted, he might have beat away till doomsday.
The constant firing was too much for the sound of a
single drum; but when the firing ceased, I thought I never
heard a drum equal to it – the most delightful music to us
all. (*Military Journal of Major Ebenezer Denny*)

Sarah Osborn, wife of an American soldier who traveled with the army
(referred to below as "deponent"):

They dug entrenchments nearer and nearer to Yorktown
every night or two till the last. While digging that, the enemy
fired very heavy till about nine o'clock next morning, then
stopped, and the drums from the enemy beat excessively.
Deponent was a little way off in Colonel Van Schaick's or
the officers' marquee and a number of officers were present,
among whom was Captain Gregg, who, on account of
infirmities, did not go out much to do duty.

The drums continued beating, and all at once the officers
hurrahed and swung their hats, and deponent asked them,
"What is the matter now?"

One of them replied, "Are not you soldier enough to
know what it means?"

Deponent replied, "No."

They then replied, "The British have surrendered."

Deponent, having provisions ready, carried the same
down to the entrenchments that morning, and four of the
soldiers whom she was in the habit of cooking for ate their
breakfasts. (More here)

Washington replied to Cornwallis:

My Lord, I have had the honour of receiving your lordship's
letter of this date. An ardent desire to save the effusion
of human blood will readily incline me to listen to such
terms, for the surrender of your posts and garrisons at
York and Gloucester, as are admissible. I wish, previous

to the meeting of the commissioners, that your lordship's proposals, in writing, may be sent to the American lines; for which purpose, a suspension of hostilities during two hours from the delivery of this letter will be granted. I have the honour to be, &c. (More here)

Cornwallis's proposals arrived at allied lines at about 4:30 p.m.

The time limited for sending my answer will not admit of entering into the detail of articles; but the basis of my proposals will be, that the garrisons of York and Gloucester shall be prisoners of war with the customary honours; and, for the conveniency of the individuals which I have the honour to command, that the British shall be sent to Britain, and the Germans to Germany, under engagement not to serve against France, America, or their allies, until released, or regularly exchanged: That all arms and public stores shall be delivered up to you; but that the usual indulgence of side arms to officers, and of retaining private property, shall be granted to officers and soldiers: And that the interest of several individuals, in civil capacities and connected with us [i.e., Loyalists], shall be attended to. If your excellency thinks that a continuance of the suspension of hostilities will be necessary to transmit your answer, I shall have no objection to the hour that you may propose. ... (More here)

Sergeant Joseph Plumb Martin (American):

We waited with anxiety the termination of the armistice and as the time drew nearer our anxiety increased. The time at length arrived—it passed, and all remained quiet. And now we concluded that we had obtained what we had taken so much pains for, for which we had encountered so many dangers, and had so anxiously wished. Before night we were informed that the British had surrendered and that the siege was ended. (More here)

OCTOBER 18: NEGOTIATING THE TERMS OF SURRENDER

Events of the day

• The last three British warships reached Sandy Hook, and four ships crossed the bar into the open sea. And still, none of the combatants at Yorktown knew where this fleet was.

• Negotiators for the allies and the British hammered out the terms of surrender. The Articles of Capitulation were presented to Washington for his approval at around midnight.

Corporal Stephan Popp (German in British service):

Quiet all day, while flags of truce were coming and going, negotiating terms of surrender. (*Popp's Journal, 1777-1783*)

Lt.-Col. Saint George Tucker (American):

[Yesterday] Lord Cornwallis being allow'd but two hours sent out another Flag to request further time to digest his proposals—It has been granted and Hostilities have ceased ever since five OClock [on the 17th]. It was pleasing to contrast the last night with the preceeding—A solemn stillness prevaild—the night was remarkably clear & the sky decorated with ten thousand stars—numberless Meteors gleaming thro' the Atmosphere afforded a pleasing resemblance to the Bombs which had exhibited a noble Firework the night before, but happily divested of all their Horror.

At dawn of day [on the 18th] the British gave us a serenade with the Bag pipe, I believe, & were answered by the French with the Band of the Regiment of Deux Ponts. As Soon as the Sun rose one of the most striking pictures of War was display'd that Imagination can paint—From the point of Rock Battery on one side our Lines compleatly mann'd and our Works crowded with soldiers were exhibited to view—opposite these at the Distance of two hundred yards you were presented with a sight of the British Works; their parapets crowded with officers looking at those who were assembled at the top of our Works—the Secretary's house with one of the Corners broke off, & many large holes thro the Roof & Walls part of which seem'd tottering with their Weight afforded a striking Instance of the Destruction occasioned by War …

This was the Scene which ushered in the Day when the pride of Britain was to be humbled in a greater Degree than it had ever been before, unless at the Surrender of [British general John] Burgoyne [at Saratoga, in 1777]—It is remarkable that the proposals for a surrender of Lord Cornwallis's Army were made on the Anniversary of that important Event … (More here)

Washington to Cornwallis, during the morning of the 18th:

> My Lord, to avoid unnecessary discussions and delays, I shall at once, in answer to your lordship's letter of yesterday, declare the general basis upon which a definitive treaty of capitulation may take place.
>
> The garrisons of York and Gloucester, including the seamen, as you propose, shall be received prisoners of war. The condition annexed, of sending the British and German troops to the parts of Europe to which they respectively belong, is inadmissible: Instead of this, they will be marched to such parts of the country as can most conveniently provide for their subsistence; and the benevolent treatment of the prisoners, which is invariably observed by the Americans, will be extended to them. The same honours will be granted to the surrendering army as were granted to the garrison of Charlestown. [See note below.]
>
> The shipping and boats in the two harbours, with all their guns, stores, tackling, furniture, and apparel, shall be delivered in their present state to an officer of the navy appointed to take possession of them.
>
> The artillery, arms, accoutrements, military chest, and public stores of every denomination, shall be delivered, unimpaired, to the heads of the departments to which they respectively belong.
>
> The officers shall be indulged in retaining their side arms; and the officers and soldiers may preserve their baggage and effects, with this reserve, that property taken in the country [i.e., property plundered from Americans] will be reclaimed.
>
> With regard to the individuals in civil capacities [i.e., the Loyalists], whose interest your lordship wishes may be attended to, until they are more particularly described, nothing definitive can be settled.
>
> I have to add, that I expect the sick and wounded will be supplied with their own hospital stores, and be attended by British surgeons, particularly charged with the care of them.
>
> Your lordship will be pleased to signify your determination, either to accept or reject the proposals now offered, in the course of two hours from the delivery of this letter, that commissioners may be appointed to digest the

articles of capitulation, or a renewal of hostilities may take place. I have the honour to be, &c. (More here)

NOTE: On May 12, 1780, some 5,000 besieged Americans at Charleston, under General Benjamin Lincoln, surrendered to a British force of 14,000 under Sir Henry Clinton and his second-in-command, General Charles Cornwallis. The Americans were denied the "honors of war." By the customs of 18th-century warfare, since the Americans had gallantly defended their position and had asked for terms of surrender before they were overrun by force, they should have been allowed to leave with colors (national and regimental flags) flying and drums beating. Their military band should have been permitted to play one of the British army's national songs. Such honors were a brief, gentlemanly recognition of the valor of the defeated, before they became prisoners of war. The British under Clinton and Cornwallis refused to allow the Americans the honors of war. This insult had not been forgotten: General Benjamin Lincoln was Washington's second-in-command at Yorktown, and the siege of Charleston had ended a mere 17 months earlier.

Cornwallis to Washington:

> I agree to open a treaty of capitulation up on the basis of the garrisons of York and Gloucester, including seamen, being prisoners of war, without annexing the condition of their being sent to Europe ... I shall in particular desire, that the Bonetta sloop of war may be left entirely at my disposal, from the hour that the capitulation is signed, to receive an aid de camp to carry my dispatches to Sir Henry Clinton. Such soldiers as I may think proper to send as passengers in her, to be manned with fifty men of her own crew, and to be permitted to sail, without examination, when my dispatches are ready ...
>
> If you chuse to proceed to negociation on these grounds, I shall appoint two field officers of my army to meet two officers from you, at any time and place that you think proper, to digest the articles of capitulation. I have the honour to be, &c. (More here)

For the rest of the day, the negotiators—Lt.-Col. John Laurens and the Viscount de Noailles (for the Americans and French) and Major Alexander Ross and Lt.-Col. Thomas Dundas (for the British)—hammered out the terms of surrender.

James Thacher (American):

> It is a circumstance deserving of remark, that Colonel Laurens, who is stipulating for the surrender of a British nobleman, at the head of a royal army, is the son of Mr. Henry Laurens, our ambassador to Holland, who, being captured on his voyage, is now in close confinement in the tower of London. (More here)

Laurens had been taken a prisoner of war at Charleston. He insisted that the British be denied the honors of war at Yorktown*:

> Having placed the terms on which a capitulation would be granted before Colonel Ross, that gentleman observed, "This is a harsh article." "Which article," said Colonel Laurens.
>
> "The troops shall march out with colors cased, and drums beating a British or German march."
>
> "Yes sir," replied Colonel L., with some sang froid, "it is a harsh article."
>
> "Then, Colonel Laurens, if that is your opinion, why is it here?"
>
> "Your question, Col. Ross, compels an observation which I would have suppressed. You seem to forget, sir, that I was a capitulant at Charleston—where General Lincoln, after a brave defence of six weeks' open trenches, by a very inconsiderable garrison, against the British army and fleet, under Sir Henry Clinton and Admiral Arbuthnot, and when your lines of approach were within pistol-shot of our field works, was refused any other terms for his gallant garrison, than marching out with colors cased and drums NOT beating a British or a German march." "But," rejoined Col. Ross, "my Lord Cornwallis did not command at Charleston." "There, Sir," said Col. Laurens, "you extort another declaration. It is not the individual that is here considered; it is the Nation. This remains an article or I cease to be a Commissioner." (More here)

* NOTE: This story was recorded by Major William Jackson. Laurens and Jackson were both raised in South Carolina and fought at Charleston. They spent months working together during the embassy to France in early 1781, Laurens as special minister, Jackson as his secretary. When Laurens returned to the United States, Jackson remained in France to arrange the purchase and shipment of munitions

and other supplies. He returned to the U.S. in February 1782, and presumably heard about Yorktown from his friend Laurens—who would, I assume, have been particularly happy to tell a fellow prisoner from Charleston how the British had been denied the honors of war. More on Jackson coming up in Chapter 38.

Alexander to Eliza:

> Your letter of the 3d. of September my angel never reached me till to day. My uneasiness at not hearing from you is abated by the sweet prospect of soon taking you in my arms. Your father will tell you the news. Tomorrow Cornwallis and his army are ours. In two days after I shall in all probability set out for Albany, and I hope to embrace you in three weeks from this time. Conceive my love by your own feelings, how delightful this prospect is to me. Only in your heart and in my own can any image be found of my happiness upon the occasion. I have no time to enlarge. Let the intilligence I give compensate for the shortness of my letter. Give my love to your Mama to Mrs. Carter [Angelica] to Peggy and to all the family.
>
> Adieu My Charming beloved wife, I kiss you a thousand times, Adieu, My love
>
> A Hamilton (Letter here)

MORE

• I'll put a list of the primary sources that I know of at the end of the next chapter. Meanwhile, thanks to Michael Newton (author of *Alexander Hamilton: The Formative Years*) for providing me with several that aren't readily available.

CHAPTER 37
Yorktown: October 19, 1781, and the Aftermath

According to eyewitness accounts of the British surrender at York-town on October 19, 1781, the British were valiant enemies, coward-ly, and drunk; the Americans were ragged, brave, and snide; and the French ... well, according to every single source, the French were beautifully dressed. *Ça va sans dire.* (NOTE: on Yorktown, see also Chapters 34 and 36.)

OCTOBER 19: "THE BRITISH ARMY WHICH SO LATELY SPREAD DISMAY AND DESOLATION ... DISROBED OF ALL THEIR TERRORS"

Events of the day

• In the morning, Washington sent the Articles of Capitulation to Cornwallis, with the requirement that he sign by 11 a.m. Why the rush? There was still a chance that the British fleet would sail into Chesapeake Bay at any moment: Washington did not allow Cornwallis to stall. Washington signed the Articles soon after Cornwallis.

• At 2 p.m., the British marched half or three-quarters of a mile, through a double file of French and American troops, to a field outside Yorktown. There they surrendered their weapons, then marched back into Yorktown. Cornwallis, claiming sickness, sent General Charles O'Hara to preside over the surrender.

Third of the Articles of Capitulation:

> The garrison of York will march out to a place to be appointed in front of the posts, at two o'clock precisely, with shouldered arms, colours cased, and drums beating a British or German march. They are then to ground their arms, and return to their encampments, where they will remain until they are dispatched to the places of their destination. (More here; on the honors of war, see Chapter 36)

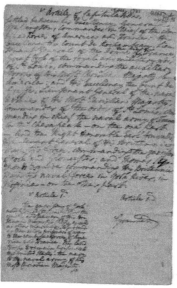

Page from the Articles of Capitulation, signed October 19, 1781, at Yorktown.

Corporal Stephan Popp (German in British service):

> The terms of surrender were finally agreed on. ... Everything was done in a regular military way. We were heartily glad the siege was over, for we all thought there would be another attack ... During the siege the enemy had fired more than 8000 great bombs, of from 100 to 150 and 200 pounds. On the day of the surrender Corporal Popp was promoted to Lieutenant. ...
>
> Of munitions of war there were left only 23 kegs of powder.
>
> At 3-4 p.m. all of Lord Cornwallis' troops, with all our personal effects and our side arms, colors covered, marched out of our lines on the Williamsburg road, between the Regiments of the enemy, which were all drawn up, with colors flying and bands playing,—our drums beating,—the French were on our right in parade, their General at the head, – fine looking young fellows the soldiers were,—on our left the Americans, mostly regular, but the Virginia militia too,—but to look on them and on the others was like day and night.
>
> We were astonished at the great force and we were only a Corporal's Guard compared to their overwhelming

numbers. They were well supplied and equipped in every way. (*Popp's Journal, 1777-1783*)

Johann Doelha (German in British service):

In the afternoon of the 19th of October, between 3 and 4 o'clock all the troops marched out of the lines and camp with bag and baggage, muskets and side arms, with standards cased, but with drums and fifes playing. Brigadier General O'Hara led us out and surrendered us ...

On the right flank, every regiment of the French paraded white silk colors adorned with 3 silver lilies; beyond the colors stood drummers and fifers and in front of the colors the Haubisten [band] which made splendid music. In general the French troops appeared very well, they were good looking, tall, well-washed men ... To our left as we marched out, or on the left flank, stood the American troops drawn up on parade with their generals, Washington, Gates, Green and Wayne. They stood in 3 ranks, first the regular troops which also had Haubisten and musicians making beautiful music and appeared tolerable enough. After them were the militia from Virginia and Maryland who looked rather badly tattered and worn.

We, now prisoners, saw all these troops standing 3 ranks deep in a line over an English miles long, with wonder and great astonishment at the great multitude, which had

Surrender at Yorktown, 1781, from a French print

besieged us. One saw, indeed, that they could have devoured us who were only a corporal's guard compared with them. The lines of both armies were drawn out nearly 2 English miles. One can imagine that an army of more than 40,000 men, also when it is paraded in 2 lines 3 ranks deep, requires space. [NOTE: The combined American and French forces totaled at most some 19,000.] The enemy was much amazed at our small force as we marched out as they had supposed us numerous. ...

As everything was now over, we marched back through the two armies—but in silence—into our lines and camp, having nothing more than our few effects in the packs on our backs. All spirit and courage which at other times animated the soldiers had slipped from us, especially inasmuch as the Americans greatly jeered at us like conquerors as we marched back through the armies. ("The Doehla Journal," translated by Robert J. Tilden, William and Mary Quarterly 2nd series, 22:3 [July 1942], p. 257-9)

James Thacher (American):

This is to us a most glorious day; but to the English, one of bitter chagrin and disappointment. Preparations are now making to receive as captives that vindictive, haughty commander, and that victorious army, who, by their robberies and murders, have so long been a scourge to our brethren of the Southern states. Being on horseback, I anticipate a full share of satisfaction in viewing the various movements in the interesting scene ...

The royal troops, while marching through the line formed by the allied army, exhibited a decent and neat appearance, as respects arms and clothing, for their commander opened his store, and directed every soldier to be furnished with a new suit complete, prior to the capitulation. But in their line of march we remarked a disorderly and unsoldierly conduct, their step was irregular, and their ranks frequently broken. (More here)

Lt. William Feltman (American):

The British army marched out and grounded their arms in front of our line. Our whole army drew up for them to march through, the French army on their right and the American army on their left. The British prisoners all appeared to be much in liquor. (More here)

Baron Ludwig von Closen (German in French service):

In passing between the two armies, they showed the greatest scorn for the Americans, who, to tell the truth, were eclipsed by our army in splendor of appearance and dress, for most of these unfortunate persons were clad in small jackets of white cloth, dirty and ragged, and a number of them were almost barefoot. The English had given them the *nickname* of Yankee Doodle. What does it matter! an intelligent man would say. These people are much more praise-worthy and brave to fight as they do, when they are so poorly supplied with everything. *(The Revolutionary War Journal of Baron Ludwig von Closen 1780-1783, trans. & ed. Evelyn M. Acomb)*

Lt.-Col. Saint George Tucker (American):

This Morning at nine oClock the Articles of Capitulation were signed and exchanged—At retreat beating last night the British play'd the Tune of "Welcome Brother Debtor"—to their conquerors the tune was by no means dissagreeable— ...

Our Army was drawn up in a Line on each side of the road ... the Americans on the right, the French on the left. Thro' these Lines the whole British Army march'd their Drums in Front beating a slow March. Their Colours furl'd and Cased. I am told they were restricted by the capitulation from beating a French or American march. General Lincoln with his Aids conducted them—Having passed thro' our whole Army they grounded their Arms & march'd back again thro' the Army a second Time into the Town—The sight was too pleasing to an American to admit of Description— (More here)

Lt.-Col. Henry Lee (American):

Valiant troops yielding up their arms after fighting in defence of a cause dear to them (because the cause of their country), under a leader who, throughout the war, in every grade and in every situation to which he had been called, appeared the Hector of his host. Battle after battle had he fought; climate after climate had he endured; towns had yielded to his mandate, posts were abandoned at his approach; armies were conquered by his prowess; one nearly exterminated, another chased from the confines of South Carolina beyond the Dan into Virginia, and a third severely chastised in that State on the shores of James River. But here even he, in the midst of his splendid career, found his conqueror.

The road through which they marched was lined with spectators, French and American. On one side the commander-in-chief, surrounded by his suite and the American staff, took his station; on the other side, opposite to him, was the Count de Rochambeau, in like manner attended. The captive army approached, moving slowly in column with grace and precision. Universal silence was observed amid the vast concourse, and the utmost decency prevailed: exhibiting in demeanor an awful sense of the vicissitudes of human life, mingled with commiseration for the unhappy. The head of the column approached the commander-in-chief; O'Hara, mistaking the circle, turned to that on his left, for the purpose of paying his respects to the commander-in-chief, and requesting further orders; when, quickly discovering his error, with much embarrassment in his countenance he flew across the road, and, advancing up to Washington, asked pardon for his mistake, apologized for the absence of Lord

British surrendering arms at Yorktown, from a German print.

Cornwallis, and begged to know his further pleasure. The General, feeling his embarrassment, relieved it by referring him with much politeness to General Lincoln ...

Every eye was turned, searching for the British commander-in-chief, anxious to look at that man, heretofore so much the object of their dread. All were disappointed. Cornwallis held himself back from the humiliating scene; obeying sensations which his great character ought to have stifled. He had been unfortunate, not from any false step or deficiency of exertion on his part, but from the infatuated policy of his superior [General Henry Clinton], and the united power of his enemy, brought to bear upon him alone. There was nothing with which he could reproach himself ; there was nothing with which he could reproach his brave and faithful army: why not, then, appear at its head in the day of misfortune, as he had always done in the day of triumph? The British general in this instance deviated from his usual line of conduct, dimming the splendor of his long and brilliant career. (From Johnston, pp. 176-177)

Colonel Fontaine (American):

I had the happiness to see that British army which so lately spread dismay and desolation through all our country, march forth on the 20th inst. [19th] at 3 o'clock through our whole army, drawn up in two lines about 20 yards distance and return disrobed of all their terrors, so humbled and so struck at the appearance of our troops, that their knees seemed to tremble, and you could not see a platoon that marched in any order. Such a noble figure did our array make, that I scarce know which drew my attention most. You could not have heard a whisper or seen the least motion throughout our whole line, but every countenance was erect, and expressed a serene cheerfulness. Cornwallis pretended to be ill, and imposed the mortifying duty of leading forth the captives on Gen. O'Hara. Their own officers acknowledge them to be the flower of the British troops, but I do not think they at all exceeded in appearance our own or the French. The latter, you may be assured, are very different from the ideas formerly inculcated in us of a people living on frogs and coarse vegetables. Finer troops I never saw. His Lordship's defence I think was rather feeble. His surrender was eight or ten days sooner than the most sanguine expected, though his force and resources were much greater than we conceived. (Quoted in Johnston, pp. 177-8)

Lt. Ebenezer Denny (American):

The British army parade and march out with their colors furled; drums beat as if they did not care how. Grounded their arms and returned to town. Much confusion and riot among the British through the day; many of the soldiers were intoxicated; several attempts in course of the night to break open stores; an American sentinel killed by a British soldier with a bayonet; our patrols kept busy. Glad to be relieved from this disagreeable station. Negroes lie about, sick and dying, in every stage of the small pox. Never was in so filthy a place—some handsome houses, but prodigiously shattered. Vast heaps of shot and shells lying about in every quarter, which came from our works. The shells did not burst, as was expected. Returns of British soldiers, prisoners six thousand, and seamen about one thousand. (More here)

Sergeant Joseph Plumb Martin (American):

The next day we were ordered to put ourselves in as good order as our circumstances would admit, to see (what was the completion of our present wishes) the British army march out and stack their arms. The trenches, where they crossed the road leading to the town, were leveled and all things put in order for this grand exhibition. After breakfast, on the nineteenth, we were marched onto the ground and paraded on the right-hand side of the road, and the French forces on the left. We waited two or three hours before the British made their appearance. They were not always so dilatory, but they were compelled at last, by necessity, to appear, all armed, with bayonets fixed, drums beating, and faces lengthening. They were led by General [Charles] O'Hara, with the American General Lincoln on his right, the Americans and French beating a march as they passed out between them. It was a noble sight to us, and the more so, as it seemed to promise a speedy conclusion to the contest. The British did not make so good an appearance as the German forces, but there was certainly some allowance to be made in their favor. The English felt their honor wounded, the Germans did not greatly care whose hands they were in. The British paid the Americans, seemingly, but little attention as they passed them, but they eyed the French with considerable malice depicted in their countenances. (More here)

Sara Osborn, wife of an American soldier ("deponent" in the selection below):

Deponent stood on one side of the road and the American officers upon the other side when the British officers came out of the town and rode up to the American officers and delivered up [their swords, which the deponent] thinks were returned again, and the British officers rode right on before the army, who marched out beating and playing a melancholy tune, their drums covered with black handkerchiefs and their fifes with black ribbands tied around them, into an old field and there grounded their arms and then returned into town again to await their destiny. Deponent recollects seeing a great many American officers, some on horseback and some on foot, but cannot call them all by name. (More here. For further details on covering the drums and tying ribands on the fifes, see the "More" heading below.)

Colonel Daniel Trabue (American):

The news [of the surrender] went far and near, and a vast number of people from Different towns and the country came forward to see the great and mighty sight.

The British had a very large gate in the South side of their fort, and on that side was a level old field. Our army was placed in a solid square column about half a mile or more around the fort gate ; it was a great sight. Part of our line was Continental Troops, part was Militia, and part was French. On the out-side of this column of soldiery was a vast number of spectators, mostly in carriages such as chariots, Fayatons, chairs, and gigs, also some common wagons. The carriages were full of gentlemen, ladies and children, besides a number on horse-back, and some on foot. Some had come as far as the city of Richmond, which was upwards of 70 miles. There were many thousands of these spectators.

General Washington and some of the officers with their aids were about the center of this vast column, immediately before the gate, and about 1/2 or 3/4 of a mile Distant. About the middle of the Day the big gate opened, and the red Coats marched out by Platoons in a solid column with some of their Officers. Our Officers, soldiers and spectators said "Did you ever see the like," and many words were spoken but not loud.

It was the most Tremendous and most admirable Sight that I ever saw. The countenances of our Officers, and soldiers all seemed to claim some credit for the great prize; and the countenances of the spectators seemed to say, also, that they deserved credit. It was truly a wonderful sight to see so many British coming out in their red coats to ground their arms. They marched straight up to General Washington, and gave up their swords and ground their arms or stacked them, and then returned to the Fort. ...

That night I noticed that the officers and soldiers could scarcely talk for laughing, and they could scarcely walk for jumping and Dancing and singing as they went about. ...

The Continental Officers and soldiers guarded the Gates of the Fort, and none of the militia were allowed to go in the Fort; one reason was the small-pox was bad there. I had a relative who was a Continental Officer. He was Lieutenant John Trabue; the very next day I went with him all over the Fort. It seemed to be nearly one mile in length by 1/4 mile in width. It was truly a Dreadfully shocking sight to see the damage our bomb-shells had Done. When a shell fell on the ground it would sink under the ground so Deep that when it burst it would throw up a wagon load, or even more of Dirt; and when it fell on a house it Tore it to pieces. The British had a number of holes and Pits Dug all over the Fort, some large and some small with timber in the top edge; when the soldiers would see a shell coming near them they could jump in one of the pits and squat Down until it had burst.

They had some large holes under ground [i.e., caves] where Lord Cornwallis, and some of the nobles staid. They called them bomb-proof, but with all their caution a vast number of them were killed.

I have been told by some of the soldiers since, that there was always some one on the watch. They could see a shell coming, and at times there was Dreadful scampering, and sometimes they would come so often, they were much beset.

Trumbull, Surrender at Lord Cornwallis, painted 1819-1820. According to Trumbull's key to the painting, Hamilton is on the right (standing next to a horse) and John Laurens is to our right of Hamilton.

Mr. Jacob Phillip told me a while before they surrendered they lost 40 men every hour. They threw a number of their arms and cannon in the Deep water.

When a shell would fall on any hard place, so that it would not go under the ground, a soldier would go to it and knock off the fiz, or neck, and then it would not burst. The soldier then received a shilling for that act. They said they did not care much about their life, but that the shilling would buy spirits! ...

The British Officers and Tories looked much dejected, and they had sad countenances, as I saw them passing I hardly heard them say a word. I thought the English soldiers, and Hessians Did not seem to Care much about it.

Everything in the Fort looked gloomy and sad. Lord Cornwallis and his other Officers looked not only sad, but ashamed. They had lived under the ground like ground Hogs [i.e., in caves]. The negroes looked condemned, for the British had promised them their freedom, but instead of freedom they made them haul wagons, by hand, with timber to build their works, and made them work very hard with spades.

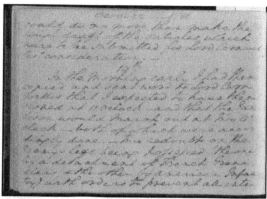

Washington's diary for October 19, 1781. Image: _Library of Congress_ (p. 5)

I left their Fort and went to our army, and what a Great Contrast our men presented. They were pert and lively, and still rejoicing. ... (More here)

Washington to Thomas McKean, President of the Continental Congress:

I have the Honor to inform Congress, that a Reduction of the British Army under the Command of Lord Cornwallis, is most happily effected—The unremitting Ardor which actuated every Officer & Soldier in the combined Army on this Occasion, has principally led to this Important Event, at an earlier period than my most sanguine Hopes had induced me to expect. ... (More here)

Commander-in-Chief George Washington's diary entry for October 19, 1781. (Just the facts, ma'am. Damn, I love GW.)

In the morning early I had [the Articles of Capitulation] copied and sent word to Lord Cornwallis that I expected to have them signed at 11 o'clock, and that the garrison would march out at two o'clock, both of which were accordingly done, the redoubts on the enemy's left being possessed, the one by a detachment of French Grenadiers, & the other by American Infantry with orders to prevent an intercourse between the army & country and the town, while officers in the several departments were employed in taking acct. of the public stores &c. (More here)

OCTOBER 20: THE FINAL TALLY

Events of the day

• In accordance with the Articles of Capitulation, the sloop *Bonetta* sailed for New York, carrying Cornwallis's report to Clinton and as many loyalists and soldiers as it could hold.

• Casualties at Yorktown: on the American and French side, fewer than 100 killed, about 300 wounded; on the British side, 200-300 killed, 300-600 wounded. About 7,500 British and their German auxiliaries were taken prisoner.

• Among the articles surrendered: 82 ships (mostly small); 191 cannon, mortars, and howitzers; 2,749 cannon balls; 693 bombs, grenades, and canister shot; 23 kegs of powder, each 120 lbs. (but considerably more was lost in the explosion of a powder magazine the night of the 18th).

OCTOBER 24: THE BRITISH FLEET ARRIVES FROM NEW YORK

The British fleet, which had departed New York harbor on the 19th, arrived off the coast of Virginia after five days at sea. Near Chesapeake Bay it met a small ship whose passengers and crew informed General Clinton that Cornwallis had surrendered on the 19th. The fleet cruised the area for five days seeking confirmation, then sailed back to New York on October 29.

Comte de Rochambeau:

> All the details of the operation were hardly concluded when the strong English squadron of twenty-seven sail, including the three of fifty [guns], appeared off Cape Henry on the twenty-seventh. It had on board a corps of troops under the joint command of General Clinton and Prince Frederick Henry [NOTE: actually Prince William Henry, Duke of Gloucester and Edinburgh, King George III's younger brother]. After making sure that the aid they carried was useless, they stood out to sea. The fleet of M. de Grasse left on November 4 ... (Rochambeau, "Memoire de la Guerre en Amerique," ed. Claude C. Sturgill, The Virginia Magazine of History and Biography 78:1, part 1 (Jan. 1970), p. 63)

NOVEMBER 25: "OH GOD! IT IS ALL OVER!"

News of Cornwallis's surrender at Yorktown arrived in London on November 25, 1781. Sir Nathaniel William Wraxall described the effect of the news on Lord North, Britain's prime minister:

> The First Minister's firmness and even his presence of mind gave way for a time under this awful disaster. I asked Lord George afterward how he took the communication when made to him ? "As he would have taken a ball in his breast," replied Lord George. For he opened his arms exclaiming wildly as he paced up and down the apartment, during a few minutes, "Oh God ! it is all over !" Words which he repeated many times, under emotions of the deepest agitation and distress. (Quoted in Johnston, pp. 179-180)

EYEWITNESS ACCOUNTS OF YORKTOWN

Thanks to Michael Newton, author of *Alexander Hamilton: The Formative Years*, for helping me expand my list of sources. If you know of others, email me at DuranteDianne@gmail.com.

Journals (written at the time of the siege)

• Denny, Lt. Ebenezer (American): *Military Journal of Major Ebenezer Denny*

• Doehla, Johann (German in British service): "The Doehla Journal," translated by Robert J. Tilden, *William and Mary Quarterly*, 2nd series, 22:3 (July 1942), pp. 229-274

• Feltman, Lt. William (American): *The Journal of Lieut. William Feltman, of the First Pennsylvania Regiment*

• Popp, Col. Stephan (German in British service): *Popp's Journal, 1777-1783*

• Thacher, James (American surgeon): *Military Journal of the American Revolution*

• Tucker, Lt-Col. St. George (American): "Journal of the Siege of Yorktown"

Letters

• Cornwallis, General Charles (British): letters to Commander-in-Chief Henry Clinton, reprinted in Tarleton's *A History of the Campaigns of 1780 and 1781*

• Hamilton, Lt. Col. Alexander (American): letter to Elizabeth Schuyler Hamilton of October 12, report written October 15 regarding the attack on Redoubt 10, and letter to Elizabeth on October 18

• Washington, George (American): search the Founders Archive for letters written in September and October 1781

Narratives written an indefinite time later

• Fontaine, Col. (American): quoted in Henry Phelps Johnston, *The Yorktown Campaign and the Surrender of Cornwallis, 1781* (Philadelphia, 1881)

• Lafayette, Marquis de (French): *Memoirs, Correspondence and Manuscripts of General Lafayette*

• Lee, Lt.-Col. Henry (American): quoted in Johnston, *The Yorktown Campaign and the Surrender of Cornwallis, 1781*

• Martin, Sergeant Joseph Plumb (American): section of his narrative on Yorktown

• Osborn, Sarah (American, wife of a soldier): deposition filed in 1837

• Rochambeau, Comte / Admiral (French): "Memoire de la Guerre en Amerique," ed. Claude C. Sturgill, *The Virginia Magazine of History and Biography* 78:1, part 1 (Jan. 1970), p. 63

• Tarleton, Lt.-General Banastre (British): *A History of the Campaigns of 1780 and 1781*

• Trabue, Col. Daniel (American): *Colonial Men and Times, containing the Journal of Col. Daniel Trabue*

MORE

• I wondered about Sarah Osborn's account of black-draped drums and fifes with black ribands. SFC Jay Martin of the United States Army Old Guard Fife and Drum Corps kindly replied to my query:

> Her account comes from her submission for a pension. Individuals who did not have an official record of service to verify their service were required to provide a detailed account of their activities/contributions to the war. The obvious issue with these narrative accounts is that they were given decades after the fact and are subject to false, embellished or tainted (by stories heard or read in the interim) recollections.

Several other accounts address the marching out of the British troops to the sound of drums. The others that I have read do not mention the drums being covered. One description that comes up a couple of times is the drums playing a 'slow march'. This would be a slow, understated march / rhythm typical of a somber occasion like a funeral. But her account is the only one I have read that describes the drums being covered.

Covering drums in black cloth for funeral processions was certainly done in that era and is still sometimes done today. So, as far as 100% accuracy as you know, we cannot say. But, as you asked is it possible, certainly.

Having said that, I'm sure there is a history buff or two out there who will tell you absolutely not because it was not specified in "X" or "Y" manuals. In reality, just like today, commanders and troops exercised a certain amount of discretion or improvisation in the moment.

In short, if one was trying to represent the event with as much accuracy as possible, I would stay away from covering the drums because we don't know. If one was trying to add to the drama, or weight of the scene being depicted, I feel covering the drums in black would certainly fall with in very reasonable artistic license.

• Did you notice that I didn't mention the British playing "The World Turned Upside Down"? Clever you. More on that in Chapter 38.

CHAPTER 38

Yorktown: "The World Turned Upside Down"?

Chernow's *Alexander Hamilton*, Fleming's *Beat the Drum: The Siege of Yorktown*, and dozens of other scholarly works state that at York-town on October 19, 1781, when the British marched out to surren-der to the Americans and French, they played "The World Turned Upside Down." In *Hamilton: The Revolution*, Lin-Manuel Miranda commented :

> Per Chernow, this was the name of the tune the British sang as they retreated. I sought out the actual song and it's … well, it's a drinking song. It's sprightly and lively and fun to sing with a pint in your hand, but didn't serve me musically. So I wrote my own melody for it. But God, what a great sentiment for the end of the war and the birth of this moment. (*Hamilton: The Revolution*, p. 122 n. 8)

The lyrics of a 1646 poem called "The World Turned Upside Down," which laments the quashing of Christmas cheer by Oliver Cromwell and the Puritans, are here. First stanza:

> Listen to me and you shall hear, news hath not been
> this thousand year:
> Since Herod, Caesar, and many more, you never
> heard the like before.
> Holy-dayes are despis'd, new fashions are devis'd.
> Old Christmas is kickt out of Town.
> Yet let's be content, and the times lament, you see
> the world turn'd upside down.

An instrumental version of the popular melody to which that poem was sung is here, as a MIDI file (with a different set of lyrics).

Now: I'm both a historian and a lover of art. In *Hamilton: An Amer-ican Musical*, Miranda's "The World Turned Upside Down" works brilliantly as the conclusion to the Revolutionary War sequence. Art-Lover Dianne doesn't care whether a tune by that name was actually played at Yorktown on October 19, 1781.

But Historian Dianne yearns to know!

PRIMARY SOURCES ON MUSIC PLAYED AT YORKTOWN

As you'll have noticed by now, I'm obsessed with primary sources. I've read every eyewitness source I could find on Yorktown (list at the end of Chapter 37). Short version: I've seen no reference in any of them to the British playing "The World Turned Upside Down."

Long version: here are the sources that mention fifes, drums, marches, and/or music.

Third of the Articles of Capitulation:

> The garrison of York will march out to a place to be appointed in front of the posts, at two o'clock precisely, with shouldered arms, colours cased, and drums beating a British or German march. ... (More here)

Lt.-Col. Saint George Tucker (American), from his journal for October 19, 1781:

> Our Army was drawn up in a Line on each side of the road ... the Americans on the right, the French on the left. Thro' these Lines the whole British Army march'd their Drums in Front beating a slow March. Their Colours furl'd and Cased. I am told they were restricted by the capitulation from beating a French or American march. (More here)

Johann Doelha (German in service of the British), from his journal:

> In the afternoon of the 19th of October, between 3 and 4 o'clock all the troops marched out of the lines and camp with bag and baggage, muskets and side arms, with standards cased, but with drums and fifes playing. ...
>
> We marched out Williams Street, or down the road which leads to Williamsburg, in column with shouldered muskets, through the whole enemy army, with our drummers beating a march. [The editor, Tilden, says in footnote 52: "A lively, old English air: 'The World Turned Upside Down.']
>
> On the right flank, every regiment of the French paraded white silk colors adorned with 3 silver lilies; beyond the colors stood drummers and fifers and in front of the colors the Haubisten [band] which made splendid music. ... [The Americans] stood in 3 ranks, first the regular troops which also had Haubisten and musicians making beautiful music and appeared tolerable enough. ("The Doehla

Journal," translated by Robert J. Tilden, William and Mary Quarterly 2nd series, 22:3 [July 1942], p. 257-8)

Col. Stephan Popp (German in British service), from his journal:

> At 3-4 p.m. all of Lord Cornwallis' troops, with all our personal effects and our side arms, colors covered, marched out of our lines on the Williamsburg road, between the Regiments of the enemy, which were all drawn up, with colors flying and bands playing,—our drums beating ... (Popp's Journal, 1777-1783)

Lt. Ebenezer Denny (American), from his journal:

> The British army parade and march out with their colors furled; drums beat as if they did not care how. Grounded their arms and returned to town. (More here)

Sergeant Joseph Plumb Martin (American), narrative published in 1830:

> We waited two or three hours before the British made their appearance. They were not always so dilatory, but they were compelled at last, by necessity, to appear, all armed, with bayonets fixed, drums beating, and faces lengthening. They were led by General [Charles] O'Hara, with the American General Lincoln on his right, the Americans and French beating a march as they passed out between them. (More here)

Sara Osborn, wife of an American soldier, memories recorded in 1837:

> [T]he British officers rode right on before the army, who marched out beating and playing a melancholy tune, their drums covered with black handkerchiefs and their fifes with black ribbands tied around them, into an old field and there grounded their arms. (More here)

So: according to the eyewitnesses, the British played fifes and drums. Nobody sang. The eyewitness accounts mention no specific tunes. Nor do any contemporary newspaper accounts about Yorktown state what music was played (according to Schrader p. 184: more on him below).

WILLIAM JACKSON ON "THE WORLD TURNED UPSIDE DOWN"

The earliest published source to mention "The World Turned Upside Down" being played by the British at Yorktown dates to 1828. In Alexander Garden's *Anecdotes of the American Revolution, Second Series,* pp. 12-19 are entitled "Embassy of Lieut. Col. Laurens to France, in 1781." Garden introduces the section thus:

> I do not think that I can follow up the interesting document immediately preceding [regarding the Mecklenburg Resolves], in a more appropriate manner, or afford a higher treat to my readers, than by giving a particular account of the spirited conduct of Lieut. Colonel Laurens, when set by Congress as a Special Minister to France, in the year 1781. Of its authenticity there can be no doubt. It was received by me in 1822, from my friend Major Wm. Jackson, of Philadelphia, who had been appointed at the request of the Lieutenant Colonel, Secretary of the Mission. It is due to Maj. Jackson, to give the statement in his own interesting and appropriate language.

What do we know about Major William Jackson (1759-1828)? He grew up in South Carolina. In early 1781, he was named secretary to John Laurens, whose mission was to persuade King Louis XVI to send yet more money and more soldiers in support of the American cause. Garden's *Anecdotes* includes Jackson's vivid account of Laurens's interactions with Louis XVI, his ministers, and Benjamin Franklin.

John Laurens returned to the United States in mid-1781, in time to join the Continental Army at the Siege of Yorktown. There he negotiated the Articles of Capitulation on behalf of the Americans. In the manuscript printed in the *Anecdotes,* Jackson recounts the dialogue between Laurens and Ross regarding the "harsh article" by which the British were denied the honors of war (quoted in Chapter 36). Then Jackson concludes his section on Yorktown:

> The result [of the negotiations]was conformed to this just retribution. The British army marched out with colours cased, and drums beating a British or a German march. The march they chose was—"The world turned up side down." (More here)

After returning from the embassy to France, Jackson served as assistant secretary of War (1782-1783), and in 1787 as secretary to the

Constitutional Convention. (He was nominated for the post by Alexander Hamilton!) From 1789 to 1790, he was one of George Washington's secretaries.

In short: Jackson was a prominent figure, and he was still alive in 1828, when the *Anecdotes* appeared. He was not a cipher to whom Garden would have attributed a fake manuscript chock full of interesting stories.

PROBLEMS WITH JACKSON'S ACCOUNT

But ... there are reasons to look askance at Jackson's account. The most notable is that *Jackson was not at Yorktown.* He didn't return to America until February 1782, four months after the surrender. He may well have had a catch-up session with Laurens soon after that: they were friends and fellow South Carolinians. Laurens wasn't killed in a skirmish until August 1782. So yes, Jackson might have gotten his details about Yorktown from an eyewitness. But he doesn't say he's recording a second-hand story, which in my mind counts against him. It's possible he's giving an accurate account, but not at all certain.

Aside from the fact that Jackson wasn't an eyewitness at Yorktown, there's another problem. Jackson's account wasn't published until 47 years after Yorktown, and Jackson was apparently not the most meticulous of notekeepers. In 1787 he lobbied to be appointed secretary of the Constitutional Convention. When John Quincy Adams was collecting information on the Convention years later, he huffed that Jackson's notes were "no better than the daily minutes from which the regular Journal ought to have been but never was made out" (quoted in Schrader, p. 186).

So: Jackson is the only source for this story; he was not an eyewitness at Yorktown; he didn't report the story until some 40 years after the event; and his note-keeping abilities weren't great.

Arthur Schrader, who spent decades researching 18th-century American music, points out several other problems with Jackson's statement that "The march they chose was 'The world turned up side down'."

1. Eighteenth-century military marches were short. It must have taken several hours for thousands of British soldiers to march out of Yorktown and surrender their arms. It's unlikely that only one tune was played during all that time.

2. Music for rank-and-file soldiers was provided by a fife and drum for each company within a regiment. It's unlikely that all of those fifers and drummers were playing a single song.

3. "The World Turned Upside Down" was not a recognized song in the late 18th century. In popular music, it was typical for many different texts to be set to a single familiar piece of music. For example: the poem "The Defence of Fort McHenry" (a.k.a. "The Star-Spangled Banner") was written by Francis Scott Key in 1814 to be sung to a tune that was widely familiar under the name "To Anacreon in Heaven." Only if a new text became extraordinarily popular did it bump the old lyrics, as the "Star-Spangled Banner" bumped "To Anacreon". Schrader argues that there is no evidence for such an association of text with tune for the 1646 poem "The World Turned Upside Down."

    > So far as we know, no eighteenth-century Briton talked or wrote about a "World Turned Upside Down" tune; no one printed it into a book, magazine, or sheet music; no Briton copied it into a manuscript or named it as the tune for a topical text; and no one pirated it. Therefore, even if there was a "World Turned Upside Down" tune in eighteenth-century Britain, it was not well enough known to be "recognized" at Yorktown … (Schrader p. 195)

4. For the British to play "The World Turned Upside Down" would have required, notes Schrader, "a self-deprecating humor the British did not otherwise display at Yorktown" (p. 193). True: in none of the eyewitness accounts do the British seem to be regarding their defeat with irony or amusement.

I'm inclined to agree with Schrader that the story of "The World Turned Upside Down" being played at Yorktown is apocryphal, and that its widespread acceptance is due to the story being "too good to reject and too trivial to bother checking out" (Schrader p. 184).

SOURCES

• Schrader, Arthur. "'The World Turned Upside Down': A Yorktown March, or Music to Surrender By." *American Music,* 16:2 (1998), 180-216. Retrieved from http://www.jstor.org/stable/3052564 doi:1

• On Major William Jackson, see Harry M. Ward. "Jackson, William," in American National Biography Online (Access Date: Fri Sep 30 2016), and Charles W. Littell, "Major William Jackson, Secretary of the Federal Convention," *Pennsylvania Magazine of History and Biography* 2 (1878): 353-69. The earliest excerpt from Jackson's narrative that I've yet seen is in the *American Review,* vol. I (1827), pp. 424-6. It includes only the description of the mission to France, and is attributed to "the respectable secretary of the mission, yet alive, in Philadelphia."

• Background: Joseph L. Trudeau, "Music In The Continental Army" (Masters thesis 2014).

• In a post from 2015, "*Hamilton* Turns the World Upside Down," Janet McKinney (a music archivist at the Library of Congress) notes that the Library of Congress has a file on "The World Turned Upside Down" that has been built up by librarians over the course of fifty years. The earliest reference any of them has found to "The World Turned Upside Down" being played at Yorktown is Garden's 1828 *Anecdotes.*

MORE

• Hamilton consulted William Jackson after Hamilton was accused of speculating with Treasury funds: this eventually resulted in the Reynolds Pamphlet: see Chapter 63C.

CHAPTER 39A

Hamilton Back in New York, 1781-1782

In October 1781, immediately after the British surrendered at York-town, Hamilton set off on the three-week trip to Albany, arriving there in November. By December 29, 1781, he was writing to his friend Major Nicholas Fish to chide him about his love life:

> I am sorry you seem to have broken your resolution so finally respecting a certain matter; as since I have been here, I have had reason to believe you were mistaken in your original suspicions. Several officers have reported here that you have openly professed to renounce the connexion—I imagine it has reached the family and I am told Miss is in great distress. 'Tis probable by this time your doubts are removed. Mr. G went lately into the Jerseys. I conjecture his errand was to see you; and I dare say you will understand each other. At all events you must be cautious in this matter, or your character will run some risk, and you are sensible how injurious it might be to have the reputation of levity in a delicate point. The Girls [Angelica, Peggy, Eliza?] have got it among them that this is not your first infidelity.

The Schuyler Mansion in Albany. Photo: Matt Wade Photography / Wikipedia.

And at the end:

> I have been very sick—I am still alternately in and out of
> bed. How are you after your Southern fatigues? (More here)

It's a sign of how ill he was that Hamilton—who was an energetic
correspondent—wrote so few lengthy letters in the last two months
of 1781. The Founders Archives has only one long letter, written in
response to one from the Vicomte de Noailles, regarding Cornwallis:

> Without speaking of a cave [see Chapter 37, Trabue's
> description], and those other reports so injurious to Lord
> Cornwallis, which have been circulated only to flatter those
> weak minds who take pleasure in lessening the real merit
> of an enemy, I chuse rather to find the cause of our victory
> in the superior number of good and regular troops, in the
> uninterrupted harmony of the two nations [France and the
> United States], and their equal desire to be celebrated in
> the annals of history, for an ardent love of great and heroic
> actions. ...
>
> We have seen a General in America unjustly accus'd; but
> where shall we find an instance in history that a General
> has been praised after a defeat, without deserving it. I have
> seen that army so haughty in its success; not an emotion
> of the soldiers escap'd me; and I observed every sign of
> mortification with pleasure. I insinuated myself into their
> confidence, but could not hear a word to the prejudice of
> Lord Cornwallis. The soldiers were the echo of their officers
> ... (More here)

Hamilton was back in New York, but living in Albany at the Schuyler
family mansion rather than in Manhattan, which was still occupied by
the British. News of Cornwallis's surrender reached London in November 1781 ("Oh God ! it is all over!": see end of Chapter 37), but
peace negotiations didn't begin until the resignation of Lord North
as prime minister in March 1782. The British finally evacuated New
York City in November 1783.

HAMILTON RESIGNS FROM ACTIVE MILITARY SERVICE

In January 1782, Secretary of War Benjamin Lincoln put Hamilton on
the list of officers to be retained in the army, because of his "superi-
or abilities & knowledge" (see here, n. 3). But Hamilton apparently decided to cut his losses with the military. He wrote to General

Washington on March 1, stating that he wished to keep his rank but renounce claims to pay—although of course he would be available should his country need him. I suspect his unusually convoluted prose is a reflection of how annoyed he got merely from thinking about how long it took him to get a command in 1781. (See Chapter 30.)

> Sir,
>
> Your Excellency will, I am persuaded, readily admit the force of this sentiment, that though it is the duty of a good citizen to devote his services to the public, when it has occasion for them, he cannot with propriety, or delicacy to himself, obtrude them, when it either has, or appears to have none. The difficulties I experienced last campaign in obtaining a command will not suffer me to make any further application on that head.
>
> As I have many reasons to consider my being employed hereafter in a precarious light, the bare possibility of rendering an equivalent will not justify to my scruples the receiving any future emoluments from my commission. I therefore renounce from this time all claim to the compensations attached to my military station during the war or after it. But I have motives which will not permit me to resolve on a total resignation. I sincerely hope a prosperous train of affairs may continue to make it no inconvenience to decline the services of persons, whose zeal, in worse times, was found not altogether useless; but as the most promising appearances are often reversed by unforeseen disasters, and as unfortunate events may again make the same zeal of some value, I am unwilling to put it out of my power to renew my exertions in the common cause, in the line, in which I have hitherto acted. I shall accordingly retain my rank while I am permitted to do it, and take this opportunity to declare, that I shall be at all times ready to obey the call of the public, in any capacity civil, or military (consistent with what I owe to myself) in which there may be a prospect of my contributing to the final attainment of the object for which I embarked in the service.
>
> I have the honor to be   very Respectfully,
> Yr. Excellency's   Most Obedient servant
>   A Hamilton (More here)

ALEXANDER AND ELIZA'S FIRST CHILD

In a letter written shortly afterward to Richard Kidder Meade, a fellow former aide-de-camp, he is his usual charming self—delighted to be a father, and matchmaking his son Philip with Meade's new-born daughter.

> An half hour since brought me the pleasure of your letter of December last. It went to Albany and came from thence to this place [Philadelphia]. I heartily felicitate you on the birth of your daughter. I can well conceive your happiness upon that occasion, by that which I feel in a similar one.
>
> Indeed the sensations of a tender father of the child, of a beloved mother can only be conceived by those who have experienced them.
>
> Your heart, my Meade, is peculiarly formed for enjoyments of this kind, you have every right to be a happy husband, a happy father, you have every prospect of being so. I hope your felicity may never be interrupted.
>
> You cannot imagine how entirely domestic I am growing. I lose all taste for the pursuits of ambition, I sigh for nothing but the company of my wife and my baby. The ties of duty alone or imagined duty keep me from renouncing public life altogether. It is however probable I may not be any longer actively engaged in it.
>
> I have explained to you the difficulties which I met with in obtaining a command last campaign. I thought it incompatible with the delicacy due to myself to make any application this [1782] campaign. I have expressed this Sentiment in a letter to the General and retaining my rank only, have relinquished the emoluments of my commission, declaring myself notwithstanding ready at all times to obey the calls of the Public. I do not expect to hear any of these unless the State of our Affairs, should change for the worse and lest by any unforeseen accident that should happen, I choose to keep myself in a situation again to contribute my aid. This prevents a total resignation.
>
> You were right in supposing I neglected to prepare what I promised you at Philadelphia. The truth is, I was in such a hurry to get home that I could think of nothing else. As I set out tomorrow morning for Albany, I cannot from this place send you the matter you wish.

Imagine my Dear Friend what pleasure it must give Eliza & myself to know that Mrs. Meade interests herself in us, without a personal acquaintance we have been long attached to her. My visit at [Mrs. Meade's uncle in Philadelphia?] Mr. Fitzhughs confirmed my partiality. Betsy is so fond of your family that she proposes to form a match between her Boy & your girl provided you will engage to make the latter as amiable as her mother.

Truly My Dear Meade, I often regret that fortune has cast our residence at such a distance from each other. [Meade lived in Virginia.] It would be a serious addition to my happiness if we lived where I could see you every day but fate has determined it otherwise. I am a little hurried & can only request in addition that you will present me most affectionately to Mrs. Meade & believe me to be with the warmest & most unalterable friendship

Yrs   A Hamilton (March 1782; more here)

Next up: Alexander studies for the bar.

CHAPTER 39B
Yorktown, 235 Years Ago:
"Here Cannons Flash, Bombs Glance,
and Bullets Fly"

In honor of the 235th anniversary of the British surrender at Yorktown, here's a poem mocking Cornwallis that was originally published in Philadelphia on October 11, 1781. At that point, the American and French allies had been besieging Yorktown for about two weeks. At the end of the text, I've identified the names and terms that are underlined—but you can get the gist without knowing them.

"An Epistle from Lord Cornwallis to Sir Henry Clinton"

From clouds of smoke, and flames that round me glow,
To you, dear Clinton, I disclose my woe;
Here cannons flash, bombs glance, and bullets fly;
Not Satan's self endures such misery.
Was I fore-doomed, like **Korah**, to expire,
Hurl'd to perdition in a blaze of fire?
With these blue flames can mortal man contend?
What arms can aid me, or what walls defend?
Even to these gates last night a phantom strode,
And trailed me, trembling, to his dark abode;
Aghast I stood, struck motionless and dumb,
Seized with the horrors of the world to come.
Were but my power as might as my rage,
Far different battles would Cornwallis wage;
Beneath his sword yon threatening hosts should groan,
The earth should quake with thunders all his own;
O crocodile! had I thy flinty hide,
Swords to defy, and glance thy balls aside,
By my own powers would I rout the foe,
With my own javelin would I work their woe;
But fate's averse, and heaven's supreme decree
Hell's serpent formed more excellent than me.

Has heaven in secret, for some crime, decreed,
That I should suffer and my soldiers bleed?
Or is it by the jealous skies concealed,
That I must bend, and they ignobly yield?
Ah! no,—the thought o'erwhelms my soul with grief, –
Come, bold **Sir Harry**, come to my relief;
Come thou, brave man, whom rebel's tombstones call
But Briton's graves,—come **Digby**, devil and all;
Come friendly **William**, with thy potent aid,
Can George's blood by Frenchmen be dismayed?
From a King's brother once Scots rebels run,
And shall not these be routed by a son?
Come with your ships to this disastrous shore,
Come, or I sink,—and sink to rise no more;
By every motive that can sway the brave,
Haste, and my feeble, fainting army save;
Come, and lost empire o'er the deep regain,
Chastise these upstarts that usurp the main;
I see their first rates to the charge advance,
I see lost **Iris** wears the flags of France;
There a strict rule the wakeful Frenchman keeps;
There, undisturbed by dogs, **Lord Rawdon** sleeps!
Tir'd with long acting on this bloody stage,
Sick of the follies, of a wrangling age, –
Come with your fleet, and help me to retire
To Britain's coast, the land of my desire, –
For me the foe their certain captive deem,
And every school-boy takes me for his theme, –
Long, much too long, has this hard service tryed,
Bespattered still, bedevil'd and bely'd,
With the first chance that favoring fortune sends
I'll fly, converted, from this land of fiends;
Then, like **Burgoyne**, as fortunate at least,
Slip on the surplice, and be dubbed a priest.

NOTES

Korah: rebelled against Moses; God smote him and 249 accomplices with fire, then caused the earth to swallow up their allies and plague to strike 14,700 others who objected to Korah's fate. See Numbers 16:1-41.

Sir Harry: Henry Clinton, commander-in-chief of the British in North America. Since September, he had been promising to sail to Virginia to relieve Cornwallis. The fleet set sail on October 19, and arrived five days after Cornwallis's surrender.

Digby: Admiral Robert Digby, commander of the British fleet in North America

William: Prince William Henry, Duke of Gloucester and Edinburgh, King George III's younger brother; he arrived in New York with Digby in September 1781. This anonymous author refers to him as George III's son, as does the Comte de Rochambeau (Chapter 37).

Iris: messenger of the Greek gods; associated with victory

Lord Rawdon: Francis Rawdon (later 1st Marquess of Hastings). After Cornwallis marched north to Virginia earlier in 1781, Rawdon was in charge of British forces in the Deep South. He resigned due to illness in July 1781, and was captured by De Grasse's fleet on his way back to Britain. No clue what "undisturbed by dogs" refers to.

Burgoyne: General John Burgoyne. At Saratoga on October 17, 1777, he surrendered 5,800 British troops to the Americans under General Horatio Gates. It was the greatest American victory in the war to date. As far as I can tell, he did *not* become a priest.

MORE

• This poem was originally published in *The Philadelphia Freemason's Journal,* October 11, 1781. It was reprinted in <u>Edwin Martin Stone,</u> *Our French allies: Rochambeau and his army, Lafayette and his devotion, D'Estaing, De Ternay, Barras, De Grasse, and their fleets, in the great war of the American Revolution, from 1778 to 1782, including military operations in Rhode Island, the surrender of Yorktown, sketches of French and American officers, and incidents of social life in Newport, Providence, and elsewhere; with numerous illustrations.* (Providence, 1884).

CHAPTER 40

Hamilton Studies Law, 1782

By late December 1781, Alexander Hamilton was recovering from the Yorktown campaign at the Schuyler family mansion in Albany—still so exhausted that he hardly wrote any letters (see Chapter 39A). If you accept 1757 as his year of birth, he turned 25 on January 11, 1782. Eleven days later, his son Philip was born. Hamilton wrote to Richard Kidder Meade in early March:

> You cannot imagine how entirely domestic I am growing. I lose all taste for the pursuits of ambition, I sigh for nothing but the company of my wife and my baby. (More here)

That same month, the New York State legislature kicked him into action.

LEGAL TRAINING IN THE EIGHTEENTH CENTURY

In the eighteenth century, an aspiring lawyer in New York State would have become an apprentice in a law office. There he would have copied a variety of legal documents, read legal treatises, and assisted the lawyer with increasingly more complicated tasks. In the 1760s, the clerkship in New York lasted five years. In 1778, the New York State Supreme Court set the requirement at three years, to be followed by a bar examination. (Julius Goebel, Jr., introduction to *Practical Proceedings in the Supreme Court of the State of New York*, pp. 10-12: henceforth *PP*)

On January 18, 1782, the New York State legislature passed a law aimed at would-be lawyers who had served in the military: "such young gentlemen who had directed their studies to the profession of the law but upon the breaking out of the present war had entered the army" (*PP* p. xii). These men would be allowed to take the bar exam without serving a three-year clerkship—but *only* until April 30, 1782. Hamilton submitted a petition for a six-month extension, and got to work. (Per Goebel in *PP*, citing 3 *PAH* 82; documents not located in Founders Archives.)

Hamilton was not, in fact, among those who had "directed their studies to the profession of the law" before the Revolution. King's College did not offer a course in law. But Hamilton's writings during the Revolutionary War show that he had read many works on the law of nations (Goebel, *PP* p. 13). So his main task in early 1782 was to become familiar with New York State's convoluted laws: a mish-mash of a vast body of English precedents with an array of local statutes and court rulings.

HAMILTON'S *PRACTICAL PROCEEDINGS*

As part of his self-designed crash course for the bar exam, Hamilton wrote out his own handbook for legal studies. The original is lost, but two early manuscript copies survive.

How, you ask, do we know this is Hamilton's work?

1. Hamilton's friend Robert Troup, another aspiring lawyer, recalled (in the 1820s): "The General [Hamilton] invited me to spend the ensuing summer with him, in his family, with the double view of pursuing my legal studies, and instructing him in the practice. I accepted the General's invitation, and domesticated myself with him for three months; during which period, he acquired a thorough knowledge of the practice, and wrote a Treatise on it; which served as an instructive grammar to future students, and has been the ground work of subsequent practical treatises by others on a larger scale." (Nathan Schachner, "Alexander Hamilton Viewed by His Friends: The Narratives of Robert Troup and Hercules Mulligan," *The William and Mary Quartery* 4:2 [April 1947], p. 215.) Hamilton's son, John Church Hamilton, quoted Troup and added, in 1834: "There are men, now living, who copied this manual as their guide." (J.C. Hamilton, *Life of Hamilton*, 1834; in the 1840 edition, see v. I, p. 398, note.)

2. *Practical Proceedings* exists in at least two manuscript copies. The earliest one, probably copied by Abraham Van Vechten at Albany during the 1780s, has "Hamilton's Proceedings" written in manuscript on the back cover, and "by Alex. Hamilton" on the first page. The latest statute referred to in its text dates to 1781. That fits the time Hamilton was studying for the bar.

3. William <u>Wyche's</u> *Supreme Court Practice*, 1794, was the first law handbook printed in New York State. In its preface, Wyche refers to "Some practical sketches in manuscript, one passing under the name of a personage of high respectability" (quoted in

Goebel, *PP* p. 5). Hamilton, as secretary of the Treasury, would certainly qualify.

4. *Practical Proceedings* appears to be the work of a novice at the law. The writer often makes conjectures rather than statements: for example, "I suppose the rule is ..." (*PP* p. 30), "The most accurate Rule with respect to holding the Defendant to special Bail seems to be ..." (*PP* p. 43). Goebel, in his introduction to the first printed edition of *Practical Proceedings,* states: "Thus, by circumstances, Hamilton's manual was a thing of his own making. It bears all the earmarks of student work, not that of a practitioner seasoned in New York law. Indeed, the cursory fashion in which Hamilton deals with some of the thirty-eight topics into which the work is divided bears a striking resemblance to the sort of synthesis which a law student might devise today if interested in procedural aspects of law for a particular examination. Furthermore, the lack of any orderly sequence in the arrangement of the topics suggests that the writing on a particular subject was done after reading some book and searching out cases or statutes, and the heading next following might well derive from a second source." (*PP* p. 16)

I'm withholding judgment on that "lack of orderly sequence." By 1782, Hamilton had a reputation as a writer. If he had wanted this work to appear in print, he would have had no problem finding a publisher. Since he didn't publish *Practical Proceedings,* we don't know to what extent he edited it, and what organization he would have used. He might have just shared with Vechten or someone else a pile of notes on separate pages.

Practical Proceedings: first page of the Vechten manuscript.

So what's in *Practical Proceedings*? The first part has short summaries of actions such as bail, warrants of attorneys, *profert in curia, habeas corpus,* and *certoriari.* The second part is a series of "exhibits," which includes copies of standard forms used by lawyers at this period: *capias, latitat, distringas,* plea of *nil debet,* and more. Goebel states that this two-part arrangement makes *Practical Proceedings* "a link between old ways of remembrancing and the new era of the printed practice books, of which Wyche's [1794] work was the first" (*PP* p. 10).

I don't recommend you run out and buy a copy of *Practical Proceedings,* even if you adore Alexander Hamilton. Unless the history of law is your specialty, *PP* will make your eyes roll. Here's a sample passage, under the heading "Judgment & Execution":

> If the Party has Confessed Judgment with a <u>cessat Executio</u> entered on the Roll, no *Sci: fa:* will be necessary, and the Court will Oblige the Party to Confirm to the Record, and will compel him to make Restitution, if Contrary thereto he takes out Execution, before the *Cassat* is expired: but if there be an agreement for a Stay of Execution extraneous to the Record, the Court will take no Notice of it. (*PP* pp. 68-69)

In the midst of all those *profert in curia, habeas corpus,* and *capias* ... yes, there is something uniquely Hamiltonian in the *Practical Proceedings.* But it's in the concept and the methodology rather than the content. Hamilton is a big-picture guy, a forest-and-trees guy, a man who can accurately remember a vast amount of detail, but who always pulls back to set it in a broader context: national, international, political, ethical, or historical. We've seen that in the *Vindication,* 1774 (Chapter 14), the *Continentalist* essays of 1781 (Chapter 31), and in the long letter on public finances that he sent to Robert <u>Morris</u> in April 1781. In *Practical Proceedings,* he compares present to past laws:

> It has been held till lately, that no Person can be made Defendant but he who was, or had at the Time been in Possession ... but this in a late Case reported in Burrows seems to have been over ruled ... (*PP* p. 102)

He also considers the overall purpose of the law as well as specific laws:

> [T]he Court ... having lately acquired a more liberal Cast begin to have some faint Idea that the end of Suits at Law is

to Investigate the Merits of the Cause, and not to entangle in
the Nets of technical Terms. (*PP* p. 49)

Rather than memorizing forms and actions by rote, Hamilton is trying
to integrate his knowledge so that it becomes a logical whole—and
hence easier to remember. It's an uncommon breadth of vision for a
25-year-old. (Thanks to lawyer Pooja Nair of It's Hamiltime for her
feedback on my comments on Hamilton's approach to studying law,
and to Rand Scholet of the Alexander Hamilton Awareness Society for
introducing me to Pooja.)

MORRIS ASKS HAMILTON TO BE TAX RECEIVER FOR NEW YORK STATE

Hamilton's letter to George Washington of March 1, 1782, in which he
kept his military rank but refused further pay (see Chapter 39), must
have been spurred partly by Hamilton's sudden need to immerse himself in legal studies. He said as much a few months later in a letter to
Robert Morris, U.S. superintendent of Finance. Morris had asked if
Hamilton would accept the position of receiver of taxes for New York
State. Here's Hamilton's response (May 18, 1782):

> My military situation has indeed become so negative that I
> have no motive to continue in it; and if my services could
> be of importance to the public in any civil line I should
> chearfully obey its command. But the plan which I have
> marked out to myself is the profession of the law; and I am
> now engaged in a course of studies for that purpose. Time is
> so precious to me that I could not put myself in the way of
> any interruptions unless for an object of consequence to the
> public or to myself. The present [tax receiver position] is not
> of this nature. (More here)

HAMILTON PRACTICES LAW

In July 1782, Hamilton was admitted to the bar as an attorney qualified
to practice before the Supreme Court of the State of New York. Three
months later he was admitted as counsel. By October 1783, he was
qualified as a solicitor and counsel in Chancery (Goebels in *PP*, p. 13,
citing 2 *PAH* 684, 3 *PAH* 122 and 3 *PAH* 189).

I will chearfully admit that I don't grasp the distinctions between
those levels: anyone want to enlighten me? (DuranteDianne@gmail.
com).

MORE

• The manuscript of the *Practical Proceedings* published in 2004 was owned by the *New York Law Journal.* In 2014, they auctioned it off via Doyle Galleries for a whopping $43,750. Details here. The hardcover of *Practical Proceedings* is listed on Amazon at $1,941.21. I'll be happy to sell you my copy (slight wear to d.j., a few light pencil annotations in margin) for a mere $1,841.21 ... Or you could try ViaLibri.

• And you thought our jury duty was inconvenient. From *Practical Proceedings:* "When the Jurors are sworn they must have no Conversation or Intercourse with any Person whatever, they must not leave the Bar without Leave of the Court or without the Attendance of a Constable. When they Leave the Bar they must have Communication with no one except to say whether they have or have not agreed upon their Verdict; they may Neither eat nor drink nor have Fire or Candle without Leave of the Court. If they eat or drink at their own Expence this is fineable; If at the Expence of the Party for whom they find it vitiates their Verdict. If they Cast Lots or throw Dice or by any other Hazard determine the Cause, the Verdict is bad." (*PP* pp. 89-90).

CHAPTER 41

The State of the Union after Yorktown, 1782

In early 1782, the Siege of Yorktown was over, but the British government had not yet admitted defeat. Without hindsight, it was impossible
to know whether or not the Revolutionary War would continue. How
do you plan your life when the state of your nation is in such flux?

HAMILTON ON THE STATE OF THE NATION

In a long letter written during the spring of 1782 to the Vicomte de
Noailles, who had served with him at Yorktown, Hamilton gave an
overview of the United States six months after Cornwallis's surrender—including how the government established by the Articles of
Confederation was faring.

> The period since you left us has been too barren of events to
> enable me to impart any thing worth attention. The enemy
> continues in possession of Charleston and Savannah ...
> Many are sanguine in believing that all the southern posts
> will be evacuated, and that a fleet of transports is actually
> gone to bring the garrisons away; for my part, I have doubts
> upon the subject. [NOTE: The British evacuated Savannah
> in July 1782 and Charleston in December 1782.] My politics
> are, that while the present [British] ministry can maintain
> their seats and procure supplies, they will prosecute the
> war on the mere chance of events; and that while this is the
> plan, they will not evacuate posts so essential as points of
> departure, from whence, on any favourable turn of affairs,
> to renew their attack on our most vulnerable side; nor would
> they relinquish objects that would be so useful to them,
> should the worst happen in a final negotiation.
>
> [General Henry] Clinton, it is said, is cutting a canal
> across New-York island, through the low ground about a mile
> and a half from the city. This will be an additional obstacle;
> but if we have otherwise the necessary means to operate, it

will not be an insurmountable one. I do not hear that he is constructing any other new works of consequence. To you who are so thoroughly acquainted with the military posture of things in this country, I need not say that the activity of the next campaign must absolutely depend on effectual succours from France. I am convinced we shall have a powerful advocate in you. La Fayette, we know, will bring the whole house with him if he can.

There has been no material change in our internal situation since you left us [in late December 1781]. The capital successes we have had, have served rather to increase the hopes than the exertions of the particular states. But in one respect we are in a mending way. Our financier [Robert Morris] has hitherto conducted himself with great ability, has acquired an entire personal confidence, revived in some measure the public credit, and is conciliating fast the support of the moneyed men.

His operations have hitherto hinged chiefly on the seasonable aids from your country; but he is urging the establishment of permanent funds among ourselves; and though, from the nature and temper of our governments, his applications will meet with a dilatory compliance, it is to be hoped they will by degrees succeed. The institution of a bank has been very serviceable to him. The commercial interest, finding great advantages in it, and anticipating much greater, is disposed to promote the plan; and nothing but moderate funds, permanently pledged for the security of lenders, is wanting to make it an engine of the most extensive and solid utility.

By the last advices, there is reason to believe the delinquent states will shortly comply with the requisition of congress for a duty on our imports. This will be a great resource to Mr. Morris, but it will not alone be sufficient.

Upon the whole, however, if the war continues another year, it will be necessary that congress should again recur to the generosity of France for pecuniary assistance. The plans of the financier cannot be so matured as to enable us by any possibility to dispense with this; and if he should fail for want of support, we must replunge into that confusion and distress which had like to have proved fatal to us, and out of which we are slowly emerging. The cure in a relapse would be infinitely more difficult than ever. (More here)

FINANCIAL STATUS OF THE UNITED STATES

When we left Hamilton in Chapter 40, he had decided to study law, and was designing a crash course for himself. In July 1782, he passed the bar. But being Alexander, he also had several other irons in the fire.

Between May 1781, when he resigned from Washington's staff, and September 1781, when he camped out with the army at Yorktown, Hamilton published four issues of *The Continentalist* (see Chapter 31). In them he argued in favor of a strong central government. On April 18 and July 4, 1782, the final two issues appeared, introduced by a wry note:

> The succeeding numbers of the Continentalist were written last fall, but accidentally got out of the possession of the writer. He has lately recovered them, and he gives them to the public more to finish the development of his plan, than from any hope that the temper of the times will adopt his ideas. (Here, n. 1)

In *Continentalist* no. 5, Hamilton contended that the nation must preserve its balance of trade. His opening salvo berated those who believe government has no part in commerce:

> There are some, who maintain, that trade will regulate itself, and is not to be benefitted by the encouragements, or restraints of government. Such persons will imagine, that there is no need of a common directing power. This is one of those wild speculative paradoxes, which have grown into credit among us, contrary to the uniform practice and sense of the most enlightened nations. Contradicted by the numerous institutions and laws, that exist every where for the benefit of trade, by the pains taken to cultivate particular branches and to discourage others, by the known advantages derived from those measures, and by the palpable evils that would attend their discontinuance—it must be rejected by every man acquainted with commercial history. Commerce, like other things, has its fixed principles, according to which it must be regulated; if these are understood and observed, it will be promoted by the attention of government, if

unknown, or violated, it will be injured—but it is the same with every other part of administration.

> To preserve the ballance of trade in favour of a nation ought to be a leading aim of its policy. (More here)

NOTE: This is straight mercantilist theory, which assumes wealth is a zero-sum game, and that a nation must have a favorable balance of trade in order to survive and prosper. To justify laissez-faire capitalism at its root, one needs arguments that depend on philosophy, not economics: and the philosophy wasn't worked out until quite a long time after 1782. (More on Hamilton and laissez-faire in Chapter 62).

In *Continentalist* no. 5, Hamilton goes on to justify his argument for government regulation of trade with examples of how England, France, and the Dutch governments encouraged trade. Then he explains why the individual states in America cannot be expected to do the same. In *Continentalist* no. 6, Hamilton discusses the different types of tax (property, poll, customs). He ends the series with a swipe at the states and their petty squabbling:

> There is something noble and magnificent in the perspective of a great Fœderal Republic, closely linked in the pursuit of a common interest, tranquil and prosperous at home, respectable abroad; but there is something proportionably diminutive and contemptible in the prospect of a number of petty states, with the appearance only of union, jarring, jealous and perverse, without any determined direction, fluctuating and unhappy at home, weak and insignificant by their dissentions, in the eyes of other nations. Happy America! if those, to whom thou hast intrusted the guardianship of thy infancy, know how to provide for thy future repose; but miserable and undone, if their negligence or ignorance permits the spirit of discord to erect her banners on the ruins of thy tranquillity! (More here)

HAMILTON'S FIRST POLITICAL POST: TAX RECEIVER FOR NEW YORK STATE

But wait: there's more. While Hamilton studied for the bar, kept up his correspondence, and submitted the last two *Continentalist* essays for publication, he was also taking on his first civilian job in government. On May 18, 1782, he turned down an offer from Robert Morris (the U.S. Superintendent of Finances) to become tax receiver for New

York State. The tax receiver (a position created by Morris) was to be responsible for collecting taxes and turning over the federal government's share. His pay would be a small percentage of tax revenues.

In the letter below, notice that in the midst of his frenetic legal studies, Hamilton has somehow got his hands on the approximate amount of taxes due from New York to the federal government. He's also assessed the likelihood that the taxes will be paid.

And by the way ... *this is 1782*. There is no Internet, no Express Mail, no telephone; no planes, trains, cars. To get this information, Hamilton had to either drop his legal studies and gallop off to Poughkeepsie in hopes of digging up the information on his own—or he had to reach out to the sort of prominent men who might know it. Based on his considerable correspondence, I suspect that Hamilton had spent a lot of time building such relationships, so that when he asked questions, he got prompt replies.

> My military situation has indeed become so negative that I have no motive to continue in it; and if my services could be of importance to the public in any civil line I should chearfully obey its command. But the plan which I have marked out to myself is the profession of the law; and I am now engaged in a course of studies for that purpose. Time is so precious to me that I could not put myself in the way of any interruptions unless for an object of consequence to the public or to myself. The present is not of this nature. Such are the circumstances of this state, the benefit arising from the office you propose would not during the war exceed yearly one hundred pounds; for unfortunately, I am persuaded it will not pay annually into the Continental treasury above forty thousand pounds; and on a peace establishment this will not be for sometime to come much more than doubled. You will perceive Sir that an engagement of this kind does not correspond with my views and does not afford a sufficient inducement to relinquish them.
>
> I am not the less sensible to the obliging motives which dictated the offer, and it will be an additional one to that respect and esteem with which I have the honor to be very truly Sir   Yr. most Obed & humble servant (More here)

Morris apparently wanted Hamilton in the tax-receiver position enough to make another offer. He promised Hamilton not .25% of

Portrait of Robert Morris by Robert Edge Pine, ca. 1785

taxes collected, but .25% of taxes *due*. Hamilton replied on June 17, 1782 (about a month before he took the bar):

> The explanation you give of your intention in your late offer makes it an object that will fully compensate for the time it will deduct from my other occupations. In accepting it I have only one scruple, arising from a doubt whether the service I can render in the present state of things will be an equivalent for the compensation. The whole system (if it may be so called) of taxation in this state is radically vicious, burthensome to the people and unproductive to government. As the matter now stands there seems to be little for a Continental Receiver to do. The whole business appears to be thrown into the hands of the County treasurers. ... There is only one way in which I can imagine a prospect of being materially useful that is in seconding your applications to the State. In popular assemblies much may sometimes be brought about by personal discussions, by entering into details and combating objections as they rise. If it should at any time be thought adviseable by you to empower me to act in this capacity, I shall be happy to do every thing that depends on me to effectuate your views. ...
>
> It is of primary moment to me as soon as possible to take my station in the law, and on this consideration I am pressing to qualify myself for admission the next term which will be the latter end of July. After this if you should

think an interview with me necessary I will wait upon you in Philadelphia. In the mean time I shall be happy to receive your instructions, and shall direct my attention more particularly to acquiring whatever information may be useful to my future operations. ... A meeting of the Legislature is summoned early in the next month [July 1782] at which, if I previously receive your orders, it may be possible to put matters in train. (More here)

By the end of July—the same month he passed the bar—Hamilton had accepted the position of tax receiver for New York State, and had begun operating with the same ferocious efficiency he displayed on Washington's staff. He wrote to Gerard Bancker, treasurer of the state of New York, asking for details on the taxes New York owed to the federal government (here). He followed up with a letter to Governor George Clinton asking for his cooperation regarding taxes, using a combination of flattery and shame.

Your Excellency must have been too sensible of the necessity of enabling the Director of the Finance of the United States to form a just judgment of the true state of our affairs to have omitted any measure in your power to procure the fullest information on the several matters submitted to you and I am persuaded the business is in such a train that little will be left for me to do. (More here)

He wrote to the county treasurers of New York State in much the same vein on August 5, 1782:

When I assure you I want this information for an important purpose I doubt not you will forward it to me as speedily as it can be prepared and with as much accuracy as circumstances will permit ... (More here)

Meanwhile, on August 1, 1782, Hamilton (as "Receiver of Continental Taxes for the State of New-York") published a statement in the *New-York Packet* that he had received no monies from New York State. Perhaps he hoped to shame the state's politicians into action.

CORRUPTION IN NEW YORK

On August 13, 1782, barely three months after he began to consider the position of tax receiver and a only few weeks after he assumed the post, Hamilton sent Morris a 4,000-word "full view of the situation and temper of this state." He estimated the damage to New York State's economy from the war:

> It will not be difficult to conceive this, when we consider, that five out of the fourteen counties of which the state was composed, including the capital, are in the hands of the enemy—that two and part of a third have revolted—two others have been desolated, the greater part, by the ravages of the enemy and of our own troops—and the remaining four have more or less suffered partial injuries from the same causes. Adding the fragments of some to repair the losses of others, the efficient property, strength and force of the state will consist in little more than four counties.

New York, says Hamilton, made great expenditures during the war (sometimes "from want of judgment, at others from necessity"), and the resultant taxes have "both distressed and disgusted the people." Its frontier is in danger of attack by Indians and British. With New York City under enemy control, there is no foreign trade. The balance of trade is against New York, and cash is exceedingly scarce.

Furthermore, the New York State government is in bad shape.

> Here we find the general disease which infects all our constitutions, an excess of popularity. There is no order that has a will of its own. The inquiry constantly is what will please not what will benefit the people. In such a government there can be nothing but temporary expedient, fickleness and folly.
>
> Nothwithstanding the obvious defects of this system, notwithstanding experience has shown it to be iniquitous and ineffectual and that all attempts to amend it without totally changing it are fruitless, notwithstanding there is a pretty general discontent from the inequality of the taxes, still ancient habits, ignorance, the spirit of the times, the opportunity afforded to some popular characters of skreening themselves by intriguing with the assessors, have hitherto proved an over-match for common sense and common justice as well as the manifest advantage of the State and of the United States.

Hamilton proceeds to give Morris brief, witty, amusing sketches of the main figures in New York government. For example:

> [Judge Pain] is a man of strong natural parts and as strong prejudices; his zeal is fiery, his obstinacy unconquerable. He is as primitive in his notions, as in his appearance. Without education, he wants more knowlege, or more tractableness.

Oh, dear, don't we all know people like that?

Hamilton sums up his report to Morris with an estimate of how much New York State will collect in tax revenues, and how much of that total Morris might reasonably expect to have for the federal government. (More here)

From August until early November, Hamilton did his utmost to collect taxes, sending frequent updates to Robert Morris (9/28/1782 10/5/1782, 10/9/1782). On November 9, 1782, he had the pleasure of publishing in the *New York Packet* that he had received on behalf of the federal government $6,434.10.

By that time, Hamilton was about to resign his position as tax receiver for New York State: he had bigger fish to fry. At some point in July, he went to the state legislature, as he had offered to do in his letter to Morris of mid-June: "In popular assemblies much may sometimes be brought about by personal discussions, by entering into details and combating objections as they rise … A meeting of the Legislature is summoned early in the next month [July] at which … it may be possible to put matters in train" (here). I haven't seen any contemporary account of Hamilton's visit to the state legislators. Whatever he said, it made such an impression that in July, they appointed him as one of New York's five delegates to the Confederation Congress in Philadelphia.

As of the first Monday of November, 1782, Hamilton was moving back onto the national stage.

MORE

• The year 1782 makes me think of the last two lines of O'Shaughnessy's "Ode": "For each age is a dream that is dying, / Or one that is coming to birth." If you're thinking you've heard me quote the "Ode" before, you're right. Rereading my essay "On Studying History" reminds me, pleasantly, of the days when I homeschooled my daughter; and, less pleasantly, that if I had time and leisure (is that redundant?), I could write a blow-you-all-away history textbook.

CHAPTER 42
John Laurens Dies in South Carolina, August 1782

In July 1782, Alexander Hamilton passed the bar in New York State, became the state's tax receiver, and was appointed a delegate for New York State to the Continental Congress, in the session that would meet in November 1782. His first-born son Philip was six months old. Meanwhile, Hamilton kept up his correspondence, including letters to Lt.-Col. John Laurens, with whom he'd become friends when they served together on Washington's staff. (More on Laurens in Chapter 4.)

After a trip to France as envoy extraordinary in early 1781, John Laurens had returned to the United States in time for the Siege of York-town. There he helped set the terms of capitulation for Cornwallis and his men. (See here.) In early 1782, Laurens briefly served on the South Carolina legislature, then rejoined the army under General Nathanael Greene near Charleston, South Carolina. In early August, he wrote to his long-time friend:

> I am indebted to you, my dear Hamilton, for two letters; the first from Albany, as masterly a piece of cynicism as ever was penned, the other from Philadelphia, dated the 2d March [NOTE: neither of these letters survives]; in both, you mention a design of retiring, which makes me exceedingly unhappy. I would not wish to have you for a moment withdrawn from the public service; at the same time, my friendship for you, and knowlege of your value to the United States, make me most ardently desire, that you should fill only the first offices of the Republic. I was flattered with an account of your being elected a delegate from N. York, and am much mortified not to hear it confirmed by yourself. I must confess to you, that, at the present state of the War, I shd. prefer your going into Congress, and from thence, becoming a Minister plenipotentiary for peace, to your remaining in the Army, where the dull System of seniority and the Tableau would prevent you from having the important commands

to which you are entitled; but at any rate I wd. not have you renounce your rank in the Army, unless you entered the career above-mentioned. Your private affairs cannot require such immediate and close attention; you speak like a pater familias surrounded with a numerous progeny.

I had, in fact, resumed the black project, as you were informed, and urged the matter very strenuously, both to our privy council and legislative body; but I was out-voted, having only reason on my side, and being opposed by a triple-headed monster that shed the baneful influence of Avarice, prejudice, and pusillanimity in all our Assemblies. It was some consolation to me, however, to find that philosophy and truth had made some little progress since my last effort, as I obtained twice as many suffrages as before. (More here; the end of the letter is missing, but might have included the paragraph quoted by John C. Hamilton, here)

The "black project" is Laurens's proposal to grant slaves in South Carolina freedom if they volunteered to serve in the American army (Chapter 4).

Hamilton replied to Laurens from Albany on August 15, 1782:

I received with great Pleasure, My Dear Laurens, the letter which you wrote me in ___ [blank in manuscript] last.

Your wishes in one respect are gratified; this state has pretty unanimously delegated me to Congress. My time of service commences in November. It is not probable it

Miniature of John Laurens by Charles Wilson Peale

will result in what you mention [i.e., an appointment as a minister plenipotentiary]. I hope it is too late. We have great reason to flatter ourselves peace on our own terms is upon the carpet. The making it is in good hands. It is said your father is exchanged for Cornwallis and gone to Paris to meet the other commissioners and that Grenville on the part of England has made a second trip there, in the last instance, vested with Plenipotentiary powers. [See the Founders Archive notes on the actual peace commissioners.]

I fear there may be obstacles but I hope they may be surmounted.

Peace made, My Dear friend, a new scene opens. The object then will be to make our independence a blessing. To do this we must secure our union on solid foundations; an herculean task and to effect which mountains of prejudice must be levelled!

It requires all the virtue and all the abilities of the Country. Quit your sword my friend, put on the toga, come to Congress. We know each others sentiments, our views are the same: we have fought side by side to make America free, let us hand in hand struggle to make her happy.

Remember me to General Greene with all the warmth of a sincere attachment.

Yrs for ever

A Hamilton (More here)

Hamilton's friend probably never received that letter. Laurens was stationed outside Charleston, which the British continued to occupy while peace negotiations were under way. On August 27, 1782, he was killed in a skirmish near the city.

We don't know how Hamilton found out, but he knew by October 12, 1782, when he wrote to General Nathanael Greene, Laurens's commander:

Dr General

It is an age since I have either written to you or received a line from you; yet I persuade myself you have not been the less convinced of my affectionate attachment and warm participation in all those events which have given you that place in your countrys esteem and approbation which I have known you to deserve while your enemies and rivals were most active in sullying your reputation.

You will perhaps learn before this reaches you that I have been appointed a member of Congress. I expect to go to Philadelphia in the ensuing month, where I shall be happy to correspond with you with our ancient confidence and I shall entreat you not to confine your observations to military subjects but to take in the whole scope of national concerns. I am sure your ideas will be useful to me and to the public.

I feel the deepest affliction at the news we have just received of the loss of our dear and inestimable friend Laurens. His career of virtue is at an end. How strangely are human affairs conducted, that so many excellent qualities could not ensure a more happy fate? The world will feel the loss of a man who has left few like him behind, and America of a citizen whose heart realized that patriotism of which others only talk. I feel the loss of a friend I truly and most tenderly loved, and one of a very small number.

I take the liberty to inclose you a letter to Mr. Kane Executor to the estate of Mr. Lavine a half brother of mine who died some time since in South Carolina. ...

I am Dr. Sir, truly Yr. friend & ser

A Hamilton (More here)

Several weeks later (November 3, 1782), Hamilton wrote to the Marquis de Lafayette from Albany:

I have been taught dayly to expect your return. This I should not have done from my own calculations; for I saw no prospect but of an inactive campaign, and you had much better be intriguing for your hobby horse at Paris than loitering away your time here. ...

I have been employed for the last ten months in rocking the cradle and studying the art of fleecing my neighbours. I am now a Grave Counsellor at law, and shall soon be a grand member of Congress. The Legislature at their last session took it into their heads to name me pretty unanimously one of their delegates. I am going to throw away a few months more in public life and then I retire a simple citizen and good paterfamilias. I set out for Philadelphia in a few days. You see the disposition I am in. You are condemned to run the race of ambition all your life. I am already tired of the career and dare to leave it.

But you would not give a pin for my letter unless politics or war made a part of it. You tell me they are employed in building a peace; And other accounts say it is nearly finished; I hope the work may meet with no interruptions: it is necessary for America; especially if your army is taken from us as we are told will soon be the case. That was an essential point d'appui; Though money was the primum mobile of our finances, which must now lose the little activity lately given them, our trade is prodigiously cramped. These states are in no humour for continuing exertions; if the war lasts, it must be carried on by external succours. I make no apology for the inertness of this country. I detest it; but since it exists I am sorry to see other resources diminish.

Your Ministers ought to know best what they are doing; but if the war goes on and the removal of the army does not prove an unwise measure I renounce all future pretensions to judgment. I think however the circumstances of the enemy oblige them to peace. ...

There is no probability that I shall be one of the Commissioners for peace. It is a thing I do not desire myself and which I imagine other people will not desire.

Our army is now in excellent order but small. ...

Adieu

General & Mrs. Schuyler & Mrs. Hamilton all join warmly in the most affectionate remembrances to you. As to myself I am in truth yours pour la vie

AH

I wrote a long letter to the Viscount De Noailles whom I also love. Has he received it? Is the worthy Gouvion well? has he succeeded? how is it with our friend Gimat? how is it with General Du Portail, all those men are men of merit & interest my best wishes.

Poor Laurens; he has fallen a sacrifice to his ardor in a trifling skirmish in South Carolina. You know how truly I loved him and will judge how much I regret him.

I will write you again soon after my arrival at Philadelphia.

(More here)

MORE

• <u>This collection</u> of John's letters to his father (latest dated 1778) in-cludes a photo of John Laurens' grave marker.

• Henry Laurens, John's father, was at this time in Europe, having been captured by the British on his way to France, and then exchanged for Lord Cornwallis. He would have heard of his son's death while he was still abroad, probably at least a month after the fact. In <u>Hamilton: The Revolution</u> (p. 131), Alexander hears of John's death through a letter from Henry Laurens that's read aloud by Eliza: "On Tuesday the 27th, my son was killed in a gunfight against British troops retreating from South Carolina. As you know, John dreamed of emancipating and recruiting 3,000 men for the first all-black military regiment. His dream of freedom for these men dies with him." Henry Laurens was probably not the first to notify Alexander of John's death—round-trip messages to Europe would take at least two months—but as a theatri-cal device, the letter from Henry Laurens works perfectly well. (If it's an actual letter, I haven't been able to find it: let me know if you have.)

CHAPTER 43
How Does History Differ from Art?

Last week, I intended to write on Hamilton's 1782-1783 term in Congress, but got distracted by Hamilton's role in the Newburgh Conspiracy (March 1783), which could have led to a military coup by Washington's officers.

This week, I intended to write on the Newburgh Conspiracy, but decided I don't know the context well enough. I've read the letters Hamilton and Washington exchanged at this period, but ... What other delegates to Congress did Washington correspond with from February to April 1783? What do James Madison's notes say regarding Congress's debates about pay for the army? What did Hamilton write to others besides Washington during that period? Who were the leaders in Congress at that time, especially the nationalists?

All of which will help me judge the accuracy of Knott and Williams's statement that "Hamilton played a sordid role in the Newburgh conspiracy" (*Washington and Hamilton: The Alliance That Forged America)*.

While I tackle that, this week's post is a rough transcription of the intro to the talk I gave last week, "Hamilton: Man and Musical."

HISTORY

I write on both art and history, so I'll start with a question too few people ask: what's the difference between art and history?

History starts with the whole world, past and present, almost up to this moment. As a historian, I choose a topic and search out the relevant facts. I look for actions and motivation, cause and effect, long-term consequences. My job is not to collect and then regurgitate the facts—it's to make a coherent narrative out of them. If I find facts that seem to conflict, I must seek a way to reconcile them. At the very least, if there are inconsistencies in the record, I have to mention them.

As a historian, I'm part of a dialogue. When I uncover new information or when others do, the narrative has to be revised to include it. That's why history—even when it deals with events 200 or 2,000 years ago—is never finished, sealed, and locked away for safekeeping.

There's always the chance that new evidence will pop up, or that we can make a more precise integration of the known facts, or that we'll find a new way to to apply a lesson from history to our own life and times.

ART

On the other hand, an artwork such as a musical is a self-contained world, complete in itself. Whatever the influences the artist had in music, whatever references he used for his story ... when the curtain rises, the work has to stand on its own. Why? Because art has a different purpose from history.

Art doesn't teach us facts or lessons. It shows us the artist's point of view about life: what matters, what's important, how the world can and ought to be. The artist shows us that by his choice of characters, by their actions and words, and by who's smiling when the curtain drops. If you're addicted to *Hamilton: An American Musical* and/or have its soundtrack on a repeating loop, then some aspect of it is showing you the world as you think it is or ought to be.

The medium of any artwork imposes certain restrictions. For a musical, the artist has to tell the story within two or three hours. In a musical based on someone's life, that will require eliminating many events: no song about the Newburgh Conspiracy! It may also mean shifting the timeline. Hamilton didn't actually meet all three of his best buds at once, in a bar.

So: history is an ongoing attempt to find the truth about the past, to make sense of it, and to learn from it. An artwork is a self-contained world that shows you what the artist thinks is important.

I consider *Hamilton: An American Musical* a brilliant work of art. I love Hamilton's character (his energy, drive, and self-confidence) and the way he creates his own destiny. I love the supplementary characters, the pacing, and the words words words words. (I'm a writer. Whaddaya expect?)

As a historian, I'm amazed by the number of accurate details and important historical issues Lin-Manuel Miranda managed to work into 2 3/4 hours. Yes, there are changes in Hamilton's life that I'd come down on like a ton of bricks (a very polite ton of bricks) if I saw them in a scholarly work. In a musical, such changes are completely acceptable.

But I didn't write this talk because I fell in love with the musical. My niche in art history is outdoor sculpture in New York City. My original talk on Hamilton, back in 2004, was provoked by the fact that there are four outdoor sculptures of Hamilton in New York—more than of anyone else except George Washington.

My goal in writing the talk was to find out what Hamilton did, what ideas drove him to those actions, and why his actions mattered. The most important part of that talk was twenty or so substantial quotes that let Hamilton speak for himself about what he thought and valued. For the current version of the talk, I've kept the quotes (I'd be delighted to have volunteers to read these), added pictures, and worked in lines from the musical. Please feel free to sing when I give you a cue!

MORE

• Two of the Hamilton sculptures (nos. 2 and 4 below) are discussed in *Outdoor Monuments of Manhattan: A Historical Guide.*

• My take on art is based on the views of Ayn Rand. For her definition, see here. I've discussed the nature of art in the introduction to *Innovators in Sculpture,* and in many of the essays in *Outdoor Monuments of Manhattan: A Historical Guide.*

Sculptures of Alexander Hamilton in Manhattan. 1) Carl Conrads, 1880. Central Park near the Metropolitan Museum of Art. 2) William Ordway Partridge, 1892. 287 Convent Ave. (between West 141st and 142nd Sts.). 3) Partridge, 1908. Columbia University. 4) Adolph Weinman, 1941. Museum of the City of New York.

CHAPTER 44A

The Newburgh Mutiny, Spring 1783

As I read about the 1782-1783 session of the Continental Congress, I started to wonder whether New York State's legislature sent Alexander Hamilton as a delegate to Congress because they were so impressed with him ... or because no one else wanted to go. Hamilton himself admitted to good intentions, but not high expectations. "I do not hope to reform the State," he told <u>Richard Kidder Meade</u> in August, "although I shall endeavour to do all the good I can."

In November 1782, Hamilton resigned his position as tax receiver for the State of New York (see Chapter 41) and rode off to Philadelphia. En route, he dashed off a letter to Eliza (11/18/1782):

> I am perfectly well, and as happy as I can be when absent from you. Remember your promise; don't fail to write me by every post. I shall be miserable if I do not hear once a week from you and my precious infant. You both grow dearer to me every day. I would give the world for a kiss from either of you.
>
> Adieu My precious charmer   Yr tender A H
> (more <u>here</u>)

A month later (12/18/1782), he was desperate for her company:

> I begin to be insupportably anxious to see you again. I hope this pleasure may not be long delayed. I wish you to take advantage of the first good snow that promises to carry you through, to get as far as Mr. Cortland's at Persepenni [Parsippany?]. ...
>
> When you are in the Jerseys write me of your arrival and I will come for you. Write me indeed when you will set out. I do not know whom you will get to travel with you. I am loth that you should make so long a journey alone.
>
> For God's sake take care of my child on the journey. I am very apprehensive on his account. ... (More <u>here</u>)

Lovesick he might be, but Hamilton was soon making his presence felt in Congress. In early December, he successfully moved that Robert Morris, superintendent of Finance, tell the state legislatures that they must ante up payments on the war debt. A few days later, Hamilton was chairman of the committee that tried to persuade tiny, recalcitrant Rhode Island to agree to an import duty, so that the United States could begin to pay off its vociferous creditors. (See Kent's *Memoirs*, pp. 283-88 in the printed version).

Meanwhile ...

PEACE NEGOTIATIONS WITH GREAT BRITAIN, LATE 1782

John Adams wrote to Abigail from Paris on 11/8/1782:

> G.B. has Shifted Suddenly about, and from persecuting Us with unrelenting Bowells [Say WHAT, John?], has unconditionally and unequivocally acknowledged Us a Sovereign State and independant Nation. (More here)

By November 30, 1782, the British had hashed out a preliminary treaty with Adams, Benjamin Franklin, John Jay, and Henry Laurens. The draft acknowledged "the Said United States ... to be free, Sovereign, and independent States ... [and Great Britain] relinquishes all claims to the Government, Propriety and territorial Rights of the Same, and every Part thereof." It set boundaries with Canada and in the west (at the Mississippi River) and granted Americans fishing rights off Newfoundland. The draft treaty also promised that creditors on both sides would be allowed to collect money owed to them (Article 4) and that Congress would "earnestly recommend" to the states that they restore property confiscated from British loyalists (Article 5). No confiscations or prosecutions were to be commenced against those who took part in the war (Article 6). King George would withdraw his armies, garrisons, and fleets from "every Port, Place and Harbour" of the United States (Article 7). (More here)

THE ARMY DEMANDS ITS PAY

With the prospect of peace, many of the states felt there was no further need for a national government or a standing army. Hence the states were even less willing to provide the funds they had promised to Congress.

But the members of the Continental Army had not been paid for years. Knowing from bitter experience how difficult it was to pry

Pennsylvania State House (later known as Independence Hall) in the 1770s. Image: Wikipedia

funds out of Congress, some of them were inclined not to go home until they had received their pay. In November 1782, officers from Massachusetts began collecting a list of grievances. The officers of the Sixth Regiment wrote:

> We believe that we engaged to serve the public, not as slaves at discretion for life, but as freemen upon contract for a definite period; that in order to make any contract binding on one party, the stipulations must be fulfilled by the other, or at least endeavors manifested by the other for their fulfillment. We flatter ourselves that no endeavors, or actual exertions have been wanting on our part to fulfil the contract with the public, or even to answer their most sanguine expectations. But at the close of the sixth year of the contract we have not received more than one-sixth part of our pay. (Quoted in Hatch, <u>Administration of the Revolutionary Army</u>, p. 149)

The Massachusetts officers soon invited the officers of New Hampshire, Connecticut, New York, and New Jersey (all in winter quarters with Washington in <u>Newburgh</u>, N.Y.) to join them in writing a memorial to Congress. The finished document included an oblique threat:

> Our distresses are now brought to a point. We have borne all that men can bear—our property is expended—our private resources are at an end, and our friends are wearied out and disgusted with our incessant applications. We therefore most seriously and earnestly beg, that a supply of money may be forwarded to the army as soon as possible. The uneasiness of the soldiers, for want of pay, is great and dangerous; any further experiments on their patience may have fatal effects. (<u>Hatch, p. 150</u>)

Major-General McDougall, Lt.-Col. Brooks, and Col. Ogden rode off to Philadelphia with this memorial. After some private discussions with members of Congress, they formally presented it on January 6, 1783. Robert Morris, superintendent of Finances, told them that payment at present was impossible: Congress had no money. McDougall and Brooks both responded that the officers were ready to resort to extreme measures, in part because they were irritated that civil officers (Congress, for example) were never left unpaid.

A Congressional committee report written by Hamilton ordered that the superintendent of Finances would, "as soon as the condition of the treasury permitted, furnish pay in such amounts as he thought proper; and that the States should be recommended immediately to settle accounts with their respective lines [soldiers] up to August 1, 1780." (Quoted in Hatch, p. 155.)

But of course the national treasury had no prospects of income, and Congress had no power to force the states to provide it.

HAMILTON IN CONGRESS

Hamilton had a unique perspective on this situation. He had served in the army for six years: he sympathized with his fellow soldiers. He had been a tax receiver in New York State for four months: he knew how difficult it was to raise funds for the federal government. As a new member of Congress, he had observed first-hand the sort of ineffectual wrangling that went on there. In six issues of his *Continentalist* series (1781-1782), he had argued in favor of a more powerful national government.

On January 12, 1783—within a week of when McDougall, Brooks and Ogden presented their memorial—Hamilton sent one of his regular updates to George Clinton, governor of New York State.

> We have now here a deputation from the army, and feel a mortification of a total disability to comply with their just expectations. If, however, the matter is taken up in a proper manner, I think their application may be turned to a good account. Every day proves more & more the insufficiency of the confederation. (More here)

According to the notes of James Madison (who was Hamilton's ally at this point), Hamilton made the same point to Congress

> As the energy of the fœderal Govt. was evidently short of the degree necessary for pervading & uniting the States it was

expedient to introduce the influence of officers deriving their emoluments from & consequently interested in supporting the power of Congress. (More here)

Notice that he's explicitly saying the army's demands might *support* Congress—that is, support a stronger national government.

HAMILTON CORRESPONDS WITH WASHINGTON

Hamilton made the same points to Washington. He had not been in touch with Washington for over a year, but from February through April 1783, the two exchanged a spate of letters. They agree, again and again, that the soldiers should be paid and that the national government should be stronger.

Before we get to those letters: Since 1970 or so, there has been a move to place Hamilton at the center of a 1783 conspiracy (the "Newburgh Conspiracy") to use military force to overthrow the government. As it happens, I read one such interpretation just before I started to draft this post, and it skewed my first perusal of the letters. After reading Michael Newton's very persuasive post on the Newburgh Conspiracy (more on that at the end of this chapter), the Hamilton-Washington correspondence looked quite different.

So while as a rule I try to cut the length of the excerpts in these posts, I'm giving long excerpts here—it's more difficult to twist long passages than snippets—and stating my interpretation of each. If you don't know about the modern interpretation of the Newburgh Conspiracy, this may seem like overkill; but I think it's necessary, and I'm the one writing, dammit.

Washington's headquarters at Newburgh, N.Y. Image: Wikipedia

Below is most of Hamilton's letter to Washington of 2/13/1783. As we know from the *Vindication,* from the *Continentalist* essays, and from his correspondence with Robert Morris, the Vicomte de Noailles, and others (Chapters 14, 31, 41), Hamilton was extremely adept at gathering facts, looking for principles, and giving a big-picture summary. Doubtless it was one of the skills that made Washington value him so highly as an aide. Here is Hamilton doing that again, from his new perspective in Congress.

Sir

Flattering myself that your knowlege of me will induce you to receive the observations I make as dictated by a regard to the public good, I take the liberty to suggest to you my ideas on some matters of delicacy and importance. I view the present juncture as a very interesting one. I need not observe how far the temper and situation of the army make it so. The state of our finances was perhaps never more critical. I am under injunctions which will not permit me to disclose some facts that would at once demonstrate this position, but I think it probable you will be possessed of them through another channel. It is however certain that there has scarcely been a period of the revolution which called more for wisdom and decision in Congress. Unfortunately for us we are a body not governed by reason or foresight but by circumstances. It is probable we shall not take the proper measures, and if we do not a few months may open an embarrassing scene. This will be the case whether we have peace or a continuance of the war.

If the war continues it would seem that the army must in June subsist [i.e., support] itself to defend the country; if peace should take place it will subsist itself to procure justice to itself. It appears to be a prevailing opinion in the army that the disposition to recompence their services will cease with the necessity for them, and that if they once lay down their arms, they will part with the means of obtaining justice. It is to be lamented that appearances afford too much ground for their distrust.

It becomes a serious inquiry what will be the true line of policy. The claims of the army urged with moderation, but with firmness, may operate on those weak minds which are influenced by their apprehensions more than their judgments; so as to produce a concurrence in the measures

which the exigencies of affairs demand. They may add
weight to the applications of Congress to the several states.
So far an useful turn may be given to them. But the difficulty
will be to keep a complaining and suffering army within the
bounds of moderation.

This Your Excellency's influence must effect. In order
to [do] it, it will be adviseable not to discountenance their
endeavours to procure redress, but rather by the intervention
of confidential and prudent persons, to take the direction of
them. This however must not appear: it is of moment to the
public tranquillity that Your Excellency should preserve the
confidence of the army without losing that of the people. This
will enable you in case of extremity to guide the torrent, and
bring order perhaps even good, out of confusion. 'Tis a part
that requires address; but 'tis one which your own situation
as well as the welfare of the community points out.

So: Congress is a mess. It probably won't pay the army. Maybe the
army's claims "urged with moderation and fairness" will help push
Congress into action, but it's crucial that the commander-in-chief keep
the army from getting out of control.

And now we get to the reason Hamilton is writing: the matter of
"delicacy and importance." He's giving Washington a warning. Hamilton has heard talk in Philadelphia that the army considers Washington to be only a lukewarm advocate of the army's rights. Watch your
back, sir.

> I will not conceal from Your Excellency a truth which it is
> necessary you should know. An idea is propagated in the
> army that delicacy carried to an extreme prevents your
> espousing its interests with sufficient warmth. The falsehood
> of this opinion no one can be better acquainted with than
> myself; but it is not the less mischievous for being false. Its
> tendency is to impair that influence, which you may exert
> with advantage, should any commotions unhappily ensue,
> to moderate the pretensions of the army and make their
> conduct correspond with their duty. (More here)

In the next paragraph, Hamilton reminds Washington that his long-
term goal is to get the finances of the United States in order, so that the
nation can survive:

> The great desideratum at present is the establishment of
> general funds, which alone can do justice to the Creditors

of the United States (of whom the army forms the most meritorious class), restore public credit and supply the future wants of government. This is the object of all men of sense; in this the influence of the army, properly directed, may cooperate. (More here)

A few days after he wrote this letter, Hamilton said at an evening get-together (with James Madison taking notes, as usual):

Mr. Hamilton & Mr. Peters who had the best knowledge of the temper, transactions & views of the army, informed the company that it was certain that the army had secretly determined not to lay down their arms until due provision & a satisfactory prospect should be afforded on the subject of their pay; that there was reason to expect that a public declaration to this effect would soon be made; that plans had been agitated if not formed for subsisting themselves after such declaration; that as a proof of their earnestness on this subject the Comander was already become extremely unpopular among almost all ranks from his known dislike to every unlawful proceeding, that this unpopularity was daily increasing & industriously promoted by many leading characters; that his choice of unfit & indiscreet persons into his family [i.e., military staff] was the pretext and with some a real motive; but the substantial one a desire to displace him from the respect & confidence of the army in order to substitute Genl. ___ [name heavily scored in manuscript] as the conductor of their efforts to obtain justice. Mr. Hamilton said that he knew Genl. Washington intimately and perfectly, that his extreme reserve, mixed sometimes with a degree of asperity of temper both of which were said to have increased of late, had contributed to the decline of his popularity; but that his virtue his patriotism & his firmness would it might be depended upon never yield to any dishonorable or disloyal plans into which he might be called; that he would sooner suffer himself to be cut into pieces; that he, (Mr. Hamilton) knowing this to be his true character wished him to be the conductor of the army in their plans for redress, in order that they might be moderated & directed to proper objects, & exclude some other leader who might foment and misguide their councils; that with this view he had taken the liberty to write to the Genl. on this subject and to recommend such a policy to him. (More here)

Hamilton is telling the members of Congress the same facts he told Washington: the army should be paid, the army is disgruntled, and Washington will keep them in check. And a bit more: there is "some other leader," a general whose name is crossed out in Madison's notes, who may lead the army astray if Washington is pushed out.

Washington thanked Hamilton for the head's-up on 3/4/1783:

> I have received your favor of February—& thank you for the information & observations it has conveyed to me … [W] here there is a want of information there must be chance medley and a man may be upon the brink of a precipice before he is aware of his danger, when a little fore knowledge might enable him to avoid it.
>
> The predicament in which I stand as Citizen & Soldier, is as critical and delicate as can well be conceived—It has been the Subject of many contemplative hours. The Sufferings of a complaining Army on one hand,— & the inability of Congress & tardiness of the States on the other are the forebodings of evil and may be productive of events which are more to be depricated than prevented. …
>
> The Contents of your letter is known only to my self— Your prudence will be at no less to know what use to make of these Sentiments— I am Dr Sir Yrs &c . GW (More here)

THE ANONYMOUS LETTER AT NEWBURGH AND WASHINGTON'S RESPONSE

A few days later (3/10/1783), an anonymous letter was circulated among the army at Newburgh, urging the officers to meet and draft an ultimatum to Congress. The "Address to the Officers" or "Newburgh Address" is a remarkable piece of rhetoric: even from the excerpt below, you can see how it must have inflamed emotions among the soldiers. (As with most rhetoric, it's better read aloud, and surely would have been at Newburgh.)

> After a pursuit of seven long years, the object for which we set out is at length brought within our reach!—Yes, my friends, that suffering courage of yours, was active once— it has conducted the United States of America through a doubtful and a bloody war! It has placed her in the chair of independency, and peace returns again to bless—whom? A country willing to redress your wrongs, cherish your worth,

and reward your services; a country courting your return to private life, with tears of gratitude, and smiles of admiration; longing to divide with you that independency which your gallantry has given, and those riches which your wounds have preserved? Is this the case? or is it rather, a country that tramples upon your rights, disdains your cries, and insults your distresses? Have you not, more than once, suggested your wishes, and made known your wants to Congress? Wants and wishes which gratitude and policy should have anticipated, rather than evaded. And have you not lately, in the meek language of entreating memorial, begged from their justice, what you would no longer expect from their favour? ...

[C]arry your appeal from the justice to the fears of government—change the milk and water style of your last [December 1782] memorial; assume a bolder tone— decent, but lively—spirited and determined; and suspect the man who would advise to more moderation and longer forbearance. ...

[Tell Congress] that in any political event, the army has its alternative. If peace, that nothing shall separate you from your arms but death [i.e., tell them that you will not go home without your pay]; if war, that courting the auspices and inviting the directions of your illustrious leader, you will retire to some unsettled country, smile in your turn, and "mock when their fear cometh on" [i.e., tell them that you won't protect them from their enemies any more].
(More here)

The anonymous writer never says, "Let's overthrow the government"—but he does suggest that the soldiers should remain armed in peacetime if they are not paid. One of the first lessons in handling a gun is that you don't pick it up unless you're willing to use it. This is a threat of civil war, of the army vs. the civilian government, and Washington and Hamilton assumed that. (See GW's 3/12/1783 letter below, "civil horror," and Hamilton on 3/17/1783 below, "the horrors of a civil war.")

Washington was suspicious of this sudden explosion of anger among his troops: he thought someone in Philadelphia had lit the fuse. On 3/12/1783, two days after the anonymous letter began circulating, he wrote to Hamilton:

When I wrote to you last we were in a state of tranquility,
but after the arrival of a certain Gentleman, who shall
be nameless at present, from Philadelphia, a storm very
suddenly arose with unfavourable prognostics; which tho'
diverted for a moment is not yet blown over, nor is it in my
power to point to the issue. ...

There is something very misterious in this business. It
appears, reports have been propagated in Philadelphia, that
dangerous combinations were forming in the Army; and
this at a time when there was not a syllable of the kind in
agitation in Camp. It also appears, that upon the arrival in
Camp of the Gentleman above alluded to such sentiments as
these were immediately circulated: That it was universally
expected the army would not disband untill they had
obtained justice; That the public creditors looked up to them
for Redress of their own grievances, wd afford them every
aid, and even join them in the Field if necessary; That some
members of Congress wished the measure might take effect,
in order to compel the public, particularly the delinquent
States, to do justice; with many other suggestions of a
similar nature.

From this, and a variety of other considerations, it is
firmly believed, by some, the scheme was not only planned
but also digested and matured in Philadelphia; but in my
opinion shall be suspended till I have a better ground to
found one on. The matter was managed with great art;
for as soon as the Minds of the Officers were thought to
be prepared for the transaction, the anonymous invitations
and address to the Officers were put in circulation, through
every state line in the army. I was obliged therefore, in
order to arrest on the spot, the foot that stood wavering on
a tremendous precipice; to prevent the Officers from being
taken by surprize while the passions were all inflamed, and
to rescue them from plunging themselves into a gulph of
Civil horror from which there might be no receding, to issue
the order of the 11th. This was done upon the principle
that it is easier to divert from a wrong, and point to a right
path, than it is to recall the hasty and fatal steps which have
been already taken. ...

Let me beseech you therefore, my good Sir, to urge this
matter earnestly, and without further delay. The situation of

> these Gentlemen I do verily believe, is distressing beyond
> description. It is affirmed to me, that a large part of them have
> no better prospect before them than a Goal [jail], if they are
> turned loose without liquidation of accts. and an assurance of
> that justice to which they are so worthily entitled. To prevail
> on the Delegates of those States through whose means these
> difficulties occur, it may, in my opinion, with propriety be
> suggested to them, if any disastrous consequences should
> follow, by reason of their delinquency, that they must be
> answerable to God & their Country for the ineffable horrors
> which may be occasioned thereby. (More here)

So: someone came to Newburgh from Philadelphia, told the officers
and men that no one expected them to disband, and called for them to
issue an ultimatum. The officers, at fever pitch, scheduled the meeting. Washington ordered the meeting postponed for a few days to give
them time to cool down. Hamilton should tell "the Delegates of those
States" that have been preventing the army from being paid that if the
army does get out of control, it'll be on their heads.

Not only is Washington corresponding with Hamilton: he's treat-
ing Hamilton as his inside man in Congress, the guy who can pass on
to fellow delegates what's really happening at Newburgh and what
Washington thinks of the situation. (I wonder if there were any other
former members of Washington's staff in Congress at this point? No
time to check that.)

At the officers' meeting on March 15, Washington did indeed talk
his men back from the precipice. He's not appealing to emotions the
way the anonymous author of the Newburgh Address did, but he ain't
too shabby at getting the audience on his side.

> I was among the first who embarked in the cause of our
> common country; as I have never left your side one moment,
> but when called from you on public duty; as I have been
> the constant companion and witness of your distresses, and
> not among the last to feel and acknowledge your merits;
> as I have ever considered my own military reputation as
> inseparably connected with that of the army; as my heart has
> ever expanded with joy, when I have heard its praises, and
> my indignation has arisen when the mouth of detraction has
> been opened against it, it can scarcely be supposed, at this
> late stage of the war, that I am indifferent to its interests. But
> how are they to be promoted? ...

    With respect to the advice given by the author, to suspect the man who shall recommend moderate measures and longer forbearance, I spurn it, as every man who regards that liberty and reveres that justice for which we contend, undoubtedly must; for, if men are to be precluded from offering their sentiments on a matter which may involve the most serious and alarming consequences that can invite the consideration of mankind, reason is of no use to us. The freedom of speech may be taken away, and, dumb and silent, we may be led, like sheep, to the slaughter. I cannot, in justice to my own belief, and what I have great reason to conceive is the intention of Congress, conclude this address, without giving it as my decided opinion, that that honorable body entertain exalted sentiments of the services of the army, and from a full conviction of its merits and sufferings, will do it compleat justice: that their endeavours to discover and establish funds for this purpose have been unwearied, and will not cease till they have succeeded, I have not a doubt. ...

    Let me conjure you, in the name of our common country, as you value your own sacred honor, as you respect the rights of humanity, and as you regard the military and national character of America, to express your utmost horror and detestation of the man, who wishes, under any specious pretences, to overturn the liberties of our country; and who wickedly attempts to open the flood-gates of civil discord, and deluge our rising empire in blood. (More here)

An eyewitness account of the speech proves (did we need proof?) that Washington was as savvy in a meeting as on a battlefield.

    After he had concluded his address, he said, that, as a corroborating testimony of the good disposition in Congress towards the army, he would communicate to them a letter received from a worthy member of that body, and one who on all occasions had ever approved himself their fast friend [Hamilton, perhaps? See Washington's letter of 4/16/1783, below]. This was an exceedingly sensible letter; and, while it pointed out the difficulties and embarrassments of Congress, it held up very forcibly the idea that the army should, at all events, be generously dealt with. ...

    His Excellency, after reading the first paragraph, made a short pause, took out his spectacles, and begged the indulgence of his audience while he put them on, observing at the same time, that he had grown gray in their service, and now found himself growing blind. There was something so natural, so unaffected, in this appeal, as rendered it superior to the most studied oratory; it forced its way to the heart, and you might see sensibility moisten every eye. (*Journals of Major Samuel Shaw*; more here)

Hamilton wrote to Washington on 3/17/1783, still sharing his concerns about the army and the nation, commending Washington for his ability to keep the army under control, and stating again that the army's demands might do some good, *if* they're temperate (i.e., if they don't overthrow the government!).

I am happy to find You coincide in opinion with me on the conduct proper to be observed by yourself. I am persuaded more and more it is that which is most consistent with your own reputation and the public safety. ...

I cannot forbear adding that if no excesses take place I shall not be sorry that ill-humours have appeared. I shall not regret importunity, if temperate, from the army.

There are good intentions in the Majority of Congress; but there is not sufficient wisdom or decision. There are dangerous prejudices in the particular states opposed to those measures which alone can give stability & prosperity to the Union. There is a fatal opposition to Continental views. Necessity alone can work a reform. But how apply it and how keep it within salutary bounds? ...

As to any combination of Force it would only be productive of the horrors of a civil war, might end in the ruin of the Country & would certainly end in the ruin of the army. (More here)

On 3/25/1783, Hamilton wrote to Washington on behalf of Congress, reminding him that Congress had no ability to demand funds from the states, and that once the peace treaty was signed, the army would have to be disbanded, since a standing army during peacetime was illegal.

For Washington's eyes only, Hamilton sent another letter on 3/25/1783. He urges the army to moderation, but he has to admit, privately and with mortification, that he doesn't think Congress will pay them.

The inclosed [i.e., the letter on behalf of Congress] I write more in a public than in a private capacity. Here I write as a citizen zealous for the true happiness of this country—as a soldier who feels what is due to an army which has suffered everything and done much for the safety of America.

I sincerely wish ingratitude was not so natural to the human heart as it is. I sincerely wish there were no seeds of it in those who direct the councils of the United States. But while I urge the army to moderation and advise your Excellency to take the direction of their discontents and endeavor to confine them within the bounds of duty I cannot as an honest man conceal from you that I am afraid their distrusts have too much foundation. Republican jealousy has in it a principle of hostility to an army whatever be their merits, whatever be their claims to the gratitude of the community. It acknowledges their services with unwillingness and rewards them with reluctance. I see this temper though smothered with great care involuntarily breaking out upon too many occasions. I often feel a mortification which it would be impolitic to express that sets my passions at variance with my reason. Too many I perceive if they could do it with safety or color would be glad to elude the just pretensions of the army. (More here)

Washington replied to Hamilton on 3/31/1783, agreeing that the weakness of the government under the Articles of Confederation has been the cause of innumerable problems.

No Man in the United States is, or can be more deeply impressed with the necessity of a reform in our present Confederation than myself—No Man perhaps has felt the bad efects of it more sensibly; for to the defects thereof, & want of Powers in Congress may justly be ascribed the prolongation of the War, & consequently the Expences occasioned by it. More than half the perplexities I have experienced in the course of My command, and almost the whole of the difficulties & distress of, the Army, have there origin here. (More here)

But, Washington told Hamilton a few days later (4/4/1783), there are rumors that some in Congress want to use the army's grievances as a political weapon; and the army is a dangerous toy to play with.

I read your private letter of the 25th with pain, & contemplated the picture it had drawn with a astonishment & honor [horror?]—but I will yet hope for the best. The idea of redress by force is too chimerical to have had a place in the imagination of any serious Mind in this Army ...

I will now, in strict confidence, mention a matter which may be useful for you to be informed of. It is that some Men (& leading ones too) in this Army, are beginning to entertain suspicions that Congress, or some Members of it, regardless of the past sufferings & present distress—maugre the justice which is due to them—& the returns which a grateful people should make to Men who certainly have contributed more than any other class to the establishment of Independency, are to be made use of as mere Puppits to establish Continental funds—& that rather than not succeed in this measure, or weaken their ground, they would make a sacrafice of the Army and all its interests.

I have two reasons for mentioning this matter to you—the one is, that the Army (considering the irritable state it is in— its sufferings—& composition) is a dangerous instrument to play with. the other, that every possible means consistant with their own views (which certainly are moderate) should be essayed to get it disbanded without delay. (More here)

Hamilton to Washington, 4/8/1783:

The idea of not attempting to separate the army before the settlement of accounts corresponds with my proposition. That of endeavouring to let them have some pay had also appaeared to me indispensable. ...

There are two classes of men Sir in Congress of very Different views—one attached to state, the other to Continental politics ... (More here)

Washington notes the dangers of local prejudices and tells Hamilton that the army considers him a friend (4/16/1783):

That no Man can be more opposed to state funds & local prejudices than myself, the whole tenor of my conduct has been one continual evidence of—No Man perhaps has had better opportunities to see & to feel the pernicious tendency of the latter than I have. and I endeavor (I hope not altogether ineffectually) to inculcate them upon the officers of the

Army upon all proper occasions; but their feelings are to be attended to & soothed; and they assured that if Continental funds cannot be established, they will be recommended to their respective states for payment. Justice must be done them.

I should do injustice to Report & what I believe to be the opinion of the Army were I not to inform you, that they consider you as a friend, zealous to serve them, and one who has espoused their interests in Congress upon every proper occasion. (More here)

THE TREATY OF PARIS

The Treaty of Paris was signed on January 20, 1783. Word of it reached America on March 12, and Congress ratified the treaty on April 15. Washington delayed his official announcement to the army at Newburgh until April 19, the eighth anniversary of the Battles of Lexington and Concord, which began the Revolutionary War.

Congress ordered Washington to disband the army, giving each soldier three months' pay. However, Congress's funds were so short that in order to pay the soldiers, wealthy Robert Morris, superintendent of Finances, issued $800,000 in personal notes.

Washington wrote to Hamilton again on 4/22/1783, after he had released the British prisoners in accordance with the draft peace treaty. The army still had not been paid and was still resentful.

[C]ircumstances as things now are, I wish most fervently that all the Troops which are not retained for a Peace Establishment were to be discharged immediately—or such of them at least as do not incline to await the Settlement of their Accts. If they continue here, their claims, I can plainly perceive, will encrease; & our perplexities multiply. ...

And here, my dear Colo. Hamilton, let me assure you, that it would not be more difficult to still the raging Billows in a tempestuous Gale, than to convince the Officers of this Army of the justice or policy of paying men in Civil Offices full wages, when they cannot obtain a Sixtieth part of their dues. I am not unapprised of the arguments which are made use of upon this occasion, to discriminate the cases; but they really are futile ... (More here)

The soldiers under Washington's leadership at Newburgh disbanded peacefully. The soldiers in Philadelphia ... well, that's another story, and Hamilton's in the thick of it again.

A 'SORDID ROLE'?

In Chapter 43, I quoted Knott and Williams's statement that "Hamilton played a sordid role in the Newburgh conspiracy. ... The unpaid Continental army, led by a small group of conspirators, posed what was potentially the greatest threat to the fledgling American republic. The plotters comprised a group of nationalists who used the army to menace the civilian government to achieve a stronger political and economic union." (*Washington and Hamilton: The Alliance That Forged America,* location 1937 in the Kindle version).

Since I've been focusing on primary sources rather than secondary scholarship, I had no context for that statement. Thanks yet again to Rand Scholet (a.k.a. the Hamilton Hub), who mentioned Michael Newton's research on the Newburgh Conspiracy, and to Michael, who was kind enough to let me read his unpublished talk on the subject, and then kind enough to work the talk into a blog post so I could cite it.

Michael argues persuasively that the "sordid" interpretation—Hamilton as part of a cabal manipulating the army—came from a suspicious source decades after the fact. It didn't begin to appear in the scholarly works until 1970, and the article that spurred it was highly speculative. I won't steal Michael's thunder: go read his blog post.

When reading the Hamilton-Washington letters of this period, the point I kept stumbling over was Hamilton's repeated statements (to Clinton, to fellow Congressmen, to Washington) that the army's demands might be used to strengthen the ineffectual national government. The best analogy for what he's proposing is, I think, a politician who uses a rising crime rate to argue for more cops on city streets. That's quite legitimate, as opposed to a name-your-supervillain who sees a rising crime rate as an opportunity to gather a gang of thugs and take over the city.

The tone of the letters between Hamilton and Washington suggests to me that they're using each other for moral and political support and for tactical advice—not manipulating the hell out of each other. If you can justify a different interpretation after reading their letters, publish your findings and send me a link! (DuranteDianne@gmail.com)

CHAPTER 44B

Hamilton and Company at 48 Wall Street

At 48 Wall Street, in the <u>Museum of American Finance</u>, I was recently delighted to discover a series of eight huge murals whose content and style I like very much. Think <u>N.C. Wyeth</u> meets Ayn Rand.

BACKGROUND: THE BANK OF NEW YORK

The Bank of New York opened for business in June 1784, less than a year after the British evacuated New York City at the end of the Revolutionary War. (Details on the establishment of BNY are <u>here</u>). Among the bank's founders were Alexander McDougall, Isaac Roosevelt, Gulian VerPlanck, and Alexander Hamilton. Hamilton remained a member of the board and BNY's legal advisor until he was appointed secretary of the Treasury in 1789.

BNY's first headquarters was Walton House. According to the *Columbia Historical Portrait of New York* (invaluable!), Walton House was on Pearl Street between Peck Slip and Dover Street, near the present-day entrance ramp to the Brooklyn Bridge.

In 1797, BNY moved to a brand new two-story Georgian-style building at the corner of Wall and William Streets. Its cornerstone is preserved on the facade of 48 Wall Street.

Hamilton may have attended the laying of the cornerstone on June 22, 1797 ... or he might have been otherwise occupied. In June 1797, James Callender accused him of speculation as secretary of the Treasury. Hamilton's response: *Observations on Certain Documents Contained in nos. V & VI of "The History of the United States for the Year 1796,"* better known as the "Reynolds Pamphlet" (see Chapters 63A, 63B, 63C). He signed it July 1797.

EXTERIOR OF 48 WALL ST.

The building presently at 48 Wall Street was constructed in 1927 as the new headquarters of the Bank of New York. (BNY remained there until 1998, when it acquired Irving Trust and moved to 1 Wall Street.) Architect Benjamin Wistar Morris designed 48 Wall in a conservative style—Colonial Revival—that suited his very conservative client.

Left: Walton House, the original Bank of New York headquarters. Right: second Bank of New York headquarters, 1797-1927.

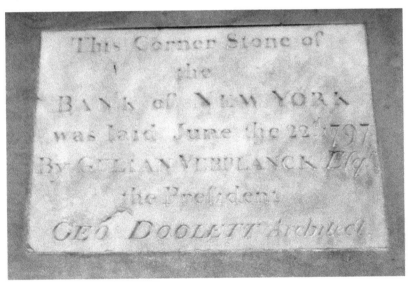

Cornerstone of the first Bank of New York building, on the west end of 48 Wall St., laid on June 22, 1797. Photo copyright © 2016 Dianne L. Durante

INTERIOR OF 48 WALL ST.

The original banking hall (now part of the Museum of American Finance) is reached by a gorgeous marble staircase, elliptical and cantilevered.

Beneath the banking hall's 30-foot ceilings and huge chandeliers are eight arched murals related to the Bank of New York and to commerce. J. Monroe Hewlett, an architect as well as a mural painter, completed them around 1929. The style is reminiscent of the works of N.C. Wyeth, one of my favorite 20th-century artist/

48 Wall Street, lower floors, tower with eagle (the Federalists would have approved!), and matching subway entrance. Photos copyright © 2016 Dianne L. Durante

Stairs in main lobby; BNY logo at top of stairs; former banking hall at 48 Wall Street.

illustrators. Hewlett's grand-daughter <u>Angelsea Parkhurst Newman</u> noted that Hewlett also executed a series of murals in the auditorium of the Carnegie Institution in Washington that "depict a group of heroic figures—astronomers, geographers, and explorers—typifying the researchers of the institution." (It drives me mad that I can't find images of those online.) On Hewlett's career, see also the <u>Lehman College Art Gallery site</u>.

The mural sequence runs from left to right. The three across the back (north) wall honor the earliest presidents of the Bank of New York. Five more along the right-hand (east) wall celebrate industry and commerce.

Before you look at these, please note that **the photos do not do them justice**. The images are rather dark and grainy, because I use a handheld 12 MP Canon Powershot that's a couple years old. They ought to be photographed with a serious camera of 30+ MP, a tripod, and supplementary lighting. Best substitute: visit the <u>Museum of American Finance</u> and see them in person!

FOUNDERS' MURALS (NORTH WALL)

On the first mural, the grisaille (gray-and-white) portrait relief front and center honors General Alexander McDougall (d. 1786), first president of the Bank of New York. He was a hero in colonial New York for his opposition to the Crown, and during the Revolutionary War rose to the rank of major-general. We met him in Chapter 44A, delivering a memorial from the army at Newburgh to Congress in Philadelphia in January 1783.

The building pictured is Walton House,

First mural. Photo copyright © 2016 Dianne L. Durante

Second mural. Photo copyright © 2016 Dianne L. Durante

Third mural. Photo copyright © 2016 Dianne L. Durante

BNY's first home. (See the image at the beginning of this chapter.) The spectators in the foreground (anachronistically) are Dutch burghers, or perhaps early English settlers.

Beneath this painting runs the text of the advertisement of February 23, 1784, that established the Bank of New York: "It appearing to be the disposition of the gentlemen in this city to establish a bank on the liberal principles, the stock to consist of specie only, they are therefore hereby invited to meet tomorrow evening at six-o-clock when a plan will be submitted to their consideration."

The second mural has a portrait relief of Isaac Roosevelt (d. 1794), BNY's second president, 1786-1791. Aside from being a co-founder of BNY, he helped found the New York Chamber of Commerce and the Society of the New York Hospital (the city's first hospital). Like McDougall, Roosevelt was a Federalist and an ally of

366

Hamilton. Franklin Delano Roosevelt was his great-great-grandson.

The building in the background is the original Federal Hall: Washington was inaugurated there in April 1789, during Roosevelt's tenure as president of BNY. See the contemporary engraving here. The spectators this time are proper eighteenth-century gentlemen. The figure standing near the center, with a scroll in his hand, is probably Alexander Hamilton. The face looks very much like Hamilton's as it appeared on the $10 bill beginning in 1929, around the time these murals were painted.

Fourth mural. Photo copyright © 2016 Dianne L. Durante

The third mural has a relief portrait of Gulian Verplanck (d. 1799), third president of BNY, of which he was also a co-founder. Like McDougall, Roosevelt, and Hamilton, he was a Federalist.

The building in the background is the 1797 BNY headquarters at Wall and William Streets. (See image near the beginning of this

Fifth mural: "Agriculture and Mining." Photo copyright © 2016 Dianne L. Durante

Sixth mural: "National Credit 1861."
Photo copyright © 2016
Dianne L. Durante

Seventh mural: "Steam Transportation."
Photo copyright © 2016
Dianne L. Durante

chapter. The spectators at the left and right seem to be pioneers—appropriate, since Americans began pushing West even before Jefferson purchased the Louisiana Territory in 1803.

INDUSTRY AND COMMERCE MURALS (EAST WALL)

The fourth mural celebrates foreign trade. Docks jutted out all around the lower end of Manhattan in the 19th century.

The fifth mural celebrates agriculture and mining. The building is the original Merchants Exchange (1827), at 55 Wall Street, a block east of William Street. A 15-foot tall sculpture of Alexander Hamilton was dedicated inside the building in 1835. Both building and sculpture were reduced to rubble a few months later, in the Great Fire of 1835. In honor of agriculture, there's a man with a horse and plow planting crops on Wall Street (!) and a man at left with a sheaf of

wheat. In honor of min-
ing, the man on the right
pans for gold.

The sixth mural is
captioned "National
Credit, 1861." In the
background is Federal
Hall at Wall and Broad
Streets, built in 1842
as the United States
Customs House. It was
erected on the site of
the building (pictured
in the second mural) on
whose balcony Wash-
ington was inaugurated.
At the left is a Union
soldier, at the right a
black man raising a flag.
Down Wall Street (go
West!) bumps a covered
wagon.

Eighth mural: "Steel - Electricity."
Photo copyright © 2016
Dianne L. Durante

The seventh mural celebrates steam transportation. On the west
side, the railroads may once have run that close to the docks. The
spectator at right appears to be wearing America's most enduring con-
tribution to fashion, Levi's jeans (est. 1853).

The eighth and final mural celebrates steel and electricity with my
favorite of the eight images: a steamship passing beneath the Brooklyn Bridge (completed 1883).

MORE

• I've taken information on McDougall, Roosevelt, VerPlanck, and
the Bank of New York mostly from the *Encyclopedia of New York
City,* another invaluable work.

• Information on the Museum of American Finance is here, including
a page on 48 Wall Street.

• Information on 48 Wall Street from the Skyscraper Museum
is here (search "48"). See also "The Rise of Wall Street."

CHAPTER 45
Alexander Hamilton: A Brief Biography

I've just published a new edition of *Alexander Hamilton: A Brief Biography,* which I first released as a Kindle book in 2012.

How brief is it? At 18,000 words, halfway between the length of Hamilton's "Reynolds Pamphlet" and his first *Report on Public Credit*. I've kept the casual tone of the two-hour talk on which this book is based: it's an easy read.

What's in it for you?

1. Substantial quotes from Hamilton's writings let you see how Hamilton's mind worked.
2. Dozens of early images let you picture his life and times.
3. History not your strong point? A timeline sets Hamilton's life in the context of events in the United States and in Europe.
4. Start small: *Alexander Hamilton: A Brief Biography* is 90% shorter than Chernow's *Hamilton*. If you want to get an overview of the important events of Hamilton's life and the ideas that drove him, this is a great place to start. If you find you're curious about details of Hamilton's life, such as his "death wish", why he resigned from Washington's staff, his role in the Newburgh Conspiracy, or the Reynolds affair (to name just a few), cross-references my two-volume *Alexander Hamilton: A Friend to America* make it easy to learn more.

Bonus: Descriptions and multiple photos of the four sculptures of Hamilton in Manhattan are in a separate chapter at the end.

If you're a fan of *Hamilton: An American Musical,* this biography will give you more reasons to love the man and the musical. If you're a history geek, it will give you a unique view of Hamilton and the other Founding Fathers.

BRIEF TABLE OF CONTENTS

CHAPTER 46

The Pennsylvania Mutiny, Summer 1783

*In which Alexander Hamilton lectures Governor George Clinton
on keeping one's word, faces off against mutineers and John Dickinson,
and, along with the entire Continental Congress, flees Philadelphia.*

We last saw Alexander Hamilton corresponding with George Washington regarding the Newburgh Conspiracy (Chapter 44A). In mid-March 1783, Washington talked his troops away from the brink of mutiny and a possible coup. On April 19, he announced to them that hostilities with Great Britain were suspended, because a draft peace treaty had been approved by Congress.

And the music swells as the spotlight comes up on the American flag, unfurling in the breeze while the patriots celebrate their hard-won victory?

Not exactly.

FINDING PAY FOR THE ARMY

Congress was still scrabbling to find even three months' pay for the soldiers. In practice, that task fell mostly on Robert Morris, superintendent of Finances (the equivalent of secretary of the Treasury). He was so sick of it that he threatened to resign. On 5/1/1783, he noted in his diary:

> The Honble. Mr. Hamilton, Mr. Fitzsimmons, Mr. Wilson Mr. Carrol Mr. Gorham and Mr. Osgood called to Confer with and Convince me of the Propriety of continuing in this Office untill the Army are disbanded and Peace Arrangements take place &c. To all their Arguments I opposed my Observations on the Conduct of Congress towards me; And I wish for nothing so much as to be relieved from this cursed Scene of Drudgery and Vexation. (More here, note 3)

Under the Articles of Confederation, Congress could do nothing but beg the states to send money. On 5/2/1783 they passed a motion proposed by Hamilton:

> Whereas it is the desire of Congress when the reduction of the army shall take place to enable the officers and soldiers to return to their respective homes with convenience and satisfaction, for which purpose it will be indispensable to advance them a part of their pay before they leave the field ... Therefore Resolved that the respective states be called upon in the most earnest manner, to make every effort in their power to forward the collection of taxes, that such a sum may without delay be paid into the common treasury as will be adequate to the public exigencies; and that Congress confidently rely, for an immediate and efficacious attention to the present requisition, upon the disposition of their constituents not only to do justice to those brave men, who have suffered and sacrificed so much in the cause of their country, and whose distresses must be extreme should they be sent from the field without the payment of a part of their well earned dues; but also to enable Congress to maintain the faith and reputation of the United States; both which are seriously concerned in relieving the necessities of a meritorious army and fulfulling the public stipulations. (More here)

Two weeks later (5/14/1783), Hamilton sent an update on Congress's most recent actions to Governor of New York George Clinton. Hamilton sounds exactly like a patriot and a man of honor who's trying to persuade a pragmatic politician to abide by his promises – in this case, to see that New York pays the money it owes to the federal government.

> I hope our state will consent to the plan proposed; because it is her interest at all events to promote the payment of the public debt on Continental funds (independent of the general considerations of Union & propriety). ... [T]here are superior motives that ought to operate in every state, the obligations of national faith honor and reputation.
>
> Individuals have been already too long sacrificed to public convenience. It will be shocking and indeed an eternal reproach to this country, if we begin the peaceable enjoyment of our independence by a violation of all the principles of honesty & true policy. (More here)

In the first in a series of such requests to Governor Clinton, Hamilton asks: please send someone else to represent New York.

> I wish two other Gentlemen of the delegation may appear as soon as possible for it would be very injurious to me to remain much longer here. Having no future view in public life, I owe it to myself without delay to enter upon the care of my private concerns in earnest. (More here)

HAMILTON REBUKES GOVERNOR CLINTON

On 6/1/1783, Hamilton wrote to Clinton again: "I wish your Excellency would urge a couple of gentlemen to come on, as it becomes highly inconvenient to me to remain here and as I have staid the full time to be expected." He also discusses at length an issue that will become important for his law practice within the next year.

Here's what you need to know to appreciate this letter as much as I do.

- In early March 1783, the New York State legislature passed the "Trespass Act." Under it, patriots who fled New York City were permitted to bring suit against loyalists who had occupied the deserted property. It didn't matter if the loyalists had done so under the direct orders of the British army. There was no legal appeal of the verdict. (Entire text of the Trespass Act is here.)

- Hamilton is 26 years old. He's a junior delegate to the weak federal legislature. He's lecturing—almost giving orders to—Governor Clinton, who is 18 years his senior and holds the highest office in one of the most important states in the union. To make it even more interesting, the candidate whom Clinton had defeated in 1777 for the governorship was Hamilton's father-in-law, Philip Schuyler. Clinton remained governor until 1795, and from 1805-1812 was vice president under Jefferson and then Madison, which tells you where on the political spectrum his sympathies lie.

Hamilton writes to Clinton:

> I observe with great regret the intemperate proceedings among the people in different parts of the state in violation of a treaty the faithful observance of which so deeply interests the United States. Surely the state of New York with its capital and its frontier posts (on which its important

fur-trade depends) in the hands of the British troops ought to take care that nothing is done to furnish a pretext on the other side, even for delaying much less for refusing the execution of the treaty. We may imagine that the situation of Great Britain puts her under a necessity at all events of fulfilling her engagements and cultivating the good will of this country. This is no doubt her true policy; but when we feel that passion makes us depart from the dictates of reason, when we have seen that passion has had so much influence in the conduct of the British councils in the whole course of the war—when we recollect that those who govern them are men like ourselves and alike subject to passions & resentments—when we reflect also that all the great men in England are not United in the liberal scheme of policy with respect to this Country and that in the anarchy which prevails, there is no knowing to whom the reins of government may be committed when we recollect how little in a condition we are to enforce a compliance without claims—we ought certainly to be cautious in what manner we act, especially when we in particular have so much at stake, and should not openly provoke a breach of faith on the other side, by setting the example.

An important distinction is not sufficiently attended to— the 5th article is recommendatory [i.e., it suggests that the states return property confiscated from loyalists], the sixth positive. There is no option on the part of the particular states as to any future confiscations prosecutions or injuries of any kind to person liberty or property on account of any thing done in the war. ... No part of the 6th [article] can be departed from by them without a direct breach of public faith and of the confederation. ...

In the eye of a foreign nation, if our engagements are broken, it is of no moment whether it is for the want of good intention in the government or for want of power to restrain its subjects. ... I am told that indictments continue to be brought under the former confiscation laws; a palpable infraction if true of the 6th article of the treaty to which an immediate stop ought no doubt to be put.

It has been said by some men that the operation of this treaty is suspended 'till the definitive treaty—a plain subterfuge. Whatever is clearly expressed in the provisional or preliminary treaty is as binding from the moment it is made as the definitive treaty …

I have omitted saying any thing of the impolicy of inducing by our severity a great number of useful [former loyalist] citizens, whose situations do not make them a proper object of resentment to abandon the country to form settlements that will hereafter become our rivals animated with a hatred to us which will descend to their posterity. (More here)

So while he's still in Congress, in Philadelphia, Hamilton is already considering the implications for business of chasing former loyalists out of New York.

A week after writing that letter to Governor Clinton, Hamilton sent a letter to General Nathanael Green in which his exasperation with politics-as-usual is obvious (6/10/1783):

I expect to leave this shortly for that place [Albany] and to remain there 'till New York is evacuated; on which event I shall set down there seriously on the business of making my fortune. …

There is so little disposition either in or out of Congress to give solidity to our national system that there is no motive to a man to lose his time in the public service; who has no other view than to promote its welfare. Experience must convince us that our present establishments are Utopian before we shall be ready to part with them for better. (More here)

ANOTHER MUTINY

In early June, just as Hamilton was preparing to leave, a mutiny erupted—not, this time, with Washington's army in Newburgh, but in the seat of Congress, Philadelphia.

In the spring of 1783, Robert Morris told Congress that given the dearth of federal revenue, they could either give the soldiers several months' back pay (as promised), or keep the troops under arms until the treaty was finally signed—but not both. Congress resolved on May 26 to send the soldiers on furlough, even though no money was available to pay them. When the soldiers stationed in Philadelphia learned of this resolution, they sent a message to Congress (6/12/1783) asserting that they refused to go on furlough or be discharged until they had received their payment.

More soldiers marched in from Lancaster. The mutineers were now several hundred strong, and controlled the city's supply of arms and ammunition. On June 16, Alexander Hamilton and two other Congressmen were appointed to confer with John Dickinson and the Supreme Executive Council of Pennsylvania regarding what actions to take against the mutineers.

On June 21, a group of soldiers marched, under arms, to the State House (now Independence Hall), where the Council was meeting on the second floor and the Continental Congress was in emergency session on the first. Outside their windows, the delegates to Congress could see citizens of Philadelphia cheering the mutineers as local tavern-keepers provided them with liquor.

John Dickinson and the Council refused to call out the local militia to protect Congress against the mutineers. Congress decamped to Princeton, New Jersey, on June 24. The mutineers backed down the following day. There was no bloodshed and no property damage during the Pennsylvania Mutiny of 1783. The mutineers who were convicted were given full pardons by Congress.

That's the basic story, but there are a slew of unresolved questions about this mutiny. How far in advance was it planned? Was there a mastermind behind it? (General Horatio Gates's close associate John Armstrong, Jr., who wrote the Newburgh Address, had recently been appointed secretary of the Supreme Executive Council ... Hmmm. See Chapter 44A, and especially this post by Michael Newton on Armstrong.) Did the mutineers mean to demand satisfaction of their grievances from Congress, or from the Supreme Executive Council and Dickinson? Did they intend to rob the Bank of North America? Why did Dickinson and the Supreme Executive Council refuse protection to Congress?

Pennsylvania State House (now Independence Hall) in the 1770s. Image: Wikipedia

Whatever the answers to those questions, and despite the fact that the mutiny turned out to be bloodless, in Hamilton's eyes it was no trifling affair. He wrote a few months later to John Dickinson:

> This was not to be considered as the disorderly riot of an unarmed mob but as the deliberate mutiny of an incensed soldiery carried to the utmost point of outrage short of assassination. The licentiousness of an army is to be dreaded in every government; but in a republic it is more particularly to be restrained, and when directed against the civil authority to be checked with energy and punished with severity. The merits and sufferings of the troops might be a proper motive for mitigating punishment when it was in the power of the government to inflict it—but it was no reason for relaxing in the measures necessary to arrive at that situation. Its authority was first to be vindicated and then its clemency to be displayed.
>
> The rights of government are as essential to be defended as the rights of individuals. The security of the one is inseparable from that of the other. And indeed in every new government, especially of the popular kind the great danger is that public authority will not be sufficiently respected. (More here)

Back in 1775, Hamilton told John Jay his fear of what might happen if democracy turned into rule by the mob: "When the minds of [the unthinking populace] are loosened from their attachment to ancient establishments and interests, they seem to grow giddy and are apt more or less to run into anarchy." In June 1783, with armed mutineers outside the State House and the citizens of Philadelphia cheering them on, he must have wondered if his nightmare was coming true.

On 6/29/1783, Hamilton once again updated Governor Clinton:

> You will have heared of a mutiny among the soldiers stationed in the barracks of Philadelphia, and of their having surrounded the state house where Congress was sitting. Fortunately no mischief insued. There was an insolent message sent to the Council. It was at once determined that should any propositions be made to Congress they would not take them into consideration whatever extremities might ensue, while they were surrounded by an armed force. ...
>
> The conduct of the executive of this state was to the last degree weak & disgusting. In short they pretended it was out

of their power to bring out the militia, without making the experiment.

This feebleness on their part determined the removal of Congress from a place where they could receive no support; and I believe they will not easily be induced to return.... (More here)

Hamilton was right about that. One of the long-term consequences of the Pennsylvania Mutiny was that Congress didn't return to Philadelphia until 1787.

ALEXANDER TO ELIZA: "IN A VERY SHORT TIME I HOPE WE SHALL BE HAPPILY SETTLED IN NEW YORK"

Hamilton wrote to Eliza on 7/22/1783:

I wrote you my beloved Betsey by the last post, which I hope will not meet with the fate that many others of my letters must have met with. I count upon setting out to see you in four days; but I have been so frequently disappointed by unforeseen events, that I shall not be without apprehensions of being detained, 'till I have begun my journey. The members of Congress are very pressing with me not to go away at this time as the house is thin, and as the definitive treaty is momently expected.

Tell your father that Mr. Rivington in a letter to the South Carolina delegates has given information coming to him from Admiral Arbuthnot, that the Mercury-frigate is arrived at New York with the definitive treaty, and that the city was to be evacuated yesterday by the treaty. [NOTE: It wasn't evacuated until November 25, 1783.]

I am strongly urged to stay a few days for the ratification of the treaty; at all events however I will not be long from My Betsey.

I give you joy my angel of the happy conclusion of the important work in which your country has been engaged. Now in a very short time I hope we shall be happily settled in New York.

My love to your father. Kiss my boy a thousand times. A thousand loves to yourself.

A Hamilton (More here)

In a letter to John Jay three days later (7/25/1783), Hamilton summed up the state of the country and of Congress, and his own future plans.

> The peace which exceeds in the goodness of its terms, the expectations of the most sanguine does the highest honor to those who made it. It is the more agreeable, as the time was come, when thinking men began to be seriously alarmed at the internal embarrassments and exhausted state of this country. The New England people talk of making you an annual fish-offering as an acknowlegement of your exertions for the participation of the fisheries.
>
> We have now happily concluded the great work of independence, but much remains to be done to reach the fruits of it. Our prospects are not flattering. Every day proves the inefficacy of the present confederation, yet the common danger being removed, we are receding instead of advancing in a disposition to amend its defects. The road to popularity in each state is to inspire jealousies of the power of Congress, though nothing can be more apparent than that they have no power; and that for the want of it, the resources of the country during the war could not be drawn out, and we at this moment experience all the mischiefs of a bankrupt and ruined credit. It is to be hoped that when prejudice and folly have run themselves out of breath we may return to reason and correct our errors.
>
> After having served in the field during the war, I have been making a short apprenticeship in Congress; but the evacuation of New York approaching, I am preparing to take leave of public life to enter into the practice of the law. ...

(More here)

ANGELICA IN LONDON

In the same letter, Hamilton added a request that John Jay be hospitable to Angelica and her husband (John Barker Church, a.k.a. Carter):

> The bearer of this is Mr. Carter, who with Mrs. Carter are making a jaunt to Europe. I presume you have heard of my connection in the family. Your acquaintance with Mr Carter makes it unnecessary I should request your civilities to him, which my friendship for him would otherwise do in the warmest manner. I anticipate the pleasure which Mrs.

Jay and Mrs. Carter will enjoy in the society of each other, possessed as they both are of every quality to please and endear. ... (More here)

LESSONS OF THE PENNSYLVANIA MUTINY

The Pennsylvania Mutiny of 1783 never made it to my ninth-grade civics class back in Pennsylvania, but it had several important repercussions, aside from Congress's change of residence. It was a face-to-face confrontation of the federal government with one of the strongest states. It was an object lesson in federal sovereignty: after Dickinson failed to call out the militia to protect Congress, Congress realized that it needed exclusive jurisdiction over the federal capital—hence (eventually) the creation of the District of Columbia. And of course the mutiny was yet another proof of the weakness of the federal government under the Articles of Confederation.

In July 1783, Hamilton drafted a resolution for Congress listing twelve defects of the Confederation of the United States. Among them:

- The federal government does not have enough "efficacious authority" to accomplish anything.

- The legislative and executive powers are held by the same body, "contrary to the most approved and well founded maxims of free government which require that the legislative, executive and judicial authorities should be deposited in distinct and separate hands."

- There is no nationwide judiciary power, so states pass whatever laws they please: "the national treaties will be liable to be infringed [Note: Hamilton is probably thinking of the prosecution of loyalists in New York], the national faith to be violated and the public tranquillity to be disturbed."

- Congress is responsible for defense but can't impose taxes, "rendering that power, so essential to the existence of the union, nugatory."

- Congress is authorized to borrow money or print it on the credit of the United States, but since it has no power to collect money, that means "a continuance of the injustice and mischiefs of an unfunded debt, and first or last the annihilation of public credit."

- Congress cannot adequately protect the country because it must rely on independently run state militias, to the "great confusion of the military department."

- Congress has no power to regulate trade, which means the states do as they please, including interfering with foreign trade.

- Nothing can be passed unless at least nine states concur, "a rule destructive of vigour, consistency or expedition in the administration of affairs."

Hamilton's draft concludes (blanks are in the original):

> Hence, resolved: that it be earnestly recommended to the several states to appoint a convention to meet at ___ on the day of ___ with full powers to revise the confederation and to adopt and propose such alterations as to them shall appear necessary to be finally approved or rejected by the states respectively—and that a Committee of ___ be appointed to prepare an address upon the subject. (More here)

Hamilton's note on the document states, "Resolution intended to be submitted to Congress at Princeton in 1783; but abandoned for want of support."

I wonder how this compares to the Annapolis Resolution of 1786, which Hamilton drafted and which resulted in the Constitutional Convention? Presently I'll find out. If you're impatient, the Annapolis Resolution is here.

Hamilton finally set off for Albany on July 29, 1783.

MORE

• Two thoroughly researched articles on the Pennsylvania Mutiny of 1783, with extensive references to primary sources, are Kenneth R. Bowling, "New Light on the Philadelphia Mutiny of 1783: Federal-State Confrontation at the Close of the War for Independence," *The Pennsylvania Magazine of History and Biography*, October 1977; and Mary A.Y. Gallagher, "Reinterpreting the 'Very Trifling Mutiny' at Philadelphia in June 1783," *The Pennsylvania Magazine of History and Biography*, January/April 1995.

• Hamilton's 5,000-word letter to Dickinson, which he apparently wrote in September 1783 but didn't send, gives a detailed account of the Mutiny.

REFERENCES

These links are available online at
http://diannedurantewriter.com/ hafav1/

p. 2 For more on the author, visit
> http://diannedurantewriter.com/about/

p. 2 Amazon Author Page for Dianne L. Durante
> https://www.amazon.com/Dianne-L.-Durante/e/B001JS9VDO/ref=ntt_dp_epwbk_0

p. 2 write a review on Amazon --> CHECK LINK
> https://www.amazon.com/gp/product/B0079J4D62/ref=as_li_qf_sp_asin_tl?ie=UTF8&-camp=1789&creative=9325&creativeASIN=B0079J4D62&linkCode=as2&tag=forgot-tendeli-20

INTRODUCTION

p. 5 *Alexander Hamilton: A Brief Biography*
> http://amzn.to/2zT6Twx

p. 5 Ron Chernow's *Alexander Hamilton*
> http://amzn.to/2xlDeMa

p. 5 *Hamilton: An American Musical*
> http://www.hamiltonbroadway.com/

CHAPTER 1: My World Turned Upside Down

p. 6 "Alexander Hamilton"
> https://www.youtube.com/watch?v=P7rcAVy6sh8

p. 9 *Outdoor Monuments of Manhattan: A Historical Guide*
> http://forgottendelights.com/outdoormonumentsofmanhattan.html AND
> http://amzn.to/2zT6Twx

p. 9 Monuments of Manhattan:
> Samples on the web
> https://www.forgottendelights.com/MonumentsOfManhattanRelease.html
> iPhone samples
> https://itunes.apple.com/us/app/preview-monuments-of-manhattan-videoguide/id953895848
> iPhone purchase
> https://itunes.apple.com/us/app/monuments-of-manhattan-videoguide/id953900277
> Android samples
> https://www.amazon.com/Preview-Monuments-Manhattan-Guides-VideoGuide/dp/B00JSYTZHS/
> Android purchase
> https://www.amazon.com/Guides-Who-Know-Monuments-Videoguide/dp/B00LMGVISY/

CHAPTER 2: The Hurricane Letter, 1772

p. 10 "Alexander Hamilton"
   https://www.youtube.com/watch?v=P7rcAVy6sh8

p. 14 see here for notes
   http://founders.archives.gov/documents/Hamilton/01-01-02-0042

CHAPTER 3: Aaron Burr (1756-1836)

p. 16 here
   http://founders.archives.gov/documents/Hamilton/01-01-02-0002

p. 16 Gore Vidal's *Burr*
   http://amzn.to/2hGBaVj

p. 17 American National Biography
   http://www.anb.org/

p. 17 "Sinners in the Hands of an Angry God"
   http://digitalcommons.unl.edu/cgi/viewcontent.cgi?article=1053&context=etas

p. 18 Eliza Bowen Jumel
   http://cbrowder.blogspot.com/2014/05/125-remarkable-women-eliza-jumel.html

p. 18 Morris-Jumel Mansion
   http://www.morrisjumel.org/

p. 18 National Archives Founders Online
   http://founders.archives.gov/

CHAPTER 4: John Laurens (1754-1782)

p. 20 Ayn Rand, who rejected racism
   https://campus.aynrand.org/works/1963/01/01/racism/page1

p. 22 "Your Dutiful Son, John Laurens"
   https://archive.org/stream/yourDutifulSonJohnLaurens-Ex-cerptsFromHisCorrespondenceWithHis/John-Laurens#page/n0/mode/2up

p. 23 selection of Laurens's letters
   https://archive.org/stream/yourDutifulSonJohnLaurens-Ex-cerptsFromHisCorrespondenceWithHis/John-Laurens#page/n0/mode/2up

p. 23 Founders Archive
   http://founders.archives.gov/

CHAPTER 5: Marquis de Lafayette (1757-1834)

p. 25 Well worth reading, here
   http://founders.archives.gov/documents/Hamilton/01-05-02-0202

p. 26 Letter of Lafayette to George Washington, 3/15/1792, from George Washington, *The Writings* (1858), v. 10, p. 502-4
   https://books.google.com/books?id=vcJJAAAAcAAJ&lpg=PA502&ots=oE_Wshy-uNk&dq=Although%20warlike%20preparations%20are%20going%20on%2C%20

it%20is%20very%20doubtful%20whether%20our%20neighbours%20will%20
attempt%20to%20stifle%20so%20very%20catching%20a%20thing%20as%20
liberty&pg=PA504#v=onepage&q&f=false

p. 27 imprisonment at Olmutz

http://sites.lafayette.edu/olmutz/

p. 27 *The Young Rebels*

https://en.wikipedia.org/wiki/The_Young_Rebels

p. 27 *Outdoor Monuments of Manhattan: A Historical Guide*

http://forgottendelights.com/outdoormonumentsofmanhattan.html and
http://amzn.to/2B7IFx4

p. 27 Monuments of Manhattan: see note for Ch. 1, p. 9

p. 28 NYC Parks Dept. page here

http://www.nycgovparks.org/parks/lafayette-square/history

p. 28 *Daily Beast* article here

http://untappedcities.com/2014/05/09/
seeing-double-bartholdis-lafayette-and-washington/

p. 28 Green in Morristown, New Jersey

http://morristowngreen.com/

p. 28 StudioEIS

https://en.wikipedia.org/wiki/StudioEIS

CHAPTER 6: Hercules Mulligan (1740-1825)

p. 31 letter of 11/26/1775

http://founders.archives.gov/documents/Hamilton/01-01-02-0060

p. 32 Dr. Cooper's description

http://spenserians.cath.vt.edu/BiographyRecord.php?action=GET&bioid=34389

p. 34 Founders Online

http://founders.archives.gov/documents/Hamilton/01-20-02-0022

p. 34 Fox News

http://www.foxnews.com/opinion/2012/07/04/this-july-4-let-thank-forgotten-revolution-ary-war-hero.html

p. 34 *The Daily Beast*

http://www.thedailybeast.com/articles/2016/02/06/hercules-mulligan-the-spy-who-saved-george-washington-twice.html

p. 34 Irish emigrants

http://thewildgeese.irish/profiles/blogs/ham

p. 34 *New York Journal*

http://fultonhistory.com/my%20photo%20albums/All%20Newspapers/New%20
York%20NY%20Journal%20or%20General%20Advertiser/New%20York%20NY%20
Journal%20or%20General%20Advertiser%201773-1775/index2.html

p. 34 Chernow

http://amzn.to/2xlDeMa

p. 34 Hamilton's letter to John Jay on mobs

http://founders.archives.gov/documents/Hamilton/01-01-02-0060

CHAPTER 7: Hamilton-Related Places to Visit

p. 35 *New York Times* article of 3/6/16
http://www.nytimes.com/2016/03/06/fashion/hamilton-fans-grave-broadway.html?_r=1

p. 37 the Grange
http://www.nps.gov/hagr/index.htm

p. 39 PDF on ForgottenDelights.com
http://www.forgottendelights.com/HamiltonTour.pdf

p. 39 excerpt from *Outdoor Monuments*
http://www.forgottendelights.com/hamctrlpk_2.html

p. 39 Monuments of Manhattan app: see notes for Chapter 1, p. 9

p. 39 "More" page for *Hamilton* in Central Park
http://www.forgottendelights.com/omomapp/omomreal/hamctrlpk.html

p. 39 "More" page for *Hamilton* near the Grange
http://www.forgottendelights.com/omomapp/omomreal/hamgrange.html

p. 43 Monuments of Manhattan: see notes to Chapter 1, p. 9

p. 43 Jefferson here and here
http://www.forgottendelights.com/omomapp/omomreal/jefferson.html
http://www.forgottendelights.com/jefferson2.html

p. 43 For more on this sculpture [*Hamilton* at MCNY], see ForgottenDelights
http://www.forgottendelights.com/HamiltonMCNY.html

p. 43 Museum of American Finance
http://www.moaf.org/index

p. 43 see Hamilton (without Burr)
http://media.gettyimages.com/photos/bronze-statue-of-alexander-hamilton-appoint-ed-the-first-secretary-of-picture-id457413913

p. 43 Morristown Green
http://morristowngreen.com/

p. 43 Paterson Great Falls
http://www.nps.gov/pagr/learn/photosmultimedia/multimedia.htm

p. 44 Alexander Hamilton Awareness Society
http://the-aha-society.com/

p. 44 Wikipedia article on NCC
https://en.wikipedia.org/wiki/National_Constitution_Center

p. 44 Wikimedia page on NCC
https://commons.wikimedia.org/wiki/Category:National_Constitution_Center

p. 44 NCC's site
http://constitutioncenter.org/visit/visitors-guide/

p. 44 Kristen Visbal
http://visbalsculpture.com/americancapeinfo.html

p. 44 this page
http://heyhamilton.com/about/alexander-hamilton/

p. 47 Smithsonian American Art Museum's Art Inventories Catalog
http://siris-artinventories.si.edu/ipac20/ipac.jsp?session=1N5N878X49220.2787&pro-file=ariall&menu=search&submenu=power&ts=1457878649271

p. 47 *Alexander Hamilton: A Brief Biography*
http://amzn.to/2zT6Twx

p. 47 *Outdoor Monuments of Manhattan*
http://forgottendelights.com/outdoormonumentsofmanhattan.html AND
http://amzn.to/2zT6Twx

p. 47 Monuments of Manhattan: see Chapter 1, p. 9

p. 47 handy list is here
http://diannedurantewriter.com/
new-york-city-sculptures-of-figures-from-american-history-active-before-1800

p. 47 *Alexander Hamilton: A Brief Biography*
http://amzn.to/2zT6Twx

CHAPTER 8: Hamilton's First Published Political Writing, 1774

p. 49 Founders Online
http://founders.archives.gov/documents/Hamilton/01-01-02-0054

p. 50 Founders Online
http://founders.archives.gov/documents/Hamilton/01-01-02-0054

p. 51 *Alexander Hamilton: The Formative Years*
http://amzn.to/2ixMlQQ

p. 51 This article has fascinating details
https://allthingsliberty.com/2014/09/the-statue-of-george-iii/

p. 51 horse's tail
http://www.nyhistory.org/exhibit/fragment-equestrian-statue-king-george-iii-tail

p. 51 New-York Historical Society
http://www.nyhistory.org/

p. 52 sketched reconstruction
http://www.nyhistory.org/exhibit/
equestrian-statue-king-george-iii-bowling-green-new-york-city-0

p. 52 modern reconstruction (3D!) see this post
http://diannedurantewriter.com/king-george-iii-born-again-in-new-york-city/

p. 52 "Shook Ones Part 2"
https://www.youtube.com/watch?v=PosV5zVNWlc

p. 52 lyrics here
https://play.google.com/music/preview/Tdqnxrkht6z3xy2ok7wq4jxpzmy?lyr-
ics=1&utm_source=google&utm_medium=search&utm_campaign=lyrics&pcam-
paignid=kp-lyrics&u=0

p. 52 "Going Back to Cali"
https://www.youtube.com/watch?v=FdizL4on-Rc

p. 52 "You've Got to Be Carefully Taught"
https://www.youtube.com/watch?v=OAZ8yOFFbAc

p. 52 "Hey, hey, we're the Monkees"
https://www.youtube.com/watch?v=ksJ6QP8BYn0

p. 53 literary devices
https://quizlet.com/871457/poetry-terms-flash-cards/

p. 70 excellent blog post by Daytonian in Manhattan
> http://daytoninmanhattan.blogspot.com/2012/11/the-lost-thomas-paine-house-no-309.html

p. 70 blog post by Forgotten New York
> http://forgotten-ny.com/1999/05/a-paine-in-the-village/

CHAPTER 12: Angelica Schuyler (1756-1814)

p. 72 *Washington Crossing the Delaware*
> http://www.metmuseum.org/art/collection/search/11417

p. 72 portrait in the New-York Historical Society
> http://www.nyhistory.org/exhibit/mrs-philip-john-schuyler-1734-1803

p. 73 Trumbull's *Declaration of Independence*
> https://commons.wikimedia.org/wiki/File:Declaration_independence.jpg

p. 73 Trumbull's *Washington Before the Battle of Trenton*
> https://en.wikipedia.org/wiki/John_Trumbull#/media/File:General_George_Washington_at_Trenton_by_John_Trumbull.jpeg

p. 73 Trumbull's *Surrender of Lord Cornwallis at Yorktown*
> https://commons.wikimedia.org/wiki/File:Surrender_of_Lord_Cornwallis.jpg

p. 73 J.P. Morgan Chase
> http://www.bloombergview.com/articles/2012-05-03/the-violent-scandalous-origins-of-jpmorgan-chase

p. 74 *An Intimate Life of Alexander Hamilton*
> http://tinyurl.com/yder9t38

p. 75 This one from Hamilton, dated 12/6/1787
> http://founders.archives.gov/documents/Hamilton/01-04-02-0172

p. 76 More here (Jefferson to Angelica)
> https://founders.archives.gov/documents/Jefferson/01-12-02-0638

p. 76 this letter of 12/4/1798
> https://www.pinterest.com/pin/319192692311639191/

p. 76 This site claims
> http://www.findagrave.com/cgi-bin/fg.cgi?page=gr&GRid=7558791

p. 76 *A Guide to the Papers of Angelica Schuyler Church*
> http://ead.lib.virginia.edu/vivaxtf/view?docId=uva-sc/viu00003.xml;query=;

p. 77 elegant 17th-century teapot
> http://www.nyhistory.org/exhibit/teapot-50

p. 77 American National Biography
> http://www.anb.org/

p. 77 Chernow
> http://amzn.to/2xlDeMa

p. 77 Newton
> http://amzn.to/2ixMlQQ

p. 77 GQueues
> https://www.gqueues.com/

p. 77 on this WordPress site

https://angelicaschuylerchurch.wordpress.com/2012/03/26/role-of-angelica-schuy-ler-church-in-political-and-patronage-matters-with-hamilton-and-jefferson/

p. 77 "Muse and Confidante"

https://www.lib.virginia.edu/exhibits/church/index.html

p. 77 charming fangirl blog post

http://exhibit-no-restraint.tumblr.com/post/133827127864/in-which-my-fangirling-over-hamilton-reaches-new

p. 77 "More Between Heaven and Earth"

http://billmadison.blogspot.com/2013/11/preview-more-between-jefferson-cosway.html

p. 77 Salon-Sanctuary

http://www.salonsanctuary.org/

p. 77 the jaw-droppingly beautiful costumes

https://www.facebook.com/SalonSanctuaryConcerts/photos/a.10152958214409268.1073741849.141029109267/10152958312579268/?-type=1&theater

CHAPTER 13: New York, New York (1624-1783)

p. 79 Shorto

http://amzn.to/2hEF3d8

p. 80 for more than a very few days. (More here)

I cannot find the source of this quote. It is driving me mad.

p. 82 *Nathan Hale*

http://www.forgottendelights.com/hale_aob.html

p. 83 New York after the British evacuation (pics here)

http://www.forgottendelights.com/omomapp/omomreal/washusq.html

p. 83 *AIA Guide to New York City*

http://amzn.to/2zSZZbm

p. 84 Ellis's *The Epic of New York City*

http://amzn.to/2hP6ogC

p. 85 Daytonian in Manhattan

http://daytoninmanhattan.blogspot.com/2014/10/the-lost-1763-rhinelander-sugar-house.html

p. 85 this chilling description

http://query.nytimes.com/mem/archive-free/pdf?res=9902E1DE1438E334BC4E52DFB7678389649FDE

p. 86 Prison Ship Martyrs' Monument

https://en.wikipedia.org/wiki/Prison_Ship_Martyrs%27_Monument

p. 86 Morris-Jumel Mansion

http://www.morrisjumel.org/

p. 87 Hessian Hut

http://www.nycgovparks.org/parks/dyckman-house-museum/highlights/9753

p. 87 Daytonian in Manhattan

http://daytoninmanhattan.blogspot.com/2010/12/1783-dyckman-farmhouse-broad-way-and.html

p. 88 forms here

> https://books.google.com/books?id=Ya8FAAAAMAAJ&lpg=PA17&dq=small%20 burgher%20status%20in%20nyc&pg=PA17#v=onepage&q=small%20burgher%20 status%20in%20nyc&f=false

p. 88 Articles of Capitulation

> http://www.thirteen.org/dutchny/interactives/document-dutch-articles-of-surrender/

p. 88 interview with historian David McCullough

> http://www.nytimes.com/2005/12/23/travel/escapes/new-yorks-revolutionary-war-sites-just-squint-and-its-1776.html?_r=0

p. 88 Shorto's *Island at the Center of the World*
> http://amzn.to/2hEF3d8

p. 88 Ellis's *The Epic of New York City*
> http://amzn.to/2hP6ogC

p. 88 *Gotham: A History of New York to 1898*
> http://amzn.to/2hMpkwi

p. 88 handy list is here
> http://www.forgottendelights.com/pre1800.pdf

CHAPTER 14: Hamilton vs. Seabury, 1774-1775

p. 89 *Free Thoughts on the Proceedings of the Continental Congress*
> https://archive.org/details/cihm_20488

p. 89 *Full Vindication*
> http://founders.archives.gov/documents/Hamilton/01-01-02-0054

p. 94 Library of America edition of Hamilton's works
> http://amzn.to/2zSUxVE

p. 95 one of his more famous letters
> http://founders.archives.gov/documents/Hamilton/01-01-02-0060

p. 95 American National Biography
> http://anb.org/articles/home.html

p. 95 this article
> https://allthingsliberty.com/2013/07/reverend-seaburys-pamphlet-war/

CHAPTER 15: A Revue of Royal & Revolutionary Rhetoric, 1756-1776

p. 96 *Journal of George Washington*
> https://ia802609.us.archive.org/17/items/journalofmajorge00wash/journalofmajorge00wash_bw.pdf

p. 96 Battle of Kunersdorf
> https://en.wikipedia.org/wiki/Battle_of_Kunersdorf

p. 97 Stamp Act
> http://avalon.law.yale.edu/18th_century/stamp_act_1765.asp

p. 97 Declaratory Act
> http://www.constitution.org/bcp/decl_act.htm

p. 98 Townshend Acts
> http://avalon.law.yale.edu/18th_century/townsend_act_1767.asp

p. 98 Captain Preston

http://www.let.rug.nl/usa/documents/1751-1775/captain-prestons-account-of-the-boston-massacre-march-5-1770.php

p. 98 anonymous report printed in Boston

http://www.let.rug.nl/usa/documents/1751-1775/anonymous-account-of-the-boston-massacre-march-5-1770.php

p. 99 Sons of Liberty in Boston

https://books.google.com/books?id=NiNCAAAAIAAJ&lpg=PA255&ots=mCsUCwnX-zD&dq=THAT%20worst%20of%20plagues%2C%20the%20detested%20T%20E%20A%20shipped%20for%20this%20port%20by%20the%20East%20India%20Company%2C&pg=PA255#v=onepage&q=THAT%20worst%20of%20plagues,%20the%20detested%20T%20E%20A%20shipped%20for%20this%20port%20by%20the%20East%20India%20Company,&f=false

p. 99 surrounding it here

http://americainclass.org/sources/makingrevolution/crisis/text6/teaactresponse.pdf

p. 100 Benjamin Franklin quote

http://americainclass.org/sources/makingrevolution/crisis/text6/teaactresponse.pdf

p. 100 states the rights

http://avalon.law.yale.edu/18th_century/resolves.asp

p. 100 *The Farmer Refuted*

http://founders.archives.gov/documents/Hamilton/01-01-02-0057

p. 101 Congress to George Washington

https://memory.loc.gov/cgi-bin/query/r?ammem/hlaw:@field(DOCID+@lit(jc00238))

p. 101 Olive Branch Petition

https://en.wikisource.org/wiki/Olive_Branch_Petition

p. 101 different musical

http://www.imdb.com/title/tt0068156/

p. 101 Proclamation of Rebellion

http://www.britannia.com/history/docs/procreb.html

p. 102 King elaborates on the Proclamation of Rebellion

http://www.loc.gov/teachers/classroommaterials/presentationsandactivities/presentations/timeline/amrev/shots/address.html

p. 103 Constitutional Congress responds

http://www.loc.gov/teachers/classroommaterials/presentationsandactivities/presentations/timeline/amrev/shots/responds.html

p. 104 Paine's pamphlet is here

http://www.gutenberg.org/files/147/147-h/147-h.htm

p. 105 full text here

http://www.archives.gov/exhibits/charters/declaration.html

p. 106 letter of abdication

https://parliamentum.org/2011/08/09/george-iii-and-the-loss-of-the-american-colonies/

p. 106 *Boston Tea Party Opera*

http://www.bostonteapartyopera.com/

CHAPTER 16: Hamilton Joins Washington's Staff, 1776

p. 108 Washington to Hancock

http://founders.archives.gov/documents/Washington/03-05-02-0192

p. 109 Washington wrote to Congress

http://founders.archives.gov/documents/Washington/03-05-02-0337

p. 110 aides-de-camp

https://en.wikipedia.org/wiki/Washington%27s_Aides-de-Camp

p. 110 Paul Johnson's brief biography of Washington

http://www.amazon.com/George-Washington-Founding-Father-Eminent/
dp/0060753676/ref=as_li_ss_tl?ie=UTF8&qid=1463225512&sr=8-1&keywords=paul+-
johnson+george+washington&linkCode=ll1&tag=forgottendeli-20&linkId=b-
4841b1925ebd33640f665f1d7564729

p. 110 Ford Mansion

https://www.nps.gov/morr/learn/historyculture/ford-mansion-washingtons-headquarters.
htm

p. 111 charming illustration

http://founders.archives.gov/documents/Washington/03-05-02-0218

p. 111 Addison's *Cato*

http://www.amazon.com/s/ref=as_li_ss_tl?url=search-alias%3Daps&field-keywords=ad-
dison+cato&linkCode=ll2&tag=forgottendeli-20&linkId=1f6f291442aef742d298d-
1ef54f50536

p. 111 credited with inspiring famous lines

https://en.wikipedia.org/wiki/Cato,_a_Tragedy

p. 111 Pergamon exhibition

http://diannedurantewriter.com/sculpture/
pergamon-exhibition-metropolitan-museum-favorites-9/

p. 112 opposition to the theater here

https://allthingsliberty.com/2013/12/congress-bans-theatre/

p. 112 Mount Vernon

http://www.mountvernon.org/

p. 112 StudioEIS

http://www.studioeis.com/

p. 112 "Coming Soon to Mount Vernon, 3 Georges"

http://www.nytimes.com/2006/02/17/politics/17george.html?_r=0

p. 112 "Putting a Face on the First President"

http://www.scientificamerican.com/article/putting-a-face-on-the-fir/

p. 112 This video shows the lyrics

https://www.youtube.com/watch?v=wYZM__VdEjk

p. 112 the 1983 movie

http://www.imdb.com/title/tt0086112/

p. 112 *Ruddigore*

https://www.youtube.com/watch?v=zmBri9kvptE

CHAPTER 17: The Battle of Long Island and the American Retreat, 1776

p. 113 [caption] Lord Howe's HMS *Eagle* is top right. More here

    http://www.morgan-nj.org/blog/sample-page/revolutionary-war-times/
the-battle-of-long-island/

p. 114 full text here

    http://founders.archives.gov/documents/Washington/03-05-02-0127

p. 115 glacial moraine in Brooklyn

    http://drpeterjdadamo.com/GBM/2011/01/05/in-the-beginning/

p. 116 that song

    https://en.wikipedia.org/wiki/The_Grand_Old_Duke_of_York

p. 116 animated here

    https://www.youtube.com/watch?v=QRMBwZjuGEU

p. 117 Old Stone House

    http://theoldstonehouse.org/

p. 118 online here

    http://americainclass.org/sources/makingrevolution/war/text6/pensionnarratives.pdf

p. 119 monument to the Maryland 400

    http://forgotten-ny.com/2014/02/the-maryland-monument-prospect-park/

p. 120 Go. Washington (more here)

    http://founders.archives.gov/documents/Washington/03-06-02-0144

p. 120 my most sincere wish (more here)

    http://founders.archives.gov/documents/Washington/03-06-02-0228

p. 120 Morris-Jumel Mansion

    http://www.morrisjumel.org/

p. 121 [caption] British Headquarters Map

    https://welikia.org/about/how-it-all-began/

p. 122 Your Most Obedt. Sert. (More here)

    http://founders.archives.gov/documents/Washington/03-06-02-0251

p. 122 Flexner's biography of Washington

    http://www.amazon.com/Washington-Indispensable-James-Thomas-Flexner/
dp/0316286168/ref=as_li_ss_tl?ie=UTF8&qid=1463839842&sr=8-1&keywords=flex-
ner+washington&linkCode=lll&tag=forgottendeli-20&linkId=56a380cfe3fb1ec926d-
1c10af2cf850e

p. 122 McCullough's *1776*

    http://www.amazon.com/1776-David-McCullough/dp/0743226720/ref=as_li_
ss_tl?ie=UTF8&qid=1463839896&sr=8-1&keywords=mccullough+1776&-
linkCode=lll&tag=forgottendeli-20&linkId=43f41bdd4fd49759c0daaa97dea4f447

p. 122 Honor and Liberties of their Country (More here)

    http://founders.archives.gov/documents/Washington/03-06-02-0256

p. 124 Go. Washington (More here)

    http://founders.archives.gov/documents/Washington/03-06-02-0454

CHAPTER 18: Hamilton as a Bachelor
and Meeting Elizabeth Schuyler, 1777-1780

p. 125 William Livingston

http://www.findagrave.com/cgi-bin/fg.cgi?page=gr&GRid=3278

p. 125 May 24, 1797; quoted here

https://angelicaschuylerchurch.wordpress.com/2012/03/26/role-of-angelica-schuy-ler-church-in-political-and-patronage-matters-with-hamilton-and-jefferson/

p. 126 [caption] Find-a-Grave

http://www.findagrave.com/cgi-bin/fg.cgi?page=gr&GRid=101281226

p. 128 Alexr. Hamilton (More here)

http://founders.archives.gov/documents/Hamilton/01-01-02-0128

p. 130 A Hamilton (More here)

http://founders.archives.gov/documents/Hamilton/01-02-02-0100

p. 130 James McHenry in 1782

https://books.google.com/books?id=BW-AAAAAIAAJ&pg=PA45&lpg=PA45&d-q=charms+in+all+companies.+no+one+has+seen+her,+of+either+sex&-source=bl&ots=vgFSk4rdkI&sig=twnPI3wvownvOhGj6a_HBqxVm5Y&hl=en&sa=X-&ved=0ahUKEwiR2_LSs_DMAhVMWx4KHV2GAgAQ6AEIHzAA#v=onep-age&q=charms%20in%20all%20companies.%20no%20one%20has%20seen%20her%2C%20of%20either%20sex&f=false

p. 131 [caption] Elizabeth Schuyler Hamilton at Museum of the City of New York.

http://collections.mcny.org/C.aspx?VP3=SearchResult&VBID=24UAYWRZBTF-WQ&SMLS=1&RW=1286&RH=633

p. 133 what survives is here

http://founders.archives.gov/documents/Hamilton/01-02-02-0613

p. 133 Ph. Schuyler (More here)

http://founders.archives.gov/documents/Hamilton/01-02-02-0642

p. 135 assurances of their love (More here)

http://founders.archives.gov/documents/Hamilton/01-02-02-0742

p. 135 *Much Ado About Nothing*

http://shakespeare.mit.edu/much_ado/full.html

p. 135 See this site

http://www.alexanderhamiltonexhibition.org/about/teachers/HamiltonHighSchool.pdf

CHAPTER 19: Alexander and Eliza's Engagement and Wedding, 1780

p. 137 Adieu my love (More here)

http://founders.archives.gov/documents/Hamilton/01-02-02-0747

p. 138 [caption] *Intimate Life of Alexander Hamilton*

https://books.google.com/books?id=YmgoAAAAYAAJ&pg=PA126&lpg=PA126&d-q=Before+no+mortal+ever+knew+A+love+like+mine+so+tender,+true,&-source=bl&ots=MbbrdJa6pO&sig=w3aXrvSUg1UJwsrtCo1grnMeXuE&hl=en&sa=X-&ved=0ahUKEwighpnn54vNAhXLdj4KHcllD1UQ6AEIPDAH#v=onepage&q&f=false

p. 141 first opportunity (More here)

http://founders.archives.gov/documents/Hamilton/01-02-02-0834

p. 143 A Hamilton (More here)

http://founders.archives.gov/documents/Hamilton/01-02-02-0839

p. 158 [caption] Inscription is transcribed here
   https://commons.wikimedia.org/wiki/File:Bennett_Park_New_York_Manhattan_Fort_
   Washington_Memorial_Mark.jpg

p. 159 without me ... (More here)
   http://founders.archives.gov/documents/Washington/03-07-02-0171

p. 160 vanished. (More here)
   http://amarch.lib.niu.edu/islandora/object/niu-amarch%3A104112

p. 160 their Aid. (More here)
   http://founders.archives.gov/documents/Washington/03-07-02-0267

p. 161 [caption] Capture of Major General Charles Lee by the British
   http://gwpapers.virginia.edu/history/topics/major-general-charles-lee/

p. 162 [caption] George H. Moore's 1860 publication
   https://archive.org/stream/mrleesplanmarch201moor#page/n29/mode/2up

p. 162 document and background here
   https://archive.org/stream/mrleesplanmarch201moor#page/87/mode/2up

p. 162 read the rest: here
   https://en.wikisource.org/wiki/The_American_Crisis

p. 164 relieve or prevent (More here)
   http://memory.loc.gov/cgi-bin/query/r?ammem/mgw:@field(DOCID+@lit(gw100200))

p. 164 "fall flat down." (More here)
   https://books.google.com/books?id=Tj5_kGy_QEMC&pg=PA267&lpg=PA267&d-
   q=our+whole+frame+is+shattered.+we+are+tottering+and+without+the+immedi-
   ate+exertions&source=bl&ots=VKJ23jPe-e&sig=Do2X1p3vWwyZznPyIDDGedx-
   CF8M&hl=en&sa=X&ved=0ahUKEwis7bm1_LHNAhUJLSYKHftUASIQ6AEIH-
   DAA#v=onepage&q=our%20whole%20frame%20is%20shattered.%20we%20are%20
   tottering%20and%20without%20the%20immediate%20exertions&f=false

p. 165 *Valiant Ambition*
   http://amzn.to/2Bcezsa

CHAPTER 23: The Battle of Monmouth, June 1778

p. 167 Dr General Yours (More here)
   http://founders.archives.gov/documents/Washington/03-15-02-0574

p. 167 serving under him (More here)
   http://founders.archives.gov/documents/Washington/03-15-02-0593

p. 168 that gentleman's character (More here)
   http://founders.archives.gov/documents/Washington/03-15-02-0586

p. 168 near Englishtown (letter here)
   http://founders.archives.gov/GEWN-03-15-02-0606

p. 169 before-mentioned defile (More here)
   http://www.americanheritage.com/content/private-yankee-doodle?page=8

p. 171 Charles Lee (More here)
   http://founders.archives.gov/documents/Washington/03-15-02-0651

p. 171 Go: Washington (More here)
   http://founders.archives.gov/documents/Washington/03-15-02-0652

p. 171 Charles Lee (More here)
http://founders.archives.gov/GEWN-03-15-02-0653

p. 172 Go: Washington (More here)
http://founders.archives.gov/documents/Washington/03-15-02-0655

p. 175 silence at midnight
http://www.readtheconstitutionstupid.com/en/2012-01-27-19-34-40/2012-02-09-15-37-
19/2012-02-09-15-37-20/2022-1778-letter-of-john-laurens-to-henry-laurens-regarding-
the-battle-of-monmouth

p. 178 unpardonable (More here)
http://founders.archives.gov/documents/Hamilton/01-01-02-0499

p. 178 Molly Pitcher
https://en.wikipedia.org/wiki/Molly_Pitcher

p. 179 Joseph Plumb Martin
https://en.wikisource.org/wiki/The_Adventures_Of_A_Revolutionary_Soldier

CHAPTER 24: Charles Lee on Trial, July-August 1778

p. 179 full transcript is here
https://babel.hathitrust.org/cgi/pt?id=loc.ark:/13960/t73t9z740;view=1up;seq=11

p. 180 printed transcript of the Lee court-martial
https://babel.hathitrust.org/cgi/pt?id=loc.ark:/13960/t73t9z740;view=1up;seq=11

p. 187 Lee's court martial (full text as PDF)
https://babel.hathitrust.org/cgi/pt?id=loc.ark:/13960/t73t9z740;view=1up;seq=11

CHAPTER 25: A Modern Hamilton Portrait

p. 188 auction in Philadelphia, at Freeman's
http://www.invaluable.com/catalog/searchLots.cfm?scp=u&catalogRef=&sh-
w=50&ord=0&img=1&olF=1&houseRef=&houseLetter=A&artist-
Ref=&aID=0&areaID=&countryID=&regionID=&stateID=&fdt=&tdt=&fr=0&to=0-
&wa=Frudakis&wp=&wo=&nw=&upcoming=0&rp=&hi=&rem=FALSE&ns=1&isS-
C=0&row=1&isBIN=

p. 188 Zenos's website here
http://www.zenosfrudakis.com/sculpture/alexander-hamilton

p. 188 full 3-D effect is here
https://youtu.be/N4sBi8MQ1Kc

p. 189 *Freedom* details
http://www.zenosfrudakis.com/freedom-sculpture/

CHAPTER 26: Meanwhile: Aaron Burr, 1778-1783

p. 191 *Memoirs of Aaron Burr*
https://archive.org/details/memoirsaaronbur00davigoog

p. 192 A. Burr (More here)
http://founders.archives.gov/documents/Washington/03-17-02-0561

p. 192 do your duty (More here, n.1)
http://founders.archives.gov/documents/Washington/03-17-02-0561

p. 192 adversity (More here)

https://books.google.com/books?id=bDwMAAAAIAAJ&lpg=PA151&ots=Dfpx-
tuzWon&dq=Our%20being%20the%20subject%20of%20much%20inquiry%2C%20
conjecture%2C%20and%20calumny&pg=PA151#v=onepage&q=Our%20
being%20the%20subject%20of%20much%20inquiry,%20conjecture,%20and%20
calumny&f=false

p. 193 Burr's courtship is here

http://www.historiaobscura.com/
the-courtship-of-theodosia-bartow-prevost-and-aaron-burr/

p. 193 WikiTree

http://www.wikitree.com/wiki/Bartow-24

p. 193 on the site of the Hermitage

http://www.thehermitage.org/programs/programs_school.html

p. 193 home is a museum: the Hermitage

http://www.thehermitage.org/

CHAPTER 27: Dueling Codes, Part 1

p. 194 PBS page on the "Code Duello"

http://www.pbs.org/wgbh/amex/duel/sfeature/rulesofdueling.html

p. 196 under the title *The Duelling Code*

http://amzn.to/2mT021c

p. 196 *Some Short and Useful Reflections upon Duelling*

https://play.google.com/store/books/
details?id=peEwAQAAMAAJ&rdid=book-peEwAQAAMAAJ&rdot=1

p. 196 *The Only Approved Guide through All Stages of a Quarrel*

http://amzn.to/2hLdHSY

p. 198 publishing reprints

http://amzn.to/2jg7M8F

p. 198 PBS page

http://www.pbs.org/wgbh/amex/duel/sfeature/rulesofdueling.html

p. 198 *The Code of Honor*

https://archive.org/details/codeofhonororrul00wils

p. 198 *American Quarterly Review*

https://books.google.com/books?id=T_8RAAAAYAAJ&pg=PA134&lpg=PA134&d-
q=american+quarterly+review+jonah+barrington&source=bl&ots=nsmcnDe9f-
C&sig=yaC7yF8UqbmiudGgzRmj6YWtoeg&hl=en&sa=X&ved=0ahUKEwi-
u3KrFuObNAhVKaD4KHZXMDvYQ6AEIHzAB#v=snippet&q=ireland&f=false

p. 198 *Personal Sketches of His Own Times*

https://play.google.com/store/books/details/
Sir_Jonah_Barrington_Personal_Sketches_of_His_Own?id=WLxvnWXRehkC

p. 200 PBS page on the Code Duello

http://www.pbs.org/wgbh/amex/duel/sfeature/rulesofdueling.html

p. 201 dealer in old and rare books (Richard C. Ramer)

http://livroraro.com/

p. 201 Thimm, *Complete Bibliography of Fencing and Duelling*

> https://www.vialibri.net/cgi-bin/book_search.php?refer=start&sv=fHRoaW1tfGZlbmN-
> pbmd8fHx8&since=40&wt=20&fr=s&sort=yr&order=asc&lang=en&act=search&c-
> ty=US&hi_lo=hi&curr=USD&y=1889

p. 201 Levi and Gelli, *Bibliografia del Duello*

> https://www.vialibri.net/cgi-bin/book_search.php?refer=start&sv=fHxCaWJsaW9ncm-
> Fmw61hIGRlbCBEdWVsbG98fHx8&since=40&wt=20&fr=s&sort=yr&order=as-
> c&lang=en&act=search&cty=US&hi_lo=hi&curr=USD&y=1982

p. 202 WorldCat

> https://www.worldcat.org/

p. 202 ViaLibri

> https://www.vialibri.net/

p. 202 *Hamiltome*

> http://amzn.to/2jQTOOE

p. 202 "Ten Duel Commandments"

> https://www.youtube.com/watch?v=CAXys0fOsxg

p. 202 "Ten Crack Commandments": listen here

> https://www.youtube.com/watch?v=ZYb_8MM1tGQ

p. 202 read lyrics here

> https://play.google.com/music/preview/Tmqmb4jaujfe3vcavzkzqvk4nay?lyrics=1&utm_
> source=google&utm_medium=search&utm_campaign=lyrics&pcampaignid=kp-song-
> lyrics

CHAPTER 28: Dueling Codes, Part 2

p. 203 "The Ten Duel Commandments"

> https://www.youtube.com/watch?v=CAXys0fOsxg

p. 203 *Essai sur le duel*

> https://play.google.com/books/reader?printsec=frontcover&output=reader&id=drxY-
> AAAAcAAJ&pg=GBS.PA3

p. 204 *Down the River*

> http://quod.lib.umich.edu/cgi/t/text/text-idx?c=moa;idno=APF7327

p. 204 *The Code of Honor, or, Rules for the Government of Principals*

> https://archive.org/details/codeofhonororrul00wils

p. 205 [caption] Sabine's *Notes on Duelling*

> https://babel.hathitrust.org/cgi/pt?id=nyp.33433068177447;view=1up;seq=7;size=75

p. 206 "The Coward"

> https://play.google.com/books/reader?printsec=frontcover&output=reader&id=Py-
> 9MAAAAMAAJ&pg=GBS.PA81

p. 208 *Hamiltome*

> http://amzn.to/2jQTOOE

p. 208 Freeman, *Affairs of Honor*

> http://amzn.to/2oTbSWq

p. 208 *History of Duelling*

> https://catalog.hathitrust.org/Record/009736056

p. 208 *The Romance of Duelling*
   https://archive.org/details/romanceduelling00steigoog

p. 208 *Down the River, or Practical Lessons in the Code Duello*
   http://quod.lib.umich.edu/cgi/t/text/text-idx?c=moa;idno=APF7327

p. 208 *Gentlemen's Blood: A Thousand Years of Sword and Pistol*
   http://amzn.to/2hIRKDY

CHAPTER 29: The Lee-Laurens Duel, 1778-1779

p. 210 *Collections of the New-York Historical Society for the Year 1873,* cited as
   "NYHS Publication Fund Series 6"
   https://play.google.com/store/books/details?id=uR0XAAAAYAAJ

p. 210 Freeman, *Affairs of Honor*
   http://amzn.to/2oTbSWq

p. 210 *Washington: A Life*
   https://www.amazon.com/Washington-Life-Ron-Chernow/dp/0143119966/
   ref=as_li_ss_tl?ie=UTF8&qid=1470485081&sr=8-1&keywords=Cher-
   now%27s+Washington:+A+Life&linkCode=lll&tag=forgottendeli-20&linkId=84e3d-
   3cebeec1c18f215c6848d916276

p. 210 Lee Court Martial
   https://babel.hathitrust.org/cgi/pt?id=loc.ark:/13960/t73t9z740;view=1up;seq=11

p. 211 NYHS Publication Fund Series 6
   https://play.google.com/store/books/details?id=uR0XAAAAYAAJ

p. 213 NYHS Publication Fund Series 6
   https://play.google.com/store/books/details?id=uR0XAAAAYAAJ

p. 214 silence (More here)
   http://founders.archives.gov/documents/Hamilton/01-01-02-0673

p. 214 NYHS Publication Fund Series 6
   https://play.google.com/store/books/details?id=uR0XAAAAYAAJ

p. 216 *Life and Correspondence of Joseph Reed*
   https://play.google.com/store/books/details?id=ojujVebQcqYC

p. 216 *Valiant Ambition*
   http://amzn.to/2Bcezsa

p. 216 NYHS Publication Fund Series 6
   https://play.google.com/store/books/details?id=uR0XAAAAYAAJ

p. 216 Freeman's *Affairs of Honor*
   http://amzn.to/2oTbSWq

p. 218 of this nature (Letter here)
   https://founders.archives.gov/documents/Hamilton/01-01-02-0687

p. 219 NYHS Publication Fund Series 6
   https://play.google.com/store/books/details?id=uR0XAAAAYAAJ

p. 220 NYHS Publication Fund Series 6
   https://play.google.com/store/books/details?id=uR0XAAAAYAAJ

p. 221 *Washington's Secret War*
   https://books.google.com/books?id=RGxOCwAAQBAJ&pg=PT311&lp-
   g=PT311&dq=I%27ve+stopped+the+damned+rascal%27s+tongue+anyhow&sour-

ce=bl&ots=DemA8rTniw&sig=GFFp3tNEiWFgyYU0N3TQmOpedtl&hl=en&sa=X-
&ved=0ahUKEwjMn-eRoKrOAhWGJx4KHejNBOMQ6AEIITAB#v=one-
page&q=I've%20stopped%20the%20damned%20rascal's%20tongue%20
anyhow&f=false

CHAPTER 30: Hamilton Resigns from Washington's Staff, 1781

p. 223 Annotated letter here
http://founders.archives.gov/documents/Hamilton/01-02-02-1090

p. 226 Founders Archive version
http://founders.archives.gov/documents/Hamilton/01-02-02-1089

p. 227 (Rest of letter here)
http://founders.archives.gov/documents/Hamilton/01-02-02-1110

p. 228 *Alexander Hamilton: The Formative Years*
http://amzn.to/2ixMlQQ

p. 229 A. Hamilton (More here)
http://founders.archives.gov/documents/Hamilton/01-02-02-1178

p. 229 "Alexander Hamilton: Man and Musical" tour
http://diannedurantewriter.com/tours/
alexander-hamilton-words-images-nyc-tour-by-dianne-l-durante/

CHAPTER 31: Hamilton Tackles Economics, Summer 1781

p. 232 placed upon them (More here)
http://founders.archives.gov/documents/Washington/99-01-02-04754

p. 232 Newton, *Hamilton*
http://amzn.to/2ixMlQQ

p. 232 Marquis de Lafayette had recommended
https://founders.archives.gov/documents/
Hamilton/01-02-02-1004#ARHN-01-02-02-1004-fn-0002

p. 232 nominated by Sullivan
http://founders.archives.gov/documents/Hamilton/01-26-02-0002-0051

p. 232 seconded by Lafayette
https://founders.archives.gov/documents/
Hamilton/01-02-02-1006#ARHN-01-02-02-1006-fn-0007

p. 232 letter of 2/4/1781
http://founders.archives.gov/documents/Hamilton/01-26-02-0002-0054

p. 233 divinations to yourself (More here)
http://founders.archives.gov/documents/Hamilton/01-02-02-1150

p. 233 called the line (More here)
http://founders.archives.gov/documents/Hamilton/01-02-02-1163

p. 234 merit and abilities (More here)
http://founders.archives.gov/documents/Hamilton/01-02-02-1164

p. 234 made it so (More here)
https://founders.archives.gov/documents/Washington/99-01-02-05607

p. 234 importunity (More here)
http://founders.archives.gov/documents/Hamilton/01-02-02-1169

p. 235 *Trade and Commerce* (letter here)
> http://founders.archives.gov/documents/Hamilton/01-02-02-1152

p. 235 letter on finances
> http://founders.archives.gov/documents/Hamilton/01-02-02-1167

p. 235 letter to James Duane
> http://founders.archives.gov/documents/Hamilton/01-02-02-0838

p. 236 his 4/30/1781 letter to Morris
> http://founders.archives.gov/documents/Hamilton/01-02-02-1167

p. 239 upon these points (More here)
> http://founders.archives.gov/documents/Hamilton/01-02-02-1167

p. 239 Robt. Morris (More here)
> http://founders.archives.gov/documents/Hamilton/01-02-02-1176

p. 240 Whole issue here
> http://founders.archives.gov/documents/Hamilton/01-02-02-1179

p. 241 Whole issue here
> http://founders.archives.gov/documents/Hamilton/01-02-02-1181

p. 242 Yr. A Hamilton (More here)
> http://founders.archives.gov/documents/Hamilton/01-02-02-1180

CHAPTER 32: French Aid, 1775-1781

p. 244 Treaty of Alliance
> https://memory.loc.gov/cgi-bin/ampage?collId=llsl&fileName=008/llsl008.db&recNum=19

p. 244 Treaty of Amity and Commerce
> http://avalon.law.yale.edu/18th_century/fr1788-1.asp

p. 247 whatsoever with him (More here)
> http://founders.archives.gov/documents/Washington/99-01-02-02521

p. 247 9/26/1780; more here
> http://founders.archives.gov/documents/Washington/99-01-02-03401

p. 248 to sollicit (More here)
> http://founders.archives.gov/documents/Washington/99-01-02-05346

p. 249 my duty (More here)
> http://founders.archives.gov/documents/Washington/99-01-02-05543

p. 250 Go: Washington (More here)
> http://founders.archives.gov/documents/Washington/99-01-02-05495

p. 251 Schwerin; quoted here
> http://www.historynet.com/letters-from-wilhelm-graf-von-schwerin-eyewitness-to-siege-of-yorktown.htm

p. 253 Virginia (More here)
> http://founders.archives.gov/documents/Hamilton/01-02-02-1189

p. 253 National Park Service
> https://www.nps.gov/waro/learn/historyculture/washington-rochambeau-revolutionary-route.htm

p. 253 Museum of the American Revolution
> https://www.amrevmuseum.org/updates/reflections/washington-and-rochambeau-revolutionary-collaboration

p. 253 Xenophon Group

> http://xenophongroup.com/mcjoynt/rochamb.htm

CHAPTER 33: Alexander and Eliza's Rings, Handkerchiefs,
and Wedding Cake

p. 255 Rare Books and Manuscripts Library

> http://library.columbia.edu/locations/rbml.html

p. 255 Alexander Hamilton Awareness Society

> http://the-aha-society.com/

CHAPTER 34: Yorktown: August to Early October 1781

p. 258 appearance of defeat (quoted here)

> https://archive.org/stream/beatthelastdrumt006769mbp/beatthelastdrumt006769mbp_djvu.txt

p. 258 James McHenry

> http://msa.maryland.gov/megafile/msa/speccol/sc3500/sc3520/000800/000800/pdf/msa_sc_5458_51_3385.pdf

p. 260 hear the worst (Quoted here)

> https://books.google.com/books?id=zW8BAAAAMAAJ&pg=PA184&lpg=PA184&dq=i+would+rather+risk+an+action+than+defend+my+half-finished+work&source=bl&ots=5_HlfNAn8E&sig=2iZ3prkXljWaVYHU6DxrZwZyprI&hl=en&sa=X&ved=0ahUKEwijxoOgmerOAhWC1R4KHSTLCw4Q6AEIHzAB#v=onepage&q=i%20would%20rather%20risk%20an%20action%20than%20defend%20my%20half-finished%20work&f=false

p. 260 *Journal of Colonel Daniel Trabue*

> http://books.googleusercontent.com/books/content?req=AKW5Qaegg3NAqQULr8mIwp7GcvHOeQkxuLETWupGYlTW510Xw4jAJtO9vePrS_-EkbZQBu5Keg-MlPApGIv-JU02QhiW7QGHXl2NvtlFKljK-xXQyC2P_6YLz9i3pupRqHbtZkQN_enTm2J92RBk1eNjf7nAIoG8DU7v0zPEUnyPQBSwhYsNrgcwozpEQEkxclL3I5qoLfM48ioNQy6i8TK8UylMjGGxPuHGnxhgTJ26flmIiRlSHF9rXPZkuqUZien-evclMpNlSzaz3kU6ys_vRPrUYspRfVA

p. 261 Adieu A Hamilton (More here)

> http://founders.archives.gov/documents/Hamilton/01-02-02-1199

p. 262 U.S. Army Heritage site

> http://www.carlisle.army.mil/ahec/trail/Redoubt10/

p. 263 Revolutionary War cannon

> http://www.visitingyorktown.com/cannon.html

p. 263 howitzer

> http://www.visitingyorktown.com/howitzers.html

p. 263 mortar

> http://www.visitingyorktown.com/mortars.html

p. 263 cannon ball (More here)

> http://www.historynet.com/letters-from-wilhelm-graf-von-schwerin-eyewitness-to-siege-of-yorktown.htm

p. 263 this 1814 image

> https://commons.wikimedia.org/wiki/File:Ft._Henry_bombardement_1814.jpg

p. 263 whoever it hits (More here, p. 112)

http://books.googleusercontent.com/books/content?req=AKW5Qaegg3NAqQUL-
r8mIwp7GcvHOeQkxuLETWupGYlTW510Xw4jAJtO9vePrS_-EkbZQBu5Keg-
MlPApGIv-JU02QhiW7QGHX12NvtlFKljK-xXQyC2P_6YLz9i3pupRqHbtZk-
QN_enTm2J92RBk1eNjf7nAIoG8DU7v0zPEUnyPQBSwhYsNrgcwozpEQEkxcl-
L3I5qoLfM48ioNQy6i8TK8UylMjGGxPuHGnxhgTJ26fImIiRlSHF9rXPZkuqUZ-
ien-evclMpNlSzaz3kU6ys_vRPrUYspRfVA

p. 264 bursting of our shells (More here)

https://archive.org/stream/jamesthachermil00revorich#page/340/mode/2up/search/
meteor

p. 264 huge slaughter (More here)

http://www.revolutionarywararchives.org/redoubt10witness.html

p. 265 shotgun blast (search "grape shot")

http://www.revolutionarywararchives.org/redoubt10mystery.html

p. 265 shot off (Quoted here)

https://books.google.com/books?id=a4rlBgAAQBAJ&pg=PT190&lpg=PT190&d-
q=men+lying+nearly+everywhere+who+were+mortally+wounded,+whose+-
heads,+arms,+and+legs&source=bl&ots=NSJmgXNZE1&sig=N-JqJIqy9nWLL-
v23HMnpDoI9s0Y&hl=en&sa=X&ved=0ahUKEwjLramO3uzOAhVBEBQKHVAe-
CWAQ6AEILDAE#v=onepage&q=men%20lying%20nearly%20everywhere%20
who%20were%20mortally%20wounded%2C%20whose%20heads%2C%20
arms%2C%20and%20legs&f=false

p. 266 prisoners (More here)

http://xenophongroup.com/mcjoynt/9and10.htm

p. 267 other redoubt (More here)

http://www.gutenberg.org/files/8376/8376-h/8376-h.htm

p. 267 Fleming

https://archive.org/stream/beatthelastdrumt006769mbp/beatthelastdrumt006769mbp_
djvu.txt

p. 268 covered way (More here)

https://books.google.com/books?id=DsNOAQAAMAAJ&pg=RA1-PA408&lp-
g=RA1-PA408&dq=duncan+diary+yorktown&source=bl&ots=A4mF5kzJZS&sig=-
7lie-nqHmn_KwQL7CCdHEqyNIog&hl=en&sa=X&ved=0ahUKEwiW2s-
D3j-3OAhXDmx4KHZxoDVgQ6AEIODAG#v=onepage&q=duncan%20diary%20
yorktown&f=false

p. 269 opposition (More here)

https://books.google.com/books?id=tGhKAAAAMAAJ&pg=PA275&lpg=PA275&d-
q=the+besiegers+had+got+within+300+yards+of+them&source=bl&ots=jmYA2zi-
INY&sig=FZx9otjPA-m7AMSw_q3MaQIuF7g&hl=en&sa=X&ved=0ahUKEw-
jFw_rl-u3OAhWBJx4KHcCoBokQ6AEIHDAA#v=onepage&q=the%20besiegers%20
had%20got%20within%20300%20yards%20of%20them&f=false

p. 269 You really should read it: here

http://www.revolutionarywararchives.org/redoubt10witness.html

p. 270 ceased to resist (More here)

http://founders.archives.gov/documents/Hamilton/01-02-02-1200-0001

p. 270 after-action report

http://founders.archives.gov/documents/Hamilton/01-02-02-1200-0001

p. 270 Newton's *Alexander Hamilton: The Formative Years*

http://amzn.to/2ixMlQQ

p. 270 CORNWALLIS (More here)

> https://books.google.com/books?id=TUYUAAAAYAAJ&pg=RA1-PA190&lp-g=RA1-PA190&dq=we+shall+soon+be+exposed+to+an+assault+in+ruined+works&-source=bl&ots=X5K75OsVhC&sig=7D1ehQPs2BuTjJoFfG11j-pauRY&hl=en&sa=X-&ved=0ahUKEwiw8vnmk-3OAhWEqx4KHQK0BrQQ6AEILTAG#v=onep-age&q=we%20shall%20soon%20be%20exposed%20to%20an%20assault%20in%20ruined%20works&f=false

p. 271 Ammunition totally (More here)

> http://www.encyclopediavirginia.
> org/_Journal_of_the_Siege_of_Yorktown_by_St_George_Tucker_1781

p. 271 appropriate celebrations

> http://www.historyisfun.org/yorktown-victory-center/yorktown-victory-celebration/

p. 271 Fleming's *Beat the Last Drum*

> http://amzn.to/2zcjg3K

p. 271 Captain Stephen Olney's account

> https://books.google.com/books?id=tGhKAAAAMAAJ&pg=PA275&lpg=PA275&d-q=the+besiegers+had+got+within+300+yards+of+them&source=bl&ots=jmYA2zi-INY&sig=FZx9otjPA-m7AMSw_q3MaQIuF7g&hl=en&sa=X&ved=0ahUKEw-jFw_rl-u3OAhWBJx4KHcCoBokQ6AEIHDAA#v=onepage&q=the%20besiegers%20had%20got%20within%20300%20yards%20of%20them&f=false

p. 271 forlorn hope

> https://en.wikipedia.org/wiki/Forlorn_hope

CHAPTER 35: Alexander and Eliza's Wedding Cake, Revisited

p. 272 link to a recipe

> http://alloveralbany.com/archive/2016/08/30/
> an-18th-century-albany-wedding-cake-maybe

p. 272 The Manuscript Cookbooks Survey

> http://www.manuscriptcookbookssurvey.com/

p. 274 Leslie's cookbook

> http://digital.lib.msu.edu/projects/cookbooks/coldfusion/display.
> cfm?ID=sevf&PageNum=58

p. 274 *The Practical Housekeeper*

> http://digital.lib.msu.edu/projects/cookbooks/html/books/book_21.cfm

p. 274 Manuscripts Cookbook Survey

> http://www.manuscriptcookbookssurvey.com/

CHAPTER 36: Yorktown: October 16-18, 1781

p. 278 *A History of the Campaigns of 1780 and 1781*

> https://play.google.com/books/reader?printsec=frontcover&output=reader&id=-d1Y-AAAAMAAJ&pg=GBS.PA444

p. 278 *Popp's Journal, 1777-1783*

> https://archive.org/details/poppsjournal177700popp

p. 279 Fleming, *Beat the Last Drum*

> http://amzn.to/2zcjg3K

p. 279 drawing to a close (More here)
https://archive.org/stream/jamesthachermil00revorich#page/342/mode/2up

p. 279 *Popp's Journal*
https://archive.org/details/poppsjournal177700popp

p. 279 Tarleton's *History*
https://play.google.com/books/reader?printsec=frontcover&output=reader&id=-d1Y-AAAAMAAJ&pg=GBS.PA446

p. 280 *Military Journal of Major Ebenezer Denny*
http://deila.dickinson.edu/cdm/printview/collection/ownwords/id/8974/type/compoundobject/show/8722

p. 280 ate their breakfasts (More here)
http://historymatters.gmu.edu/d/5833/

p. 281 the honour to be, &c. (More here)
https://play.google.com/books/reader?printsec=frontcover&output=reader&id=-d1Y-AAAAMAAJ&pg=GBS.PA446

p. 281 you may propose (More here)
https://play.google.com/books/reader?printsec=frontcover&output=reader&id=-d1Y-AAAAMAAJ&pg=GBS.PA447

p. 281 seige was ended (More here)
http://historymatters.gmu.edu/d/6597/

p. 282 *Popp's Journal*
https://archive.org/details/poppsjournal177700popp

p. 282 important Event (More here)
http://www.encyclopediavirginia.org/_Journal_of_the_Siege_of_Yorktown_by_St_George_Tucker_1781

p. 283 honour to be, &c. (More here)
http://www.loc.gov/teachers/classroommaterials/presentationsandactivities/presentations/timeline/amrev/peace/yorktown.html

p. 284 honour to be, &c. (More here)
https://play.google.com/books/reader?printsec=frontcover&output=reader&id=-d1Y-AAAAMAAJ&pg=GBS.PA450

p. 285 tower of London (More here)
https://archive.org/stream/jamesthachermil00revorich#page/344/mode/2up

p. 285 Commissioner (More here)
https://babel.hathitrust.org/cgi/pt?id=nyp.33433068173875;view=1up;seq=33

p. 286 A Hamilton (Letter here)
http://founders.archives.gov/documents/Hamilton/01-02-02-1202

p. 286 *Alexander Hamilton: The Formative Years*
http://amzn.to/2ixMlQQ

CHAPTER 37: Yorktown: October 19, 1781, and the Aftermath

p. 287 destination (More here)
http://founders.archives.gov/documents/Washington/99-01-02-07199

p. 288 *Popp's Journal*
https://archive.org/details/poppsjournal177700popp

p. 290 frequently broken (More here)

    https://archive.org/stream/jamesthachermil00revorich#page/344/mode/2up

p. 290 much in liquor (More here)

    https://books.google.com/books?id=9YEsAAAAMAAJ&pg=PA22&lpg=PA22&d-
q=feltman+British+army+marched+out+and+grounded+their+arms+in+-
front+of+our+line.&source=bl&ots=oaimB-L1ji&sig=iqLHgGNDM42-_
zdEM4D-nH6AsQY&hl=en&sa=X&ved=0ahUKEwj098rR-KXPAhWMNj4KHfl-
wCcsQ6AEIHjAA#v=onepage&q&f=false

p. 291 *Revolutionary War Journal of Baron Ludwig von Closen*

    https://books.google.com/books/about/The_Revolutionary_Journal_of_Baron_Ludwi.
html?id=vEiaOwAACAAJ

p. 291 admit of Description (More here)

    http://www.encyclopediavirginia.
org/_Journal_of_the_Siege_of_Yorktown_by_St_George_Tucker_1781

p. 293 Johnston

    https://play.google.com/books/reader?printsec=frontcover&output=reader&id=rWw-
FAAAAQAAJ&pg=GBS.PA177

p. 294 one thousand (More here)

    http://deila.dickinson.edu/cdm/printview/collection/ownwords/id/8974/type/
compoundobject/show/8722

p. 294 their countenances (More here)

    http://historymatters.gmu.edu/d/6597/

p. 295 all by name (More here)

    http://historymatters.gmu.edu/d/5833/

p. 297 still rejoicing (More here)

    https://ia802205.us.archive.org/31/items/colonialmentimes00harp/colonialmentime-
s00harp.pdf

p. 297 induced me to expect (More here)

    http://www.loc.gov/teachers/classroommaterials/presentationsandactivities/presenta-
tions/timeline/amrev/peace/yorktown.html

p. 298 [caption] Washington's diary for 10/19/1781, at Library of Congress (p. 5)

    https://www.loc.gov/exhibits/treasures/trt022.html

p. 298 public stores &c. (More here)

    https://www.loc.gov/exhibits/treasures/trt022.html

p. 298 Articles of Capitulation

    http://avalon.law.yale.edu/18th_century/art_of_cap_1781.asp

p. 298 Cornwallis's report

    http://www.shsu.edu/~his_ncp/Yorktown.html

p. 299 Johnston

    https://play.google.com/books/reader?printsec=frontcover&output=reader&id=rWw-
FAAAAQAAJ&pg=GBS.PA180

p. 300 *Alexander Hamilton: The Formative Years*

    http://amzn.to/2ixMlQQ

p. 300 *Military Journal of Major Ebenezer Denny*

    http://deila.dickinson.edu/cdm/printview/collection/ownwords/id/8974/type/
compoundobject/show/8722

p. 300 *Journal of Lt. William Feltman*

https://books.google.com/books?id=9YEsAAAAMAAJ&pg=PA22&lpg=PA22&d-q=feltman+British+army+marched+out+and+grounded+their+arms+in+-front+of+our+line.&source=bl&ots=oaimB-L1ji&sig=iqLHgGNDM42-_zdEM4D-nH6AsQY&hl=en&sa=X&ved=0ahUKEwj098rR-KXPAhWMNj4KHfl-wCcsQ6AEIHjAA#v=onepage&q&f=false

p. 300 *Popp's Journal*

https://archive.org/details/poppsjournal177700popp

p. 300 Thacher, *Military Journal of the American Revolution*

https://archive.org/stream/jamesthachermil00revorich#page/342/mode/2up

p. 300 Tucker, *Journal of the Siege of Yorktown*

http://www.encyclopediavirginia.
org/_Journal_of_the_Siege_of_Yorktown_by_St_George_Tucker_1781

p. 300 Tarleton's *History of the Campaigns of 1780 and 1781*

https://play.google.com/books/reader?printsec=frontcover&output=reader&id=-d1Y-AAAAMAAJ&pg=GBS.PA444

p. 300 Hamilton, letter of 10/12/1781

http://founders.archives.gov/documents/Hamilton/01-02-02-1199

p. 300 Hamilton, report of 10/15/1781

http://founders.archives.gov/documents/Hamilton/01-02-02-1200-0001

p. 300 Hamilton, letter of 10/18/1781

http://founders.archives.gov/documents/Hamilton/01-02-02-1202

p. 300 Founders Archive

http://founders.archives.gov/

p. 300 Johnston, *The Yorktown Campaign*

https://books.google.com/books/about/The_Yorktown_Campaign_and_the_Surrender.html?id=rWwFAAAAQAAJ

p. 300 Lafayette, *Memoirs*

http://www.gutenberg.org/files/8376/8376-h/8376-h.htm

p. 301 Johnston, *The Yorktown Campaign*

https://books.google.com/books/about/The_Yorktown_Campaign_and_the_Surrender.html?id=rWwFAAAAQAAJ

p. 301 Plumb, narrative on Yorktown

http://historymatters.gmu.edu/d/6597/

p. 301 Osborn, deposition

http://historymatters.gmu.edu/d/5833/

p. 301 Tarleton, *History of the Campaigns of 1780 and 1781*

https://play.google.com/books/reader?printsec=frontcover&output=reader&id=-d1Y-AAAAMAAJ&pg=GBS.PA444

p. 301 Trabue, *Colonial Men and Times*

https://ia802205.us.archive.org/31/items/colonialmentimes00harp/colonialmentime-s00harp.pdf

p. 301 United States Army Old Guard Fife and Drum Corps

http://www.fifeanddrum.army.mil/

CHAPTER 38: Yorktown: "The World Turned Upside Down"?

p. 303 Chernow's *Alexander Hamilton*
   http://amzn.to/2oX7jgi

p. 303 Fleming's *Beat the Drum*
   http://amzn.to/2B5ghLI

p. 303 *Hamilton: The Revolution*
   http://amzn.to/2z6omOP

p. 303 and the Puritans are here
   http://www.lukehistory.com/ballads/worldup.html

p. 303 poem was sung is here
   http://www.contemplator.com/england/worldtur.html

p. 304 British or German march (More here)
   http://founders.archives.gov/documents/Washington/99-01-02-07199

p. 304 French or American march (More here)
   http://www.encyclopediavirginia.
   org/_Journal_of_the_Siege_of_Yorktown_by_St_George_Tucker_1781

p. 305 *Popp's Journal*
   https://archive.org/details/poppsjournal177700popp

p. 305 returned to town (More here)
   http://deila.dickinson.edu/cdm/printview/collection/ownwords/id/8974/type/
   compoundobject/show/8722

p. 305 between them (More here)
   http://historymatters.gmu.edu/d/6597/

p. 305 grounded their arms (More here)
   http://historymatters.gmu.edu/d/5833/

p. 306 *Anecdotes of the American Revolution*
   https://babel.hathitrust.org/cgi/pt?id=nyp.33433068173875;view=1up;seq=7

p. 306 "The world turned upside down" (More here)
   https://babel.hathitrust.org/cgi/pt?id=nyp.33433068173875;view=1up;seq=33

p. 308 Schrader: retrieved from
   http://www.jstor.org/stable/3052564 doi:1

p. 308 Ward in American National Biography Online
   http://www.anb.org/articles/02/02-00193.html

p. 308 Littel, "Major William Jackson"
   https://www.jstor.org/stable/pdf/20084360.pdf

p. 308 *American Review*
   https://babel.hathitrust.org/cgi/pt?id=uva.x004215483;view=1up;seq=437

p. 309 Trudeau, "Music in the Continental Army"
   http://digitalcommons.apus.edu/cgi/viewcontent.cgi?article=1056&context=theses

p. 309 "Hamilton Turns the World Upside Down"
   http://blogs.loc.gov/music/2015/10/hamilton-turns-the-world-upside-down/

CHAPTER 39A: Hamilton Back in New York, 1781-1782

p. 311 Southern fatigues (More here)
https://founders.archives.gov/documents/Hamilton/01-02-02-1204

p. 311 echo of their officers (More here)
http://founders.archives.gov/documents/Hamilton/01-26-02-0002-0072

p. 311 superior abilities & knowledge (see here)
http://founders.archives.gov/documents/Hamilton/01-03-02-0006

p. 312 A Hamilton (More here)
http://founders.archives.gov/documents/Hamilton/01-03-02-0006

p. 314 March 1782; more here
http://founders.archives.gov/documents/Hamilton/01-03-02-0011

CHAPTER 39B: Yorktown, 235 Years Ago:
Here Cannons Flash, Bombs Glance, and Bullets Fly

p. 317 Stone, *Our French Allies*
https://archive.org/details/ourfrenchallies00stongoog

CHAPTER 40: Hamilton Studies Law, 1782

p. 318 my baby (More here)
https://founders.archives.gov/documents/Hamilton/01-03-02-0011

p. 318 *Practical Proceedings*
http://amzn.to/2B556Tf

p. 318 Founders Archives
http://founders.archives.gov/

p. 319 *Life of Hamilton*
https://archive.org/stream/lifeofalexanderh01hami3#page/398/mode/2up/search/manual

p. 319 Wyche's *Supreme Court Practice*
https://books.google.com/books?id=C364VLeAo8gC&pg=PA605&lpg=PA605&d-
q=wyche+supreme+court+practice&source=bl&ots=M3s6eGGHjS&sig=klR-
dOPH8ibi2cPqFvfETUh8V5Qk&hl=en&sa=X&ved=0ahUKEwjl9q6R-eHPAhX-
Baz4KHdBwBkoQ6AEISzAJ#v=onepage&q=wyche%20supreme%20court%20
practice&f=false

p. 322 It's Hamiltime
https://itshamiltime.com/

p. 322 Alexander Hamilton Awareness Society
http://the-aha-society.com/

p. 322 of this nature (More here)
http://founders.archives.gov/documents/Hamilton/01-03-02-0023

p. 323 Doyle Galleries details
https://doyle.com/auctions/14ba01-new-york-city-bar-association/
catalogue/138-manuscript-hamilton-alexander-practical

p. 323 listed on Amazon
http://amzn.to/2B556Tf

p. 323 ViaLibri

    https://www.vialibri.net/cgi-bin/book_search.php?refer=start&sv=fGhhbWlsdG9uf-
HByYWN0aWNhbCBwcm9jZWVkaW5nc3x8fHw%3D&since=40&wt=20&-
fr=s&sort=yr&order=asc&lang=en&act=search&cty=US&hi_lo=hi&curr=US-
D&y=9809

CHAPTER 41: The State of the Union after Yorktown, 1782

p. 325 difficult than ever (More here)

    http://founders.archives.gov/documents/Hamilton/01-03-02-0018

p. 326 adopt his ideas (Here, n. 1)

    http://founders.archives.gov/documents/Hamilton/01-03-02-0015

p. 326 aim of its policy (More here)

    http://founders.archives.gov/documents/Hamilton/01-03-02-0015

p. 327 arguments that depend on philosophy

    https://www.aynrand.org/novels/capitalism-the-unknown-ideal#synopsis-1

p. 327 thy tranquillity (More here)

    http://founders.archives.gov/documents/Hamilton/01-03-02-0031

p. 328 humble servant (More here)

    http://founders.archives.gov/documents/Hamilton/01-03-02-0023

p. 330 matters in train (More here)

    http://founders.archives.gov/documents/Hamilton/01-03-02-0027

p. 330 federal government (here)

    http://founders.archives.gov/documents/Hamilton/01-03-02-0043

p. 330 left for me to do (More here)

    http://founders.archives.gov/documents/Hamilton/01-03-02-0049

p. 330 circumstances will permit (More here)

    http://founders.archives.gov/documents/Hamilton/01-03-02-0053

p. 330 published a statement

    http://founders.archives.gov/documents/Hamilton/01-03-02-0048

p. 330 a full view of the situation

    http://founders.archives.gov/documents/Hamilton/01-03-02-0057-0001

p. 331 federal government (More here)

    http://founders.archives.gov/documents/Hamilton/01-03-02-0057-0001

p. 332 update to Morris 9/28/1782

    http://founders.archives.gov/documents/Hamilton/01-03-02-0082

p. 332 update to Morris 10/5/1782

    http://founders.archives.gov/documents/Hamilton/01-03-02-0088

p. 332 update to Morris 10/9/1782

    http://founders.archives.gov/documents/Hamilton/01-03-02-0089

p. 332 publishing in the New York Packet

    http://founders.archives.gov/documents/Hamilton/01-03-02-0103

p. 332 "On Studying History"

    http://www.forgottendelights.com/studyinghistory.html

CHAPTER 42: John Laurens Dies in South Carolina, August 1782

p. 334 as before (More here)
http://founders.archives.gov/documents/Hamilton/01-03-02-0044

p. 334 quoted by John C. Hamilton, here
http://founders.archives.gov/documents/Hamilton/01-03-02-0045

p. 335 Founder's Archive notes
http://founders.archives.gov/documents/Hamilton/01-03-02-0058

p. 335 Yrs for ever Λ Hamilton (More here)
http://founders.archives.gov/documents/Hamilton/01-03-02-0058

p. 336 friend & ser A. Hamilton (More here)
http://founders.archives.gov/documents/Hamilton/01-03-02-0090

p. 337 arrival at Philadelphia (More here)
http://founders.archives.gov/documents/Hamilton/01-03-02-0102

p. 337 This collection of John's letters
https://archive.org/stream/yourDutifulSonJohnLaurens-Ex-cerptsFromHisCorrespondenceWithHis/John-Laurens#page/n9/mode/2up

p. 338 *Hamilton: The Revolution*
http://amzn.to/2hDKRUl

CHAPTER 43: How Does History Differ from Art?

p. 339 *Washington and Hamilton: The Alliance That Forged America*
http://amzn.to/2hOmtDm

p. 341 *Outdoor Monuments of Manhattan*
http://amzn.to/2hOyd8L

p. 341 Ayn Rand's definition of art
http://aynrandlexicon.com/lexicon/art.html

p. 341 *Innovators in Sculpture*
http://amzn.to/2iywzW3

CHAPTER 44A: The Newburgh Mutiny, Spring 1783

p. 342 told Richard Kidder Meade
http://founders.archives.gov/documents/Hamilton/01-03-02-0064

p. 342 Yr tender A H (More here)
http://founders.archives.gov/documents/Hamilton/01-03-02-0107

p. 342 on his account (More here)
http://founders.archives.gov/documents/Hamilton/01-03-02-0128

p. 343 Kent's *Memoirs*
https://archive.org/stream/memoirsandlette00kentgoog#page/n300/mode/2up

p. 343 independant nation (More here)
http://masshist.org/digitaladams/archive/doc?id=L17821108ja

p. 343 Article 7 (More here)
http://founders.archives.gov/documents/Adams/06-14-02-0058

p. 344 Hatch, *Administration of the Revolutionary Army*, p. 149

https://play.google.com/books/reader?id=RG4-AQAAMAAJ&printsec=frontcover&output=reader&hl=en&pg=GBS.PA149

p. 344 Newburgh, N.Y.

http://parks.ny.gov/historic-sites/17/details.aspx

p. 344 fatal effects (Hatch, p. 150)

https://play.google.com/books/reader?id=RG4-AQAAMAAJ&printsec=frontcover&output=reader&hl=en&pg=GBS.PA150

p. 345 Hatch, p. 155

https://books.google.com/books?id=EDYOAAAAIAAJ&pg=PA155&lpg=PA155&dq=%22as+soon+as+the+condition+of+the+treasury+permitted,+furnish+pay+in+-such+amounts+as+he+thought+proper;+and+that+the+States+should+be+recommended&source=bl&ots=9nq7F2BN7e&sig=EVbgBAmdkZADkRkUZh1Cep2f-DQY&hl=en&sa=X&ved=0ahUKEwjjqliB4KrQAhXGeCYKHa5pDqIQ6AEIHTAA

p. 345 insufficiency of the confederation (More here)

http://founders.archives.gov/documents/Hamilton/01-03-02-0144

p. 346 power of Congress (More here)

http://founders.archives.gov/documents/Hamilton/01-03-02-0148

p. 346 Newton's very persuasive post

https://thepathtotyranny.wordpress.com/2016/11/16/alexander-hamiltons-participation-in-the-newburgh-conspiracy-reexamined/

p. 348 correspond with their duty (More here)

http://founders.archives.gov/documents/Hamilton/01-03-02-0155

p. 349 may cooperate (More here)

http://founders.archives.gov/documents/Hamilton/01-03-02-0155

p. 349 policy to him (More here)

http://founders.archives.gov/documents/Hamilton/01-03-02-0163

p. 350 Yrs &c. GW (More here)

http://founders.archives.gov/documents/Washington/99-01-02-10767

p. 351 enemies any more (More here)

http://www.varsitytutors.com/earlyamerica/milestone-events/newburgh-address-anonymous-letter

p. 353 occasioned thereby (More here)

http://founders.archives.gov/documents/Hamilton/01-03-02-0179

p. 354 empire in blood (More here)

https://en.wikisource.org/wiki/Newburgh_address

p. 354 Shaw; more here

https://archive.org/stream/journalsofmajors00shawiala/journalsofmajors00shawiala_djvu.txt

p. 355 ruin of the army

http://founders.archives.gov/documents/Hamilton/01-03-02-0182

p. 355 on 3/25/1783

http://founders.archives.gov/documents/Hamilton/01-03-02-0195

p. 356 pretensions of the army (More here)

https://books.google.com/books?id=PpQ5AQAAMAAJ&pg=PA351&lpg=PA351&dq=I+sincerely+wish+ingratitude+was+not+so+natural+to+the+hu-

man+heart+as+it+is.&source=bl&ots=jGwJOaDk3S&sig=kqWEVng_KfUdJNn-
4P1Q9TqMUpdw&hl=en&sa=X&ved=0ahUKEwi6v7-Vt5LQAhVHySYKHev-
fAmUQ6AEIIjAB#v=onepage&q&f=false

p. 356 origin here (More here)
> http://founders.archives.gov/documents/Washington/99-01-02-10968

p. 357 without delay (More here)
> http://founders.archives.gov/documents/Washington/99-01-02-10993

p. 357 Continental politics (More here)
> http://founders.archives.gov/documents/Hamilton/01-03-02-0204

p. 357 every proper occasion (More here)
> http://founders.archives.gov/documents/Washington/99-01-02-11076

p. 358 really are futile (More here)
> http://founders.archives.gov/documents/Hamilton/01-03-02-0217

p. 359 *Washington and Hamilton: The Alliance That Forged America*
> http://amzn.to/2hG1FKA

p. 359 Rand Scholet
> http://the-aha-society.com/

p. 359 Michael Newton's research
> http://michaelenewton.com/

p. 359 blog post
> https://thepathtotyranny.wordpress.com/2016/11/16/
> alexander-hamiltons-participation-in-the-newburgh-conspiracy-reexamined/

CHAPTER 44B: Hamilton and Company at 48 Wall Street

p. 360 Museum of American Finance
> http://www.moaf.org/index

p. 360 N.C. Wyeth
> https://commons.wikimedia.org/wiki/Category:N._C._Wyeth

p. 360 *Columbia Historical Portrait of New York*
> http://amzn.to/2B66YeB

p. 361 N.C. Wyeth
> https://commons.wikimedia.org/wiki/Category:N._C._Wyeth

p. 364 Angelsea Parkhurst Newman
> http://newmanservices.com/jmh/jmh_winter_2009_social_register_observer.pdf

p. 364 Lehman College Art Gallery Site
> http://www.lehman.edu/vpadvance/artgallery/publicart/bio/hewlett.html

p. 364 Museum of American Finance
> http://www.moaf.org/index

p. 368 *Encyclopedia of New York City*
> http://amzn.to/2z3X8IM

p. 368 page on 48 Wall Street
> http://www.moaf.org/news/press_access/materials/Backgroundon48WallStreet.doc

p. 368 Skyscraper Museum is here (search "48")
> http://www.skyscraper.org/webwalk/wallstreet.txt

p. 368 "The Rise of Wall Street"
> http://skyscraper.org/EXHIBITIONS/WALL_STREET/walkthrough_intro.php

CHAPTER 45: *Alexander Hamilton: A Brief Biography*

p. 369 *Alexander Hamilton: A Brief Biography*
http://amzn.to/2zT6Twx

CHAPTER 46: The Pennsylvania Mutiny, Summer 1783

p. 371 Drudgery and Vexation (More here, n. 3)
http://founders.archives.gov/documents/Hamilton/01-03-02-0224

p. 372 public stipulations (More here)
http://founders.archives.gov/documents/Hamilton/01-03-02-0229

p. 373 true policy (More here)
http://founders.archives.gov/documents/Hamilton/01-03-02-0233

p. 373 in earnest (More here)
http://founders.archives.gov/documents/Hamilton/01-03-02-0233

p. 373 Entire text of the Trespass Act is here
https://books.google.com/books?id=HWIEAAAAYAAJ&pg=PA165&lpg=PA165&d-q=to+bring+an+action+of+trespass+against+any+person+or+persons+who+-may+have+occupied&source=bl&ots=gLG2YCLfLh&sig=hdr-gE29gooGlnbn-wo0zm9XCOe8&hl=en&sa=X&ved=0ahUKEwj8qszv4tXQAhVr7IMKHS8PD-7MQ6AEIJDAC#v=onepage&q=to%20bring%20an%20action%20of%20trespass%20against%20any%20person%20or%20persons%20who%20may%20have%20occupied&f=false

p. 375 to their posterity (More here)
http://founders.archives.gov/documents/Hamilton/01-03-02-0244

p. 375 for the better (More here)
http://founders.archives.gov/documents/Hamilton/01-03-02-0249

p. 376 this post by Michael Newton
https://thepathtotyranny.wordpress.com/2016/11/16/alexander-hamiltons-participation-in-the-newburgh-conspiracy-reexamined/

p. 377 sufficiently respected (More here)
http://founders.archives.gov/documents/Hamilton/01-03-02-0288

p. 377 Hamilton told John Jay
http://founders.archives.gov/documents/Hamilton/01-01-02-0060

p. 378 induced to return (More here)
http://founders.archives.gov/documents/Hamilton/01-03-02-0259

p. 378 A Hamilton (More here)
https://founders.archives.gov/documents/Hamilton/01-03-02-0267

p. 379 practice of the law (More here)
http://founders.archives.gov/documents/Hamilton/01-03-02-0270

p. 380 please and endear (More here)
http://founders.archives.gov/documents/Hamilton/01-03-02-0270

p. 380 Hamilton drafted a resolution
http://founders.archives.gov/documents/Hamilton/01-03-02-0272

p. 381 an address upon the subject (More here)
http://founders.archives.gov/documents/Hamilton/01-03-02-0272

p. 381 Annapolis Resolution is here
http://avalon.law.yale.edu/18th_century/annapoli.asp

p. 381 "New Light on the Philadelphia Mutiny of 1783"
ttps://journals.psu.edu/pmhb/article/view/43383/43104
p. 381 "Reinterpreting the 'Very Trifling Mutiny' at Philadelphia in June 1783"
https://journals.psu.edu/pmhb/article/view/44971/44692
p. 381 letter to Dickinson
http://founders.archives.gov/documents/Hamilton/01-03-02-0288

END OF VOLUME ONE

Volume 2 of *Alexander Hamilton: A Friend to America*
continues with the years 1783 to 1804 (Chapters 47-64).

Both these volumes are companions to
Alexander Hamilton: A Brief Biography,
which includes cross-references
to all the topics covered here.

If you've enjoyed this book,
please post a review on Amazon!

CPSIA information can be obtained
at www.ICGtesting.com
Printed in the USA
FSHW02n1634230618
49446FS